An Introduction to Indian Philosophy

ALSO AVAILABLE FROM BLOOMSBURY

Exploring the Yogasutra: Philosophy and Translation, Daniel Raveh
The Bloomsbury Companion to Hindu Studies, edited by Jessica Frazier
The Bloomsbury Research Handbook of Indian Aesthetics and the Philosophy of Art, edited by Arindam Chakrabarti
The Bloomsbury Research Handbook of Indian Epistemology and Metaphysics, edited by Joerg Tuske
The Bloomsbury Research Handbook of Indian Philosophical Theories of Religion, edited by Pankaj Jain
The Bloomsbury Research Handbook to Indian Ethics, edited by Shyam Ranganathan
Understanding Asian Philosophy, Alexus McLeod
Doing Philosophy Comparatively, Timothy Connolly

An Introduction to Indian Philosophy

Hindu and Buddhist Ideas from Original Sources

Second edition

Christopher Bartley

Bloomsbury Academic
An imprint of Bloomsbury Publishing Plc

BLOOMSBURY
LONDON • NEW DELHI • NEW YORK • SYDNEY

Bloomsbury Academic
An imprint of Bloomsbury Publishing Plc

50 Bedford Square
London
WC1B 3DP
UK

1385 Broadway
New York
NY 10018
USA

www.bloomsbury.com

BLOOMSBURY and the Diana logo are trademarks of Bloomsbury Publishing Plc

First published 2015

British Library Cataloguing-in-Publication Data
A catalogue record for this book is available from the British Library.

ISBN: PB: 978-1-4725-2476-8
HB: 978-1-4725-3225-1
ePDF: 978-1-4725-2437-9
ePub: 978-1-4725-2851-3

Library of Congress Cataloging-in-Publication Data
A catalog record for this book is available from the Library of Congress.

Typeset by Deanta Global Publishing Services, Chennai, India
Printed and bound in India

For Loretta, with love

Table of Contents

Preface

This revised and augmented edition has been prompted by a number of observations made by kindly reviewers and correspondents. Colleen Coalter at Bloomsbury suggested that I revise the book and then encouraged me to do it. Mikel Burley, of the University of Leeds, went to considerable lengths in providing dozens of typographical corrections as well as making a number of valuable recommendations. He has my admiration as well as my thanks. One suggestion that has not been adopted is that the abbreviations B.C. and A.D. should be replaced by B.C.E. and C.E. Does this arise from an aversion to Latin, or is the objection to Christian civilization? I have been told that C.E. stands for 'Common Era'. But that notion is a fiction. There would be a justification for abandoning established usage were another calendar to be introduced, but merely changing the abbreviation while retaining the same calendrical system has always seemed to me rather odd.

The glossary of Sanskrit terms and the catalogue of schools, people and their works are new, but the tenor and ethos of the work remain broadly the same. Some of the more protracted translations have been removed and so many obscure points enubilated that the revisions are really quite profuse! The suggestions for further reading have of course been updated. It is hoped that the expanded table of contents will help readers to find their way around.

I have emphasized my view that the Buddhist philosophers' denial of the soul proceeds primarily from a rejection of substance ontology. It is not too late to suggest that Buddhism may be understood not only as a reaction to the Brahminical commitment to substance, but as expressing a pattern of thinking that is quite as ancient as anything to be found in Hinduism. There is somewhat more about the Upaniṣads illustrating the idea that we are individualizations of a primary reality whose nature (*ātman*) we share. The chapters about the Advaita and Viśiṣṭādvaita schools of Vedānta have been largely rewritten with a view to providing a more complete picture of the origins of that tradition.

Department of Philosophy
University of Liverpool
October 2014

Abbreviations

AKBh	*Abhidharmakośabhāṣya* of Vasubandhu (Pruden, 1988).
BG	*Bhagavad Gītā* (Johnson, 1994).
BSBh	*Brahma-Sūtra-Bhāṣya* of Śaṃkara (Thibaut, 1904).
Br.Up.	*Bṛhadāraṇyaka Upaniṣad* (Olivelle, 1998).
Ch.Up.	*Chāndogya Upaniṣad* (Olivelle, 1998).
IPK	*Īśvarapratyabhijñākārikā* of Utpaladeva (Torella, 2002).
IPKV	*Īśvarapratyabhijñāvimarśinī* of Abhinavagupta (Pandey, 1986).
MMK	*Mūlamadhyamakakārikā* of Nāgārjuna (Siderits and Katsura, 2013).
MPAV	*Mataṅgapārameśvarāgama* (*Vidyāpāda*) of Rāmakaṇṭha (Bhatt, 1977).
NIPP	*Nareśvaraparīkṣāprakāśa* of Rāmakaṇṭha.
SBh	*Śrī Bhāṣya* of Rāmānuja (Thibaut, 1904).
SK	*Sāṃkhyakārikā* (Wezler & Motegi, 1998).
SV	*Ślokavārttika* of Kumārila.
Veds	*Vedārthasaṃgraha* of Rāmānuja (van Buitenen, 1956).
VV	*Vigrahavyāvartanī* of Nāgārjuna (Bhattacharya, 1998).
YD	*Yuktidīpikā*.

Introduction

This book attempts an overview of some of the topics, themes and arguments discussed by Brahminical Hindu and Buddhist Indian philosophers. It aims to explore a variety of different theories, rather than to evaluate them or to ask whether they are true. It begins with some general considerations about the background to the different philosophical schools and tries to explain the origins of the fundamental opposition between the essentialist substance ontologies propounded by Brahmins and the event or process ontologies formulated by the Buddhists, who deny that there are any real stable natures or identities. We can see a dialectic between two world views: one asserting the primacy of foundational *Being* as the source of a cosmos regulated by universals and populated by substantial entities, and the other understanding the world as a flux of ephemeral beings in a temporal process. According to the first view, states of affairs are produced by interactions between stable continuing entities, including enduring selves. According to the second one, the world is an ever-changing flow of events, and what we treat as individual entities are convenient abstractions from relational complexes. We ourselves are no less conditioned than the things in the world with which we are involved. The first outlook is that one fundamentally is in some sense a soul or substantial self, a further fact over and above one's experiences. In short, there is a difference between you and your life. This is precisely what is repudiated by the Buddhist outlook, according to which there are just life histories. There is no 'real me'. Terms like 'self' and 'person' are convenient abbreviations for the ways in which embodied persons behave in the world.[1]

I am not apologizing when I say that this book is a survey of some of the Indian traditions. The field is vast and there is so much to be explored. I have tried to describe what the traditions deem the fundamentals, and it is to be hoped that readers will be moved to consult more specialized works and read the original sources so as to form their own views. Suggestions about further reading are to be found at the end of each chapter.

In classical India, philosophy was understood as contributing to human well-being by freeing people from misconceptions about themselves and the world. Hindus especially conceived the final goal of religion as a form of freedom (*mokṣa*) from natural limitations (*saṃsāra*) outside the conditions of space and time, albeit one that can be enjoyed proleptically in the here and now (*jīvan-mukti* or liberation while living). Philosophies, as well as religious traditions, understood themselves as paths to well-being.

Where the religious contexts of those who engaged in critical, reflective and argumentative philosophy are concerned, we have to reckon with a tremendous variety of beliefs and practices. Neither 'Hinduism' nor 'Buddhism' is really homogeneous. It is difficult to know where to begin: you can always go back further. In the course of the second millennium B.C., Aryan migrations into the north-west of the subcontinent introduced the Vedic religious culture and the fourfold natural hierarchy of *varṇas* (Brahmins, warriors, farmers and servants) that was superimposed on the indigenous system of *jātis*. It appears that originally the ritual cult was concerned with propitiating with offerings the many deities in the Vedic pantheon. Their favour thus secured would yield mundane and supra-mundane rewards. Rituals performed by members of the Brahmin caste were understood as yielding benefits for both the individual and the community. But there developed an outlook that the continuation of the cosmos, the regularity of the seasons and the rising of the sun were not merely marked or celebrated by ritual acts but actually depended upon ritual. What the rituals effected was too important to be left to the choices of ultimately uncontrollable capricious divinities. So rituals came to be thought of as automatic mechanisms, in the course of which the mention of deities' names was but a formulaic aspect of the process. The relegated gods existed only in name. The Brahmins unilaterally declare themselves the gods in human form. From the point of view of the individual, the benefit of the ritual was understood in terms of the accumulation of merit that would be enjoyed at some point in the future, in this or a subsequent life, perhaps even in paradise (*svarga*). This notion of consequentiality may be seen as influencing the development of the notion of *karma*, which is basically a recognition that one's intentional, deliberate actions generate a sort of residue that awaits fruition in this life or in a subsequent life.[2] The notion of repeated births is a presupposition shared by Brahmins and Buddhists (not to mention the Jainas, who are outside the scope of this work. For an overview of their beliefs, see my essay 'Jainism' (Bartley 2001).). Everyone agreed that the process of rebirth goes on and on, is fundamentally unsatisfactory and is to be escaped from. Habitual actions create dispositions, and it is believed that we have a massive accumulation of dispositions to act and experience in certain ways, which is called 'the subtle body'. Hindus say that the latter attaches to the soul, and Buddhists say that it is just the bundle of dispositions that is reborn, there being no soul. Either way, it is reborn. It is reborn in an embryo produced by a couple whose circumstances provide an appropriate context for the actualization of a dominant set of potential dispositions. Inheritance is karmic, not genetic. *Karma* does not determine the future directly: rather, it lies in wait for circumstances appropriate for its actualization in one's experience. It is *karma* that *personalizes* and propels individuals through a series of births in the here and now.

One's *karma* is believed to fix the initial conditions of one's life and also its length. A soul associated with a stock of dispositions where virtue predominates will be reincarnated in a Brahmin womb. The process continues until one achieves *mokṣa* – release from the round of death and rebirth, and for the majority that is but a remote prospect. Whatever the quantum of good *karma* accumulated by an individual, it will still become exhausted. Felicity is always temporary. Release or liberation is always understood as irreversible freedom from rebirth. This freedom from rebirth, the ultimate goal of religious praxis, is what is called by Brahmins '*mokṣa*' or '*mukti*' and by Buddhists as '*nirvāṇa*', although as we shall see, their understanding of what it means is very different.

Hindus believe that we are immortal by nature: that is to say, one is essentially an indestructible soul or spirit that is contingently attached to an embodied life. This life, in the sense of this assembly of interests and identifications, will not continue after my death. Death is the destruction of the natural organism that includes the ego (*ahaṃkāra* – embodied personal individuality in terms of which unenlightened beings misidentify themselves), mind (*buddhi*) and memory. At death, the psychologically continuous stream of phenomenal and intentional mental states that I call 'mine' ceases. When Hindus say that the soul continues, they usually mean the permanent background consciousness that accompanies all mental states. The soul is still but you at a level deeper than the everyday sense of yourself as an embodied centre of awareness and memory, other than rational and affective mental processes.

For there to be rebirth and the anticipation of future benefits, Brahmins regarded it as essential that there be a permanent and stable identity (*ātman*) to which the *karma* pertains, so that the instigator of the performance could be the one who enjoyed its consequences. The status of this 'self' (*ātman*) in the natural hierarchy of being was maintained, and hopefully improved, by the spiritual purity of the persona with which it was associated. The system of castes, whether the endogamous and commensal *jātis* that have a monopoly on specific trades and professions or their interpretation in the *varṇa* framework, is a hierarchy determined by spiritual purity. The hierarchy accords with and expresses the cosmic order that is both natural and right (*dharma*). Each caste has its own set of duties (*dharma*). The Brahmins insisted that it was better to do one's own *dharma* badly than that of another well.[3] *Dharma* is not thought of as a universal morality applicable and accessible to all. Rather it is a matter of performing duties that are dictated by one's station in life. The Brahmins' purity derived from obedience to the rules bearing upon every aspect of life that are encoded in texts prescribing social and religious duties (the *Dharma-Śāstras*).[4] The rules chart a safe passage through a universe populated by dangerous forces that are looking for an opportunity to occupy the body and mind of those who are negligent of their observance. Spiritual purity is purchased at the price of moral heteronomy, and the Brahmin's life is one of anxiety and inhibition.[5] Daily ritual, as well as personal and social duties (*dharmas*), confers meaning on the life of the orthodox 'twice-born' Hindu. It is clear that the mainstream Vedic orthodoxy perpetuated by lineages of what are known as '*smārta*' (traditionalist) Brahmins is more than a matter of personal or shared religious allegiance. For much of its history, India has been politically fragmented into hundreds of small kingdoms. In the absence of a centralized monarchical institution, the integrating factor promoting harmonious coexistence, agreed expectations, shared values and trust between different states throughout the sub-continent was the Vedic *religion* with its established rituals, social norms and Sanskrit language. Hence the anxiety occasioned by departures from the common identity conferred by participation in the mainstream Vedic cults. Such departures were potentially subversive of civil order.

Some aspects of the philosophical articulations and defences of this mainstream orthodoxy (*smārta*), especially against Buddhist versions of the views that there is no genuine permanence and no persisting self, are described in the chapters on Mīmāṃsā ritualism and the Nyāya-Vaiśeṣika metaphysical pluralism.

The discipline of *yoga*, whose philosophy is described in the chapter on Sāṃkhya-Yoga, aims to calm the mind so that it may become fit for a non-discursive awareness of reality as it really is. This begins with control of the body and develops mental discipline through meditation, with a view to freedom from determination by natural causality. Obviously such practice is compatible with participation in ritual acts, but it may be detached from that form of religiosity in the case of those who have become convinced that ritual practice is ultimately ineffective as a means to final salvation, understood as freedom from repeated births. The model of human experience here is that which is called 'mind' (*manas*) co-ordinates information received via the sense-faculties. For the most part, we are passive in relation to sensation and the feelings it evokes. Moreover, mental attention is often diffuse and not really focused. When our mind and senses are not controlled, we are living purely on the level of sensation. The ideal is to discipline the senses by bringing the *manas* under the control of what is called *buddhi* (usually not very helpfully translated as 'the intellect') and to focus attention on one's inner identity (*ātman*). Such a person is called '*yukta*' or integrated:

> When a person lacks understanding and his mind is out of control, he is subject to the senses that are like bad horses of a charioteer. But when a person has understanding and his mind is under control, his senses are subdued like good horses.[6]

> When the five sensory cognitions and the mind are stilled and reason (*buddhi*) is steady, they call this the highest state. They call *yoga* a firm grip on the senses. One is then free from distractions.[7]

> He should sit still as a piece of wood. Collecting his sense-faculties, he should focus his mind steeped in meditation. He should not hear with his ears nor see with his eyes. He should not long for the objects of the sense-faculties. He should focus the mind within for it wanders in and out of the five doors and has no stable foundation.[8]

A different outlook (described in the chapter on Advaita Vedānta) says that insight or gnosis alone is necessary for salvation. This is the view of those individuals who have chosen the path of renunciation (*saṃnyāsa*) of the everyday social relations life of the adult male householder with his duties of wealth creation, procreation and the performance and patronage of rituals. Renouncers have come to the conclusion that the interminable performance of rituals cannot conduce to final well-being. They think that rituals and yoga may be helpful preliminaries, but they are insufficient in themselves for freedom from rebirth, which can only be approached through concentrated meditation leading to insight into one's true identity. *Saṃnyāsa* is formalized through a special type of initiation ritual for the removal of inherited caste status. Initially a trend subversive of social order, renunciation became integrated into the mainstream religion and was classified as the fourth stage of life (*āśrama*) subsequent to those of celibate studentship, being a householder and retirement or 'forest-dwelling'. Renouncers are homeless wanderers committed to celibacy. They possess only a saffron robe, begging bowl and staff. They are dedicated to achieving liberation from rebirth through *insight* into the nature of a soul that is a reality beyond space and time, and the ultimate source of all reality (the *brahman*).[9]

Nevertheless, renunciation has always been controversial, and for some people renouncers are objects of fear and suspicion. There is a resistance to the idea that anyone should quit the established social order and the rituals commanded by the Vedas, and go it alone. So some traditions hold that the performance of social and ritual duty is mandatory: what one should renounce is desire for the results of the rituals. That outlook is clearly expressed in the *Bhagavad Gītā*, one of whose messages is 'If you must renounce something, renounce the fruits of action!'[10]

Others (see the chapters about Viśiṣṭādvaita Vedānta and Dvaita Vedānta) believe that whole-hearted and deeply felt devotion (*bhakti*) to a personal deity is rewarded by divine favour (*prasāda*) and heavenly felicity. The self is understood as an essentially dependent servant of God whose fulfilment is to be found in enjoyment of the divinity. This is not a late development but is apparent as early as the *Śvetāśvatara Upaniṣad*:

> The Lord supports this whole world consisting of the perishable and the imperishable, the manifest and the unmanifest that are linked together. The soul who is different from the Lord is bound because he is the experiencer of the fruits of *karma*. Having known God, he is released from all bonds. The one God rules over the material cosmos and the soul. By contemplating him, by uniting with him and in the end sharing his way of being, the material world ceases. When one has known God, the bonds are destroyed, when the afflictions (*kleśa*) have dwindled away, there is an end to birth and death.[11]

As well as what is generally recognized as mainstream orthodox *smārta* Brahmanism, there are traditions that base themselves not on the Vedic corpus but on divinely revealed scriptures called Tantras or Āgamas. These are monotheistic ritual cults, whose praxis includes forms of yoga and meditation. The deities are Śiva, the Goddess and Viṣṇu. Tantrism is the subject of the chapter about the Śaiva and Śākta cults.

Further reading

A. L. Basham, *The Wonder that was India: A Survey of the Culture of the Indian Sub-Continent Before the Coming of the Muslims*, is an interesting and comprehensive overview.

Gavin Flood's *Introduction to Hinduism* and Julius Lipner's *Hindus* are both informative and stimulating.

Louis Dumont (1980), 'World Renunciation in Indian Religions' has been very influential. Dumont argues that the key to understanding Indian religion is to be found in the dialogue between the householder and the renouncer. The latter, he says, represents the closest Indian equivalent to the European notion of *the* individual as the bearer of values. The monograph, *Homo Hierarchicus*, is a fundamental contribution to Indian sociology. Olivelle (1993) is about the four stages of life. Olivelle (1996) translates texts bearing on *Renunciation in Hinduism*.

For a translation of the *Bhagavad Gītā*, see Johnson (1994). For the *Upaniṣads*, Olivelle (1998) provides an informative introduction, texts, translations and illuminating annotations. What is called the *Mokṣa-dharma* (composed while Buddhism was developing) in the *Mahābhārata Book XII* offers an insight into the spiritual outlook of the Brahminical renouncers. There is a text and translation in Wynne (2009).

On devotional religiosity see Hardy (1983), which is unlikely to be superseded. J. A. B. van Buitenen's 'On the Archaism in the Bhāgavata Purāṇa' (Chapter XIX of Rocher (1988)) applies M. N. Srinivas' theory about the process of 'Sanskritization' to *bhakti* religion.

Notes

1. As the late Dr Joseph Needham used to observe, the Buddhist ethos is encapsulated in the French proverb 'Tout passe, tout lasse, tout casse'.
2. *Mutatis mutandis*, this account applies to Buddhism as well. One modification to note is that Buddhism has always insisted that *karma* is a matter of what one intends. (My own view is that this is what most Hindus think too.)

3. *Bhagavad Gītā* 3.35.
4. Olivelle (2005) and Olivelle (1999).
5. These ideas are from Sanderson (1985).
6. *Kaṭha Upaniṣad* 3.5-6 in Olivelle (1998).
7. *Kaṭha Upaniṣad* 6.10-11.
8. *Mahābhārata* 12.195.5f in Wynne (2009).
9. See Louis Dumont's 'World Renunciation in Indian Religions', reprinted as Appendix B to *Homo Hierarchicus* (Dumont 1980).
10. Johnson (1994). See especially Chs 2–4.
11. *Śvetāśvatara Upaniṣad* 1.8-11 (in Olivelle 1998).

1

Foundations of Brahmanism: Vedas and Upaniṣads

Chapter Outline

The primacy of substance

Orthodox Hinduism bases itself on scriptures called the Vedas. These were composed in the course of the Aryan migrations into northern India: population shifts occurring from around 2000 to 1100 B.C. They are called the Rig Veda, the Sāma Veda, the Yajur Veda and the Atharva Veda and are regarded by mainstream orthodox Hindus not as human (or divine) compositions but as a simply given timeless and infallible source of knowledge about religious and social duties. Enactment of those duties brings us into harmony with the natural universal order (*dharma*). The eternal sounds of the sacred canon are held to have been discerned by seven primordial 'seers' who transmitted them to subsequent generations. Priestly Brahmin families preserve the different traditions of recitation of the sacred sounds. The basic component of each of the four Vedas is its collection (*saṃhitā*) of verses (*mantra*), evocative of the divinities whose sonic forms they are, which are used in rituals. Attached to each collection are works called '*Brāhmaṇas*' that prescribe, describe and elucidate the purposes of the sacrificial rituals performed by Brahmin priests and their householder patrons. They include explanations of the meanings of the ritual actions, and posit correspondences between aspects of the rites and features of the cosmos including the social structure and the human body. It was believed that ritual performance orders, sustains and perpetuates the universe, creating new time and ensuring the regular succession of the seasons. Most rituals involve some sort of oblation to divine powers, thrown into a sacred fire. Agni, the god of fire, delivered the offerings to the other gods whose favour would confer benefits such as children, healthy cattle, a good harvest, long life, prosperity, wealth and martial success. Some obligatory rites are to be performed at crucial junctions of each day; some are seasonal requirements, and others are performed by people with specific ends in view.

Also included under the heading 'Veda' are the 'Āraṇyakas' ('Forest Books') that speculate about the 'inner' meaning of the rituals. These are closely associated with what are called the Upaniṣads. The latter were composed by Brahmins who had probably renounced the actual performance of ritual. The view was that the mental re-enactment of the meaning of the ritual is just as effective as its overt performance. These compositions contain many reflective explorations of fundamental metaphysical questions and encompass a diversity of viewpoints. I treat them as a starting point because they mark a departure from purely mythological ways of thinking. For example, a hymn belonging to the Rig Veda explains the creation of the cosmos and the establishment of the caste-based social order as the consequences of the dismemberment of a primeval giant.[1] Broadly speaking, the Upaniṣad thinkers ask where the giant came from and realize that the answer 'another giant' is not the sort of explanation that they are looking for. That explanation would be one that answered the question, 'why is there something rather than nothing?'

Such matters are also to be found in the hymns of the Rig Veda. These hymns celebrate and propitiate gods mostly associated with natural forces. Their cosmogonic hymns speak of the gods such as Indra and Varuṇa establishing inhabitable space and creating sustainable order out of chaos. They were used by Brahmins in rituals whose aim was the perpetuation of the cosmos. The questions about Being – Why is there something rather than nothing? Where did it all come from? – feature there, if not prominently. One line of thought says that there is an original One, beyond being and non-being. Another idea is that Being (*sat*) arises from non-Being (*asat*).[2] Since everyone knows that nothing comes from nothing, 'non-Being' probably meant an amorphous, undifferentiated state in which are no things, no names and forms, no entities and kinds, no structures or organizing principles. 'Being' would then by contrast be a cosmos of differentiated, identifiable, organized realities, necessarily including sentient beings capable of registering information and making discriminations. But as we shall soon see, this notion of the priority of non-being was rejected by what might tentatively be called the dominant tradition of Upaniṣadic thought.

There are many works bearing the name 'Upaniṣad', of which twelve are usually deemed 'major'. These were composed between 800 and 400 B.C. The doctrines they contain are many and various. For instance, the Bṛhadāraṇyaka, the vastest in extent, contains at least three cosmogonies. These texts are assemblages, recording many different views. It would be a mistake to expect consistencies in meaning throughout the postulated 'corpus'. The meanings of terms such as '*sat*', '*ātman*' and '*brahman*' differ according to context. In what follows, we shall be concerned with Brahminical concepts of substance, essence, first cause, sustaining cause and truth in the sense of the permanently real, all of which are examples of fictions according to Buddhists.

While the Upaniṣads contain many different views (including the idea that the original substance is water[3]), the idea that exercised the greatest influence on subsequent thought is that there is an ontologically independent primary reality or underlying substance. That concept was variously expressed as 'the *brahman*', '*sat*', '*ātman*' and *mahad bhūta*. This primary or original being is understood as a timeless, unconditioned and unlimited substance that needs nothing else in order to exist. *Sat*, sheer being without categorical determinations, is also the source, basis, support and final cause of all existents. It makes worlds and experiencers, mind and matter, while itself remaining intact. It is what Vedānta and Sāṃkhya thinkers, as we will see in later chapters, describe as the universal material cause (*upādāna-kāraṇa*) that is capable of self-transformation.

It is the foundational 'something other' out of which the world of entities, 'name and form', appears or unfolds.[4] The Brahminical philosophers understand it as the ungenerated source of genesis. They saw that the first principle of generation cannot itself be a generated being. Nor can it share with the empirical cosmos of finite entities, their aspects of finitude, insubstantiality and transience, birth and death. The great being is boundless (*apāram* cf Gk *apeiron*). It does not just last for a very long time: it endures eternally, outside time and space. To it are ascribed desire, thought and creative power. This first principle is alive. It is unsurpassably subtle or refined. Its generating sentient beings and environments (or worlds) is a manifestation of progressively less subtle – that is, grosser or coarser – forms of being. The 'Vital Principle' encompasses the mental and the physical, minds and matter.

This primal being has the spontaneous capacity to transform itself into a complex cosmos of individual cognizers and material things, while itself abiding unchanged. The *brahman* lacks nothing, which is why it is sometimes said to be blissful. The *brahman* is the essence of whatever actually exists. The *brahman* is the truth in the sense of the perfect reality. This reality behind and underlying all contingent, finite and mutable entities is sometimes characterized as the One, sheer Being beyond existence and non-existence. Those categories apply only to determinate entities falling within the sphere of our experience. The *brahman*, not being an identifiable individual, cannot be spoken of as 'this' or 'that'.

According to this outlook, the cosmos has immanent order and purpose (*dharma*) independently of any meanings that human beings might create for themselves. It is a leading concept of the Upaniṣads that the universal nature (*ātman/brahman/sat*) individualizes itself into sentient beings limited by space and time. They participate in the universal reality. It is what they really are, the immortal element, the 'inner guide' immanent in the heart (rather than the mind or intellect), dwelling in the body and dwelling in the sun. And thus we often find the word '*ātman*' (meaning the *nature* of something) used to mean the individualizations of the universal primary Being. Under the influence of much later Vedāntic ideas, the word '*ātman*' is often translated as 'soul', 'self' or even 'The Self'. Translation as 'soul' (essential nature of something) is fitting in some contexts, and 'self' is appropriate for reflexive usages. The reified notion 'The Self' is much more problematic. My view is that many translations of occurrences of '*ātman*' in the Upaniṣads as 'Self' are misleading.

One meaning of the word is 'breath' (*prāṇa*), a word for the vital functions of seeing, hearing, speaking and thinking. But there developed the view that we are not reducible to physical factors and functions. The principle of reasoning is that when something – such as a sentient individual cognizer – can objectify a process (e.g. human vital functioning), it cannot itself have emerged from that process although it may be involved in it. In this light, *ātman* is no longer the breath, or any one vital function or the vital functions taken collectively. *Ātman* is not a part of the human being but is that which is the source of vital functions, that which underlies them and explains their reason for being.[5] '*Ātman*' will increasingly come to mean 'essential nature' and 'soul'. This concept of essential nature is different from what we ordinarily mean by self (so we have to be careful about translating the term) or person, that is to say, a subject of experiences or a thinking, willing, feeling, acting individual. It seems that in these early texts, the term '*ātman*' basically meant fundamental Being, understood as the self-transforming source of every kind of entity. Its signification was extended to cover individualizations of the universal reality. In other words, to the questions 'what are we really?' and 'what is our nature' (*ātman*), the answer was, 'manifestations of a greater reality' (*ātman/brahman*).

Some illustrative passages from the Bṛhadāraṇyaka Upaniṣad

1.6.1 and 3: This world is tripartite: name (*nāma*), perceptible forms (*rūpam*) and action (*karma*)…. While this is a tripartite reality, it is one nature (*ātman*).

2.1.20: As a spider emits threads and as little sparks flash from fire, so do all the vital functions, all the worlds, all the gods and all basic elements arise from this primary state (*asmad-ātmanaḥ*).

2.4.5: One values a husband, not out of love for the husband: rather, it is out of love for the universal nature (*ātman*) that one values a husband. One values a wife, not out of love for the wife: rather it is out of love for the universal nature that one values a wife…. One values the whole world, not out of love for the world: rather it is out of love for the universal nature that one values the world.

2.4.12: When a lump of salt is thrown into water [of which it is a solidified form], it dissolves into the water and cannot be grasped at all. But from wherever one takes a sip, the salt is there. This Great Element (*mahad bhūtam*) is infinitely unconfined concentrated sentience (*vijñānaghana*). It emerges from the basic elements and disappears after them. So I say, after death there is no perception [because there are neither individual subjects nor objects].[6]

3.4 and 5: Explain to me the primal reality (*brahman*) that is clear and not hidden, the nature (*ātman*) that is within all.

The universal nature is also your nature.

What is the universal nature?

You cannot see the seer who sees. You cannot hear the hearer who hears. You cannot think of the thinker who thinks. You cannot perceive the perceiver who perceives objects. The universal nature is yours too.... That is what is beyond hunger and thirst, beyond sorrow and delusion, beyond old age and death. When they know this nature, Brahmins cease to desire sons, wealth and other worlds of experience, and adopt the mendicant life.

3.7: What is the inner controller of this world and the next, as well as of all beings, who controls them from within?

This nature (*ātman*) of yours who is present within but is different from the earth [fire, air, wind and other physical features], whom the earth does not know, whose body the earth is and who controls the earth from within – he is the inner controller, the immortal one.... This nature of yours who is present within but is different from all beings, whom all beings do not know, whose body is all beings and who controls all beings from within – he is the inner controller, the immortal.... This nature of yours who is present within the breath but is different from the breath [from speech, sight and other sensory and cognitive functions], whom the breath does not know, whose body is the breath and who controls the breath from within – he is the inner controller, the immortal.... That is the seer who cannot be seen, the hearer who cannot be heard, the thinker who cannot be thought of, the perceiver who cannot be perceived. There is no other who sees etc. It is this nature of yours who is the inner controller, the immortal.

4.2.4: About this nature (*ātman*) one can only say, 'it is not this' or 'it is not that'. It is incomprehensible for it cannot be grasped. It is undecaying, for it is not subject to decay.

4.3.7: What is *ātman* in humans?

It is the spirit (*puruṣa*), the vital power (*prāṇa*) consisting in perception (*vijñāna*), that which is the inner light within the heart.

4.4.6: The one who does not desire, who is without desires, who is free from desires, whose desires are fulfilled, whose only interest is in the universal nature, his vital functions do not cease. The *brahman* he is and to the *brahman* he goes.

Such a one is at peace, in control, unperturbed, patient and focused for he sees the soul in himself and he sees all things as the soul [Br.Up. 4.4.23].

4.5.6: It is this nature (*ātman*) that one should see and hear and on which one should reflect and contemplate. When this nature has been seen and heard, reflected upon and understood, everything is understood.

The sixth chapter of the Chāndogya Upaniṣad, sometimes called the '*Sad-vidyā*' or 'Knowledge about Being', is a text on the borderland of creation mythology and metaphysical speculation.[7] It begins with a sage called Uddālaka Āruṇi offering to teach his son Śvetaketu 'how one hears what has not been heard before, how one thinks the hitherto unthought and how one understands what has not been understood'. The topic is nothing less than understanding the basic nature of reality. The general form of explanation is that by knowledge of one, there is knowledge of the all. The 'one' is the primary substance (variously called *sat*, the *brahman*, *ātman*), the first cause and source of the differentiated cosmos. As the text puts it: Being is the source of all these creatures, Being is their resting place and Being is their foundation.[8] Although the precise character of this hyper-reality cannot be specified (since in this mortal life we only know its effects – ourselves included), this did not inhibit speculation.

Selections from Chāndogya Upaniṣad, chapter 6

6.1.4: It is like this: by means of one lump of clay, one understands [the substance or nature of] everything made of clay. The product is a singling out by speech, a naming, while the truth is just 'it is clay'.

6.2.1–3: In the beginning there was being (*sat*), one only and without a second.

There are some who say that only non-being (*asat*) was here originally and that existence arose from non-existence. But how is it possible that existence arose from non-existence?[9] No: *sat* alone was here originally.

And *sat* thought to itself, 'Let me become many: let me multiply myself.'

It begat heat. The heat thought, 'Let me become many: let me multiply myself.' Heat begat water.... Water begat food.

6.3.2: The same divinity (*devatā*, meaning *sat*) thought, 'Let me create various entities (*nāma-rūpa*, *lit. names and perceptible forms*) by entering these three divinities (i.e. heat, water and food) by animating them (*jīvena-ātmanā*).

I shall make each of them three-fold.' So that divinity created various entities by entering those three divinities and making each of them threefold.

Learn from me how each of these three becomes threefold.

6.4: The red colour in a fire is the manifestation of heat. The white colour in a fire is the manifestation of water. The black colour in a fire is the manifestation of food.

Thus, the apparently singular character of fire has disappeared. Any product (such as fire) is a singling out by speech, a designation, while the truth is just that it consists of the three manifestations.

6.5: Learn from me how each of these three divinities on entering a man becomes threefold. Food when consumed becomes threefold: faeces, flesh and mind. Water turns into urine, blood and breath. Heat becomes bones, marrow and speech.

[The text's detailed account of the genesis of sundry kinds of creatures is omitted here. The theme is that there is an ultimate principle and source – called Being (*sat*) whence all kinds of entities arise as combinations of the primary derivatives: heat, water and food. The source remains unchanged as it is in itself. When entities finally revert to the primal being, their individuality is annihilated.]

6.8.6: Being (*sat*) is the source of all these creatures, Being is their abode and Being is their foundation. When a man is dying, his speech merges into his mind, his mind into his vital breath and his breath into the supreme divinity (*sat*).

That which is the finest essence[10] here, that is the nature of the whole world. That is what's real, that is the primary substrate (*ātman*),[11] and that is what you are.[12]

6.9: Just as when the bees gather honey and condense into a unity the nectar from many trees, the nectars from each different tree lack the discernment 'I am from this tree' or 'I am from that tree'. Similarly, all these creatures, when they merge into Being, are not individually aware, 'I am merging into Being'. Whatever they were in the world, they merge into Being.

Whatever is the finest essence here, that is the nature of the whole world. That is what's real, that is the primary substrate (*ātman*), and that is what you are.

6.10: The easterly rivers flow towards the west and the westerly ones towards the east. Starting from the ocean, they eventually merge into the ocean. The ocean just continues in being. There they do not know 'I am this river' or 'I am that river'. In the same way, when all these creatures reach the Being that is their source, they are not individually aware that they are reaching Being. Whatever they were in the world, they become Being.

Whatever is the finest essence here, that is the nature of the whole world. That is what's real, that is the substrate (*ātman*), and that is what you are.

6.12: 'Bring me a fruit from the banyan tree.

Here it is, Sir

Cut it up

I've cut it, Sir

What do you see here?

Tiny pieces.

Cut one of them up

What do you see?

Nothing?

You cannot see the finest essence here, but it is because of that essence that this great Banyan tree stands.

That which is the finest essence is the nature shared by everything. That is what's real. That is the substrate (*ātman*) and that is what you are.'

Selections from the Taittirīya Upaniṣad

2.1.1: He who knows the *brahman* attains the highest. The *brahman* is reality, consciousness and infinite. He who knows that as hidden in the heart attains all his desires and the *brahman*.

Space was produced from that substrate (*ātman*), air was produced from space, fire from air, water from fire, the earth from water, plants from the earth, food from plants and man (*puruṣa*) from food. A man is made of the essence of food. He has a head, a left and a right, this is his nature (*ātman*).

2.2: Different from and lying within this man made from the essence of food is the nature (*ātman*) made of breath. Different from and lying within this man made from breath is the nature (*ātman*) consisting in mind: different from mind is the nature consisting in perception; different from perception is the nature consisting of bliss.

Selections from the Aitareya Upaniṣad (*ātman* as primary substrate)[13]

1. In the beginning this world was *ātman*, one alone. There was nothing else that even blinked. He thought to himself, 'Let me create the worlds.'

3.1 What is this *ātman*? Is it that by which one sees, or hears, or smells, or speaks?

3.2 Is it the heart and the mind? Is it perceiving or thinking, wisdom, memory, decision, intention? All these are just names of modes of consciousness.

3.3 It is the *brahman*, it is Indra, it is Prajāpati: it is all the gods. It is the five base elements (*pañca māhābhūtāni*): earth, wind, air, water and light. It is also all sorts of things that are mixtures of the elements. It is living beings born from eggs and wombs, from sweat and from seeds. It is horses, cattle, men and elephants. It is everything animate, moving, flying and immobile. Consciousness is the eye of all that. It is all founded on consciousness. Consciousness is the world's eye. Consciousness is the foundation and the *brahman* is consciousness.

Selections from the Kaṭha Upaniṣad

2.20: More subtle than the subtlest, greater than the greatest is the soul (*ātman*) hidden in the heart of a living being. One who is free from desires and regrets sees the greatness of the soul by the grace of the creator.

2.22: When he knows this supreme and all-pervading nature (*ātman*) as bodiless within bodies, as constant in the midst of changes, the wise man ceases to grieve.

2.23: This soul cannot be comprehended by speech, by doctrine or by intelligence. Only the one he chooses can grasp him.

3.3: Know the soul (*ātman*) to be a passenger in a chariot and the body nothing more than a chariot. Know the intellect (*buddhi*) to be the charioteer and the mind (*manas*) to be the reins.

3.4: The senses are the horses and the perceptible objects their field. That which is linked to intellect, senses and mind, the wise call the experiencer.

3.5: The man lacking wisdom and whose mind is undisciplined, his senses are out of control, as bad horses do not obey a charioteer.

3.6: But as to the wise man whose mind is disciplined, his senses are under his control, as good horses obey a charioteer.

3.7: The man who lacks wisdom is careless and impure. He does not reach the highest place and continues on the cycle of rebirth.

3.8: The wise man is diligent and pure. He reaches the highest place from which he is not born again.

3.9: He who has wisdom as his charioteer and his mind as the reins reaches the journey's end – the place of Viṣṇu.

Further reading

For Vedic Hinduism and the contents of the Vedic corpus, see Jamison and Witzel (2003). This is accessible online via Professor Witzel's website.

Rig Vedic hymns are translated in Doniger (2005).

All the Upaniṣadic passages mentioned here can be found in Olivelle (1998). There is also an Oxford University Press paperback that just has the translation.

Essays II, V–X in van Buitenen (1988) have all been influential. Chapters I and II of Halbfass (1992) are thought-provoking about the 'question of being' in India.

Questions for discussion and investigation

1. Does it really make sense to suppose that the complex cosmos has a single source?
2. Are the Upaniṣads expressions of a timeless spirituality, or do they express beliefs current at the times of this composition?

Notes

1. Rig Veda 10.90.
2. See for example Rig Veda 10.129.
3. The view of the pre-Socratic thinker, Thales.
4. 'In the beginning there was only the *brahman*, and it knew only itself in thinking, "I am the brahman." From that, everything came into being' (Bṛhadāraṇyaka Upaniṣad 1.4.10).
5. 'Soul's secret name is, "the reality of what's real", for the real constitutes the vital breaths and the soul is their essence' [Br.Up. 2.1.2].
6. The passage is obscure. It is included to illustrate the composite nature of the Upaniṣad. The Great Element (*mahad bhūtam*) usually means the first cause, of which the elements (*bhūtas*) are the primary evolutes. The picture here is one of a great being emerging out of lesser sentient and insentient factors.
7. This text will be very influential especially in the Vedānta systematizations of the Upaniṣadic teachings. It will be interpreted by Śaṃkara and his Advaitin followers in monistic, gnostic and non-theistic terms. By contrast, Rāmānuja demonstrates its compatibility with a pluralistic ontology and devotional theism. See Chapters 10–13.
8. Ch.Up. 6.8.6.
9. Note: This is a response to an ancient doctrine found in Rig Veda 10.129; Tait.Up. 2.7.1; Bṛhad.Up. 1.2.1; Ch.Up. 3.19.1: 'In the beginning this world was just non-being. What now exists came from that. It developed and formed an egg ....' Exactly what its proponents meant by '*asat*' is obscure. Presumably they did not suppose that it simply meant nothing! See above p. 11.
10. *aṇiman* means the original and most refined or subtle state from which the infinitely boundless Being transforms itself into the cosmos of localized entities.
11. *Ātman* here might be translated as 'soul' but with a universal, perhaps impersonal, connotation. It should not be taken as meaning self or person, let alone the modern reification, The Self.
12. '*Tat tvam asi*', traditionally translated as 'That thou art', and one of the Vedāntic *mahāvākyas* or key statements according to Vedānta.
13. Cf. Ch.Up. 7.25.2 and 26.1. Translation of '*ātman*' as 'self' here is implausible.

Part I

Buddhist Traditions

2

The Buddhist Ethos

Chapter Outline

What Buddhists believe

Gautama Śākyamuni, who would become known as the Buddha or 'the Enlightened One', probably lived in the fifth century B.C. Early Buddhism set its face against the notions of the *brahman* and *ātman* that we saw in the previous chapter. Buddhists think that there are no enduring, substantial realities (*anātman*/*anattā*), no essences and no fundamental principle. Buddhism teaches the essential temporality of beings (*kṣaṇika-vāda*). Things as well as times are always changing. Nothing really lasts. But there is no deeper, or higher, level of reality that is the background to or substrate of change. Everything is impersonal. There are no immutable natures and no universal properties running through reality as a whole.

The Buddha thought that the Brahminical ritual religion was pointless and rejected the authority of the Vedic scriptures on which it was founded.[1] He said that the belief that advantages are to be acquired by ritual practices is an expression of the unhealthy way of being, one that is aflame with greed, hatred and delusion. Brahmins, from their pedestal at the summit of the social hierarchy, maintain that the system of castes is a natural fact. From this point of view, one's social and one's biological identity are the same. One's caste status dictates one's morality (*sva-dharma*). The Buddha held that the caste system is nothing other than a set of social arrangements.[2] The Buddhist outlook is atheistic in that it denies that the cosmos has a single source, sustaining cause or goal.[3] If it has a reason for being and an explanation for its dispositions, it is just so that sentient beings may experience the fruits of their karmas.

Buddhists and Brahmins recognize that we are people who remain similar over time and whose futures are conditioned by our deliberate and intentional decisions and actions. They differ about whether a basic principle of identity (*ātman*) is required to explain the coherence and continuity of such persons. We might depict the Buddhist as arguing that psychological continuity is enough for personal identity. The Brahmin position is that psychological continuity presupposes personal identity and therefore cannot constitute it.[4] On several grounds, the Brahmins assert and the Buddhists reject the need for a permanent and stable inner principle in human beings:

It unifies the manifold of experiences both through time and in the present.
It explains and justifies egocentric concerns.
It explains the phenomena of memory and recognition.
It is the bearer of our determinate identity.
It underwrites the possibility of one's post-mortem survival.
It serves as the bearer of individual *karma* across lives.

But the disagreement between the Buddhists and Brahmins goes deeper than questions about personal identity. That dispute occurs in the context of much broader opposition that may be described in terms of two contrasting philosophical outlooks: on the one hand, a substance ontology according to which enduring entities are the basic constituents of the worlds, and on the other, an ontology that accords primacy to ephemeral and insubstantial processes and events (*nairātmya* – non-substantiality). If the meaning of substance encompasses both independence of everything else and enduring identity, the *anattā* doctrine is the view that there are no substances. We ordinarily suppose that there are substances because our world view is infected by ignorance (*avidyā*/*avijjā*). This is ignorance about the world's ontological structure. We interpret what is impermanent (*anitya*/*anicca*) as if it were permanent and substantial. We think in terms of change in terms of the loss or gain of properties by persisting entities defined by a core essence that remains unchanged. Buddhists deny that there is anything that basically remains the same, that there are any permanent stable identities at any level (*nairātmya-vāda*). There are no real universals or kinds, no essences constituting enduring objects, no eternal sounds or meanings. There are only sequences and clusters of momentary events (*kṣaṇika-vāda*). Whereas the Brahminical metaphysic posits Being or substance as prior to and underlying the sphere of beings and becoming, Buddhists say that there are just ephemeral beings in a flux that is really impersonal.

The Buddhist outlook is often summarized in the 'Three Jewels':

Everything is Unsatisfactory (*duḥkha/dukkha*).
Everything is Impermanent (*anitya/anicca*).
Everything is Insubstantial (*anātman/anattā*).

Buddhist philosophers typically reduce anything that is conventionally considered as a stable substance to a stream or sequence of occurrences. The Buddhist claims that thoughts purporting to be about persisting entities that may undergo qualitative changes without loss of identity can be reductively analysed into descriptions couched in terms of sequences of instantaneous or momentary events. They reject any categorical distinction between enduring substrates and properties of which they are the bearers. Rather, they understand the world to consist of temporary collocations of basic factors (*dharma*), which may be material, kinetic or mental. What is experienced as individual personality is understood as a causally explicable flux of mental and physical occurrences. What makes for the continuity of a person's life is just the occurrence of a series of suitably interconnected physical and mental events. What is called 'self' or 'soul' is not a substantial enduring entity distinct from the contents of experiences, but a construction, convenient but mistaken, out of those momentary events. The Buddhist maintains that the human subject is an essentially temporal (*kṣaṇika*) succession of phases that has somehow imputed an enduring nature to itself.

The denial that we are permanent selves or souls, selfish concern with which is the source of all our woe, follows from the global rejection of substance, from the denial that there are any enduring realities. The anti-substance view denies that reality is constituted by stable and reliable structures grounded in a single source. It denies that either the totality or individual human lives have any intelligible purpose or meaning outside themselves. There is no God who has a purpose for the world and for human lives. This may sound negative, but that was not the intention. Rather, understanding life in these terms is held to be liberating. Much that one had worried about does not really matter. One will not live forever. We do not matter nearly as much as we think we do. In fact, in the long run we do not matter at all. Perhaps it enables people to 'let go', escape from the burdens of self-concern and enjoy life while they can. Above all, it is meant to empty our heart of hatred, greed and bitterness and to engender a spirit of compassion, friendliness and generosity.

Gautama Śākyamuni, who became known as the Buddha or Enlightened One, was born into a royal family in the far north-east of the Indian subcontinent. Like many others at the time, he became disillusioned with the frustrations, superficialities and conventional expectations of normal social life. Renouncing society and the ritual religion with its eye on future benefits, he 'went from home to homelessness'.[5] He tried to live as an ascetic, practising severe austerities, in the manner of contemporaneous Jaina renouncers, with a view to acquiring spiritual insight. Finding that this did not work but only made him ill, he espoused the 'middle way' – a path of morality and meditation, between comfort and asceticism. The doctrine is also understood as the middle way between eternalism and nihilism. The former says that identity is permanent. The latter holds that universal impermanence and non-substantiality entail chaos and thus preclude ethical consequentiality. The Buddhists thought that eternalism was amoral in that the soul that it wrongly posits would in any case be independent of our moral agency. Nihilism just denies that there are bearers of moral responsibility and recipients of consequences. Avoiding all these extremes, Buddhists think that a morally significant stream of information and dispositions (*saṃskāras*) continues after the death of what has been considered as a person. To the question of whether the one who is born is the same as the one who dies, the tradition replies that it is neither the same nor different. The stream's future is not the future of that very person. Still, we should care about the stream's future and strive for its amelioration in the interests of general well-being. In short, it is better that there be more happiness than suffering, and we should all aim for that overall state of affairs regardless of the fact that we individual centres of agency and experience will not survive death.

Gautama was called 'the Buddha', meaning 'the Enlightened One' because he discovered the truths (called '*dhamma*' in the Pāli language) about the cosmos. The Buddha's teachings and spiritual journey are reported in the collections of discourses found in the Sutta-piṭaka of the Pāli Canon of scriptures. After centuries of development by oral transmission, the Pāli Canon was committed to writing in Sri Lanka during the reign of King Vaṭṭagāmanī (97–77 B.C.) at the Council of Ālokavihāra. These are the scriptures recognized as authoritative by all Buddhists, whether belonging to the Theravāda traditions found in Sri Lanka, Burma, Thailand and Cambodia, or to the Mahāyāna ones belonging to parts of India (until the twelfth century A.D.), Tibet, China and Japan. Of the differences between the two families (many of which are cultural), one might mention that the Mahāyānists ascribe quasi-divine status to the many Buddhas and accept texts additional to the Pāli Canon as authorities. It is sometimes argued that some of the alleged doctrinal differences – for example, the Mahāyānists emphasize compassion and insight, worship the Buddhas, and hold that the path to enlightenment is long and difficult – are not really differences at all but belong to the shared heritage.

The Four Noble Truths

The basic principles of the Buddha's teachings are expressed in the 'Four Noble Truths':

1 All mental and physical phenomena are unsatisfactory (*duḥkha/dukkha*).
2 Unsatisfactoriness has a cause.
3 There is an end to suffering, called *nirvāṇa* (*nibbāna*).
4 There is a path leading to *nirvāṇa*.

In more detail:

1 All mental and physical phenomena are unsatisfactory (*duḥkha/dukkha*)

Pain and suffering, frustration and disappointment characterize the eternal round of existences, the cycle of rebirth (*saṃsāra*).

Everything is unsatisfactory because all conditioned phenomena, including human lives, are impermanent (*anicca*) and insubstantial (*anattā*). In truth, there are no enduring essences or identities. The world is an impersonal process of events, in which everything is changing all the time.

Selfhood is a fiction that the fluxes of thoughts and desires conventionally called persons superimpose upon themselves. We are just as conditioned, that is to say – variable products of an interplay of forces – as the objects in the world about us.

Attempts to cling to what are in reality impermanent objects, states of affairs and relationships are bound to end in suffering.

The renouncers (*samnyāsins*) who composed the Upaniṣads thought that the key to release from rebirth (deathlessness) is the realization or recognition that there is a stable principle within oneself that is nothing other than the first principle (the *brahman*) 'behind' the cosmos. The Buddha taught that enlightenment and freedom arose from the realization that there is no such stable inner reality either at the heart of the cosmos or of the individual. There is neither a centre nor a basis. The ephemeral and insubstantial realities in which we participate are all that there is. And we too are ephemeral and insubstantial beings. The beliefs that we are substantial entities and that we really matter are mistaken.

2 Unsatisfactoriness has a cause

In fact, there are two root causes: 'thirst', a metaphor for desire and attachment, and ignorance of the way things really are.

Unenlightened actions are motivated by the fires of greed, hatred and delusion. We are burning with egocentric desires and ambitions for the future. Bundles of selfish energies, we are acquisitive, intent on possession. We seek to extend our sphere of influence, to dominate and control people and events. We are averse to anything that gets in our way. We are deluded in our beliefs that there are substantial beings that really persist.

What is sometimes called 'The doctrine of interdependent origination' (*pratītya-samutpāda*) is first and foremost presented as an account of how the whole mass of suffering comes about. The doctrine is expressed as a cycle of twelve factors, without beginning or end, because there is no first cause – the world is brute fact.

The theory is a purely naturalistic explanation: there is no reference to supernatural or other-worldly factors.

There is neither a designer nor design; there is no *telos*, final cause or purpose.

The process is impersonal: there are no references to selves or persons. The theory is intended to show that the experience of continuity within subjectless streams of experiences, bundles of selfish energies cohering as fields of forces, does not require an internal principle or soul but results from the co-operation of twelve factors.

It is a natural fact that actions and experiences occur in streams.[6]

The twelve spokes in the wheel

1 Ignorance (*avidyā/avijjā*) [the selfish, unenlightened way of living – the failure to realize that we are just aspects of a process that will inevitably be experienced as unsatisfactory]
conditioning/leading to

2 Inherited dispositions, characteristics, the self-centred 'mindset' (*saṃskāra/saṅkhāra*)
conditioning/leading to

3 Cognitions or sensory perceptions (*vijñāna*) [i.e. one's character {2} conditions how one perceives]
conditioning/leading to

4 Name and form (*nāma-rūpa*) ['name' covers sensation, thoughts, volition, perceptions; 'form' means body]
conditioning/leading to

5 Six kinds of sense-based experiences (*ṣaḍ-āyatana*)
conditioning/leading to

6 Sensory contacts with the external environment (*sparśa/phassa*)
conditioning/leading to

7 Feelings of pleasure and pain (*vedanā*)
conditioning/leading to

8 Thirst/desires (*tṛṣṇa/taṇhā*) for more experiences
conditioning/leading to

9 Appropriation or grasping (*upādāna*): [clinging to sense-based pleasures; clinging to dogmas and views; clinging to religious rituals and vows; clinging to the belief that one is an enduring soul]
conditioning/leading to

10 The process of becoming (*bhāva*): [the momentum within a stream]
conditioning/leading to

11 Rebirth
conditioning/leading to

12 Aging, death and sorrow … leading to unenlightenment (1)

3 There is an end to suffering, called *nirvāṇa (nibbāna)*

'Nirvāṇa' means 'blowing out'. Specifically, it is the end of unsatisfactory existence through the extinction of the fires of greed, hatred and delusion that generate rebirth-causing actions.... It means a tranquil and detached way of being in the world, untroubled by selfish concerns and acquisitiveness. Nirvana is the pacification of the greedy and aggressive self-perpetuating stream of experiences that has mistakenly superimposed a persisting identity on itself.

This is what early Buddhism meant by 'enlightenment'. It is nothing other than comprehension of the Four Noble Truths and their enactment in one's life. *Nirvāṇa* is a way of being in this world, rather than a supernatural realm of heaven.

As Richard Gombrich has pointed out, the use of the metaphor of fire in respect of greed, hatred and delusion is no accident. Indeed, it is more specific than the idea that everyone is burning with desires that only generate more experiences and more desires. It alludes to the three fires which the Brahminical householder was obliged to keep burning and which symbolized his life, responsibilities and attachments as a social being.[7] It represents the endless repetitions that characterize the life of the householder. The tradition is reluctant to say anything positive about *nirvāṇa* as a post-mortem state. Whatever it involves, there are no persons to experience it. The earlier tradition sees it as the extinction of greed, hatred and delusion and the end of the afflictions (ignorance, selfishness, desire for sensory gratifications, obsessive attachments and an exalted opinion of oneself).

4 There is a path to the cessation of suffering: The eightfold path of morality and meditation

The Four Noble Truths are the key to enlightenment, the eradication of self-interested motivations and oppressive emotions. But hearing the truth is not enough. It has to be acted upon, and this is where the path of morality and meditation comes in. The emphasis is on self-control, kindness and tranquillity. The goal is a 'decentring', a reversal of the predicament of *homo incurvatus in se*, via the cultivation of virtues or worthwhile dispositions of character and motivation. Fundamentally, I do not exist in any sense that matters, but it is still possible to improve this present stream by replacing anger, jealousy, greed, carelessness and sloth with equanimity, compassion, friendliness and generosity. The eightfold path is said to consist in right views, right thoughts, right speech, right action, right livelihood, right effort, right mindfulness and right concentration. Right views and thoughts are mind-purifying wisdom or insight into the fleeting and unsatisfactory nature of existence; right speech, action and livelihood are moral conduct; and right effort, mindfulness and concentration are understood as meditation.

Buddhists insist that virtue is necessary for the cultivation of meditation and insight. It is the intention (*cetanā*), more generally the attitude, with which an action is performed that is held to determine its moral quality. Moral conduct involves deliberate abstention from murder, theft, sexual promiscuity, alcohol and drugs, false and malicious speech, slander, harsh words, frivolous talk, covetousness, malice and false views. Right livelihood would preclude such occupations as arms-trading, dealing in drugs and alcohol, and butchering animals. Meditative concentration (*samādhi*) is the achievement of tranquillity through avoidance of distractions and by controlling the senses. Emphasis is placed upon mindfulness or exercising control through constant self-awareness of one's physical, mental and emotional states.

The path is the 'middle way' between the self-indulgent and ascetic lives, neither of which lead to release from the desire-fuelled series of existences. What is needed is the elimination of the basic defects of greed, hatred and delusion.

We saw that the Buddha insisted that it is the intention (*cetanā*) with which an action is performed that determines its moral quality and thus its consequences in the stream to which it belongs. He tells his followers to cultivate attitudes of non-violence, honesty, friendliness, gentleness, compassion and generosity. The right sorts of actions will follow. He did not provide a rulebook stipulating particular types of ethical actions (although his followers did for the monks) or an ethical theory. There are some basic principles: do not kill, do not steal, do not tell lies or indulge in malicious gossip, avoid sexual misdemeanours and intoxicating substances. These are universal – not caste-specific – in that they have moral application to everyone: I do not want to be assaulted and can reasonably conclude that no other sane person wants to be. There is a trend of thought running through Hinduism that there may be ways of acting that do not generate *karma*. Representative here is the idea, promoted in the *Bhagavad Gītā*, that since it is deliberately purposive actions that generate *karma*, actions done for their own or duty's sake without a view to the advantage of the agent will not generate *karma*. The Buddha thought that sentient beings could not escape from *karma*. The eightfold path recognizes this. It is sometimes argued that the outlook is consequentialist, holding that it is overall states of affairs that have moral value. Indeed, the Buddhist path aims to promote general happiness. Everyone accepts that some patterns of behaviour have better overall consequences than others. The view is that although the future of the stream that is your life is not your future, you still have reason to care about its future, as well as that of all other streams.

Moral conduct attenuates afflictions (*kleśa*) that prey upon the mind. These weaknesses are familiar ones: ignorance in the sense of indulging oneself in self-serving fantasies and believing whatever it suits one to believe; the sheer selfishness that sees itself as the centre of the world; desire for sensory gratifications; neurotic obsessions that divert attention from what matters; and an exalted opinion of one's significance in the scheme of things. The texts catalogue other impediments to spiritual progress, two of which we shall mention briefly. There is attachment to rituals, central to the Brahminical way of life, and vows, the latter being personal undertakings and commitments such as the harsh austerities that Gautama had found useless. I think that the word '*kāma*' often moralistically translated as 'lust' or 'sensual desires' was probably more specific and refers to those rituals performed by Brahmins that will yield benefits in this world for those patronizing them. The Buddha thought that all ritual performances were at heart self-interested, not to say a waste of time and effort.

The texts are rich in descriptions of and prescriptions for meditational practices, aiming at the control and finally the cessation of discursive mental activities. The Buddha described his path to enlightenment as an ascent through a hierarchy of four stages of meditations (*dhyāna*) which, far from involving ascetic rigours, are pleasant experiences:

> Then indeed, having eaten enough, having got my strength back, free from desires, free from unhelpful matters, I reached the first stage that is accompanied by thought and reflection, which is produced by discrimination and consists of joyful happiness, and remained there. But this pleasant state did not put my mind at rest.
>
> Stilling thought and reflection, I reached the second stage that is inner tranquillity, a focusing of the mind on one point, free from thought and reflection, consisting of joyful happiness that is born of concentration, and remained there. But this pleasant state …

> I reached the third stage when I became detached from joy, indifferent to pleasures and pains, attentively mindful and knew no physical pleasures. But this …
>
> From abandoning bliss and abandoning pain and thanks to the disappearance of cheerfulness and depression, I reached the fourth stage that is beyond pleasures and pains, the quintessence of equanimity and attentiveness. But this … [Majjhima Nikāya 1.247].

This is a typical account of meditation involving successive stages. It did not put his mind at rest because it stopped short of revealing the fundamental truth that our experiences are unsatisfactory because we fail to realize that there are really no individual identities and that everything is impermanent.

Meditation also has a positive goal, that is to say, the cultivation of the helpful (*kuśala*) states called the *Brahma-Vihāras*: friendliness, compassion, joy and equanimity. There is also what is called 'meditation on the four infinities' that aims at the suppression of imagination and conceptual thinking. There is a fourfold hierarchy of stages: the stage of the infinity of space, the stage of the infinity of perception, the stage of nothingness and the stage beyond conceptualization and non-conceptualization. Dwelling on notions of the infinite emphasizes the limits of conceptual thought and undermines confidence in the capacity of our minds to grasp the nature of reality. I take what is called meditation on no-thingness to refer to a state in which one is not focused on anything in particular: a reflex of the realization that there are no individual identities.[8]

Finally, morality and meditation are not understood instrumentally, as means to something different. Their complete realization is what enlightenment means. That is the *nirvāṇa* accomplished by the Buddhas. The person who successfully follows the Buddhist path is liberated while still alive.

Anattā: No substance; no soul; no self that really matters

The early Buddhists denied that there is anything *essential* to one's life. If everything is always changing, there are no fixed identities or natures. It is natural fact that a life is a series of phases of mental and physical events. A phase is a period of psychological continuity. We are just successive phases upon which a specious enduring identity is somehow superimposed. Thence arises the illusion of personal endurance.

There are, however, no personal substances. There is nothing that owns its experiences. Rather, each discrete and momentary perception is the perceiver; each discrete and momentary thought is the thinker; a feeling is what feels pleasure and pain; a memory is the rememberer. There is a life history, but no subject of that history. Put another way: there is no difference between you and your life. The Buddha and his followers denied the need for the postulation of an unchanging transcendental factor that unifies one's experiences. There is no reason to posit something that serves as a vehicle of *karma* through lives since the continuity of action and consequence is a purely natural occurrence. As Alex Watson has put it, 'Thus the Self disappears by being deconstructed both diachronically and synchronically. It is deconstructed diachronically into a plurality of distinct momentary phases; and synchronically in that even the momentary phases are not unitary because they consist of five separate constituents. *This model stresses not only the transitory and insubstantial, but also the impersonal nature of our existence. The idea of a person acting and experiencing is replaced with that of an impersonal stream of transitory mental and physical events.*'[9] [my emphasis]

The occasionally canvassed suggestion that the Buddha accepted that there is a substantial soul as a further fact separate from the interactions of the five *skandhas* may safely be dismissed. In the first place, there is no textual support. Secondly, Buddhism would not have been constituted as a distinct religious movement had its originators propounded a substance ontology. The rejection of essentialism and adoption of process ontology precludes the belief that we are souls.[10]

One view found in the Upaniṣads is that the key to the meaning of life and ultimate well-being is the realization that what one is essentially is the same as the innermost principle of the cosmos.

> The nature (*ātman*) that is free from evils, free from old age and death, from sorrow, from hunger and thirst, whose desires and intentions are ever realised, that is what is to be discovered, that is what is to be understood. When someone discovers that nature and understands it, he obtains all worlds and all his desires are fulfilled.

The text continues to say that this nature, discovery of which delivers all worlds and the satisfaction of every desire, is to be found within: it is 'this person that appears in the eye … that is immortal, that is free from fear, that is the *brahman*'.[11]

The Buddha thought that the mentality to which such thinking belongs is basically self-interested. The belief that one is a persisting entity with a specific set of interests generates anxiety, narrow-mindedness, acquisitiveness and antagonism – in other words, everything that is meant by the familiar formula 'greed, hatred and delusion'. He resists views like this by denying that there is such a thing as the soul: all we can say is that there are temporal streams of experiences and ethical consequentiality.

If what we call the person is the stream of thoughts, who is thinking them? The Buddhist view is that intrinsically self-aware subjectless thoughts are thinking themselves, as well as each other. They do not need illumination by consciousness belonging to a persisting subject. They form a continuous entity by knowing their immediate predecessors and successors. William James illuminatingly characterized an atomistic 'no-self theory' as follows: 'Each pulse of cognitive consciousness, each thought, dies away and is replaced by another. The other, among the things it knows, knows its own predecessor … saying: "Thou art mine, and part of the same self with me." Each later thought, knowing and including thus the thoughts which went before, is the final receptacle of all that they contain and own. Each Thought is thus born an owner, and dies unowned, transmitting whatever it realized as its Self to its own later proprietor.'[12]

The early Buddhist tradition reductively analysed what we understand as persons into processes consisting of five components (*skandhas*):

1 Body (*rūpa*).
2 Sensation, and feelings of pleasure and pain (*vedanā*).
3 Sense-based perceptions of objects (*vijñāna*). This is apprehension of particulars.[13]
4 Conceptual thoughts (*saṃjñā*) [thinking *that* a given object is blue or that blue is a colour]. This is apprehension of generalities.
5 Inherited dispositions of character, acts of will, mindset and habits (*saṃskāra*).

Feelings, perceptions, thoughts and volitions are all momentary events. It is noteworthy that there is no mention of consciousness purely as such. Indeed, they do not recognize what is sometimes called 'the unity of consciousness' since the notion that there is a singularity called consciousness is at home in a soul theory.

Neither singly nor collectively do these transitory factors constitute an enduring identity. There is no permanent self or person over and above the components. There is nothing that 'owns' successively occurring experiences.

The interactions of the *skandhas* produce the illusion that one is a subject looking out on the world from a privileged point of view. They generate an epiphenomenal sense of continuing selfhood, but that sense is ephemeral and insubstantial. Although it occurs, it is not really significant. But some things matter: virtues like honesty, kindness, self-control, generosity and compassion.

It is held that there is continuity of events within a stream because one event causes the origination of its successor. A taste sensation may engender a feeling of pleasure, and each may be registered by distinct thoughts. This complex may engender in the future a memory that causes a desire for the repetition of the initial pleasurable experience.

The genesis of the illusion of enduring selfhood, the appearance of unity among rapidly successive inner events, is also explained by reference to the self-revealing nature of individual perceptions, feeling, thoughts and volitions comprising a mental field. At any given moment, one's mental state is self-aware. This self-awareness of each is readily confused with that of the subsequent event. In short, they blend together and the amalgam experiences itself as a continuing reality.

It is apparent from the Pāli Canon that views about what humans really are were as multifarious during the Buddha's time as they are today. When fear of death perturbs the human spirit, we look for something to hold on to that will exist in the future. Some may think of 'a self' in personal terms as a complex of experiences that just lasts for a while. Others may believe that there is as a transcendental subject that is untouched by worldly life and destined to exist for ever. The mainstream Buddhist view is that the belief that there is some sort of lasting self is one of the varieties of grasping that only lead to distress.

The term 'person' is seen as a convenient shorthand expression for talking about a causally connected sequence of events. We unenlightened beings may make the mistake of supposing that what is merely a manner of speaking designates an enduring substance, an inner controller, an irreducible subject of experiences looking out on the world from a privileged perspective. For the Buddha, attachment to this misconception only leads to unhappiness. Buddhist praxis aims to eliminate the mistake. Belief that one is really 'a soul' leads to anxious self-concern, narrowness of vision, defensiveness and antagonism to others who are seen as barriers to the expansion of the ego. Such is the fuel of the perpetuation of the process of rebirth. If the Upaniṣadic thinkers thought that the soul was ungraspable, beyond language, so subtle as to be undetectable, the Buddha went further. There isn't anything there. We have here a radical solution to the problem of human selfishness: there is no 'self' to worry about. This goes beyond the rejection of Brahminical notions of transcendental soul. It extends to the everyday assumption that there is a unique personal essence or ego at the centre of an arena of action and concern. And take the more modest view that although the centre is nothing more than an ephemeral epiphenomenon of the experiential flux, it still matters and is worth protecting and promoting. All these beliefs, say the Buddhists, are forms of selfishness, and they too are fatal to our chances of happiness.

An early and popular scripture, the Snake Sutta in the Majjhima Nikāya, describes the familiar pathology in terms of a series of identifications that are instances of grasping or appropriation (*upādāna*):

> The unenlightened person regards the body as his, as what he is, as his nature. He regards feelings as his, as what he is, as his nature. He regards perceptions as his, as what he is, as his nature. He regards thoughts as his, as what he is, as his nature. He regards volitions and habits as his, as what he is, as his nature. He regards what he has seen, heard, known, experienced, pursued and considered as his, as what he is, as his nature.
>
> And there is the attitude, 'The world and the soul are the same, and after death this is what I shall be – permanent, enduring, eternal, immutable and I shall exist like that forever.' This view he regards as his, as what he is, as his nature.... But the enlightened person does not think in these terms and so is not anxious about something that does not exist.[14]

The point seems to be that identifying anything finite and transient, such as a stream of embodied experiences, as a persisting personal identity (an obstacle to enlightenment called '*sat-kāya-dṛṣṭi*') is bound to lead to unhappiness and anxiety. Thoughts and feelings just happen. In reality there is no one to whom they happen. There is just a 'bundle of perceptions'. The more sophisticated understanding of oneself as a transcendental subject, really exempt from worldly life and destined to exist forever, only leads to worry too. Will it really continue? The enlightened person does not think in terms of either of these egocentric frameworks, and that is the key to living without anxiety, without obsessive self-concern. The key to enlightenment and happiness is not just altruism, but the realization that there is neither soul nor a substantial ego that might justify one's selfish concerns.

The radical nature of the vision should not be underestimated. Returning to the Snake Sutta:

> When someone who does not have the view that the world and the soul are the same, and that after death he will be permanent, enduring, eternal, immutable and that he will exist like that for ever hears the Buddha's teaching about the abandonment of theories, opinions and attachment to them, the teaching that aims at the suppression of clinging obsessive attachments, the relinquishing of possessions, the end of craving, the cultivation of dispassion and the extinction of greed, hatred and delusion – he does not fear, 'I shall be annihilated. I shall be destroyed. I shall no longer exist.' He is not distressed and confused. He is not anxious about something that does not exist.[15]

A work called the Questions of King Milinda relates a dialogue about the no-self doctrine between Menander, the Greek king of Bactria (c.165–130 B.C.) in what is now Afghanistan, and a Buddhist monk called Nāgasena.[16] The text appears to be directed against a 'personalist' trend in early Buddhism according to which there emerges from the interactions of the five constituents of personality (*skandhas*) a persisting individual who is reborn.

The monk says that he is called 'Nāgasena' but that is only a name, a label, a conventional usage. It does not follow that there is a personal entity. The King replies that in that case Nāgasena lacks parents, teachers and superiors in the monastic order. It also rules out agency and moral responsibility. At this point, Nāgasena introduces the simile of the chariot. The chariot looks like a unitary whole entity, but on reflection we see that it is a mere assemblage of parts – wheels, axle and chassis. The word 'chariot' is a label, a conventional designation for what is in fact a collection. If the chariot is dismantled, we have collection of parts but no one thing that we could call the chariot. Still, it conveys us from A to B.

Analogously the name 'Nāgasena' is a conventional designation for a construct out of the five constituents of personality. No person is found, as opposed to being constructed. But the series of interactive components suffices as a vehicle of *karma* across lives.

There is no further fact over and above the fleeting components of the stream of experiences. Nevertheless, there is sufficient continuity within the stream for us to make sense of agency and moral responsibility. The Buddhist position is that moral responsibility does not depend on a permanent self that is the subject of experiences and who will enjoy future consequences.

If we are to be happy, we should be concerned about the future, even though it is not the future of my self.

The tradition has it that the Buddha deliberately left a number of questions unanswered.[17] They include whether or not the world is eternal, whether or not the world is infinite, whether self and body are the same and whether or not enlightened beings (Buddhas) exist after death (a question that can be seen as making the mistaken assumption that there are entities with determinate identities).

In refusing to answer such questions, the Buddha cannot be saying that he does not know, for the Buddhas are omniscient. Rather, he is saying that there is nothing to know. From the Buddhist point of view, such questions reflect a resistance to the disturbing teachings of momentariness and the non-substantiality of beings.

One Buddhist tradition says that thinking about such matters is not conducive to the ending of suffering and enlightenment. One cannot lead a spiritual life by virtue of believing that the world is eternal or infinite in space and time! Another view is that the questions are themselves unanswerable because they are posed in categories that are themselves distorting. The questions about the cosmos presuppose that it is such that we are in a position to view it as a single whole and that past, present and future are divisions within a single temporal framework. It is difficult to formulate the question about whether the cosmos has a finite age.

Above all, the problem is that the questions reflect a search for intellectual certainty and conviction, an attempt to comprehend and perhaps control. They imply that an absolute conception of reality, an Olympian perspective or a totally objective grasp of truth, is accessible to us. The Buddha's position seems to be that it is not the case that such a perspective is available, but even if it were, it would not help us along the path to enlightenment.

A much-quoted traditional formulation distinguishes broadly between four Buddhist philosophical positions:

> The Vaibhāṣikas say that there are realities external to minds and that they are directly perceptible.
>
> The Sautrāntikas say that there are realities external to minds and that they are inferable from the occurrence of mental representations.
>
> The Yogācāras deny that there are any realities external to minds.
>
> The Mādhyamikas deny that there are any intrinsic natures.

The next chapters will consider each of these four schools of thought.

Further reading

Bechert and Gombrich (1984) is a collection of essays covering all forms of Buddhism and is beautifully illustrated.

Rupert Gethin's *Foundations of Buddhism* is comprehensive. It is now supplementary to his invaluable *Sayings of the Buddha.* Walpola Rahula, *What the Buddha Taught,* is a classic, written from a Theravādin point of view. Steven Collins, *Selfless Persons,* is indispensable for early Buddhist (Theravādin) representations of persons. Richard Gombrich, *How Buddhism Began,* puts many things in context. Edward Conze's *Buddhist Scriptures* is a useful collection that contains the Questions of King Milinda.

Bronkhorst (2000) contains translations of much original material and connects early Buddhism with the Jaina renunciatory tradition. For the latter, Jaini (1979) and Dundas (1992) are fundamental contributions.

Mark Siderits, *Buddhism as Philosophy,* provides plenty of food for thought. The same author's *Personal Identity and Buddhist Philosophy* is an exhaustive discussion of Eastern and Western reductionist accounts of selves. Chapter 5 of Paul Williams, *Altruism and Reality,* is, to say the least, stimulating.

Questions for discussion and investigation

1. Can reductionism about persons make sense of human life?
2. If personal identity is an illusion, what is making the mistake in the first place?

Notes

1. Gombrich (1992) and (1996). See also Norman (1991).
2. v. Eltschinger (2012).
3. It is also atheistic in the sense that Buddhists do not think that the absence of God is grounds for regret.

4. Neither seriously entertains a physicalist account. The facts that the body dies and is burned rule out continuity across different lives and thereby undermine belief in *karma*.
5. The phrase is from the Pāli Canon.
6. DN II 56-64: SN II 2-4.
7. v. Gombrich (1996), pp. 65–72.
8. Bronkhorst (2000), pp. 78–95.
9. Watson (2006), pp. 56–7.
10. 'He rejected entirely the use of the word in the old animistic sense. He retained it in a personal sense, in the meaning of "oneself, himself" &c. And though, of course he acknowledged the reality of the emotional and intellectual dispositions, he refused absolutely to look upon them as a unity.' See T. W. Rhys Davids, Dialogues of the Buddha Pt I, p. 189. The translated literature is replete with formulations to the effect that 'x is/are not the self'. This leads some to suppose that the Buddha believed that there is a Self that we variously misidentify with thoughts, perceptions or the body. The formulations in question usually mean 'thoughts are insubstantial', 'feelings are insubstantial', 'physical states are insubstantial' (*anātmānaḥ*).
11. Chāndogya Upaniṣad 8.7.1ff.
12. *The Principles of Psychology*, Volume I, p. 339.
13. *Viṣayaṃ prati vijñaptir upalabdhiṃ vijñāna skandha iti ucyate* (AKBh 11.6-8). The *vijñāna skandha* is called cognition or awareness of an object.
14. Majjhima Nikāya, I 135. Gethin (2008), p. 161.
15. Majjhima Nikāya, N I 137. Gethin (2008), p. 163.
16. Milinda's Questions, trans. I. B. Horner, London PTs (1963–64).
17. Collins (1982), pp. 131–7.

3

Abhidharma Buddhism

Chapter Outline

The Monastic context

We have seen that the Buddha and his followers believed that there was no need to posit a substantial primary being as the cause of the cosmos. We have seen them deny that a substantial soul lies at the basis of personality. They hold that the terms such as 'self' and 'person' are applied to what is just a series of components. Accordingly, it is a mistake to suppose that one has an identity distinct from those ephemeral and insubstantial factors.

We have seen them claim that continuity and regularity in the cosmos and in the sphere of human experience is explained by dependent origination (*pratītya-samutpāda*). In the centuries after the Buddha's death (c.400 B.C.), divergent interpretations of the master's teachings saw the development of a plethora of sects, each with its own literature.[1] These literary works were called Abhidharmas, and they were systematic explications of the teachings discursively presented in the Pāli Canon. After approximately 200 B.C., some philosophically minded Buddhist monks set about the task of establishing the truth of insubstantiality (*nairātmya*) by reductively analysing our experiences, and the world-as-experienced, in ways that were more systematic and comprehensive than the earlier analysis of the human person into the five impermanent components of personality (*skandhas*): body, feelings, sensory perceptions, mindset and conceptual thoughts. These monks set about compiling increasingly elaborate lists and classifications of what they took to be the basic mental and physical phenomena. Through the method of sub-division into minute detail and combination, the catalogues proliferated. What motivated this enterprise? Discriminative analysis or deconstruction of composites into basic elements of reality (*dharmānām pravicaya*) was believed to be an aspect of mental cultivation and hence a meritorious activity. Vasubandhu (c.350 A.D.) says in his '*Abhidharmakośa*': There is no means of pacifying the passions without close examination of the elements of reality. It is the passions that cause the world to wander in the great ocean of rebirth (*saṃsāra*).[2]

Critical analysis leads to insight (*prajñā*) into the inherent natures of the simple elements. The world is not what it seems: it is a superficial construct out of basic factors. There's another reality behind the phenomena. Moreover, deconstruction of personality reinforces the belief that there is no soul understood as a substance or entity in its own right. The skilled practitioner dissolves the objects of attachment into their elements and eliminates desires for them. The organization of *dharmas* into categories also facilitated the drawing of distinctions between experiences that are unwholesome and lead to more suffering and virtuous ones that lead to liberation.

We know about the Theravādin and Sarvāstivādin (also called Vaibhāṣika) Abhidharma sects (*nikāya*). It is the Vaibhāṣika view that will be described here. Our most valuable source of information is a work called the *Abhidharmakośa-bhāṣya* by Vasubandhu (350–400 A.D.), which was actually written from an opposing point of view called 'Sautrāntika'.[3] The designation 'Vaibhāṣika' derives from a text called the *Mahāvibhāṣa*, itself a commentary on the *Jñānaprasthāna*, which was one of the seven treatises constituting a collection called the Abhidharma-piṭaka of the Sarvāstivāda sect.

Ontology

Sarvāstivāda means 'the theory that everything exists' (*sarva-asti-vāda*).[4] Specifically, it means that past, present and future are equally real, although only the present is actual. The questions 'What exists?' or 'What is there?' cannot be answered by merely listing objects. We need a classification of types of existents. Moreover, there has to be some criterion or standard of judging what *really* exists, and the criterion here is simplicity and irreducibility: nothing that is composed of parts is *authentically* real. If nothing composed of parts is *genuinely* real, then nor is the person that is composed of organs, faculties and diverse experiences.

As we have seen, the basic elements of which all mental and material phenomena consist are called *dharmas*.[5] The Sarvāstivādins distinguish between the primary and irreducible existence (*dravya-sat*) that belongs to the simple elements (*dharmas*) and the conventional or nominal existence (*saṃvṛti-* or *prajñapti-sat*) that belongs to whatever they comprise.[6] *Dharmas* as primary and simple realities exist in what we call the past, present and future – but strictly speaking, they exist timelessly or eternally. This is *dravya-sat* or substantial being. Their momentary occurrence as the world of our experience when they exercise their causal efficacy (*kāritram*) is *prajñapti-sat*. A parallel distinction is drawn between absolute or ultimate truth and reality (*paramārtha-satya*) and conventional/superficial truth (*saṃvṛti-satya*).[7] The latter pertains to the world as it is understood by finite beings participating in conditioned causal processes. The former means reality as it is in itself, as understood by the Buddhas, who are omniscient beings.

All causally conditioned things, spread out in space and time, and featuring in our normal experience are described as conventional realities. Anything that consists of parts, anything that can be reduced to basic elements, is said to exist by convention or nominally (*prajñapti-sat*). Such composites are by definition impermanent, existing only, as it were, 'for the time being'. The atoms composing a clay pot are primary existents, whereas the pot is a derivative 'conventional reality'. This is not to say that everyday things do not exist. They are, however, insubstantial and ephemeral. They are reducible to the basic realities of which they are composed.

Each *dharma* has a fixed essence or intrinsic nature of its own. This is called '*svabhāva*', which can be analysed as meaning 'own' (*sva*) 'being' or 'nature' (*bhāva*). It will be obvious that if the meaning of substance encompasses both independence of everything else as well as an enduring essential identity, then we have here a very strong notion of substance. *Svabhāva* means a fixed and permanent essence that does not depend upon anything else. It is this possession of a timeless, self-sufficient and permanent identity that differentiates the *dharmas* from the macroscopic aggregates that are composed of them. It is these *dharmas* as they are in themselves that are held to exist in the 'three times': future, present and past. The impermanence taught by the Buddha refers not to the nature of the elements (they are timeless essences) but to their actualizations in complexes as this world. It refers to the very quick (not quite instantaneous) exercise of efficacy here and now. The insubstantiality taught by the Buddha refers to complexes, aggregates and process, not to the elements.

Each *dharma* has its own specific mark (*svalakṣaṇa*). The latter is also its specific function (*kāritra, vṛtti, svakriyā, svabhāga*). The Sarvāstivādins thought that the impermanence taught by the Buddha referred to this functioning, but not to the essential natures of the basic elements. In the Abhidharma catalogues, the essence of a *dharma* is *specified* by reference to its function, although the essence of a *dharma* is not identical with that function. The *svabhāva* of earth atoms is solidity, that of water atoms is fluidity, and that of fire atoms is heat. It is the *svabhāva* of consciousness to apprehend objects.[8]

A *dharma* manifests its proper function for a single brief moment in an appropriate context of other dharmas and then returns to its original inert condition. We may think of the *dharmas* as they are in themselves as occupying another dimension of reality, from which they briefly migrate into our world, and to which homeland they return. The actualization, the temporal presence, of the *dharmas* in and as our world, is the exercise of their efficacy in a causal complex. Intrinsic natures are fixed (*dharma-svabhāva* is *nitya*), but the exercise of efficacy is momentary (*anitya*) and circumstantial (*kādācitka*). The Vaibhāṣikas think that it was to these momentary discharges of energy in the world of conditioned phenomena that the Buddha was referring when he spoke of universal impermanence. The exercise of efficacy when a *dharma* enters a causal complex is not a change in that *dharma*, but just its manifesting what it permanently is. Each case of momentary actualization lasts just long enough to bring about its own following moment. A *dharma* attracts the manifestation of another token of its own type. This explains stability and continuity. Efficacy may be compared to the charge on the countless identical electrons. A *dharma* is said to be in conditioned mode when it participates in a causal complex. 'Conditioned' means having the four characteristics of origination, duration, decline and impermanence (sometimes expressed as impermanence, suffering and the lack of essential identity). 'Decline', another basic reality, is what we may call entropy, and explains why the flower fades and the grass withers.

The moment of manifestation is what is called the present time. Future *dharmas* are those that have not manifested their proper function. Past *dharmas* are those that have. The *dharmas* do not just exist *at* those times but rather constitute them – time means the actualization or otherwise of *dharmas*. They exist *as* those times. Time is understood in terms of the exercise of efficacy. We see here a distinctive understanding of time and a rejection of the view of another sect called the Vibhajyavāda-Dārṣṭāntikas who held that time is a reality in its own right through which the transient conditioned elements of existence move. They say that only the *dharmas* that are present now exist, along with some retributive potencies of past intentional actions. The Vaibhāṣika view is that what we call past is those *dharmas* that have exercised their efficacy and what we call future is those *dharmas* that have not exercised that disposition. Time is not a substantial reality independent of subjects, objects and events. The *dharmas* do not 'pass through' time as though time were a separate reality. Our experience of temporal flow is in fact the replacement of *dharmas*. There is no real change on the level of the primary realities, which exist timelessly and immutably. (Some think that there is a problem in defining the present as the moment of the exercise of causal efficacy. The latter is an activity, a process that requires time. So the concept of temporal efficacy requires an independent grasp of the distinction between past, present and future.)

The functioning of the *dharmas* in complexes is regulated by one or more of six causal operations.[9] These are:

Simultaneous cause (*sahabhū-kāraṇa*)
Immediately preceding cause (*samanantara-kāraṇa*)
Homogeneous cause (*sabhāga-kāraṇa*)
Ubiquitous cause (*sarvatraga-kāraṇa*)
Moral cause (*vipāka-kāraṇa*)
Master cause (*adhipati-kāraṇa*)

Take the example of a blue surface: it consists of blue-*dharmas* that function just for long enough to attract their replacement by other blue-*dharmas*. This is a case of homogeneous causality. In other cases, a *dharma* determines a remote effect. This is particularly applicable to the future moral consequences of our actions. The morally significant aspect of an action is the intention (*cetanā*) with which it is performed. That intention is a momentary *dharma*. How is it related to its effects in the same stream when it no longer exists? The system of causes provides the explanation. If the effect occurs in the same moment, the simultaneous and immediate causes are operative. If it occurs in the next moment, the responsibility is that of the homogeneous and ubiquitous causes. When the occurrence of the effect is remote, the *vipāka-kāraṇa* is operative (and the homogeneous and ubiquitous causes may be). The Vaibhāṣika view is that what we experience as the present is the exercise of efficacy (*phala-ākṣepa-śakti*) – the power of projecting effects that belongs to a complex of *dharmas*.

Other Buddhist philosophical traditions see a problem here. The basic elements are said to have intrinsic natures. But intrinsic nature is often construed as causal power, the capacity to do something. The nature of a white atom is to contribute to a white surface and bring about a certain perception. The aim is to identify the *dharmas* in virtue of their independent self-sufficiency, their being as they are in themselves. But it seems that they are not characterized in categorical terms but rather in dispositional ones, that is to say, in terms of their capacity to interact with other *dharmas*. Strictly speaking, each is characterized in relational terms. We are not really specifying internal natures because causal powers have to do with external relations. We are not being told what the possessors of the causal powers are like in themselves. So the picture is one of a giant causal flux, but with no real explanation of the intrinsic natures of the entities related in the flux. We shall return to this point in the next chapter.

The Sarvāstivādin catalogues distinguish conditioned (*saṃskṛta*) and unconditioned *dharmas*. *Dharmas* are spoken of as conditioned when they are the constituents of causal processes. Such processes are transient and insubstantial, and all *dharmas* are impersonal. Processes are generated by the co-operating causes and conditions (called *hetu* and *pratyaya*) that we saw above. The unconditioned realities are exempt from causality. These are: space (*ākāśa*); nirvana as a result of liberating insight and nirvana as a result of meditation and virtuous conduct.

The conditioned phenomena are categorized as follows:

(i) Material phenomena (*rūpa*): bodies, sense-faculties and corresponding types of objects.

(ii) Mind (*citta*)

(iii) Mental phenomena (*caitta*):

Intentional mental acts: perceiving (via senses); judging; willing; intending; imagining; believing; considering; doubting; and remembering.

Feelings.

Moral values that belong to the fabric of reality: compassion, generosity, modesty, non-violence, trust (in the Buddhas), mindfulness, self-control and also defects such as greed, hatred, delusion, conceit and sloth [which have to be eradicated and replaced by virtuous moral *dharmas*].

(iv) 'Factors dissociated from mind' (*citta-viprayukta-dharma*) which cannot be classified as either material or mental. These are:

Traces of previous cognitions latent in the mind that furnish the contents of dreams and hallucinations.

Sentences, words and letters.

The common properties that organize living beings into the different species (*nikāya-sabhāgatā*). This is what causes perceived resemblances.

A force called *prāpti* that regulates the aggregation of particular types of *dharmas* and locates them in a specific stream.

The four general characteristics (*sāmānya-lakṣaṇa*) common to conditioned phenomena, that is, origination (*jāti*), continuation (*sthiti*), decline (*jara*) and impermanence (*anityatā*).

The Vaibhāṣika doctrine that future and past phenomena are just as real as present ones claims the authority of the Buddha's teaching. Its key assumptions are:

(i) Cognitive experiences occur only when there is interaction between one of the six faculties (five senses and mental cognition) and a real object outside the mind.

(ii) All mental acts, including memories and expectations, have existent objects external to the mind. The fact that past and future phenomena are perceived proves that they exist. Memories and future expectations refer to real objects that are not present.

(iii) The subject–object relation in awareness requires two real terms.

(iv) We cannot escape the consequences of past actions. If past actions were non-existent, they could not have future consequences.[10]

> Past and future *dharmas* exist because cognitions need real objects. When there is an object, there arises a cognition. When there is no object, there arises no cognition. If past and future *dharmas* did not exist, there would be cognitions whose objective grounds (*ālambana*) would be unreal things. Therefore there would be no cognition of the past and future because of the absence of objective grounds. If the past were non-existent, how could there be future effects of good and bad actions? For at the time when the effect arises, the efficient cause of its actualisation (*vipāka-hetu*) would no longer exist. That is why the Vaibhāṣikas hold that past and future exist.[11]

> The Sarvāstivādins say that everything – past, future and present – exists. By contrast, the Vibhajyavādins say that only the present exists, as well as past actions that have not yet yielded their consequences. [They say that] what will be future, and actions that have borne fruit do not exist.[12]

'A reality that is past has ceased to function due to impermanence. A reality that is future has not yet exercised its function. A reality that is present has originated and not yet ceased. When basic realities (*dharmas*) exercise efficacy, this is called the present. If *dharmas* do not yet exercise it, this is called the future. If efficacy has gone, this is called the past.'[13]

Mind and world

Where our interactions with the world about us are concerned, the Vaibhāṣikas and Sarvāstivādins are epistemological direct realists. Macroscopic combinations of the basic factors are the causes and direct objects of awareness (*anusaṃcayavāda*). The objects that we perceive are conglomerates of *dharmas*. We do not perceive *dharmas* – not because they are too small or outside the scope of our sense-faculties (as certain sounds are, for instance) but because they are imperceptible.

All cognitive events have existent objects. This is because a perception is defined as the product of the interaction between one of the six sense-faculties and something in the world. Dreams and hallucinations (as well as memories) have real objects. Memories, for example, relate to information about former configurations of *dharmas* – information about which is stored in the transcendent dimension. All information about the past is recorded and stored 'in a cloud'. Dream experiences and hallucinations relate to configurations of basic realities that just happen not to be actual.

Minds just reveal objects in the world: there is no subjective contribution. This realist view is called *nirākāra-vāda*, and it means that our perceptions of objects are unmediated by mental images, representations or ideas that fall as a veil between mental acts and external reality.

Indriya	*Viṣaya*	*Vijnāna*
Faculties	*Spheres*	*Experiences*
Sight	Colour/shape	Visual
Audition	Sounds	Auditory
Smell	Odours	Olfactory

Taste	Tastes	Tasting
Touch	Textures	Tactile
Mental	Cognitions	Thinking

Items in column three are products of the interaction of the corresponding pair (termed *āyatana*) in columns 1 and 2. They are described as perceptions directed towards objects (*prati-viṣaya-vijñapti*). Mind (*manas*) is also treated as a faculty. Just as we perceive physical objects by means of the senses, the mind is that by which we grasp thoughts. This covers thinking about experiences of objects, as well as states of affairs that are not present to the senses. Perceptions are always the product of an interaction between a sense-faculty and something in the world. There is no reality in its own right called 'consciousness', just a succession of cognitive events.

Ethical consequentiality and moral values

Buddhism is first and foremost an unselfish way of life rather than a theory. Buddhists believe that liberation is not possible for those who do not accept that what is conventionally called (*prajñapti*) self is only a stream of components of personality. Unenlightened people mistakenly believe in an identity that is a further fact over and above the transient flux of embodied experiences. From this attachment to the notion of soul arise the afflictions such as grasping, aversion and delusion. But the notions of self and individual personal agency are just conventional human constructs. Underlying what we call the person is a complex of components (*skandhas*) that admit of yet further reduction into the basic elements of reality. Nevertheless, a causal chain of embodied experiences is sufficient for the origin of the deluded belief that one is a persisting subject of experiences. It is the intentional actions alone that are responsible for the arising and organization of the worlds. This attribution of causality to the deeds of sentient beings is intended to exclude God, Time, Soul or Prime Matter as the causes of the cosmos.

Buddhism has a problem explaining moral consequentiality. It is difficult to see how we could lead ethical lives if only the present were real. The extension of causality to future consequences is a condition of ethical being. Moreover, we all know that the past may return to haunt us. The Buddhist insistence upon the importance of morality as the path to liberation is apparently challenged by two of its own tenets: All conditioned things are impermanent. All phenomena (*dharma*) are impersonal. If ethically significant intentional actions are conditioned events, and thus transitory and impersonal, how can they have subsequent effects in lives? It is held that it is the intention (*cetanā*) with which an action is performed that determines its moral character. An intention is a conditioned *dharma* occurring in a specific set of circumstances. This manifestation is ephemeral and insubstantial. How can such a fleeting occurrence have consequences for the 'person' who expresses it? Or, in the impersonal terms that are closer to the truth, how can it affect the future of the stream in which it occurs? If the past has become non-existent, there could be no effects in the future of previous good and bad actions. Those deeds would have been wiped out *without trace*, as it were.

The Sarvāstivāda-Vaibhāṣikas believe that information about the moral quality of actions is stored 'in suspension' as it were and independently of changing temporal process. Of course, the rationale is that the *dharmas* per se exist timelessly. It follows that moral values, qua *dharmas*, are objective in the sense that they are woven into the fabric of reality. This has the implication that in the final analysis, reality is friendly to human interests. Recognition of the objectivity of values allays fears that life is meaningless.

Suppose that in our conditioned world a generous action occurs in a stream of experiences. This is another way of saying that a generous-intention-*dharma* is made manifest or actualized in the stream. Generosity occurs in the stream, even though there is no one who is generous. The generous action might be of brief duration, but its occurrence as a factor in that stream is timelessly true. Information about the moral quality of actions is stored 'in another dimension' and will re-emerge *as* the future (of the stream in which the original action occurred).

That generous-action-*dharma* is considered as having two aspects – its public expression (*vijñapti*) and a private, unmanifest (*avijñapti*) one. These aspects too are real factors. Moreover, another type of *dharma* called *prāpti* (one of the realities dissociated from mind or *cittaviprayuktadharmas*) preserves the *avijñapti-dharma*, which is charged with the moral quality of the public action from which it has arisen, in the stream. On the occurrence of circumstances that are appropriate for the actualization (*vipāka*) of the efficacy of that merit-bearing *dharma*, the beneficial result of the generous-action-*dharma* will express itself. *Prāpti* is posited to explain how consequences occur in the appropriate stream. It explains continuity – the cohesion of *dharmas* (which is why I sometimes liken it to the more famous

Higgs boson!) – by preserving latent information (*avijñapti*) about the moral quality of acts. The preservative force of the *avijñapti-dharmas* also accounts for settled commitments such as the Buddhist discipline, as well as enduring dispositions of character.

All this is held to make sense of the mechanism underlying moral consequentiality and responsibility. The consequences of an action will occur in the same stream as the originating act. Do not ask why you should be moral. There is no 'you': there's just the present and occurrent configuration of a successive complex of factors that is calling itself 'I' at this moment. Buddhists think that supposing that morality requires persisting selves whose future prospects underwrite their present concerns is typical of the unenlightened, misery-making outlook for which it offers a remedy.

The personalists (*Pudgalavāda*)

Vasubandhu says that what vitiates other doctrines is their false belief that there is real personal identity: 'There is no salvation from other religions, because they are addicted to the false view that there is a permanent self. They do not understand that what they call self is only a label (*prajñapti*) for a series of physical and mental components (*skandha-saṃtāna*). They imagine that personal identity is a distinct reality in its own right. From this clinging to the conviction that there is a soul arise the moral defects (*kleśa*).'

His commentator Yaśomitra quotes the poet Mātṛceta:

> As long as we think in selfish terms, the series of births does not cease. Selfishness stays in the heart while there is belief in the soul. No other teacher in the world propounds the unreality of the Self. So there is no path to peace other than your teaching.

The ninth chapter of the *Abhidharmakośa-bhāṣya* is a critique of what was called the Vātsīputrīya tradition, an offshoot of the Sarvāstivāda that held that the Buddha actually did accept a form of personal identity, a self (pudgala) that is the ground and support of changing mental states, as well as the substratum of *karma*. This was, to say the least, controversial. It must be remembered that Buddhism holds that acting unselfishly is not enough if it presupposes a belief that there is still an enduring individual identity. Buddhism goes deeper and insists that not only is there no transcendental subject, but also that the concept of stable selfhood is a misconception and that the experience of persisting subjectivity is an illusion. We do not know exactly what the Vātsīputrīyas taught because their views are preserved only in the works of their opponents. I suspect that they thought that something emerged from the combinations of the constituents that was sufficient to account for moral responsibility. It could not be considered a reality in its own right (a sixth *skandha*, as it were) because the Buddha did not mention it. But it was more than merely a convenient designation (*prajñapti*) for the aggregation of the interactive constituents of personality. Perhaps it was thought of as something that emerges as part of a natural process and enjoys stability for a while. Vasubandhu responds that if this 'something' were really supervenient upon the constituents from which it emerges, it would be knowable. If it is not a newly emergent entity, it is reducible to the constituents and there is no point in positing it. Our experience can be explained as a continuum of mental (and physical) events, and there is no need to posit any sort of self as the subject that owns the experiences.

Further reading

L. Pruden (1988) is an English version of Louis de la Vallée Poussin's French translation of the Abhidharmakośa-bhāṣya.

Paul Griffiths (1986) is acute and enlightening, despite its title.

E. Frauwallner, *Studies in the Abhidharma Literature*, especially Chapter VIII, is a rich source of information.

P. S. Jaini (2001), Section IV, contains some influential articles.

Ronkin (2005) is about Theravāda metaphysics.

Alexis Sanderson, 'The Sarvāstivāda and its Critics', is illuminating.

James Duerlinger's *Indian Buddhist Theories of Persons*, translates Vasubandhu's critique of the *Pudgalavāda* soul theory in the Abhidharmakośa.

Questions for discussion and investigation

1. Can Buddhists reconcile atomistic impersonality and moral responsibility?
2. Does the Abhidharma notion of *svabhāva* conflict with Buddhist principles?

Notes

1. See Bareau (1955) and Lamotte (1988).
2. AKBh 2.20-3.2 (Cited in Griffiths [1986], p. 49).
3. The *Abhidharmakośa* describes a range of Abhidharma theories known to Vasubandhu in the second half of the fourth century A.D. His commentary, the *Abhidharmakośa-bhāṣya*, criticizes many of these views from a Sautrāntika representationalist point of view. Vasubandhu finally espouses an idealist position.
4. '*Sarva*' means 'all' or 'everything', '*asti*' means 'it is' or 'it exists' and '*vāda*' means 'theory'.
5. An etymology (*nirukta*) has it that they are so called because they support (*dhāraṇād* < √dhṛ) their own identity.
6. We need to bear in mind the plural senses of existence here. Complexes exist, but not in the same sense as simples. The simples are ultimate constituents that exist fundamentally. Composites and complexes exist derivatively or superficially.
7. There are two truths: conventional truth and ultimate truth. What is the definition of the two? If the cognition of something does not occur when that thing is broken into parts, that thing is conventionally real. For example, a pot. When it is divided into halves, the cognition of a pot does not arise. And anything that can be mentally analysed into parts is conventionally real. But in other cases, we have ultimate truth: when something is either fragmented or mentally analysed and the idea of it remains the same (Pradhan 1975: 333).
8. Pruden, 'Differentiation from the natures of others is in virtue of svabhāva' (Abhidharmakośa 1.18).
9. Frauwallner Studies.
10. 'Actions do not cease to exist even after thousands of millions of aeons. It is certain that once they reach the right moment and all the conditions are germane, they subject embodied beings to their inevitable effects.' This saying is quoted by Vasubandhu and cited by Candrakīrti ad *Mūlamadhyamakakārikā* 17.21d.
11. *Abhidharmakośa-bhāṣya* 5.25ab.
12. *Abhidharmakośa-bhāṣya* 5.25cd. We shall be looking at developments of this Vibhajyavāda view in the next chapter.

13 *Abhidharmakośa-bhāṣya* 1.20.

4

Sautrāntika Buddhism

Chapter Outline

The last chapter saw brief references to the Vibhajyavāda tradition of the Abhidharma. This outlook rose to prominence and acquired the name 'Sautrāntika' meaning 'those who are focused on the sūtras'. These conservatives maintained that it was only the Pāli *Suttas*, not the Abhidharma texts, which contained the authentic words of the Buddha. They thought that the Sarvāstivāda-Vaibhāṣikas had introduced innovations that went beyond the meaning of those sūtras. They accused them of obscuring the simplicity of the Buddha's original teaching about the impermanence (*anitya*) and insubstantiality (*anātman*) of all existents. Moreover, in the guise of the notion of *svabhāva*, they had restored the alien notions of permanence and substance. The Sautrāntikas interpret impermanence as meaning the radical momentariness of all existences, and insubstantiality as the indeterminacy of the world relative to our minds and conceptual schemes.

Ontology

The Sautrāntikas taught a doctrine of radical momentariness (*kṣaṇika-vāda*) and simplified the ontology of the Sarvāstivāda-Vaibhāṣikas. They rejected the latter's category of unconditioned phenomena, holding that space is just the absence of extended objects. They say that *nirvāṇa* is simply the non-occurrence of suffering and not a reality or state of being. They reject the category of the *citta-viprayukta-dharmas* – those that are neither mental not physical. So there are no *avijñapti-dharmas*, underpinning karmic causality by preserving effective intentions in a subliminal form, and no *prāpti* accounting for continuities within a stream of experiences by fixing the *avijñapti dharmas* therein. Also rejected are the *sāmānya-lakṣaṇas* (birth, continuation, entropy and impermanence) characterizing the brief occurrence of *dharmas* in conditioned complexes.

The Vaibhāṣikas say that the basic realities (*dharmas*) are timeless realities with unchanging essential natures (*svabhāva*). Those essences may or may not exercise their causal functions in and as the world. The Sautrāntikas abandon the concept of intrinsic nature. We can easily see how this came about. We said in the last chapter that there was a problem lurking behind the Vaibhāṣikas' apparent interpretation of intrinsic nature as causal power. The rationale for ascribing intrinsic natures to the *dharmas* is to enable their identification in virtue of their independent self-sufficiency and thus to distinguish them from the conditioned, fluid and transient macroscopic formations that they constitute. But in fact, intrinsic nature is characterized in causal terms as the capacity to interact with other *dharmas*. So each *dharma* is actually characterized in relational terms. We are not really specifying their *internal* natures in categorical terms but only in dispositional ones. Causal powers have to do with external relations. We are not being told what the possessors of the causal powers are like in themselves. So the picture becomes one of a giant causal flux, but with no explanation of the *intrinsic* natures of the entities related in the flux. This picture the Sautrāntikas are happy to accept. They retain the notion of causal power or efficacy (*kāritra/svalakṣaṇa*). They say that the causal powers rather than entities are basic, and they call these energies *svalakṣaṇa*. The rejection of the Sarvāstivāda-Vaibhāṣika notion of *svabhāva* implies the rejection of ontological distinctions between conditioned and unconditioned reality, between nominal existence (*prajñapti-sat*) and substantial existence (*dravya-sat*). Although, the distinction between the true by convention (*saṃvṛti-satya*) and the ultimate truth (*paramārtha-satya*) still applies, the refusal of *svabhāva* is the abolition of the 'two-worlds' view.

The energies are not thought of as belonging to anything else, such as a particle. They exist only for a moment, like bursts or flashes. Hence neither future nor past is real. The basic realities are unique instants that are just moments of causal efficacy. They cannot be captured by concepts or language. Their interplay supplies the uninterpreted data of sensory perceptions. Matter is the localization of energy. What we experience as extended in space and time is really a causally continuous series of momentary powers. Such complexes elicit cognitive reactions: we see blue patches, touch solid surfaces and hear prolonged sounds. It is they that are the data of acquaintance. There is a striking development here. To use an analogy: if earlier reductionism had said that there are no forests but only trees, the Sautrāntikas are saying that there aren't any individual trees either but only constructs.[1]

The Sautrāntikas insist that production by the co-operation of causes and conditions obtains at every level, 'all the way down', and does not just apply to macroscopic formations. All things are momentary in the radical sense that they exist only for the moment at which they are produced. They argue that all entities are inherently perishable, having no intrinsic tendency to continue in existence. The rationale is: Everything decays. Decay is non-existence. But non-existence has no causes. So decay needs no external cause. It must be the intrinsic nature of things to be perishable. Given that perishability is the very nature things, they cease spontaneously at the moment of their origination. Accordingly, there is no sense in speaking of real past and future phenomena, as the Vaibhāṣikas do.

It was said that localizations of energies are experienced by beings with our cognitive and perceptual faculties as matter: solid objects, expansions of colour, shapes and sounds. The *svalakṣaṇas* per se are instantaneous and hence ineffable and imperceptible. They are not the data of direct acquaintance. While the Vaibhāṣikas hold that aggregates of atoms are the direct objects of perception, the Sautrāntikas say that what we are acquainted with are mental forms that arise when clusters of *svalakṣaṇas*, purely causal potencies, somehow impart impressions of their forms (*ākāra*/*pratibhāsa*) to conscious episodes. Clusters of unique particulars are the material causes and objective supports of perceptions. When they occur in clusters or fields, they collectively make impressions on our minds. Each episode of representation is self-illuminating or self-conscious (*svasaṃvedana*, *sva-saṃvitti*) and thus has its own phenomenal or qualitative character. The energies are the ultimate and remote causes of what we interpret as experiences of a three-dimensional world of continuous objects and properties.

Although it is impossible for us to make sense of what is happening (to do so would require an other-worldly point of view out of this world), the facts that our activities are usually successful and our cognitive experience is not chaotic enable us to *infer* that there is some sort of conformity (*sarūpya*) between our representations and the behaviour of the particulars. Moreover, although we are not acquainted with the instants, we may infer that they behave in structured ways. We might consider here the case of rainbows. What we see are bands of colour in the sky. But this phenomenal representation is caused by light waves refracted off droplets of water. We do not directly see or feel the unique instants that are, as it were, the raw materials of the world. Nevertheless, they impress themselves on episodes of awareness and are imperfectly grasped through the filters of the mental images and concepts that they cause.[2] Our concepts lead us to reify what is given in sensation and suppose that we are enduring subjects confronting a world of objects, properties and structural principles.

If the contents of awareness are just mental representations, how do we know that there is an external reality? The reply is that our representations do not occur at random but are about definite objects at specific times and places. Moreover, since we have no control over much of which presents itself in our experiences, it is unlikely that mental representations have been entirely generated from within a stream of experiences. Surely they have causes other than the immediately preceding moment (*samanantara-pratyaya*) in a mental stream. The Sautrantikas conclude that the causes of our mental representations are evanescent realities external to experiences. Opponents are quick to point out that self-destructing instantaneous particulars do not last long enough to enter into even short-lived formations that could cause anything. Indeed, the view that existence means spontaneous destructibility will lead to a charge of nihilism. And we shall see that the Sautrāntika representationalism may lead to idealism, which says that there is no need to posit any material realities external to minds and that only ideas are real.

The Sautrāntika position is that meaningful experience of the external world of unique particulars is mediated by representations and articulated in concepts (*vikalpa*) and language.[3] In other words, stimuli are filtered through representations and organized in concepts. This accords with the plausible view that while sensations from objects arise in us, as mere contents of perceptual consciousness, they do not mean anything. As Frege said, sense-impressions on their own do not disclose the external world. Only concepts can make sense of the uninterpreted manifold of experience. Sensation and perception are constrained by the external domain in a way in which conceptualization is not. Concepts proliferate and float free of empirical origins. The elaborate conceptual scheme is only remotely connected with the initial stimuli that may be held to give rise to it.

The identification of objects and events is a function of our interpretation of the dynamic manifold. What counts as an object, and of course relational complexes of objects, is determined by contexts of human interests and practice, which we might call human convenience and human convention. Representation and conceptualization select salient (in the sense of relevant to human interests) features of the behaviour of the *svalakṣaṇas*. What we identify as entities is a function of how we are 'minded', and how we are minded is a function of the inheritance of concepts belonging to the stream that we are. The realist thinkers of the Brahminical Nyāya tradition (see Chapter 8) may be seen as prioritizing the identity of entities and their differences from each other. In the Buddhism of Dignāga and Dharmakīrti, we see the opposite tendency. What intellect does is to abstract from differences in things (*svalakṣaṇas*) in order to arrive at stable concepts applicable to discrete individual entities. The flux of conceptually unwrought reality is a region of instantaneous occurrences graspable only in perceptual intuition.

The notions of selfhood, caste and universal properties (as well as other categories such as substance, relations and qualities) involve concepts and linguistic categories. They are matters of human convention, dictated by our interests. Such categories are superimposed upon the amorphous sphere of *svalakṣaṇa*/energies. So they are not natural.

It is apparent that there is a big gap between the way our minds work and the way things are. Reality is not how it appears to us or as it is interpreted in our conceptual schemes. Indeed, the subject–object dichotomy is a feature of human conceptual schemes.

Ethical consequentiality

The Sautrāntikas account for karmic continuity by saying that an intentional action, albeit instantaneous, is a 'seed' that initiates a transformation in an experiential series (*citta-saṃtāna-pariṇāma-viśeṣa*). Its fruition is either reward or punishment. The originating cause need not last until its effect is realized since it is not a sustaining cause – like parents who are necessary for the origination but not the continued existence of their offspring. They argue that if an action continued to exist until its fruition, it would have to be eternal. But if it ceased to exist, it could not produce anything. A seed initiates a series beginning with germination. The fruit arises as the culmination of the series, rather than directly from the seed. But it still needs the seed to start the process. Although the series and the result depend upon the seed as the originating cause, we do not say that the seed is either annihilated or that it is eternal. Likewise, an intention initiates a series of mental events from which the consequence results. The series requires the initial intention, and the consequence arises from the series. The intention is neither annihilated nor is it eternal.

Dignāga

Dignāga (480–540 A.D.) was a Buddhist philosopher whose most important work is the *Pramāṇa-samuccaya*. He also wrote a work called 'The Examination of Objective Grounds of Cognition' (*Ālambana-parīkṣā*), extracts from which are translated below. He may be seen as belonging to the Sautrāntika development of the Ābhidharmika schools tradition of thought. He thinks that there is a real domain of ineffable instantaneous particulars external to minds, and says that what we know are only its reflections mediated by mental images and discursive concepts. If everything truly real is individual or particular, there is a gap between the way our minds work and the way the world is.

Dharmakīrti (600–660 A.D.) drew out the implications of Dignāga's ideas and exercised an inestimable influence on subsequent debates. His works include the *Pramāṇa-Vārttika*, the *Pramāṇa-Viniścaya* and the *Nyāyabindu*. His treatise called the *Proof of Other Streams of Experiences* addresses the problem of other minds and argues that there is a multiplicity of streams of experience.

Prior to Dignāga, most thinkers in the Buddhist tradition had accepted that there are three ways of knowing (*pramāṇa*): sensory perception, inference and reliable testimony (i.e. both human authorities and scriptural reports of the Buddha's teachings). Dignāga denies that testimony is an independent way of knowing in its own right and subsumes it under inference. The rationale is that we do not unquestioningly assent to what a person says but accept that their words are true only when we already believe that they are well informed, reliable and sincere. But above all, what is apparent is a repudiation of the authority of the Vedic scriptures, which are held to be a *pramāṇa* in their own right by the orthodox Brahminical traditions. It is not the Brahmin scriptures that are reliable guides to ultimate well-being, but the words and indeed the person of the Buddha.[4] The Buddha's words are trustworthy not only because they are informed by his own experiences but also because they have not been contradicted by anything in the experiences of his hearers.

In the first chapter of his *Pramāṇa-samuccaya*, Dignāga says:

> Sense-perception (*pratyakṣa*) and inference (*anumāna*) are the only two ways of knowing because what is knowable is of two sorts. Apart from the unique and ineffable particulars (*svalakṣaṇa*) and the four general features of conditioned phenomena (*sāmānya-lakṣaṇa*: birth, stasis, decline and impermanence) there is nothing else to know.
>
> Sense-perception pertains to the unique particulars, while inference pertains to whatever has the general features.
>
> Perception is free from conceptualisation (*kalpanā*).
>
> What is conceptualisation? It is the association of proper names, general terms etc. with what is given in sensation. In the case of proper names, something is characterised by association with a name such as Ḍittha. In the case of terms for kinds of beings (*jāti-śabda*), something is characterised by a universal such as 'cow'. In the case of adjectives (*guṇa-śabda*), something is characterised by a quality such as white. In the case of action-nouns something is characterised by an action such as cooking; in the case of nouns for substances, we find formations like 'staff-holder'.[5]

Thus, Dignāga divorces sensory perception (*pratyakṣa*) from thinking in concepts and words (*kalpanā*). He calls the latter 'inference' (*anumāna*). Sensory perception never involves general concepts (*sāmānya-lakṣaṇa*). Sensation is direct experience of a world that consists of fluid clusters of unique particulars (*svalakṣaṇa*).[6] Perception is always valid, revealing the world, because it precedes mental activity. So there is no scope for mental distortion. On the other hand, sensation yields only impressions, and impressions are insufficient for understanding. Because they do not share any common features, particulars are indescribable. We have here a nominalist outlook: everything truly real is individual or particular. General features are conceptually constructed by perceivers and superimposed on what is given in sensation.

Since each sense-faculty is restricted to its proper sphere, a concept such as substance can never be a deliverance of perception. I see an orange patch in front of me. I may feel a certain texture, taste a flavour and smell a scent. But what sensations do not tell me is *that there is a single object called an orange* in which all those properties are combined. *The fact that* there is such an entity is a case of conceptual construction (*kalpanā*). We see orange, but the propositionally structured thought that there is something that is orange is a distinct cognitive act.[7]

Dignāga believes that the categories of things (*padārtha*) that the Nyāya-Vaiśeṣika realists claim to be basic structures *discovered* in the world are in fact *imposed* by the workings of our minds.[8] Our minds group unique particulars together and interpret them as continuing objects that are the bearers of different types of properties. In other words, the constructive activity of minds *constitutes* objects out of the flux of sensation. In reality, there are no universals, no real stability and no entities with determinate identities. It follows that the notion of soul and the authority to the Vedic scriptures and the associated religion are all cases of human conceptual construction and not features of the real world. This will be used to argue that class – caste – characteristics are conceptual fictions. They are recognized only by those who have been socialized in the appropriate culture and language. Someone who lacked the appropriate word and concept would not be able to recognize a Brahmin on the basis of perceptual evidence alone. Caste status is not an aspect of the real world (as the Brahmins think) but belongs to the realm of human conventions.

Dignāga thinks that thought and language are inseparable. He said that conceptual thought is born out of language and language is born out of concepts. Conceptual thought and language deal in generalities (*sāmānya-lakṣaṇa*). But because there are no objective general features, even simple concepts are at one remove from reality. They are causally related to the realities and not just arbitrary fictional inventions. But as we have already said, there is a gap between how our minds work and the way things are. *More strongly, concepts are interpretations that disguise rather than disclose reality.* To put it bluntly, words neither refer to nor describe real entities, and we unenlightened beings are trapped in a web of conceptualization.

Logic is not about reality as rightly articulated in language but is a set of rules governing the moves in a conceptual language game. Dignāga says at one point: 'All this convention involving inferential reason and properties to be established is based on the distinction between property and property-possessor, which is itself imposed by the human mind: it is not grounded in anything existing outside the mind.' His contribution to an inductive theory of inference was very influential, although similar ideas are found in the works of Vasubandhu and in a text called the *Nyāyapraveśa*.[9]

Dignāga proposed that in a valid inference, we must have observed cases of an invariable connection (*avinābhāva-saṃbandha*) between the logical reason (*hetu*) and what it establishes (*sādhya*). We observe wherever the reason occurs, there the *sādhya* occurs also. This relation has to be exceptionless, rather than just a matter of causality. This condition is met, and we can be confident that we are reasoning reliably and responsibly when three factors (*trairūpya*) obtain:

The logical reason (*hetu*) must really be a property of the subject (*pakṣa*) of the inference.

The logical reason must be present in some instance (*sapakṣa*) other than the subject of the inference, which is similar to that subject in that it too possesses the thing that is to be proved (*sādhya*).

Whatever lacks the property to be proved also lacks the proving property or reason. There must be no instances (*vipakṣa*) where the proving property occurs and the property to be proved does not.

Take the inference: sounds (*pakṣa*) are impermanent (*sādhya*) because they are products (*hetu*). The invariable association is: whatever is produced is impermanent. Here the supporting example (*sapakṣa*) could be something uncontroversially impermanent such as a pot that also exhibits the property of being a product. It is open to us to cite a *vipakṣa* or actual instance illustrating the joint absence of the property to be proved and the logical reason. The atmosphere would count as such a negative example because it both lacks impermanence and is not produced by effort.

We look at Dharmakīrti's response below. Here it suffices to say that he rejects Dignāga's broadly inductive approach, based as it is on the observation of correlated instances, in favour of an account that emphasizes the internal or essential connection between the logical reason and that which is to be established.

Apoha: The 'exclusion' theory of linguistic functioning

The thinkers of the Hindu Nyāya-Vaiśeṣika realist (see Chapter 8) tradition think that objective features (universal properties, natural kinds and the individual substances belonging to them, qualities such as colours, shapes and sizes) are the grounds for the repeated applications of general terms. According to this view, we classify some individual animals as cows because they form a natural kind. The single, real universal property 'being a cow' is itself an entity common to all cows. It is what the word 'cow' fundamentally means. Our words and concepts are *informed* by mind-independent reality. It is this that explains why they are as they are.

But Dignāga is an anti-essentialist and a nominalist who says that there are no objective general features. Generalization is a function of language. There are no universals structuring and regulating a world that consists of instantaneous unique and indescribable particulars. But if there are really neither shared properties nor even resemblances, how do words and concepts function? They cannot all behave like proper names because in that case we could not say anything *about* things. The realist says that we call some animals 'cows' because they share features in virtue of belonging to the same kind. Words and concepts are anchored in reality, and their combinations reflect its structure. The word 'cow' really means an inherited essence and designates any individuals who participate in that essence. However much a buffalo may resemble a cow (and they may be superficially indistinguishable), it is not a cow. Such a referentialist theory of meaning in which nouns have meaning by standing for objects and kinds, adjectives have meaning by expressing qualities and verbs mean actions will not work if there are no objects, kinds and qualities. Dignāga's response is that words and concepts form a fabric of inherited conventional understanding in which meanings 'exclude each other' (*anya-apoha*).[10] The basic idea is that words (and concepts) do not have meaning in virtue of their *referring* to extra-linguistic realities. Rather, they are signs whose meaning derives from their roles in a framework of significances, where they stand in relations of opposition and complementarity. (Later thinkers say that *apoha* means the mutually exclusive interrelations of modes of presentations (*pratibimba*) and concepts (*vikalpa*) that determine objects and states of affairs.) A language expresses a conceptual scheme. Perhaps it may be compared to a jigsaw puzzle. The pieces are significant only when they occupy their proper places. They are useless is isolation. A word has meaning by excluding other meanings belonging to the same language. Dignāga and his followers deny that we need to posit a single real universal property shared by all individual cows as the basis of the application of the word/concept 'cow'. Mind selects groups of salient features, which it unifies and upon which it superimposes a single concept. Salience here means congeniality to human interests. A striking example is the concept 'analgesic'. Substances with distinct pharmacological properties are unified under a single concept/word because they reduce human pain symptoms.

Human conceptual schemes are the way they are because it suits human interests to articulate the play of momentary particulars in certain ways. What we have here is a theory about how language works and not a theory about the genesis of language or the acquisition of language and concepts by children. Were it the latter, it would be impossible to explain how anyone could learn the meaning of a word in the first place, because they would have to exclude an infinite range of other things. As for the former, there is no problem: we are born into a beginninglessly established linguistic community.

Self-awareness of mental events

All Buddhists deny that there is a constant experiencing subject that is distinct from the process of awareness. They analytically reduce experiences into a succession of discrete moments. But how could successive thoughts conceive of themselves as a continuum? How do we account for the phenomenon of subjectivity, the feeling that one has of oneself (*svasaṃvedana*) as a continuous centre of experiencing? Can we account for the subject–object structure of awareness? In response to such questions, Dignāga says that just as emotions are 'self-aware', so each and every perception and judgement is aware of itself (*sva-saṃvitti*): it is said to be inherently self-illuminating. A cognition simultaneously and *in virtue of the same act* cognizes its own form as well as that of what it is about. Take an awareness of something red. This awareness has two aspects: objective or the red content, and subjective – its own self-awareness – which we might express as 'what it feels like to see red'. From this a lot follows. The bifurcation of cognition into subjective and objective aspects accounts for the origin of the subject–object dichotomy without reference to an extra-mental sphere. There can be experiences of objectivity even if there is no external physical world. Reflexive mental events follow each other so quickly that they coalesce. Hence there is generated the illusion that there is a persisting subject of experiences that we call the self.

The *Ālambana-Parīkṣā*

According to the Vaibhāṣika direct realists, the objective ground (*ālambana-pratyaya*) of a thought is the reality in the world that it is about. A cognition occurs only when there is interaction between a sensory faculty and something external. According to this theory, an objective ground is both the extra-mental cause of an idea and the supplier of its representational content. A hallucination is not an objectively grounded thought. Although it has content, its cause is some defect in the perceptual system.

Dignāga believes that exposure to material things is of itself insufficient to account for our ideas. He agrees with the Vaibhāṣikas that for something to qualify as the objective ground of an awareness, it must be both the cause and the representative content of that awareness, but he does not accept that such causes have to be extra-mental material realities.

In his *Ālambana-parīkṣā*, Dignāga argues that the Vaibhāṣika atomistic *dharma* theory actually leads to the admission that the *direct* objects of perceptual awareness are internal mental forms and not mind-independent physical realities. The Vaibhāṣikas hold that we directly perceive structured masses of real atoms (*dharmas*) of various kinds and that these cause our perceptions. Like Vasubandhu, Dignāga questions the possibility of atomic aggregation. But even granting that collections of atoms may occasion the occurrence of mental representations, the atoms themselves do not figure in the subjective content of awareness. A compound of clay atoms may be one of the causes of a perception of a pot, but we do not see such a cluster of atoms. The atoms do not enter into the content of the representation: what we have is an experience of a solid, coloured extended object. It could be argued that it is a conglomerate of atoms that resembles the representative content. But the problem here is that the Vaibhāṣikas deny that conglomerates are real. So they fail to qualify as causes of anything. Dignāga concludes that an idea (a mental representation that appears as if it is about something external) can be the support of another idea. The cause of a mental representation can be another representation: thoughts may arise from other thoughts rather than directly from external objects. This coheres perfectly with the *apoha* theory described above.

Although the particulars (*svalakṣaṇa*) exist independently of minds, the direct objects of acquaintance are their representations in consciousness. He wants to persuade us that our shared, conventional framework of representations is just that, and that our thoughts and concepts do not mirror reality as it is in itself. There is a big gap between the way the world is and the way our minds work. The goal is to encourage us to realize that our everyday attachments are really just conventional constructions. Our thinking in terms of ourselves as persisting individual *subjects* confronting a world of already established propertied *objects* that await our descriptions is a basic misconception. Once such realization is achieved, we are in a position to detach ourselves from our self-centred and anxious concerns. Then we may follow the path of insight and compassion leading towards enlightenment.

The examination of objective grounds of awareness (*Ālambana-parīkṣā-vṛtti*)

People who believe that external things (*bāhyārtha*) are the objective grounds (*ālambana*) of sense-perception (*indriya-vijñapti*) suppose either that individual atoms are the support since they cause the perception or that a conglomerate of atoms is the support because such a form is the representative content of awareness.

The term 'intentional object' (*viṣaya*) means the proper form of something that is grasped in cognition, since the cognition is manifest as having that form (*ākāra*).

Even if atoms cause a sensory cognition, the atoms are not the intentional object of the cognition (just as the sensory faculties are not) because the cognition does not represent them.

Thus, the atoms are not the objective ground (which has to be both cause and content) of cognition.

As for the conglomerate of atoms, although it is what is represented in awareness, it is not the objective ground because

It is not the cause of the phenomenal representation (*ābhāsa*).

It makes sense that when something (*artha*) produces a perception (*vijñapti*) that represents it as it is (*svāvabhāsi*), that something is the objective ground. This is what has been called [in the Abhidharma] the originating condition.

But the conglomerate of atoms does not qualify as such *because it is not a reality – like the moon seeming double.*

In the case of the moon seen as double owing to a sensory defect, although the moon appears double in awareness, it is not such in reality. Likewise, the conglomerate is not the objective ground because it cannot function as a cause since it is not a real entity (*dravyataḥ asattvena*).

Thus, what appears to be external in both these cases is not a real object.

The external things called 'atom' and 'conglomerate of atoms' are not the objective grounds of awareness, because although the atoms cause the awareness, they do not feature in its representative content, and while the conglomerate appears as the content of perception, it is not the cause of the perception.

Some [realists] hold that the aggregated form is the instrumental cause of the cognition. The individual form of an atom is not the object of perception, in the same way that its solidity is not. They say that everything has many forms and that anything may be perceived in under just one of its forms. Atoms-in-combination [one of their forms] have the nature of being the originating cause of awareness when they are represented as conglomerates. Just as the real nature of solidity is not an object of visual perception, likewise the real nature of atomicity is not the object of visual perception. [We don't see atoms, but this does not detract from the fact that real conglomerates of atoms are both the causes and manifest content of perceptions.]

To this it is replied: This view cannot explain the fact that perception of a pot differs from that of a cup. There is no difference between the atoms making up those things.

But perhaps the different perceptions result from the distinct configurations of the atoms?

No. These distinct configurations are imposed (*upādhi*) by our minds. Such discriminations (*upādhi*) do not pertain to the atoms, which the realist opponent deems to be authentically real. All the atoms are identical in respect of their spherical form. And they do not have different dimensions.

The differences between the macroscopic forms of objects belong to the level of superficial reality (*saṃvṛti-satsu*).

Conventional modes of differentiation [e.g. between pots and cups] do not apply to the atoms.

Everyday objects such as pots exist superficially (*saṃvṛti-santaḥ*). Pots etc. only exist derivatively because if the atoms of which they are made are removed, the cognition whose form derives from them disappears.[11]

But this does not happen with respect to anything that is truly real.

[Conclusion]

Therefore, it makes sense that extra-mental material things are not the direct objects of sense-perceptions.

But the knowable internal form (*antarjñeyarūpam*), which appears as if external to the mind, is the object (*artha*). This is because it supplies the form of the cognition and is its support (*pratyaya*).

Given that external material things are not what perceptions are about, something internal *appearing as if external* is the objective ground (*ālambana-pratyaya*).

The internal mental form is the objective ground of awareness since it both supplies the manifest image in the cognition of the object and produces the cognition of the object.

Dharmakīrti

'Accepting the authority of the Vedas, believing in individual agency, hoping for merit from bathing, taking pride in caste, undertaking rites for the removal of evils: these are the five signs of stupidity, the destruction of intelligence.'[12] This pungent piece of invective is directed against caste Hindus who claim the authority of the Vedic scriptures for both their religious practices and their social status. Fundamental to this ideology is the belief that it is genuinely individual agents who perform rituals and reap their benefits. More broadly, it is these responsible persons who aspire to release from rebirth and the manifestation of their core identity in conditions outside space and time. The Brahminical ideology includes a belief in the reality of universals that explains and legitimates the reality of natural descent groups or kinds (*jāti*) among humans.

Dharmakīrti identifies belief that one is a substantial, permanent and personal being as a form of ignorance, indeed enchantment. Such ignorance is an effective factor that produces a specific mentality and set of behavioural dispositions (*saṃskāra*). Belief that one is an enduring being is inherited from mistaken constructions of permanent selfhood based on vestiges of the interactions of the five *skandhas* in previous lives. Hence the misconception is innate and built into our language. Thence are perpetuated the moral defects (*kleśa*) including desires, infatuations and antagonisms that cloud one's perceptions. Attachment to self is inextricably associated with the notion of 'mine', meaning not merely acquisitiveness but grasping, appropriation and clinging. There is the phenomenon of 'grasping at life': the drive to construct a personal identity and secure one's own welfare and happiness. In according a privileged status to ourselves and demanding premium treatment, we experience aversion towards whatever is felt to be inimical to our own interests – not infrequently what are imagined to be other selves. The struggle for personal happiness conceals the true nature of the moral defects so we do not see them for what they are. As long as there is clinging to self, there is rebirth.

Thankfully, the defects are impermanent and can be destroyed. Those brought about by ignorance can be eliminated by repeated practice or reinforcement in meditation of the truth that everything is insubstantial (*nairātmya*). Following the Buddhist path, including repeated meditation on the way in which self-centredness generates suffering and frustration, and on the impermanence and non-substantiality of phenomena, gradually eliminates misunderstanding and the consequent moral defects. Insight (*prajñā*) into universal non-substantiality is the proper function of a purified mind, where wisdom and compassion coincide. The elimination of misconceptions and desires that have perpetuated it is also the dissolution of the stream of experiences. You are no more.

Dharmakīrti's metaphysics

Philosophy helps by revealing that nothing real can be permanent. So there are no enduring and integrated substances, no real universals and no timeless scriptural authorities. It may also assist in the formulation of the thought that we live in thrall to an inherited and shared web of conceptualization (*kalpanā*). Dharmakīrti makes a distinction between authentically real entities (for which he uses terms like *vastu* and *svabhāva*) – that is, whatever cannot be changed by human intentions and thinking – on the one hand and whatever is determined by human conventions and social arrangements (*vyavahāra*), choices and decisions (*puruṣa-icchā-vidhāyin*) on the other. The former is the sphere of perception and the latter that of conceptual construction and convention.[13] The dichotomy coincides with the opposition between what is genuinely real (*dravya-sat*) and what is nominally real (*prajñapti-sat*), and between what is basically real (*paramārtha-sat*) and what is derivatively real (*saṃvṛti-sat*).

Dharmakīrti agreed with Dignāga that in the final analysis what we call the world is a flux of ineffable unique particulars (*svalakṣaṇa*). They are unique in the sense that each has specific location, time and form. They are perhaps better understood as energies than particles. It is by virtue of their configurations in relation to cognizers that they determine the differences in the representative content of cognitions. In a significant development of Dignāga's ideas, Dharmakīrti says that each *svalakṣaṇa* has its own causal effectiveness (*arthakriyā-sāmarthya*).[14] Instead of saying what is real by specifying some type of entities (e.g. the *svalakṣaṇa* energies or the particle-like *dharma*), he uses a criterion: only what is causally effective is real.[15] Moreover, whatever is real is directly perceptible, either actually or potentially. This is a significant aspect of causal efficacy: the capacity to produce a direct sensory perception in us.

One of many consequences is that the caste differences between human beings cannot be real, for they are not directly perceptible but rely for their apprehension upon knowledge of what are purely social conventions. Sensitivity to caste is something that has to be taught and learnt. Classes of any sort are of course generalizations (*sāmānya-lakṣaṇa*) and conceptual constructs (*kalpanā*).[16] In the words of Dharmakīrti, 'All entities are essentially separate (*vyāvṛtti* meaning *apoha*) both from things like them as well as from things unlike them because anything real is self-confined and unique. Hence distinct classes (*jāti-bheda*) which encompass particulars are conceptually constructed, being based on the exclusion of what is conceptualized as different.'[17]

The doctrine that what is substantially real endures through time maintaining its own identity as a viable whole (and that what is paradigmatically real is indestructible and immune to time's ravages) is virtually a defining mark of Brahminical realism. According to that view, thoughts and their statements in language are true when they are in conformity with established fact. Dharmakīrti maintains precisely the opposite when he stipulates that nothing permanent can be causally effective either successively or in the present because what is permanent neither changes nor engages in processes of change. According to this view, thoughts and their statements in language are true when they are practically useful.[18] Knowledge is cognition that enables us to reach our goals (*prāpakaṃ jñānaṃ pramāṇam*). A cognition is reliable, and thus knowledge when it generates successful activity.[19]

If something does not perform useful activity, then it is not a real entity. If it does perform useful activity, it is cannot be permanent. This criterion of reality rules out the existence of anything supposedly eternal and unchanging such as God, the soul and its permanent consciousness, the sounds of the Vedic scriptures, the eternal relation between Vedic words and the things they mean, universals and primal material nature (*prakṛti*) that is inert prior to its plural manifestation as the cosmos.

Dharmakīrti follows Dignāga's epistemology: only sensory perception and inference are means of knowing (*pramāṇa*). Knowledge is reliable cognition in so far as it contributes to the successful accomplishment of some purpose. It may also reveal something new: but to Dharmakīrti's mind, the instrumental function is primary and matter-of-fact truths are *revealed* in practice. Although like Dignāga he refuses to accept that testimony and language can be epistemic authorities in their own right – they are primarily thinking here of the absolute authority that the Brahmins ascribe to the uncreated Vedic scriptures – in fact, he says that language may be an instrument of knowing in the derivative sense that it communicates what are already established to be useful truths about what is to be sought after and what avoided. The Buddha and the scriptural records of his teachings are sources of knowledge in that they reveal things that would be otherwise unknown, and tell the truth about what should be pursued and what eschewed.

As we have seen, according to the Sautrāntika outlook there are no permanent realities. To be real is to be causally effective and that implies the capacity for change. But they take it for granted that were there anything permanent, it could neither act nor change. Dharmakīrti says that there is no such thing as a permanent means of knowing (*nityaṃ pramāṇam*) such as the Vedic scriptures or a divine intelligence because knowledge operates in a world of changing realities. So he denies that it is a defining mark of knowledge that it is unchanging, that it will not run away. A means of knowing cannot be unchanging because it is concerned with impermanent objects.[20] Whatever happens as part of a process cannot be permanent and unchanging. Something permanent could not be a means of knowing about what is impermanent because it could not depend upon assisting factors such as objects, subjects and instruments in the case of the knowing process. It is the particulars that are immediately given in sensory perception. The means of knowing are such because they enable us to achieve our goals in a world of ever-changing realities.

Perception and thinking

Dharmakīrti outlines his view of knowledge and perception in the first chapter of his *Nyāyabindu*:

> The accomplishment of human goals presupposes right cognition.
>
> Right cognition is twofold: perception and inference.

Perception is free from conceptualization (*kalpanā*) and is free from error.
Conceptualization is thought to involve a representation that is *capable* of being expressed in words.[21] Cognition that is both free from conceptualization and from defects is sense-perception (*pratyakṣa*) [as a means of knowing].

That has four aspects:

(a) Cognition involving the sense-faculties.
(b) Understanding (*mano-vijñānam*) produced by the sensory cognition that is its immediate cause. This process takes the initial sensory cognition of the external object as its object.
(c) All minds and mental events are reflexively aware *of themselves*.[22]
(d) Direct yogic intuition into the atomic composition of reality. This does not require sense-faculties as intermediaries.

The unique particulars (*svalakṣaṇa*) are the objects (*viṣaya*) of sensory perception.[23]

While the cognitive representation differs according to whether an object is remote or proximate, the object is still the particular.

Only the particulars are genuinely real (*paramārtha-sat*).
This is because genuine existence means having the capacity for causal efficacy.
Different from them is what is characterized by generality (*sāmānya-lakṣaṇam*).
That is the sphere of inference (*anumānasya viṣayaḥ*) because conceptual construction (kalpana) is at work. This proceeds from perceptual cognition since it refers to the same object.
It is reliable because it is in conformity (*sārūpyam*) with the object.
This is why cognition of objects leads to successful activity.

Dharmakīrti's theory about the relation between perception and the world can be understood in terms of the triad: sensation–image–concept.[24] A cluster of *svalakṣaṇas* has the power to produce the sensation of blue. Blue impressions produce an awareness having two aspects: a blue mental image (*ākāra*) and the blue mental image's being aware of itself. The image is a copy of the impressions. Constructive mental activity (*kalpanā*), conditioned by traces of prior experiences, interprets the image and produces the propositionally structured thought (*vikalpa*) that something is blue. This thought enables us to think, act and communicate. The external particulars are only the indirect objects of the thoughts that they remotely cause. But those unique instants behave in such a way that we can organize them under unifying concepts. While our concepts, involving the association of names and general properties with what is given in sensation, do not copy the fluid play of the real particulars, they represent it indirectly as a map does a territory. Perception reveals configurations of particulars, and words express concepts that range over them. Knowledge conveyed by words is thus indirect. Words express concepts agreed by convention for the purpose of communication. Given that the conventions are made after the relevant particulars have vanished, the concepts cannot apply to them directly. But since a person with the appropriate linguistically derived understanding has knowledge that conduces to the accomplishment of purposive activities, it may be concluded that words are somehow related to particulars, even if they do not tell the whole story.[25]

Sense-perception on its own has no practical application because it does not discriminate anything. Assuming that the senses are operating normally and environmental conditions do not obstruct them, sense-perception cannot be either true or false because truth and falsity apply only to judgements involving conceptual mental states. Perceptual sensation applies to reality as it is in itself (*vastu*) before we start thinking about it. But it is only when an aspect of reality has been mentally discriminated in a perceptual *judgement* (*adhyavasāya*) that we can act in relation to it. Judgements using concepts enable successful activity (i.e. are reliable) when they are causally related to the real particulars constituting events.

A *vikalpa* is a concept that the mind constructs out of the data given in sensory awareness. Cognitions involving apparently shared features of objects are conceptual interpretations based on experiences of particulars. Conceptualization involves generalizations, but there are no objective generalities. Objective reality is strictly ineffable, since it includes no general features. Like Dignāga, he wants us to realize that our conventional ways of understanding, integral to which is the notion of personal individuality, in the final analysis disguise the truth.

As we have said, to find our way around successfully, we need to make discriminations using concepts and words. Some concepts, and elaborated conceptual schemes, apply more adequately than others to objective reality: that is, they are more effective in producing successful activity. *Vikalpas* interpret and organize the data of sensation, making them intelligible and serviceable. The store of human concepts, built up from impressions derived from a beginningless series of previous experiences, is transmitted down the generations via shared language. While some complex concepts ultimately derive from sensory impressions and mental images formed from them, others, especially the idea that there is a persisting soul, are just produced by the creative imagination.

A problem arises when people overlook the purely conventional nature of what are only human ways of thinking and suppose that they correspond to, in the senses of copying or mirroring, objective realities. It is a natural mistake to suppose that our concepts are copies of reality or that our representations mirror reality as it is in itself. Since reality consists of unique particulars, general concepts cannot represent it truly. Moreover, established concepts, enshrined in language, encourage us to think that there are stable realities.

A much-quoted verse (354) from the chapter on perception of the *Pramāṇavārttika* reads:

> Cognition (*buddhi*) is itself impartite (*avibhāga*) but it appears to be differentiated into objects-known (*grāhya*), knowing subjects (*grāhaka*) and discrete cognitions because of mistaken views.[26]

Later thinkers sometimes read this in an idealist sense as an assertion that everything is internal to conscious, that only minds and ideas are real, but that it is probably not Dharmakīrti's meaning. He does not deny that there is a sphere of existence beyond human experience. He means that the conceptually posed oppositions between the perceiving subject, objects and thoughts are functions of the way our minds work and not genuine realities. It is we who contrast subjects and objects, thinking them external to each other. The differentiation of subjects, acts and objects of cognition within the one mind appears because of inherited influences of previous ideas in a beginningless and uninterrupted stream of experiences. Understanding oneself as an individual thinker facing a world of objects is a kind of self-centredness that Buddhist practice aims to eliminate. If the polar notions of object and subject are interdependent, by removing one, we remove the other. Once people have understood that the conventional view of reality as consisting of enduring objects existing independently of the minds of individual perceivers is false and that our cognitive representations are not copies of reality, they approach the realization that selfhood and its attachments are merely constructs.

Another of Dharmakīrti's statements that will be construed in an idealist sense is, 'There is no difference between blue and the cognition of it because they are always experienced together.'[27] Although later thinkers will see this claim as an endorsement of idealism, in fact it says nothing about the status of extra-mental physical reality (the reality of which is not in doubt for Dharmakīrti – it consists in the play of the energies). What Dharmakīrti may mean is that the experience of something as blue in colour is itself an *interpretation as well as a representation* of some given particulars. His point is that what we are directly acquainted with are our representation and concepts, not the mind-independent domain.

This has crucial soteriological implications: we are reminded that our understanding of reality is couched in terms of a world view or frame of reference or outlook on the world. The dominant Brahminical framework included the following elements:

The efficacy of ritual
A naturally ordered hierarchy of castes
Individual enduring objects or substances
Repeatable properties
Structuring by universals
Natural kinds
Enduring substantial souls

Dharmakīrti wants to establish the view that all of this is purely human conceptual construction, a set of conventions with no ultimate basis in reality.

The impossibility of permanence

We have seen that Dharmakīrti takes dynamic causal efficacy as criterial of reality. It follows that nothing can be permanent and static. Dharmakīrti's opponents recognize different forms of permanence (*nityatā*). By permanent, they mean both eternal and immutable. (Some realists distinguish two varieties: absolute permanence and permanence compatible with change.) Nyāya and Vaiśeṣika ascribe permanence to kinds, universals and some relations. The Mīmāṃsaka ritualists say that both the basic sound units (*varṇa*) of the Sanskrit language, the relation between a Sanskrit word and its meaning, and the Vedic scriptures, are all permanent realities. Others hold that consciousness is the permanent nature of the soul. The Sāṃkhyas, for example, say that the true nature of the soul is permanently static conscious. (Dignāga had challenged this tenet with the consideration that if the self really changes when a cognition occurs, it is impermanent. But if it does not change when cognition occurs, it is not a knowing subject.) The consensus among the various sorts of realists is that permanent realities are revealed and known by their appropriate manifestations (*vyakti*) in space and time. Individual entities are manifestations of universals. A specific usage of a word manifests a timeless meaning. The evolutes of the material nature (*prakṛti*) postulated as the universal substrative cause by the Sāṃkhyas are its manifestations. Realists argued that such manifestation does not compromise eternity and immutability. Dharmakīrti says that manifestation entails mutability. If there are universals, they could never be manifest in individuals. Similarly, if the sounds of the Vedas are permanent, we could never hear their manifestations. If the soul is eternally of the nature of awareness, it would always know everything or nothing.

Dharmakīrti examines the notion of manifestation in the context of the revelation of objects by the cognitive process. On a realist account, some form of cognitive activity, accompanied by factors such as light, is instrumental in revealing already existing realities. But according to Dharmakīrti, since everything is momentary there can be no already existing objects. Objects have to be constituted out of the data of sensation. He insists that whenever such objects are cognized, this happens as an aspect of a process. Take a stream of moments that someone may identify as constituting a pot. The stream is occurring in a dark room. Open the door and switch on the light. You see the pot. It becomes manifest. Dharmakīrti's view is that the presence of the observer (and the light) has introduced a change into the situation. The 'stream of pot moments' is not what it was. It is now involved with the light and the cognitions of the observer. The latter introduce additional factors that render the 'pot-stream' capable of producing a cognition in the observer. The manifestation or revelation of the pot is the product of the co-operation of a variety of causes upon which it depends. Now consider the possibility of the manifestation of permanent realities whose natures are supposed to be entirely self-sufficient and independent of co-operating extra factors. If the essential nature of an entity of that kind is such that it is productive, it will always produce its characteristic effects. If its essential nature is such that it is not productive, it will never produce effects. Let us apply this to consciousness: if the nature of consciousness is to actually illuminate objects, it will always illuminate everything. And in the case of universals, if being manifest as individual instances is internal to their nature, they will always be manifesting all their instances (and we will be aware of them). In the normal case of cognition (of the pot), manifestation was dependent upon co-operating causes or factors and crucially upon the introduction of an extra factor into the situation that rendered the stream of moments capable of producing an awareness. But this cannot apply in the case of allegedly permanent entities that are supposed to be in principle knowable. When Dharmakīrti concludes that their revelation is impossible, he is assuming the realist consensus that if something is real, it is in principle, if not in fact, knowable.

Logic

As we have seen, Dharmakīrti thinks that while immediate sensation relates directly to reality that consists of unique instantaneous particulars, the mental images (*ākāra*) and concepts (*vikalpa*) that they cause, and in terms of which we interpret what is given, do so indirectly. But Dharmakīrti does not think that our concepts are imaginary inventions, although some are. The instantaneous actualities behave in such a way that we can organize them under concepts. Although the natural regularity (*svabhāva-pratibandha*) between smoke and fire or that between something's being an oak and its being a tree holds primarily between two concepts, it also reflects a real state of affairs that causes us to make the connection between the concepts. Dharmakīrti says that inference does not grasp the realities directly in that it operates by determining the object in a mental representation that is not itself the object. But because the representation of the object is causally related to the real objects, we can make reliable inferences.

The key feature of a valid logical inference is the invariant association between the logical reason (*hetu*) and what is to be established (*sādhya*). Dharmakīrti says that the invariant association of As with Bs (which he also calls *avinābhāva* – 'sine qua non') must be guaranteed by a natural regularity (*svabhāva-pratibandha*). The theory of natural regularity attempts to underpin some forms of inseparable connection in the absence of objective universals. We know that the connection between the logical reason and the property to be proved could not be otherwise when the connection is either that between cause and effect (*kārya-hetu*: e.g. fire and smoke) or a case of shared nature (*tadātmya/svabhāva-hetu* – if something is an oak, then it is a tree). This necessary relation is the natural regularity. So we may infer from the fact of something's being an oak that it is a tree and from the presence of smoke to the presence of fire. This principle is applied in characteristically Buddhist arguments like 'If something is produced, it is perishable by nature'.

While Dignāga seems to have been content to allow that the idea of invariable association is the product of a finite range of observed instances, as well as the lack of counter-examples (*adarśana-mātra*), Dharmakīrti wants to strengthen the basis of inference because the inductive approach is insufficiently general and leaves open the possibility of our discovering exceptions in the future. His teacher Īśvarasena thought that our constant association of the logical reason (*hetu*) and that which is to be established (*sādhya*) was based merely on the fact of our not having observed any exceptions to the rule (*adarśana-mātra*). Dharmakīrti thought that this made the basis of inference too fragile: why should we not discover an exception in the future? Moreover, we have not surveyed every relevant instance. We do not know that there is no instance where the *hetu* occurs and the *sādhya* does not. We just have not come across one so far. This is why he argued that the inseparability of *hetu* and *sādhya* had to be grounded in the natural order of things. This means that the presence of the logical reason guarantees the presence of the property to be proved. There can be no counter-example.

We saw that causal connection is one of the two forms of natural regularity between the logical reason and what is to be proved. A causal relation is understood through positive and negative perceptions. The causal connection between smoke and fire is known when we find that smoke, which had not been present, appears when fire is introduced and that when the fire is extinguished, the smoke disappears.

Dharmakīrti applies this in a proof of the existence of streams of experience other than one's own. He argues that we have inferential knowledge of other minds. Given that in one's own case there is observation of the phenomena of language and behaviour immediately after volition or intention, and given that they are not observed in the absence of volition, one knows from one's own case that there is a cause–effect relation between volition and the occurrence of actions. The causal relation is established because we are cognizant of the relations between intention and action and know that where there is no intention there is no action. Seeing that actions separate from us occur even when we have not framed any intention, we infer intentions elsewhere to be the cause of those other actions. Thus, other minds are established. Just as I know from my own case that certain actions are preceded by certain thoughts, so I may analogously infer that similar patterns of speech and behaviour on the part of other people show that they are separate streams of experiences.

According to Dharmakīrti, the non-apprehension (*anupalabdhi*) of an entity that is in principle perceptible (*dṛśya*) establishes the absence or non-existence of that entity. This applies to the problem of other minds: from the fact that we do not perceive them, it does not follow that they do not exist because they do not fall under the category of the in-principle perceptible. But the case of the Brahminical concept of the soul (*ātman*) is different. Those who believe that the soul is a basic reality characterize it as something that should be uncontroversially knowable. Dharmakīrti and other Buddhists focus on the problems of disentangling the putative soul from the personality and its experiences. They reason that it is never known, although it is described as the sort of thing that is knowable. This non-apprehension proves its non-existence. The same pattern of reasoning is applied to the notion of Prime Matter (*prakṛti*), which is supposed by Sāṃkhyas and Vedāntins to be the ultimate source and underlying cause of all material products. But the fact that we do not see supernatural entities, such as ghosts, does not prove that they do not exist because they are by nature inaccessible to normal perception. This applies to anything inaccessible to perception by virtue of space, time or its nature.

The authority of the Buddha's teachings

Dignāga had subsumed reliable testimony, including scriptural statements about unverifiable matters, under inference as a means of knowing (*pramāṇa*). We infer that the Buddha's teachings are valid because we know that he was reliable and sincere, and above all the teaching works in practice. Dharmakīrti is more radical. He denies that any scripture concerned with the supernatural and supra-sensible matters can really have epistemic authority. Human cognitive possibilities are ordinarily restricted to objects that are actually perceptible or in principle perceptible or inferable. We have no access to the supernatural. But the religious person must be concerned with matters outside the range of our ordinary cognitive capacities. Where ordinary human authorities are lacking, he must have recourse to some scriptural authority if he is to pursue a way of life that conduces to well-being (*puruṣārtha*). So his situation is that of one who must choose which of the scriptures and which form of religious praxis to follow. The best we can do is to follow the Buddha's advice and adopt what works. We have no means of knowing about the supernatural. All we can do is hope that if a body of scriptures is a reliable guide to living well here, their teaching about what is unverifiable is trustworthy too.

Further reading

Satkari Mookerjee, *The Buddhist Philosophy of Universal Flux* is about both Dignāga and Dharmakīrti and the many disputes between their school and the Naiyāyika, Mīmāṃsaka and Sāṃkhya realists.

M. Hattori, *Dignāga, On Perception* reconstructs some texts of the first chapter of *Pramāṇa-samuccaya* and covers much more than perception.

R. Hayes, *Dignāga on the Interpretation of Signs*, has translations of chapters II and V of the *Pramāṇa-samuccaya*.

There is a translation and exposition of the *Ālambana-Parīkṣā* in Tola and Dragonetti (2004).

For the text of the *Pramāṇavārttika*, see Pandeya (1989). For that of the *Nyāyabindu* see Svami Dvarkadasa Sastri (1994).

Kajiyama (1998) translates a work belonging to the Dignāga–Dharmakīrti tradition.

John Dunne, *Foundations of Dharmakirti's Philosophy*, contains detailed treatments of ontology, epistemology, logic and the philosophy of language. There is a valuable appendix of translations. Siderits (1991) deals with the philosophy of language, especially the *apoha* theory, which has attracted much scholarly attention in recent years. The Nyāya response is to be found in Uddyotakara's commentary on *Nyāya-Sūtra* 2.2.63 (Jha 1984: 1034 ff).

Dan Arnold, *Buddhists, Brahmins and Belief* has a lot about Dignāga and Dharmakīrti, and relates them to contemporary philosophical interests.

The articles in Tom Tillemans, *Scripture, Logic and Language* combine philosophical acuity and philological expertise.

Vincent Eltschinger, *Penser l'autorité des Écritures* does much more than that and is a mine of information about Dharmakīrti's intellectual context and religious concerns. The same author's *Caste and Buddhist Philosophy* is invaluable.

Bimal Matilal, *Perception*, relates Buddhist representationalism to modern concerns.

Claus Oetke (1994), *Trairūpya*, puts Dignāga's logic in context, tracing its antecedents and relating it to Nyāya and Vaiśeṣika parallels.

See Sacks (2000) for Western parallels.

Questions for discussion and investigation

1. Does the Sautrāntika account of moral responsibility make more sense than that of the Vaibhāṣikas?
2. Is Dignāga's theory of language perception a plausible one?
3. Why does Dharmakīrti think that truth is the same as successful practice?
4. Are they committed to the view that only the present is real? Is this a sensible way of thinking about experience and the world?
5. Is the postulation of unique instants very different from modern physicists' talk about subatomic particles?

Notes

1. They may have a point. Does a tree have real boundaries? What we treat as its surfaces are fluid regions of interaction with an environment.
2. See Matilal (1986) 309–21.
3. More precisely – but perhaps too precisely – *kalpanā* means conceptual construction, especially of individual *entities*, *parikalpanā* means elaboration, *vikalpa* means *dichotomization*, *adhyavasāya* means judgements and *utprekṣā* means imagination.
4. Eltschinger (2007) and van Bijlert 120ff.
5. Hattori (1968).
6. 'The range of the senses is form that is inexpressible and which is cognisable just as it is.' PS I 5cd.
7. 'A visual perception (*cakṣur-vijñāna*) cognises blue, but is does not cognise that something is blue.' *Pramāṇasamuccaya* 1.4.
8. See Chapter 8. The Vaiśeṣika categories (*padārtha*) are substance (*dravya*), quality (*guṇa*), universal (*sāmānya*) inherence (*samavaya*), unique individuator (*viśeṣa*) and action (*kriyā*).
9. Oetke (1994).
10. 'A word expresses its own meaning through the exclusion of others' (*Śabdaṃ svārtham anyāpohena bhāṣate*).
11. V. above Ch. 3, p. (Vasubandhu).
12. Dharmakīrti's own commentary on his Pramāṇavārttika Bk1, Verse 340.
13. A cognition produced by the force of something real (*vastu-balāt*) does not depend upon convention. General ideas are not produced in that way (PV 3.45).

14. PV 2.3: *arthakriyāsamartham yat tad artha paramārthasat/anyat saṃvṛtisat proktaṃ te svasāmānya lakṣaṇe.*
15. It is worth noting that such a criterion could still hold even if nothing existed.
16. Eltschinger (2012) *passim.*
17. *Sarve bhāvāḥ svabhāvena svasvabhāvavyavasthiteḥ/ svabhāvaparabhāvābhyām yasmād vyāvṛttibhāginaḥ//tasmād yato yato'rthanānāṃ vyāvṛttis tannibandhanāḥ/jātibhedāḥ prakalpyante tadviśeṣāvagāhinaḥ* (PV 3.40-41). Of course, the meaning of the word *jāti* here is much wider than caste.
18. PV 3.213: Since there is no inherent connection between words and real things, there are no established facts based on them. They just express what speakers mean.
19. PV 1.3a: *pramāṇam avisaṃvādi jñānam arthakriyā-sthitiḥ.*
20. And a permanent relation cannot obtain between items when at least one of them is impermanent (PV 1.231. v. Eltschinger (2006), p. 256).
21. This differs from Dignāga's view that thought and language are inseparable. There is a suggestion that thought is prior to language.
22. The point here is that they do not require illumination by another conscious principle such as a conscious self. The reflexivity of awareness is used by some Brahminical thinkers as a way of proving the constant self.
23. Particular – an instant without duration in space or time. It is unique and incomparable. It cannot be cognized because cognition applies only to generalities, similarities and relations that it constructs by a synthesis of earlier and later moments.
24. Judgement or ascertainment is consequent upon perception (*pratyakṣa-pṛṣṭhalabdha-niścaya*). The thought (*pratīti*) that something is blue has the same extra-mental source as the representation (*nirbhāsam*) of blue. But it is not in virtue of the visual sensation that there is a felt awareness (*saṃvedanam*) of blue. The felt experience derives from the representation of the blue that is being experienced (Malvania 1971, p. 82; Pandita Durveka Miśra's, *Dharmottarapradīpa*, Patna.).
25. PV 3 (Sva) 92–3.
26. *Avibhāgo'pi buddhyātma-viparyāsitadarśanaiḥ/grāhya-grāhaka-saṃvitti-bhedavān iva lakṣyate.* Dignāga had said something similar. See PS.1 verse 10. The point is that a cognition is a single act or event, although it is possible to impute different aspects to it.
27. *Sahopalambhaniyamād abhedo nīla tad dhiyoḥ* (Pramāṇaviniścaya 1.55) (Vetter, p. 94.). For an example of an idealist construal of what became a 'rule', see Manorathanandin's gloss on PV II.335 (Pratyakṣaparicchedaḥ): *yat tāvan nīlādikaṃ bāhyam iti-ucyate tad jñānena sahopalambha-niyamāt tadabhinna-svabhāvam, dvicandravat.*

5

Madhyamaka Buddhism

Chapter Outline

Nāgārjuna

Nāgārjuna (c.150–200 A.D.) was a monk trained in the Abhidharma tradition, which had tried to delineate the basic forms and structures of reality. This enterprise involved categorizing mental and material phenomena into types of basically real elements (*dharma*) with intrinsic natures (*svabhāva*). Through a process of ever-increasing analysis and refinement, the monks compiled expansive catalogues listing the basic elements. In short, they were formulating what aspired to be all-embracing world views or absolute conceptions of reality from an, as it were, Olympian perspective.[1] (When Nāgārjuna says that he is not offering a *theory* or world view (*dṛṣṭi*) of his own, he may have been thinking of the Abhidharma taxonomical activity.) Nāgārjuna thought that the mistaken belief that there are entities with definite and enduring natures (*bhāva*) (i.e. substances), either at the fundamental or at the macroscopic level, only encourages us to become attached to them. The *Sarvāstivādins* were in effect aspiring to make statements about reality as a whole from a totally objective point of view. Nāgārjuna exploited the paradoxes and inconsistencies in our ways of thinking to show that unenlightened beings cannot formulate a complete and correct description of reality as it is in itself independently of any particular perspective. It follows that there is no point in our even attempting to distinguish between ultimate truth/reality and conventional truth/reality.

In the *Madhyamaka-kārikās*, Nāgārjuna subjects what realists take to be basic concepts, such as those of causality, motion, time, agency, self and substance, to destructive criticism. The concepts with which experience is organized and understood are shown to be incoherent and inconsistent; conceptual schemes are exposed as beset by internal contradictions. We are not Buddhas or fully enlightened beings, and we cannot attain a comprehensive grasp of the whole as it is in itself. The method is one of deconstruction, and Nāgārjuna wants to show that the reifying and polarizing work of conceptualization, not to say the din of chatter, conceals the truth.

His most significant philosophical works include the *Madhyamaka-kārikās*, the *Vigrahavyāvartanī* and the *Ratnāvalī*. His thought is the subject of a long exegetical tradition that continues to this day. He is sometimes difficult to understand. This is sometimes because we do not always know the specific questions to which his statements are the answer, and sometimes because of the cryptic nature of his utterances. Later interpreters include Aryadeva (c.200 A.D.), Dharmapala (c.550) and Candrakīrti (c.600). For these, see Eckel (2008) and Tillemans (2008). Śāntideva's (700–750 A.D.) *Bodhicāryāvatara*, describing the Bodhisattva's path to final enlightenment, is another influential work.

Emptiness

Abhidharmists had assumed the common-sense view that there are individual entities (*bhāva*), even if they are derivatives of more basic factors. Nāgārjuna denies that there are any such entities. He thinks that the existence of concrete particulars is just a matter of the meanings of words and concepts. In short, they too are constructs, not naturally occurrent realities. The notion of intrinsic nature or essence (*svabhāva*) attributed by the Abhidharma thinkers to the basic elements (*dharma*) is not a modest one. Intrinsic nature was held to be permanent, timeless, self-sufficient, independent of all else and unchanging. To test for *svabhāva*, we ask whether something remains the same after being broken up or analysed. So nothing that is a combination of parts can have *svabhāva*. Indeed, nothing that is composed of parts is genuinely real. The possession of such permanent unconditioned identity distinguishes the basic elements from the temporary conditioned aggregates that are the objects of everyday thought and language. In addition, it establishes the distinction between what is genuinely real (*paramārtha-sat* or *dravya-sat*) and whatever is treated as real by convention (*saṃvṛti-sat* or *prajñapti-sat*).

Nāgārjuna argues that everything is empty of intrinsic nature (*svabhāva-śūnya*).

> Whether in the cause, or in the conditioning factors, or in a complex of causes and conditions or in something else, nowhere are there found intrinsic natures of entities. This is what we mean by saying that all entities are empty. For instance the sprout is neither in the seed that is its cause, nor in the conditions such as earth, water and air taken singly or collectively, nor is it a separate reality distinct from the causes and conditions. Since there is no intrinsic nature there, the sprout lacks an intrinsic nature. Lacking intrinsic nature means that it is empty. Just as the sprout lacks an intrinsic nature and is empty, so are all entities empty because they lack intrinsic nature. [VV 1][2]

> Since there is no *dharma* that is not dependently originated, it follows that there is no *dharma* that is non-empty [of essence].[3]

It is uncontroversial for a Buddhist to say that everyday objects do not have intrinsic natures. What is distinctive about Nāgārjuna is the insistence that the *dharmas*, the ultimately real elements posited by his Ābhidharmika colleagues, do not have *svabhāva* either. They too are insubstantial.[4] The basic elements posited by the Abhidharma schools are mental constructs.[5] Were the *dharmas* to have essence, there could be no change, and if no change, no moral growth and no possibility of release from suffering.[6] The repudiation of *svabhāva* amounts to a rejection not just of the *dharma*-typologies but also of the entire Abhidharma ontology. If *svabhāva* is rejected, there is no criterion for the distinction between what is genuinely real and what is treated as real by convention. Not only does the Abhidharma distinction between what is basically real (elements or *dharmas* with intrinsic natures) and what is derivatively or conventionally real collapse, but it is impossible to differentiate between *saṃsāra* as the conditioned realm and *nirvāṇa* as the unconditioned. In fact, Nāgārjuna says that there is not the slightest difference between *saṃsāra* and *nirvāṇa*.[7] If there is a difference, it pertains to how we experience and understand things. It is the difference between insight (*prajñā*) and enchantment. He retains the distinction but does not treat it as an ontological one. Rather, the contrast is between what we take to be real and true, and the truths known by the omniscient Buddhas. There are not two worlds or two dimensions of reality, one conditioned and the other unconditioned. There is one reality that can be understood from the point of view of enlightenment, or from the point of view of conventional ways of thinking. Perhaps he means that there is no metaphysically 'deeper level' of reality where it all makes sense. The world has no ground outside itself. There is no deeper level other than what is evident, or rather, what would be evident to us if only we would see aright. A prominent theme in Chapter 24 of the *Mūlamadhyamakakārikās* is that if it is true that there is no 'other' or 'higher' dimension, it does not follow that life here is futile.

It must be emphasized that the abstract expression 'emptiness' (*śūnyatā*) just means 'absence of intrinsic nature'. It does not mean non-existence. Nāgārjuna was not a nihilist.[8] He often says that what we normally consider things, and the concepts (*vikalpa*) with which we organize our experience, are neither real nor unreal. If there are no intrinsic natures, how could there be extrinsic natures? How can there be *things* and *other things*?[9] We are losing our grip on the very notion of entity (*bhāva*). When he says in the first verse of the *Mūlamadhyamakakārikās*: 'There are no entities that have been produced either by themselves or by something else, or by both, or that have arisen spontaneously,' he means that there are *no entities whatsoever*. He does not mean we cannot account for the genesis of such entities as there may be such.

While our discursive conceptual schemes and the entities that they posit may serve our purposes to an extent (like a map), they distort our understanding and conceal the true nature of things (*tattva*). In short, concepts fall short of whatever the world is like in itself. But the fact that they do is not itself an item of information about reality. The realization that everything is empty of essence puts an end to conceptual construction. It is an antidote to the habit of reification and substantialization (*bhāva-kalpanā*) – the investiture of what is transient with constancy and the attribution of uniformity and simplicity to what is complex and variable. We cease to believe that our concepts are capturing an objective reality. Insight into emptiness, the realization that discursive thought cannot reach the truth, leads to a compassionate outlook and mental peace when one is no longer disappointed by the search for certainties. 'Emptiness' is itself said to be empty. He means that the abstraction 'emptiness' is not a real property or thing, and that there is no essence of emptiness either.

Nāgārjuna insists that the *Abhidharma* outlook is contrary to authentic Buddhist teaching about momentariness and non-substantiality according to which there are no unchanging, self-contained and self-sufficient realities. He appeals to the idea of interdependent genesis of all events (*pratītya-samutpāda*) as meaning that if everything is interdependent, then everything is empty of own nature.[10] He says that entities with essential natures would have to be uncaused or self-created, which is impossible. So there cannot be any basic elements with essences or immutable natures. Moreover, if the basic realities were *dharmas* possessing essence, the universe would be static and there would be no changes. If the unsatisfactory round of existences (*saṃsāra*) had essence or a *fixed* nature, there would be no possibility of *nirvāṇa*.[11] On the other hand, if *nirvāṇa* had essence, there would be no *saṃsāra*. Nāgārjuna also thought that if everything is interdependent, then there are no single simple objects. Hence, everything is complex. If everything is complex, there is no substance. Put simply, if there are no intrinsic natures, everything is indeterminate and we cannot form a determinate conception of reality and our place in it. (Indeed, the expressions 'everything' and 'one world' will be vacuous.) Moreover, if there are no entities, there will be no boundaries between things. As he puts it in the *Kārikās*:

> Given that all the *dharmas* are empty, what is infinite? What has a limit?[12]

A typical argument against essence is: suppose that seeing is the essence of the visual faculty, the efficient cause in a visual awareness. The visual faculty cannot see itself. Seeing, the intrinsic nature of the visual faculty, only operates in the presence of a visible object and light, and is consequent to another state of awareness. So the visual faculty's characteristic way of being actually depends upon the co-operation of a variety of conditions. Its nature is not *intrinsic* to it. But nor does seeing have a 'borrowed' or derivative nature. This is because the latter notion is parasitic upon that of *svabhāva*, and Nāgārjuna thinks that he has established that there are no *svabhāvas*.

Another argument is that if everything is impermanent, things cannot have intrinsic natures. If being young is the essence of youth and being old the essence of the elderly, what undergoes the ageing process? There is also a difficulty in formulating the relation between essence and that which has the essence. If essence is a characteristic of its bearer, the bearer must already exist. But if the bearer already is an entity, the notion of essential nature is superfluous.

A different style of argument exploits the fact that the interdependence of concepts means that they stand or fall together. Chapter 7 of the *Mūlamadhyamakakārikas* examines and rejects the Abhidharma category of the *sāmānya-lakṣaṇa-dharmas* – namely, origin, stasis, decline and impermanence – that characterize all conditioned things. Since those features are constitutive, their impossibility entails that there is no category of conditioned things. But if there is no category of conditioned things, there is no category of unconditioned ones either. Another example of the pernicious effects of dichotomizing conceptualization is that it leads people to think only in terms of extremes. Colloquially, everything has to be one thing or another. So if the concept of eternal existence is embedded in one's mentality, one is tempted to think that anything non-eternal is purely ephemeral.

A similar pattern is apparent in Chapter 8 of the *Mūlamadhyamakakārikās*, where the topic is the various factors used by grammarians and others to analyse events. Let us assume that the notion of agency, for example, is clearly defined, and let us attribute *svabhāva* – an unchanging, independent, self-sufficient nature – to the agent. Immediately we see the problem: an immutable and self-sufficient agent cannot be involved in events and has neither need nor will to participate in events intended to achieve goals.[13] If agents are not efficient causes, then the notions of effect as well as the other sorts of causes collapse. So there are no actions and no events. So there is no right and wrong if actions are impossible. If there are no outcomes, there are no paths to final release or to paradise. All activities would be pointless. We are led to despair by this nihilistic conclusion. It is the attribution of *svabhāva* that is the source of the problem. We see that an unchanging agent cannot act, and also that the denial of *svabhāva* to the agent is just as bad as the road to nihilism. The resolution is stated in verse 12: let's just say that the agent is what operates in dependence upon the action and that the action occurs in dependence upon the agent. All the factors associated with action are interdependent and inter-definable. They are just matters of human convention. It suffices to say that the agent is the one who performs the action and the action is what the agent performs. Thereby we eliminate essentialism but do not move in the direction of nihilism. It was the idea of *svabhāva* that encouraged us to think in 'all-or-nothing terms'. Nāgārjuna wanted people to understand that there is no need to attribute essence to agency (or anything else) and that its rejection does not lead to disaster. In fact, it is the middle way.

It is a view shared by the majority of Buddhist thinkers that unenlightened people think of the world as a system of interactions between more or less stable entities or substances with determinate enduring identities. This they regard as reification – a basic, inherited and shared mistake. Nāgārjuna often compares the emptiness or vanity of our conventional outlooks and beliefs to dreams, illusions and mirages that cannot be classified as real or unreal. He thought that he was recovering the Buddha's original teaching that the belief that there really are entities and persons with definite natures only encourages us to become attached to them. Nāgārjuna's analytical deconstruction of the concepts and categories in terms of which people ordinarily think is held to reveal inconsistencies and shows that conventional world views cannot be true. World views are structured by dichotomies and oppositions between concepts. Moreover, there are many competing world views: a position begets a counter-position and neither is true. Conceptual schemes proliferate, and this proliferation (*prapañca*) of persisting concepts encourages us to think that a structured reality is correspondingly diversified into individuals with substantial natures. The word for 'diversity' and 'proliferation' here is '*prapañca*', which means expansion, diffusion and ampliation.[14] It occurs in the introductory verse to the *Mūlamadhyamakakārikās* and towards the end of that collection:

> I salute the best of teachers, the fully enlightened one who taught universal interdependence according to which there is neither cessation nor origination, neither annihilation nor eternity, neither simplicity nor fragmentation, neither coming nor going, and whose teaching is the pacification (*upaśama*) of ideation (*prapañca*).
>
> This pacification (*upaśama*) of all cognitions, the pacification of ideation, is blissful (*śivaḥ*). (MMK 25.24)

Putting an end to the attempt to understand things using concepts is one thing. But is there a more positive goal? It seems that Nāgārjuna thought that he had found an ineffable and rationally incomprehensible way of life, consisting in contemplative tranquillity:

> That which is beyond the duality of being and non-being, although not beyond anything; that which is not knowledge nor an object of knowledge, which neither is nor is not, neither simple nor complex; that which is without foundation, unmanifest, incomprehensible, incomparable; that which neither arises nor disappears, is neither subject to annihilation but not eternal, that is like space in that it is inaccessible to words and cognitions.[15]

That such was Nāgārjuna's intent was believed by many of his later followers.[16] In his quest for the knowledge of truth, Bhāviveka writes:

> Supreme wisdom negates the network of conceptualisation, and it moves without moving into the clear sky of truth, which is tranquil, self-revealing, inaccessible to words and concepts, and beyond simplicity and complexity.[17]

The limitations of intellection are proclaimed in Śāntideva's celebrated *Introduction to the Bodhisattva's Path.*

> There are thought to be two truths: conventional and ultimate. What is truly real is beyond the scope of the intellect. Intellection is concealing.[18]

The commentary says that convention is that which hides and obscures knowledge of things as they really are because it conceals them behind the belief in intrinsic natures and manifests disguises.[19] Convention is synonymous with misconception, delusion and error. Intellect is concealing because its nature is conceptualization. Every concept reifies what it is about. Every concept is mistaken because it seizes on what is insubstantial.[20]

The burden of the fifteenth chapter of the *Mūlamadhyamakakārikās* is that people who think in terms of the correlative notions *svabhāva* and *parabhāva*, *bhāva* and *abhāva*, will miss the point of the Buddha's teachings.

1 It is not right to hold that intrinsic nature is produced from causes and conditions. A nature so generated would be a product.
2 But how could there be an intrinsic nature that was a product? Intrinsic nature is not manufactured and is independent of other factors.
3 If there are no intrinsic natures, how can there be derived natures (*parabhāva*)? For derivative natures presuppose intrinsic ones.
4 Without intrinsic natures and derivative natures how can there be any entities? Entity (*bhāva*) is established when there is intrinsic nature and derivative nature.
5 If entity is not established then neither is non-entity.
6 Those who see intrinsic nature and derivative nature, entity and non-entity, do not see the truth in the Buddha's teachings.
7 In the 'Instruction of Katyāyana', the extremes both 'it exists' and 'it does not exist' are eschewed by the Buddha, who understood about being and non-being.[21]
8 If existence were in virtue of essence, there would be no ceasing to be, for there is no alteration in essential nature.
9 If essence were unreal, of what would there be alteration? If essence were real, how could there be alteration?

10 The thought 'it exists' is grasping at eternalism: 'it does not exist' is the nihilist extreme. The wise should avoid thinking in terms of permanent existence versus non-existence.

11 The view that whatever exists essentially cannot cease to exist [exists necessarily] entails eternalism. The idea that something that does not exist now existed previously entails nihilism.

Verses from Nāgārjuna's *Ratnāvalī*

Chapter I

When we live well following the righteous path, the attainment of the ultimate good follows. Those who practise the perfect life gradually achieve the ultimate good. [3]

Living well is happiness, and freedom from rebirth is the ultimate good. Trust in the Buddha's teaching and insight are the means to that good. If he has trust, a person may share the path. If he has insight [into emptiness], he knows truly. Of the two, insight is the most important, but trust comes first. [4–5]

One who does not transgress the path because he is led by his own desires, antagonisms, anxiety and delusions is to be considered trusting. [6]

The unenlightened person is frightened when he hears the teachings '*I* am not', '*I* shall not be', 'Nothing belongs to me nor ever will.' [26]

The Buddha has said that such fears are the result of a mistaken belief in personal identity and possessiveness. [27]

In reality, it is a mistake to think in terms of 'I' and 'mine' because neither thought occurs when one has understood how things really are. [28]

The interactions of the five components (*skandhas*) arise from the sense of personal individuality (*ahaṃkāra*). Personal individuality is not a genuine reality. If the seed of something is unreal, how can its sprout be real? [29]

When it is seen that the components are unreal, the sense of individuality is given up. From the giving up of that, the *skandhas* no longer arise. [30]

Just as one sees the reflection of one's face in a mirror, although it is not the real thing, so one conceives individual personality on the basis of the components, although it is not a genuine reality like the reflection of one's face in the mirror. [31–32]

> Just as there appears no reflection of one's face without a mirror, so without the five components individual personality does not appear. [33]
>
> While there is grasping at the components, there is the thought 'I'. When there is belief in personal individuality there is *karma* and rebirth. [34]
>
> [Just as a mirage looks like water, but is neither water nor really anything, so the components look like a persisting self but they are not really a self. [54]]
>
> The individual person cannot be *produced* either *by itself*, or *by another*, or *by both itself and another*. Nor is it not eternal. When one realizes this, personal individuality vanishes and thence *karma* and rebirth. [37]

The pattern of thought here is applied in all manner of contexts. Nothing can bring itself into being. It would have to exist already in order to do so. So it is either eternal, without beginning or end (which does not apply to many things!), or dependent for its genesis on extraneous factors. But it makes no sense to say that an entity is produced by others. This is because a cause is a cause only in relation to an effect. But if what we are calling the effect does not yet exist, it is absurd to specify something as its cause. If there are no causes, there are no effects. In addition, we are helping ourselves to the notion of 'other things'. Where do they come from? If there is no intrinsic nature, how would there be the correlative extrinsic nature? (MMK 22.4) The assumption that there are 'other things' is question begging. The formulation 'not by itself and another' follows from the first two.

> Followers of the *Upaniṣadic* tradition do not worry when they say that familiar worldly life will not exist in the state of liberation. So why are they afraid when we say that there are no absolutely real entities here either? [40]
>
> In the state of release (*mokṣa*) there are neither individual identities nor the five components. But if such a state is dear to you, why do you resist the elimination of the self and the components in this life? [41]
>
> It is not the case that *nirvāṇa* is non-existent. But what could constitute it as an entity? *Nirvāṇa* is beyond the concepts of being and non-being. [42]

[*Nirvāṇa* is not to be understood as a state or place that is concealed by the world. It is a mistake to reify *nirvāṇa* and think of it as *something* that exists as a sort of parallel universe. We return to the original message of the Buddha: *Nirvāṇa* is just the extinction of the fires of greed, hatred and delusion.]

> In brief, the nihilist theory denies that actions have consequences. This false view is immoral and leads to hell. [43]
>
> In brief, the true view is that actions have consequences. This correct view brings merit and rebirth in good states. [44]
>
> When thanks to insight one has ceased to think in terms of what is and what is not, one no longer thinks in terms of merit and demerit. The good say that this is freedom (*mokṣa*) that is beyond good and bad births. [45]
>
> If a cause is produced before its effect or simultaneously with it, in reality it is not a cause. The concept of origination is incoherent, either from the absolute or from the conventional point of view. [47]

[As we said above: since something is identified as a cause only when it produces an effect, if the relevant factor pre-exists the effect, it cannot be considered as the cause. It can only be considered as the cause after the time when the effect has come into existence, and in that case its causal function is superfluous. Nāgārjuna is not saying that there are no entities. He is saying that they are not essentially identifiable as causes and effects.]

> Causal relations may be expressed like this: when A is present, B arises. For instance, when we have the idea of long, that of short arises. When something is produced, there is production of something else – such as radiance after the production of a lamp. [48]
>
> If there is no short, there can be no long. There can be no radiance if no lamp is produced. [49]
>
> When one understands causality like this, it does not lead to nihilism. [50]

This is a classic statement of interdependent origination (*pratītya-samutpāda*). Regularity is just a matter of one thing following another. There is no need to posit invisible and innate causal powers. The point here is that an attempt to understand causality in terms of the transformation of essential natures (or any other metaphysical account such as *satkāryavāda* or *asatkāryavāda*) is bound to fail and that disillusionment may lead to nihilism.

We move on to the problem of saying anything sensible about the 'ontological status' of the cosmos or about reality as a whole 'as it is in itself':

> The world does not come into existence. It does not go out of existence. It does not remain static even for an instant. How can we say that the world as a whole, to which the categories of past, present and future do not apply, is real? [63]

> In truth, since the temporal framework does not apply to either the world or to *nirvāṇa*, how can we specify a real difference between the two? [64]
>
> Given that there is no duration, there is neither origination nor cessation. So how can the world be produced, endure and cease. [65]

Just as the concept of production cannot apply to the cosmos taken as a whole, nor can that of time and the correlative notions of origination, endurance and cessation. The cosmos cannot have a starting point in time, if time is a measure of change and times are relations between things in the cosmos.

Next we see a characteristic example of Nāgārjuna's arguments against the Abhidharma:

> How can existence be non-temporal if things are always changing? If it is not the case that things are always changing, how can we account for their variability? [66]
>
> If everything is momentary, how do things get older? But if things are not momentary, in the sense that they remain the same, how do they get older? [68]

We move on to a critique of the metaphysic of essential temporality – the view that existence can really be reductively analysed into basic moments:

> If an instant has an end, it must be supposed to have a beginning and a middle. Given that the instant consists of three parts, it cannot be a basic reality. [69]
>
> Beginnings, middles and ends must be considered like the instant (i.e. similarly reducible, so there is an infinite regress). The conjunction 'being a beginning, a middle and an end' does not exist from itself or from something else. [70]
>
> No atom is simple since it has many sides. No atom lacks sides (if it did, it could not be connected with others). The ideas of unity and plurality are mutually dependent, as are those of existence and non-existence. [71]

This anticipates criticisms of the notion of atomic aggregation into larger entities. The point is that if atoms combine, they cannot be simple or atomic, which is a contradiction. Nāgārjuna is saying that analytic reductionism as practised by the Ābhidharmikas fails since we cannot identify basic units. The later idealist argument will be that we cannot make sense of physical matter.

Chapter II

As the Kadalī tree and all its parts when split down the middle is not anything, likewise with the person when it is analysed into components. [1]

Hence the enlightened ones have said that all *dharmas* lack intrinsic natures. They have ascertained the real nature of the components and seen that they are not substantial. [2]

Neither substance nor non-substance is found in reality. The Buddha did not espouse either the substantialist viewpoint or the anti-essentialist viewpoint. [3]

The Buddha has stated that what is observed and what is stated in scriptures is neither true nor false. When there is an argument, there is a counter-argument and neither is absolutely true. [4]

The universe is really beyond the categories of truth and falsity. In truth, we cannot say 'it is' or 'it is not'. [5]

How could the omniscient Buddha affirm of the world about which no true statement is possible that it has an end, or that it is infinite, or that it is really plural or that it is non-differentiated? [6]

People ask how many Buddhas have been, will come and are here now. But the notion of a limit on the number of beings presupposes the threefold temporal framework. [7]

There is no cause of the growth of the world. Decay is relative to the threefold temporal framework. [8]

In this consists the depth of the teaching that is a secret from ordinary people: that the world is like a magical illusion is the essence of the teaching of the Buddha. [9]

An elephant conjured up by magic may appear, and it may seem to have a beginning and end. But really it has no beginning and end. [10]

Likewise we see apparent beginnings and ends of things in the world. But in reality there are neither fixed beginnings nor ends. [11]

As a magic elephant comes from nowhere and goes nowhere, being due to a conjuror's pretence, it does not last as a reality. [12]

Likewise the world is like an illusion that comes from nowhere and goes to nowhere. It does not last as a reality since it is only mental delusion. [13]

> What then is the meaning of this world organized by the three times? It cannot be said to be or not to be, except from the conventional standpoint. [14]
>
> Therefore the Buddha did not say whether it is finite or infinite, plural or single. [15]

The Refutation of Objections

Nāgārjuna wrote an important work called 'The Refutation of Objections' (*Vigrahavyāvartanī*) in response to criticism levelled at his method by followers of the Nyāya school.[22] He envisages an opponent who says that the proposition that all entities lack intrinsic natures itself lacks one and thus cannot deny anything. If he admits that the proposition has an intrinsic nature, he is contradicting himself [VV 1–2].

What does it mean to say that a statement lacks an intrinsic nature? When a statement is true, it is an example of language operating as an instrument of knowledge (*pramāṇa*). Nāgārjuna is supposing that the opponent holds that the essence of a *pramāṇa* consists in its power (*śakti*) to be an instrumental cause that establishes the truth about things. So the point is that if a *pramāṇa* lacks intrinsic nature, it also lacks that capacity.

Nāgārjuna replies that the opponent has not understood the meaning of emptiness. Entities that are interdependently originated are empty of intrinsic natures because they are dependent upon causes and conditions. His proposition is indeed empty in this sense. But everyday objects, albeit empty, perform their functions successfully. The same applies to his proposition. Essence is not a precondition of functioning in an ever-changing world. The statement has a therapeutic value for people who take it for granted that things have essences.

There is also the objection from the Nyāya school that Nāgārjuna cannot show that all things are empty, since such a demonstration requires that there are valid means of knowing (*pramāṇas*: i.e. perception, inference and testimony). The objects of the *pramāṇas* must exist too, because one cannot negate what does not exist. The opponent says:

> 'You deny the reality of things after you have apprehended them by perception, but you also say that the perception by which entities are cognized is not a reality.' [VV 5]

Nāgārjuna replies:

> ‘If I apprehended an object by perception or inference or testimony, I could then affirm or deny things about it. But I don’t do that so the objection is not sound.’ [VV 30]
>
> If you hold that objects are established by means of knowing (*pramāṇa*), tell me how you establish those means of knowing. [VV 31]
>
> If the *pramāṇas* are established by other *pramāṇas*, there is an infinite regress. There is neither beginning, nor middle nor end. [VV 32]
>
> If you think that *pramāṇas* are established without *pramāṇas*, you have abandoned your own doctrine. [VV 33]
>
> A *pramāṇa* cannot establish itself, because something cannot exercise its characteristic activity upon itself. [VV 34-39]
>
> If the means of knowing are self-established, they are established independently of the objects known. Self-establishment does not require anything else. [VV 40]
>
> If you think that the means of knowing are established independently of the objects known, then those means of knowing are not means of knowing about anything. [VV 41]
>
> If the *pramāṇas* are established only in relation to the objects known, the objects known are not established by the *pramāṇas*. [VV 43]
>
> If the objects known are established independently of the means of knowing, what is the point in seeking to establish the *pramāṇas*? [VV 44]
>
> If you hold that the objects of knowing are established by the means of knowing and that the means of knowing are established by the objects of knowing, you cannot establish either. [VV 46]
>
> If the *pramāṇas* are established by the objects known, and if those objects have to be established by *pramāṇas*, then, because the *pramāṇas* have not been established, the objects have not been established either. So how will the objects known establish the means of knowing? [VV 48]

Further reading

There are stimulating introductions to Madhyamaka thought by David Burton (1999) and Jan Westerhoff (2009). Chapter III of Paul Williams's *Mahāyāna Buddhism* is helpful. His *Altruism and Reality* is mostly about the *Bodhicaryāvatāra*. See especially Chapter V, T. R. V. Murti, *The Central Conception of Buddhism*.

The best translation of the *Madhyamakakārikās* is Mark Siderits and Shoryu Katsura, *Nāgārjuna's Middle Way*. This supersedes all previous English translations and comes with explanatory notes.

The *Bodhicaryāvatāra* is translated in Crosby and Skilton (1996) and Wallace.

Bhattacharya (1998) translates the *Vigrahavyāvartanī*. See also Westerhoff (2010).

Lindtner (1982) contains much helpful explanatory material, as well as texts and some translations.

Hahn (1982) has the text of the *Ratnāvalī*. There is a translation by G. Tucci in the *Journal of the Royal Asiatic Society*, 66 (1934) and 68 (1936).

For engagement with Nyāya over the question of the *pramāṇas*, see especially Uddyotakara's commentary on *Nyāya-Sūtra* 2.1.8-19. This is translated in Jha (1984), p. 606ff.

Questions for discussion and investigation

1. Why does Nāgārjuna think that the Abhidharma distinction between the absolute and conventional dimensions of reality collapses?
2. Is Nāgārjuna entitled to make any truth-claims?

Notes

1. For the notion of the 'absolute conception', see Williams (1978), *passim*.
2. Bhattacharya (1978), p. 42.
3. MMK 24.19.

4. *yathā tvayā mahāyāne dharma-nairātmyam ātmanā viditam* (*Acintyastava*, verse 2).
5. *kalpanā-mātram ity asmāt sarva-dharmāḥ prakāśitāh* (*Acintyastava*, verse 36).
6. 'If the afflictions (*kleśa*) were intrinsically real, how could they be removed? Who can remove essence?' (MMK 23.24).
7. MMK 25.19.
8. *Śūnyatā ca na ca ucchedaḥ saṃsāraś ca na śāśvatam* (MMK 17.20a).
9. *Yadi nāsti svabhāvaś ca parabhāvaḥ kathaṃ bhavet.*
10. 'Whatever is interdependently originated, that is empty [of essence]. Emptiness is a concept. Such is the middle way' (MMK 24.18).
11. 'There is no end to suffering that is permanently existent. But you rule out cessation by maintaining intrinsic nature' (MMK 24.23).
12. *Śūnyeṣu sarvadharmeṣu kim anantaṃ kim antavat* (MMK 25.22a).
13. A substantial (unchanging and independent) factor does not produce a real object. An insubstantial factor does not intend an insubstantial goal.

    A substantial agent does not participate in events, so there is no agent with respect to the goal. There is no activity on the part of something substantial, so the agent (*kartā*) would have no goal.

    If an insubstantial factor brought about an insubstantial goal, the object would lack an efficient cause and the agent would not be an efficient cause.

    If there is no efficient cause, there would be neither effect nor instrumental causes. Given their absence, there would be no action, agent or instrumental cause (MMK 8 1-4).
14. The process may also be understood as reification or the assumption that every substantive designates a substance.
15. *Acintyastava*, verses 37–9.
16. Others (called *Prāsaṅgika-Mādhyamikas*) thought that the purpose of the teaching was purely negative – the destructive criticism of any and every point of view. Those who thought that Nāgārjuna taught some positive doctrines (such as the anti-essentialist idea that there is no substance) are called *Svātantrikas*. The debate was largely conducted in Tibet. See Edelglass (2009), Ch. 11.
17. Eckel (2008), 41–2.
18. Vaidya (1960), p. 170.
19. Vaidya (1960), p. 171.
20. Vaidya (1960), p. 177.
21. Siderits and Katsura (2013), p. 160, say that according to the commentators, the point is that there is always a middle way. For any pair of opposing views, one can deny one without adopting the other. So one could deny permanence without committing oneself to the view that everything is instantaneous.
22. The text is in Bhattacharya (1998).

6

Yogācāra Buddhism

Chapter Outline

Buddhist idealism: Mind-only

Some Buddhists are metaphysical idealists who deny that there are any material or physical realities existing independently of minds. This viewpoint differs from the family of views sometimes called epistemic idealism, which holds that while there are mind-independent physical entities, we have no cognitive access to them. The thinkers whose ideas are the subject of this chapter say that there are neither enduring selves nor an external world but only constructs of selfhood, agency and objectivity deriving from a storehouse of vestiges of previous experiences. There are no realities other than ideas and no persisting subjects of experience to which those ideas belong. We must bear in mind here that these philosophers were also monks, practising profound meditation every day. The point is reflected in the designation of this tradition as 'Yogācāra', which means, 'the practice of yoga'.[1] One of the meanings of 'yoga' here is the dissolution of individual experience consequent upon an end to thinking in terms of the dichotomy between subject and object. Meditation often involves experiencing what are purely thought-forms as if external to the mind. It is not surprising that such people should be especially open to the possibility that what we ordinarily take to be external realities are but projections of consciousness.

The Buddhist idealists have a lively sense that the ways in which we experience what we unenlightened beings call the external world are conditioned by personal and subjective factors. Our mindset or world view determines how we see the world. What makes one person's perception of a state of affairs different from that of another is the moods, emotions and memories that one brings to bear in the circumstances. This is illustrated by the point that when hungry ghosts see a body of water, they see a mass of pus. But humans see it as a crystal stream and drink from it. Such observations about the subjective constitution of experience do not in themselves license any conclusions about the ontological status of the physical world. But we shall see that these Buddhists present metaphysical arguments against the possibility of material substance as well as epistemic ones against the intelligibility of the concept. The latter arguments focus upon the problem of describing a mind-independent world without thinking about it.

The central figure here is Vasubandhu who lived during the period c.350–400 A.D. Trained in Vaibhāṣika-Sarvāstivāda methods of analysis and meditation, he wrote a work called the *Abhidharmakośa-bhāṣya* which is a critical survey from a Sautrāntika point of view of those Buddhist realist schools. Another work is the *Karmasiddhiprakaraṇa*, which is a Sautrāntika critique of realist notions of how *karma* operates, and an attempt to reconcile atomistic impersonality with moral responsibility and consequentiality. It appears that he moved from a representationalist to an idealist philosophical position and wrote the *Madhyāntavibhāgaśāstra*, the *Trisvabhāvanirdeśa*, the *Viṃśatikā* and the *Triṃśikā* from that point of view. His commentator Sthiramati lived around 550 A.D.

The Sautrāntika representationalists think that it makes sense to suppose that while most of our perceptual representations (*ākāra/pratibhāsa*) have external physical causes, the latter are not objects of direct acquaintance. But perceptions do not mirror or picture their external counterparts since the world really consists of a flux of unique momentary particulars (*svalakṣaṇa*) and as such does not feature in the content of awareness. That there is an external world is not a conclusion of perception (*bāhyārtha-pratyakṣa*) but one of inference (*bāhyārtha-anumeya*) that there has to be something that causes those experiences over whose occurrence we have no control. We can see how the view that the immediate objects of acquaintance are representations that are internal to minds may readily encourage an idealist outlook. The possibility that emerges is that the world is purely mental, especially if it is held that there is some commonality of form or nature (*sārūpya*) between perceptions and their objective correlatives. If the experience – *in its subjective phenomenal character* – of seeing yellow is somehow really *like* external reality, it follows that external reality too has the nature of experience. On the other hand, it might be argued that the gulf between what is supposedly given in sensation and its interpretation in concepts, thoughts and judgements is very wide. The Sautrāntikas held that we are not directly acquainted with objects in the world, and that conceptual and discursive thinking does not reach out to the world. The following question arises: if the existence of that world can only be certified by inference (itself a mental activity), why suppose that there is an extra-mental physical dimension to reality? If the manifest content of experience is determined by our minds rather than objects in the world, we might wonder what sense can be given to the notion of a mind-independent reality. Surely it is falling out of the picture. The reasoning is:

A flux of ineffable particulars is supposed to be given in sensation. But neither sensation nor imagination nor conceptual and discursive thought grasp the nature of what is given *as it really is*. The given is posited in vague and formal terms as something that has a purely instrumental causal role in the genesis of imagination and discursive thinking. But thought actually conceals the true nature of things. It is not obvious that such an unknown uninterpreted given need be postulated at all.

Considerations like these seem to be the impetus behind Vasubandhu's move towards idealism or view that only the mental factors of existence (*vijñapti-dharma*) are real. Vasubandhu came to reject the Sautrāntika view that we can validly infer that there is an extra-mental reality as the cause of our perceptual sensations. We do not need to posit a material dimension of reality in order to explain the character of experiences. Everything is a transformation of consciousness (*vijñāna-pariṇāma*). There are no physical objects. The occurrence of experiences can be readily and economically explained by the revival of traces of prior experiences (*vāsanā* or *saṃskāra*) within a stream. The traces of experiences are preserved in what is called the 'storehouse-consciousness' (*ālaya-vijñāna*)[2].

The Vaibhāṣika realists hold that all mental acts have existent objects external to the mind because perceptual experience is by definition the product of interaction between a sense-faculty and an external object. Vasubandhu argues that dreams and hallucinations show that this is not true. The occurrence of perceptions seemingly about an external world does not *necessarily* depend upon mind-independent realities. If we can point to cases of perceptual experience, phenomenologically indistinguishable from ordinary ones, that occur without extra-mental objects, may it not be possible that all such experiences lack present and external objects?[3]

The occurrence of dreams, hallucinations and visualization of what is not present to the senses does not of itself prove that there are no extra-mental objects. What these phenomena show is the possibility of cognitions that have meaningful content although they lack external objects. The next stage is to show that what we ordinarily take to be material objects composed of particles do not exist. Vasubandhu argued against the very coherence of the notion of material substance. He rejected the Vaibhāṣika view that we are directly aware of objects made up of real physical atoms. Atoms are partless and indivisible. As such they cannot join together. But if we insist that atoms come together, they must have parts. If they coalesce, there will be no increase in extent because they lack extension. If they have no extension, they cannot combine to form larger objects. If they have dimension, they will be divisible and this undermines atomism. Atoms are by definition indivisible. Anything extended is divisible: whatever is indivisible is unextended. If there are no atoms, there cannot be any wholes distinct from their parts.

A lot of weight is put on the 'dream argument'. There is a sense in which it is irrefutable. Any refutation may be part of a dream.[4] A realist about the external world might object that we are not simply aware of objects outside the mind, but also of their occurrence in a three-dimensional and temporally ordered framework. To this, Vasubandhu responds that experience of such determination occurs in dreams as well. Again the 'dream argument' may be used against the consideration that our experience of separate objects as occupying three-dimensional space is a basic phenomenological fact. In addition, in response to the argument that it appears that there are many minds experiencing the same objective environment, Vasubandhu appeals to the Buddhist notions of hells, which are shared hallucinations.

Like all Buddhists, Vasubandhu believes that it is the intentional actions of sentient beings that are responsible for the diversity and organization of the cosmos. Indeed, the worlds exist only as environments in which the consequences of actions are to be experienced. The Abhidharma thinkers understand this realm to be basically constituted by the material and mental elements (*dharmas*) of existence. The idealists reject the category of material elements and hold that only the mental elements are real. Lives are streams of perceptions (*vijñapti*) ever emerging from a universal mental storehouse (*ālaya-vijñāna*) of vestiges impressed by previous actions.[5] These self-conscious ideas may mistakenly conceive themselves as individual subjectivities, viewing ideas as other than themselves and as constituting other streams. What is described as the polluted or corrupted egocentric mentality has four modalities: This is always polluted and corrupted by four defects: belief that there is a permanent self (*ātma-dṛṣṭi*), delusions about oneself (*ātma-moha*), an exaggerated sense of one's importance (*ātma-māna*) and self-love (*ātma-sneha*). The emergent transformations of consciousness influence one another and generate a conceptual scheme or 'world view'. Thanks to the ongoing revival of vestiges of prior actions, there is a constant supply of new experiences. Because it is the nature of minds to create representations of objects, unenlightened people habitually assume that those objects exist independently of consciousness when they are in reality internal to it.

Vasubandhu thinks that individual events in a mental series are aware of themselves (*sva-saṃvitti*). By this, he means that an awareness is simultaneously and in virtue of the same act self-cognized or self-illuminating, just as a lamp illuminates itself while illuminating an object. This tenet of the reflexivity of mental events is important to the idealist outlook. If each mental event is its own subject, there is no need to invoke the notion of soul or centre of consciousness as the witness or experiencer of mental states. The intrinsic reflexivity of cognition is also taken to mean that the polarity of subject and object is purely internal to awareness. The subject–object polarity does not require that cognitions are about things in the external world, because if a cognition has two aspects, one could be about the other. So there is another reason for the claim that we cannot infer the existence of physical objects on the basis of the occurrence of experiences that are intentional in form.

Central to the Yogācāras' soteriological concerns is the conviction that our everyday environment and ways of life are a mirage concealing an authentic reality. Enchanted by the mirage, unenlightened people lead lives contaminated by selfish attachments, aversions and delusions. At the most basic level, people are attached to the objects of sensation and indeed may be said to live on the level of sensation, whereas enlightened people are detached from the objects of sense and realize that the world to which we are attached is but a fabric of appearances. The unenlightened mind is veiled by moral, emotional and intellectual defects (*kleśa*), foremost among which are cravings, antagonisms and failures in understanding. These defects spring from seeds embedded in streams of consciousness. They suppress the pure factors that are conducive to salvation and whose cultivation promotes a *transformation of mind* and conduct. Internalization of the teaching that the elements lack enduring identities (*dharma-nairātmya*) produces a non-discursive, direct intuition into the nature of unconditioned reality in which subject–object dichotomy disappears. Intensification of this intuition destroys all the defects, together with their seeds, in a stream of experience. Enlightenment means freedom from desires, aversions and delusions, primarily the delusion that one is fundamentally an enduring, substantial soul, a 'further fact' over and above the stream of one's psycho-physical continuity. This is a form of detachment more radical than a refusal of the satisfactions of sensory experience. It is the realization that one does not really matter. The wise have internalized the view that ordinary experience is of a mind-independent physical world only because ideas project themselves as if external. We have seen the basic tenet that what are ordinarily considered to be material objects do not exist independently of awareness. That they appear to do so is because ideas project themselves as if external. The Yogācāra tradition calls this the imaginative construction of unreal phenomena (*abhūta-parikalpa*). This expression may also mean the dichotomization of consciousness into subjects and objects of awareness (*grāhya-grāhaka-vikalpa*).[6]

Philosophy enriched by meditation is antidote to the misconception that we are individual subjects receiving sensory impressions from a realm of material objects that are entities in their own right independently of constructive consciousness. We have seen that the Yogācārins hold that no sense can be made of the direct realist view that the perceiving mind confronts an independently existing domain of physical objects. They claim this because atomism as an account of a purportedly material domain that is external to minds is incoherent. All the Buddhist thinkers aim to provide a rationale for why we should not be self-centred. A structural feature of the unenlightened mentality is its opposing subjects and objects (*grāhya-grāhaka-vikalpa*). Above all, it embodies at least three delusions: first, that the world is really as it appears to us; secondly, that it exists for our satisfaction; and thirdly, the basic misconception that we really are the enduring individual identities that we unreflectingly take ourselves to be.

There is an internal relation between this mentality and the misconception that people and things have timeless essences, permanent identities or unchanging natures. It does not matter whether what are considered objects are mental or physical. The real point of 'ideas-only' (*vijñapti-mātra*) is to help us to internalize and act upon the truth that there are no individual subjects of awareness confronting things and each other as objects. The notion of the apprehending subject is relative to that of there being mind-independent entities. Once it is realized that what we think of as objects are not stable external entities, our everyday understanding of cognition is transformed. Since subject and object are interdependent, the subjective element is also eliminated. In short, the Buddhist idealists want to eliminate thinking in terms of the pervasive subject–object polarity (*grāhya-grāhaka-bhāva*, literally grasped–grasper relation) which conditions our outlook on life.

Extracts from Vasubandhu's 'Twenty Verses Proving that only Mental Phenomena are Real' (*Vijñapti-mātratā-siddhi*)

According to Mahāyāna, it is established that the three realms are only mental (*vijñapti-mātra*). The words *cittam*, *manas*, *vijñāna* and *vijñapti* are synonyms. *Cittam* includes all mental events (*caitta*). 'Only' excludes material forms.

If awareness of objects depended on causation by external objects, hallucinations and delusions would not be possible. Consciousness appears in the guise of external perceptible objects. Ideas of objects are sufficient. They arise from a sub-conscious store of mental seeds and traces of prior experiences. The Ābhidharmikas say that all cognitions have real objects. The first verse responds to this by saying that some thoughts have unreal objects. The point is that reference to an extra-mental feature is not a necessary feature of awareness. If some thoughts can have significance in the absence of any external object, the question arises whether we are right to assume that there are really any extra-mental items.

1 All this is just ideas, because there is manifestation of non-existent objects – as when someone with cataracts sees non-existent cobwebs.

Here the realist opponent says:

> **2** If an idea is not caused by an external object, it would not be determined by time and place, there would be no shared experiences and ideas would lack practical consequences.

If there could be awareness of colour and shape in the absence of an external object with colour and shape, such awareness has not been caused by an external object. So why is it produced at a specific place and not anywhere? And why does it arise at that place at a specific time and not always?

And why is it produced in the streams of experience of all who are present at that time and place and not just in one, just as the illusory appearances occur in the experiential stream of those with cataracts and not in others?

And why are the hairs and bees seen by cataract-sufferers not causally effective? Things seen in dreams do not perform the functions of their counterparts in the waking state. Fictional cities don't do anything because they do not exist.

Hence, in the absence of external objects, spatio-temporal determination, shared experiences and causal efficacy are unintelligible.

Vasubandhu's Reply:

> **3** Spatio-temporal determination is established in dreams; evil spirits in immaterial hells share experiences, for they all see rivers of pus.

In dreams too, things are seen at specific places and times. So spatio-temporal determination is established without external objects. Beings in hell, who are there because of similar maturation of *karma*, all see rivers of filth. Thus, there is shared experience although the objects of awareness are not physical realities.

> **4** [The real is the causally effective] and there is production of effects as in wet dreams. Again in the case of hell, all see the hell-guards and are punished by them.

In erotic dreams, there is emission of semen without intercourse. As a consequence of the maturation of parallel karma, all the denizens of hell suffer, although the guards who inflict pains are not physical.

> **6** If you allow that the experiences of individuals in hell are the products of purely mental karmic traces, why not admit that this applies to all experiences?

7 The imprint left by the action is supposed to be in one place and the effect of the action elsewhere. Why is the effect not said to be where the imprint is?

Why not admit that both karmic traces and their effects are transformations of consciousness and just in the mind?

The opponent replies: Because of the tradition. If the representation of colour and shape etc. were just thought-forms, and colour and shape were not physical objects, the Buddha would not have taught that they were independent of minds.

8 The teaching of reality of colour and shape etc. was intended to be on a level that the hearers could understand.
9 The seed of its own from which the cognition arises and the representation of its object are the two bases of experience taught by the Buddha.

What does this mean?

An idea whose content is a representation of colour and shape arises from a specific transformation of consciousness called its seed. In the case of such an idea, the Buddha referred to that seed and the representation respectively as the eye and as the reality of colour and shape.

But why did he teach in this way?

10 To lead us to the truth that people do not have enduring natures. Put another way, the teaching that only ideas and minds are real leads to internalization of the truth that there are no *dharmas* with permanent identities – as commonly supposed.

This teaches the insubstantiality of persons. From the interaction of sense-faculties and objects, the six types of awareness occur. But there is no single subject of experience or one who thinks – there are only the perceptions.

How does this teach the insubstantiality of *dharmas*? By knowing that there is no *dharma* that really has colour and shape, and that a cognition (*vijñapti*) is just a representation of colour and shape.

Objection: If there are no *dharmas*, there are no cognitions either.

Reply: The claim that the *dharmas* are insubstantial is not the same as the claim that there are no *dharmas*. The unenlightened wrongly suppose that the *dharmas* have intrinsic nature (*svabhāva*) and that there is a real difference between subjects and objects (*grāhya-grāhaka*). This is what is meant by the denial of their substantiality. The correct understanding of insubstantiality is in terms of the 'perceptions-only' theory or the denial of material substance.

Material substance is impossible because:

11 The object in awareness is not a single whole. It is not a multiplicity that is composed of many atoms. Nor is it a conglomeration of atoms. This is because the existence of atoms is not established.

12 Given its simultaneous connection with six other atoms, the atom would have six parts. If the six occupy the same place, they would have the same size as one.

Opponent: We Kāshmiri Vaibhāṣikas say that the atoms do not unite because they are without parts. Don't attribute this mistake to us! But conglomerates of atoms are connected.

But is the conglomerate a separate reality?

13 If the atoms do not join together, how do they form conglomerates? One cannot establish conglomeration just because the atoms are simple!

An interpretation of the Thirty Verses on Consciousness

Vasubandhu also wrote a short treatise, called the Triṃśikā or 'Thirty Verses', which is a reflection upon the structure of consciousness and the phenomenology of experience. He begins by saying that the words 'identity' (*ātman*) and 'element of existence' (*dharma*) are variously applied to what are really modifications of consciousness (*vijñāna-pariṇāma*). This transformation is threefold. There is fruition of traces of prior experiences deposited in the storehouse-consciousness (*ālaya-vijñānam*). The receptive mind conditions mental phenomena (*caitta*) including sensations, perceptions, attentiveness, feelings and intentions. The second modality is reflecting upon about ideas (*mano-vijñānam*) belonging to the storehouse. This is always polluted and corrupted by four defects: belief that there is a permanent self (*ātma-dṛṣṭi*), delusions about oneself (*ātma-moha*), an exaggerated sense of one's importance (*ātma-māna*) and self-love (*ātma-sneha*). This egocentric mental mode is a function of the mental phenomena. It is transcended in enlightened beings [5b-7]. The third modality is that of perceptions of objects (*vijñapti-viṣaya*). These are conditioned by a range of mental phenomena: sensation, desire, memory and reflection. They may be affected either by virtuous factors such as faith, shame, lack of greed, hostility and delusions, energy and non-violence or by harmful ones [8–14].

The transformations of consciousness are mental constructs (*vikalpa*). What is thus constructed does not exist independently. So everything is really just ideas [17]. The emergent transformations of consciousness influence one another and generate a conceptual scheme or 'world view'. Thanks to the ongoing revival of vestiges of prior actions, there is a constant supply of new experiences [18–19].

What common sense regards as independent entities or objects (*vastu*) are mental constructs. Such constructed natures (*parikalpita-svabhāva*) do not exist in their own right [20]. Mental construction is produced by causes and conditions, and hence its nature is dependent or conditioned (*paratantra-svabhāva*). There is a perfected or unconditioned mind (*pariniṣpanna-svabhāva*) that is exempt from such conditioning [21].

It is rationally undecidable whether the perfected mind is the same as or different from the conditioned mind. This is because the conditioned mind, the process of mental construction, is just a feature, *qua* activity, of the unconditioned mind. Furthermore, as long as the conditioned state is not understood as such, we can have no conception of an unconditioned state. Immersed *in* the unenlightened mode of awareness, there is no possibility of the conditioned mind's realizing its limited nature out of its own resources. It simply lacks the ability to attain an external, neutral perspective upon itself [22].

What are called the three natures are not intrinsically determined [23].

It is a mistake to attribute an independent identity (*svabhāva*) to the products of mental construction, to the process of mental construction or to the perfected or unconditioned mind [24].

The permanent and true nature of the elements (*dharma*) is purely mental [25].

As long as one does not realize that reality is purely mental, the subject–object mentality persists [26].

Merely confronting an object and supposing 'this is just an idea' is not an experience of the mind-only state [27].

When thinking does not apprehend any objective correlatives (*ālambana*), then it is established in the mind-only state. In the absence of objects of thought, there is no grasping [28].

This is supernatural direct intuition, beyond the mind (*citta*), beyond thinking. This is the transformation of the storehouse-consciousness, immune from afflictions and obscurations [29].

Meditation

We began this chapter with an observation that the idealist philosophers were also monks, devoted to the practice of contemplation. What follows is an example of the way in which various philosophical theories may inform soteriological practice. The extract is from Kamalaṣīla's *Bhāvanākrama I.*[7]

> Contemplation uninformed by wisdom is fruitless for one who believes that he is an enduring entity.
>
> The light of wisdom is required to annihilate the seeds of delusion.
>
> Here is a brief description of the process of the cultivation of wisdom:
>
> 'Ascending to the level of mind-only (*citta-mātram*), one no longer imagines external entities.
>
> Settled on that level, one goes beyond mind-only.
>
> Having gone beyond mind-only, one reaches the level of the non-representative mind.
>
> The yogin who is settled in the non-representative mind sees the great vehicle (*mahāyāna*).
>
> When he is purified and tranquil, thanks to his vows, he attains a state where there is no effort and intuits the truth that there is no metaphysical substance.'[8]
>
> The meaning is: first the yogin should examine the material *dharmas* that are imagined by others to be external objects. He should ask, 'are they other than consciousness, or does consciousness just appear in these ways, as in a dream?' There he should examine them as atoms, supposing them to be external to consciousness. Having scrutinized them thoroughly, the yogin does not perceive external objects anymore. To him not perceiving external objects, the thought occurs, 'All this is just ideas: there are no external objects.'
>
> '*Ascending to the level of mind-only, one no longer imagines external entities*' means that he abandons thoughts of material *dharmas*. He should consider them as non-existent because such things are in principle perceptible (*upalabdhilakṣaṇaprāpti*) but are never perceived as existing.
>
> Once he has ceased to believe in the reality of material *dharmas*, he should turn his attention to the non-material ones. He should reflect, 'Given that there are no objects, there is no perceiving subject either because the perceiver depends upon the perceived. If mind is not polarised into perceiver and perceived, mind is not twofold.'

He will rest in non-dual awareness, free from representations of subject and object.

Since entities cannot originate from either themselves or from others, he will reflect that non-representative non-dual awareness is itself without substance, given the unreality of perceiver and perceived from which it is inseparable. He will abandon attachment to the belief that non-dual awareness is a substantial reality.

Once in that state, he becomes settled in the realization that no *dharmas* have intrinsic nature (*svabhāva*). Once settled there, he enjoys non-discursive contemplation (*nirvikalpaka-samādhi*) because he has arrived at the supreme *condition*. Once the yogin is settled in the non-representative knowledge of non-duality, he sees the great vehicle (*mahāyāna*). The great vehicle is the vision of the ultimate truth. The ultimate truth means understanding the nature of the *dharmas* by the eye of wisdom. What is the nature of the supreme vision? It is not-seeing all the *dharmas*!

* * *

The Yogācārins' conception of ultimate reality – and ultimate well-being – is succinctly presented by Mokṣākaragupta in his Tarkabhāṣā:

'If there are no external objects, what is the ultimate reality?'

'The ultimate reality is undifferentiated consciousness, free from stains such as the dichotomy between perceiver and perceived. As it has been said, 'There is nothing other than perception that can be experienced. Consciousness is not experienced by anything other than itself. Since consciousness is free from perceiver and perceived, it illuminates itself.'

'External objects are not existent, as the unenlightened imagine. The mind, seething with traces of prior experiences, projects the appearances of external objects.'[9]

Further reading

Text and translation of the 'Twenty Verses' in Tola and Dragonetti (2004) and Wood (1991). For the 'Thirty Verses', see Wood.

Chapter IV of Paul Williams, *Mahāyāna Buddhism* (1989) and Chapter Seven of Carpenter (2014) are enlightening. Vasubandhu is the subject of a monograph by Jonathan Gold, *Paving the Great Way: Vasubandhu's Unifying Buddhist Philosophy.*

Questions for discussion and investigation

1. Why do the idealists deny the reality of matter? Is it just because they want to encourage us to be detached from things?
2. Has Vasubandhu succeeded in showing that there is no physical reality?

Notes

1. Other names include *citta-mātra*, which means 'mind-only', and *vijñāna-vāda* or consciousness-doctrine, as well as *vijñapti-mātra* (perceptions-only). The import of each is the denial of material substance.
2. According to the Madhyamikas, this is a case of the reification of experiences and the invention of a universal mind. They say that it is impossible to overcome the subject–object and grasper–grasped dichotomies as long as one posits such a reality in its own right. See Eckel (2008).
3. Succinctly put by the orthodox Brahmin writer Śabara (400 A.D.) when he ascribes to his Buddhist opponent the view that 'Cognition is devoid of external objects. How come? Because we do not perceive object and cognition as different in form' (*śūnyas tu pratyayaḥ. Katham. Arthajñānayor ākārabhedaṃ na upalabhāmahe.* Frauwallner [1968], p. 28).
4. It was common currency among those who denied that perceptions require physical objective correlatives. Śabara, for instance, epitomizes an idealist view as 'Is it not the case that *every* cognition lacks objective grounds – as in dreams?' (*nanu sarva eva nirālambanaḥ svapnavat pratyayaḥ.* Frauwallner [1968], p. 26).
5. The storehouse includes the full gamut of internal and external experiences: sensations, memories, desires, feelings and intentions.
6. A line of idealist thought, traced back to a revelation by the Bodhisattva Maitreya to Vasubandhu's brother Asaṅga, says that the conditioned realm of our experience manifests 'the mental construction of the unreal' (*abhūta-parikalpa*). The word '*bhūta*' means reality or 'a reality'. The negative prefix 'a' is probably being used in the sense of 'mistaken for'. So *abhūta* actually has a more subtle meaning than 'unreal' or 'non-existent'. What it means is 'what is mistaken for reality'. On this reading, the 'mental creation of what is mistaken for reality' means the same as *bhāva-kalpanā* or 'the imaginative

construction of entities' where 'entity' means a stable object (or subject) with intrinsic properties whose identity is determined independently of its relations to others. So *abhūta-parikalpa* means that what we ordinarily understand and treat as objects and subjects are abstractions from a matrix of relations. Also mentally constructed and hence not authentically real is the dichotomy of subject and object (*grāhya-grāhaka-vikalpa*). The notion of emptiness (*śūnyatā*) is taken to mean falsity of the subject–object polarity that structures our unenlightened understanding. Vasubandhu's commentator Sthiramati (c.550 A.D.) in his Madhyāntavibhāgaṭīkā appears to move towards a kind of absolute idealism, according to which everything is a manifestation of an unconditioned fundamental reality that is the ultimate substrate of the process called the 'Construction of Phenomena' (*abhūta-parikalpa*). The unconditioned reality is the *precondition* of the experiences of subjectivity and objectivity, of minds and things. As such, it transcends them, and is neither mental nor physical while manifesting itself as both.

7. pp. 185–6 in the GRETIL online edition.
8. From the Laṅkāvatārasūtra.
9. Kajiyama (1998), p. 147.

Part II

Hindu Traditions

7

Nyāya and Vaiśeṣika

Chapter Outline

The world at our fingertips

Nyāya-Vaiśeṣika is a form of direct realism about an objective mind-independent world of enduring objects, properties and relations. The tradition holds that when we are thinking rationally, our concepts and language mirror external reality. Nyāya-Vaiśeṣika is one of the Brahminical lines of defence against the Buddhist reduction of objects to temporal phases, and their rejection of constant factors such as universals, kinds and enduring subjects of experiences. Their metaphysic is what is sometimes called a 'substance ontology' according to which the world consists of enduring individual entities that are the bearers of universal and specific properties. It is the interactions of these 'basic particulars' that generate processes and events. By contrast, the Buddhist event or process ontology says that there is just a system of relations where things are interdependent (*pratītya-samutpāda*). For the Buddhists, there are no stable persisting identities or substances (*nairātmya*). Nothing really lasts (*kṣaṇikatva*). There are no universal properties that run through the whole of reality. Thinking in terms of persisting individual entities is mental construction out of what is in fact a fluid process. But for the Nyāya-Vaiśeṣika philosophers, reality is an intelligible framework of stable structures and persisting individual substances. For centuries, Nyāya-Vaiśeṣika thinkers formulated metaphysics and epistemologies that were designed as bulwarks against the anti-substantialist Buddhist outlook.

Nyāya direct realism says that cognitions are informational states that depend upon and disclose objects in the world (*artha-prakāśa-buddhi*) that are *given* to us. It is a form of externalism – the view that cognitions are necessarily, and not just causally, dependent upon external objects.[1] Perceptions are not a veil of representations intervening between cognizing subjects and the world. We are always and already 'outside ourselves' with the entities that we encounter and which belong to a world invested with meaning prior to our discoveries. The world is as it appears to common sense: stable objects in a three-dimensional spatial framework existing independently of our perceptions. The Nyāya-Vaiśeṣikas believe that their system of categories describes the structure of reality as it is in itself. They accept a correspondence theory of truth according to which there is a structural isomorphism between true thoughts and states of affairs that obtain. Genuine universals (*jāti, sāmānya*), qualities (*guṇa*) and relations determine the phenomenal, causal and logical organization of the world of individual substances (*dravya*). They fix the actual states obtaining as the world. Real properties that qualify objects, as well as real relations (*samavāya* and *saṃyoga*) play a basic role in the objective, non-arbitrary classification of the world.

Actually there are two traditions here, but they were never far apart. Nyāya was originally concerned with epistemology and valid reasoning. It describes itself as an investigation of matters established by the means of knowing, including inference that is based on perception and testimony.

Vaiśeṣika was originally more concerned with metaphysical questions about the constitution of the cosmos and established the system of categories that will shortly be described.[2] By the time of Udayana (c.1050–1100 A.D.), the two had coalesced, and what follows is a synthetic overview of some of their concepts and categories. Any attempt to delineate our world view in a categorial scheme will run into problems. Inconsistencies are bound to arise. The Navya-Nyāya thinkers, the most influential of whom are Gaṅgeśa and Raghunātha, attempt resolutions of some of the problems and introduce clarifications and innovations. Their writings are very difficult, and I have not attempted to say much about them here.[3]

Early Nyāya says that we reach the Highest Good by understanding the truth about the reliable methods of knowing (*pramāṇa*), the knowable objects (*prameya*) and the various forms of argument and debate. In other words, the truth (*pramā*) will set us free. Freedom here results from the elimination of misconceptions, activities, rebirth and suffering. The description of the system of categories in which the knowable objects are organized will be followed by an account of the methods of knowing.

Metaphysics: The system of categories (*padārtha*)

Anything falling under one of the categories is existent, and in principle knowable and nameable.

The categories are as follows:

Dravya – substances – simple and complex
Guṇa – qualities
Karma – actions/motions/movements

The above three are all categories of particulars that fall under universal properties inhering in them.

Sāmānya – general properties encompassing both real universal properties and kinds (*jāti*), as well as certain imposed or imputed properties (*upādhi*). Only *jātis* are genuinely real *padārthas*. By contrast, imputed properties or *upādhis* are just concepts.
Viśeṣa – unique particularities or *individual* essence
Samavāya – the relation of inherence
Abhāva – absences

The category of substance: *Dravya*

Substances are stable existences that retain their identity over time.[4] Some substances are simple (e.g. 'souls' and material atoms), while others are *integrated* wholes (*avayavin*), novel entities generated from the coalescence of their parts. Many Buddhists say that it is the fundamentals that are genuinely real: the trees before the forest, the carbon atoms before the diamond, the five components before the human person, the parts before the car. They seek to reduce things to their simple and basic constituents. By contrast, the Nyāya-Vaiśeṣikas say that objective reality is compatible with any degree of complexity. Genuine existence belongs to whole entities. Each substance is a manifestation (*vyakti*) of a genuine universal property. They occur as natural or artificial kinds. Some are products and thus perishable, while others are eternal. At the first moment of its existence, a substance has no qualities or movements. But it has a universal property. An individual cow is nothing unless it is an instance of the generic property 'cowness'.

Earth, water, air and fire are simple substances. Combinations of their atoms in varying proportions constitute non-permanent physical entities. Atoms are uncreated, indivisible and indestructible. If there was infinite divisibility, a mountain would have the same size as a mustard seed! The cosmos comes about when the godhead imposes repeatable structures upon these raw materials.

The atmosphere is a substance. It occurs everywhere. It is the medium through which sounds are transmitted. It is single and thus does not manifest a genuine universal property.

Time and space are substances. In themselves, they are single, eternal and omnipresent. Space explains the structuring of our experience in terms of right and left, up and down, east and west, and distance and proximity. Such experiences are grounded in stable objective structures independent of our minds. Although time is single, we interpret it in terms of conditions (*upādhi*) such as past, present and future, earlier and later, and its passing slowly or quickly. But these concepts do not really affect it.

Subjects of experience (*ātman*)

Where Nyāya and Vaiśeṣika are concerned, the word 'ā*tman*' might be best translated as 'principle of identity', but I shall also usually say 'subject'. It is a type of substance that is the ultimate subject of cognitions, emotions, desires and efforts, as well as the bearer of good and bad *karma*. These essentially individual subjects are eternal and non-spatial, but each is embodied differently and has a series of life histories through time. Subjects are not essentially conscious (which is why I am avoiding calling them selves or souls), but they enjoy mental lives when embodied. Cognitions, as well as desires, feelings, intentions and personal characteristics, are contingent properties of subjects that occur only when the latter belong to an objective environment. Such subjects are non-physical and non-conscious principles of identity that have been posited to explain our abilities to remember and to synthesize the present variety of experiences into a unity. A life is a series of embodied experiences, but something supra-experiential is required to impart unity and coherence to the stream, indeed to constitute the manifold of experiences as one stream. That something is the *ātman*.

The existence of such a principle of identity is established by inference. Not being of the nature of consciousness, it cannot reveal itself, and it cannot be known by introspection. The subject is not manifest in conscious acts. The latter are entirely intentional or attentive to objects outside the mind. The basic argument for the existence of the enduring subjects is that the Vaiśeṣika categorial system decrees that thoughts, pleasures, desires, dislikes, intentions as well as virtues and vices are all qualities (*guṇa*) and as such cannot stand alone and need a substrate. There must be a continuous subject to which they belong, and this is the substantial *ātman*.

There are other arguments for the existence of an enduring principle of personal identity in the face of the Buddhist reduction of persons to a causally connected stream of embodied experiences. There are a number of background assumptions to be borne in mind. What one remembers depends on what one perceived or learnt earlier. One does not remember the experiences of other people. The Brahmins insist that the guarantor of personal identity must be a further fact over and above a stream of connected experiences. As we have said, it is not conscious by nature. It is something that underlies the stream of personality or individual character. It is the precondition for the relatedness of experiences occurring at different times. It is also the prerequisite for the coherence of the manifold of present experience.

One argument for persisting identity is that there must be a suitable vehicle for the preservation of memory traces of previous experiences. Something has to hold the stream together. Bundles of perceptions have to be bound by something. There is also the argument from experiential memory – remembering a state of affairs in which one has participated. Sometimes I can recover the sense of what it was like to enjoy a past experience: it is like being there once again. For this to be possible, there has to be some factor that makes possible the connection of present experience and memory, namely the same subject to which each belongs. There is also the argument from recognition. I can only recognize the building that houses the Liverpool University Department of Philosophy as the same one that I saw yesterday if the building is still there and if the subject of yesterday's experience is the same as today's.

The unification of perceptions belonging to different sensory faculties requires not just a single object but also a single factor that integrates them.[5] I can simultaneously see, smell, taste and feel an orange. The experience is given as a unity. But each sensory faculty has a distinct sphere of operation. Some other factor must be unifying the perceptions. That something is the mind (*manas*), and its constancy is underpinned by its association with the *ātman*.

There is also the argument from the desire to enjoy again something remembered. I see an orange and really want to eat it because I recall its delicious flavour. This complex mental synthesis (*pratisaṃdhāna*) must belong to a single subject that synthesizes diverse experiential events (present cognition of the object, previous cognition of the object, the recollection of the pleasure it gave, desire to enjoy it again). They cannot synthesize themselves if each is momentary, confined to its own sphere and thus not cognizant of the others. If it is claimed that they synthesize each other, cognitions will become assimilated to each other. There would no longer be a series of discrete individual factors constituting the stream of experiences. So we need some further factor that explains unification across sensory faculties, the connection through time between my present sight of the orange and my recognition of the orange as similar to one previously tasted, and the connection between the earlier experience, the present desire and the anticipation of the experience of eating the orange. It is significant that we do not have the experiences and then connect them with a single subject. Experience is presented as a ready-made unity.

The Buddhist may say that cases of mental synthesis arise in virtue of the cause–effect relation between momentary cognitions in a single series, and so there is no need to posit a single cognizer. The response is that even if there can be a cause–effect relation between different momentary mental events, this would not explain the phenomenon of memory. For a mental event to be experienced *as a memory*, there has to be an enduring subject. A prior experience of pleasure in a stream would be precisely that. It would not be remembered from the present perspective as *what had been* a pleasant experience. Just as one person does not remember what was experienced by another, so one discrete, fleeting and self-confined cognition cannot *remember* the content of another.

The Buddhist attempt to explain all of the above phenomena in terms of a stream of experiences impersonally related as cause and effect is not really satisfactory. There has to be something that holds the stream together, something that, as it were, underpins the causality. It is not clear whether the Buddhist account can explain synthetic experiences (*pratisaṃdhāna*) if Buddhists understand one mental event in a series as the cause of the next only in the sense that one precedes the other. But such a relationship can occur between events occurring in different series. Something stronger than causality is required – namely, the mental events are all related to something else.

There has to be something in relation to which an experience is identified as past, another present and another anticipated as future. Something has to unify the manifold of current experiences. Experience flows: we are always aware of it changing through time. But change is only possible if there is some stable factor that undergoes it. The Buddhist is actually talking about successive replacements rather than change. An enduring principle of identity, the subject of experiences, is the most economical explanation of the phenomena.

The reductionist theory that psychological continuity is nothing but a basically impersonal continuum of causes and effects has a persistent allure, despite its physicalist and functionalist animus. But there are some considerations that should make us think twice about the explanatory sufficiency of causality here. It is uncontroversial that causal relations sometimes hold between experiences. It may perhaps be the case that a causal account can be given of the formation of personality or character when this is regarded as in some sense an achievement or culmination of what went before. But a lot of changes, fragmentation or disintegration of experiences over time is consistent with there still being a single person. As Bishop Butler responded to Locke, a person is more than what they remember.[6] It might be possible to give an objectifying purely causal description of the psychological processes of an animal that is not a person – one that cannot use the pronoun 'I'. In the case of a personal individual stream of experiences, it is plausible to say that sometimes a present experience (causally) elicits a memory. But the reductionist account says that the relations between experiences within a single stream ('series person') are all causal ones. This is questionable. It is not clear that in every case of experience B following experience A, the relation is causal. But the basic being of the subject (that which is meant by *ātman*) is a *given*. It is not a product or an achievement, but the precondition of any such accomplishments. This basic subject is expressed in first-personal 'I-thoughts', and the relevant connections here are not causal ones. The first-personal, autobiographical continuity of human persons is not given in causal terms. If I think, 'I was born in Heswall' and 'I now live in Liverpool', I can truly conclude, 'I was born in Heswall and now live in Liverpool.' That conclusion has nothing to do with causation but is a matter of inferential entailment. The inference is valid because the two features are states of the same person. So it is not obvious that the unity of a person's mental life is to be explained in causal terms. Causal connections between experiences are insufficient to constitute or produce a continuum. The connections hold because of the character of the relation between thoughts, and that relation derives from their being states of the same person. The reductionist view is that personal identity is an illusion that is constructed out of experiences. We then mistakenly invest this illusory identity with an enduring character. The basic objection is this: how can construction, mistaken or otherwise, happen if there is nothing capable of doing the constructing in the first place?

Because having experiences is an accidental product of being embodied in some environment, the released state is one of unconsciousness. Unappetizing as this sounds, the Nyāya-Vaiśeṣika thinkers observe that at least you cannot want anything. Moreover, there is no such thing as pure happiness since happiness is always pervaded by fear of its loss. Later writers, perhaps under the influence of forms of Vedānta, mollify the position and say that the released state is, somehow or other, blissful.

Mind (*manas*) is a faculty that is instrumental in our having sensorily derived thoughts, feelings, desires and intentions. Each embodied subject, the vehicle of experiential continuity, is contingently connected with a mind. The sensory receptors transmit a range of information about the objective environment to the *manas*, which operates as a central processor co-ordinating that information and selecting what is relevant to the present state of the organism. Since the operation of each of the senses is restricted to its own proper sphere, another factor is required to explain the co-ordination of sensory experience, so that we can simultaneously touch what we see.

The *manas* is instrumental in the conversion of some stimuli into feelings, the translation of some items of cognitive input into conscious thoughts with practical applications (storing some as memories), and the transformation of some affective responses into acts of will. Thoughts, perceptions, feelings and intentions thus become temporary properties attaching to the constant subject, and a centre of knowing, agency and experience is generated.

The category *Guṇa* (qualities)

These are characteristics belonging only to substances or enduring objects. Substances can undergo changes in respect of their qualities and still remain the same. The loss or gain of an integral part, however, results in a new substance.

Some *guṇas* are sensible properties: colours, tastes, smells, touch, sounds (each exclusively related to the appropriate sense organ). Other natural features include dimension, temporal and spatial relations of proximity and remoteness, weight, fluidity, numbers, as well as the relations conjunction and, its counterpart, disjunction. Others are non-physical properties specific to embodied selves: cognitions, pleasures, pains, desires, antipathies, conscious efforts, spiritual merit and demerit, and inherited character traits.

Guṇas are unrepeatable particular occurrences. The blue specific to my shirt is a different instance from the blue specific to my pen, although the two shades may be identical. Redness is not a quality but the universal (*jāti*) common to all instances of red. Since a colour pervades the whole substance in which it inheres, seeing an object's colour implies seeing the entire object.

Numbers are properties only of substances. But every entity has the number-quality 'one', which is treated as a special case. In each pair of objects, there is the specific quality of *two ness*, although neither is double. (Duality is a universal inhering in each case of *two ness*.) All larger numbers relate to collections of objects in a special way by a relation called 'encompassing' (*paryāpti*). They are trying to do justice to everyday expressions like 'the number of trees in the forest'. Whatever the number is, it does not apply to each of the trees individually. They did not consider the possibility that numbers apply to concepts.

If qualities only belong to substances, and numbers are qualities, there cannot be a number of numbers or of any other quality. Nor can we consistently say that universals are one. In response to this, the Navya-Nyāya thinker Raghunātha says that numbers belong to a separate category of their own. Indeed, Bhāsarvajña had said that numbers are not qualities but relations of identity and difference. What this means is that when we say that a *jāti* is one or that the atmosphere is one, we are not attributing a property. Indeed, the only attributive use of 'one' is to say that something is integrated or that it is identical with itself. When we say that a *jāti* is one, what is meant is that it is unanalysable.[7]

Conjunction (*saṃyoga*) is a temporary relation of contact between two separate objects.

Cognitions (*buddhi, jñāna, upalabdhi*) are 'transparent' in the sense that there is no subjective contribution to awareness. Cognitions just illuminate objects (*artha-prakāśa*), external to minds. They are functional psychological properties, playing a causal role in interpersonal communications. The inclusion of cognition in the categorial schema is a feature of the naturalistic and dualistic world view, which denies that consciousness is absolutely fundamental. Cognitions or informational states are particular episodes targeted on the states of affairs that cause them. As well as current engagement with the environment (*anubhava*), there is memory or the retention of information, derived from prior cognitions of objects and elicited by occurrent ones. Their realism is what is sometimes called 'externalist' in that they say that the occurrence of a cognitive episode is necessarily and not just causally dependent upon the subject's being placed in an objective environment. We saw that Buddhist thinkers characterize mental events as self-luminous or reflexive. Take an awareness of something red. This awareness has two aspects: objective or the red content, and subjective – its own self-awareness – which we might express as 'what it feels like to see red'. From this a lot follows. The bifurcation of cognition into subjective and objective aspects accounts for the origin of the subject–object dichotomy without reference to an extra-mental sphere. There can be experience of objectivity in the absence of an external physical world. In opposition to this anti-realist tendency, the Nyāya thinkers say that cognitions are not intrinsically self-aware. They recognize that many psychological episodes pass unnoticed. Sometimes we are on 'automatic pilot'. Information may be received from the environment via the senses, processed by the mind (*manas*) and stored in the memory without being consciously registered. A cognition is only elevated to the level of conscious awareness when it is introspectively objectified by another cognition (*anuvyavasāya*). This happens when one cognitive state becomes 'telescoped' by another. An objection to this is that if the elevation to consciousness of an informational state requires another psychological state, an infinite regress results.[8]

A cognitive episode qualifies as a piece of knowledge rather than an informational state when it is produced by one of the reliable methods of knowing (*pramāṇa*). A current informational state (*anubhava*) may be true or misleading. Perceptual knowledge is direct contact with an object or state of affairs. A true cognition is one in which the attribute that is possessed by the external object is a feature of the content of the cognition. A false awareness is a situation in which the actually present external object does not have the attribute that is a feature of the content of cognition, as when we think, 'This is silver' in relation to a piece of shell. The awareness refers to real silver existing elsewhere and not to a purely mental entity, as happens in hallucinations. Falsehood is exposed in practical failure. The tradition develops a sophisticated form of a direct realist epistemology holding that there is a structural isomorphism between the complex content of a true cognition and an objective state of affairs.[9]

The category *Sāmānya* (common properties)

This category includes objectively real universal properties (*jāti* – literally 'kind') that exist independently of their instances.[10] They are the basic principles that structure the world. There are also 'imposed' or 'imputed' general properties (*upādhi*), and these are understood as used arbitrarily to group a number of individuals. Genuine universal properties (*jāti*) are manifest in both natural and artificial kinds. 'Cowness', 'horseness' and 'being a Brahmin' are examples of the former. 'Potness' is an example of the latter – individual pots manifest a permanent and stable underlying structure even though they are human products. *Jātis* are manifested in the particular substances, qualities and motions, but they exist eternally and independently of their instances, which come into being, change and last for a while. *Jātis* exist objectively, independently of human thinking. They feature in our modes of thought, but they are not thereby created. As we have seen, the Nyāya-Vaiśeṣika realists think that perceptual experience of a differentiated world is prior to conceptual and linguistic classification. Universals are discovered, not invented. They are not artefacts of conceptual schemes, imposed upon an amorphous reality.

That the ontological status of genuine universals differs from that of particulars is emphasized in the definition of the universal as unitary and unanalysable (*eka*), timeless and permanent (*nitya*), and occurrent in many manifestations (*aneka-vṛtti*). It is sometimes objected that the very notion of universal properties is incoherent because they are expected to be simultaneously both one (as a self-identical) and many (as distributed in many instances). In response, the Nyāya-Vaiśeṣikas say that this sort of objection overlooks the distinctive ontological character of universals and treats them as spatial entities.

Universals occur in substances, qualities and motions by the relation of inherence (*samavāya*), but nothing inheres in them. A genuine universal is the unitary property shared by all members of a kind, rather than the class of individual objects. It is whatever makes the class to be that particular class in the first place – the shared property that makes the flesh of Brahmins, Brahmin flesh. Moreover, the universal is not the form, configuration or arrangement of parts shared by individuals, although it is manifested in the form.

The world is not an assembly of unique individuals but consists of objects belonging to kinds. To identify an object, we mention what *kind of thing* it is. According to this theory, universals are not innate ideas. Universals are not ideas abstracted from sensory impressions, and they are not general concepts formed by a process of induction. Rather, we *perceive* a real universal property whenever we see a number of objects belonging to the same kind. Given that the individuals are different, how could we identify a common form without a universal property? Although we may have seen only one elephant, we have still *perceived* the property 'being an elephant' even though we do not yet know that the individual belongs to a natural kind. This is a form of extraordinary intuition (*alaukika-pratyakṣa*) that relates to real universals. A universal is said to *pervade* the particulars in which it inheres. It produces a concept of its own nature in respect to one or more objects. When we have an inclusive cognition of a group of objects, some of which may be remembered, it is the universal that causes the recurrent cognition.

Causal regularities hold because causal relations obtain not merely between particulars (the Buddhist view) but between particulars in so far as they belong to kinds. Kinds are self-reproducing – dogs give birth to puppies and acorns produce oak trees. When we say that fire causes smoke, we mean that all fires have the capacity to be causes of smoke. We believe that every object of a certain kind may become a cause because each possesses a certain shared characteristic disposition. Moreover, generalizations based on a limited number of observations (e.g. 'wherever there is smoke, there is fire') are possible because of a connection between universals.

Nyāya-Vaiśeṣikas deny that universals are reducible to recurrent similarities. They point out that individuals of quite different kinds may be similar in certain respects. Moreover, 'similarity' is not a genuine property because resemblance means having a certain feature in common. This feature is held to be one and the same in two or more individuals. They are judged to be similar in virtue of their possessing that feature. Nor is the universal a cluster of similar features. An albino tiger is still a tiger. Something else that combines the clustered features must be posited, and that extra factor is the unitary universal. Many universals are manifested in concrete shapes (*ākṛti*) that are specific and regular arrangements of parts characteristic of a kind. When we see an individual cow that is a manifestation (*vyakti*) of the universal cowness, we also see the universal by virtue of the shape. The shape cannot be identical with the universal because it is a collection of features whose integration the presence of the universal explains.

The genuine properties are objective and natural. They are intrinsic features of the instances where they occur. They carve nature at the joints. They are discovered, neither manufactured, nor invented nor conceptually constructed. The classes of their instances are not miscellanies. It follows that not every characteristic that we understand as common to a group of individuals is a genuine universal (*jāti*). We can divide the world up in all sorts of ways, generating as many properties as suit us. We can speak of 'the community of cooks', but 'being a cook' is a contingent property and hence is not a *jāti* but an imputed property (*upādhi*). Another example is 'being a beast', which covers many different animals. This is a compound imputed property that is a synthesis of a number of features – in this case, being hairy, having a tail and having four legs. It is artificial in that it cuts across natural kinds and violates the natural order of classification. There are many black cows, but 'being a black cow' is not a genuine universal because it is an analysable property. It is not a reality over and above blackness and cowness.

In his *Kiraṇāvalī,* Udayana formulated six factors (called *jāti-bādhakas*) that enable us to distinguish *upādhis* from *jātis.*[11] They are:

1 A universal cannot belong to a single entity, such as the atmosphere.

If we attribute the property 'Being Devadatta' to an individual man called 'Devadatta', it would be a simple imposed property (*akhaṇḍopādhi*).

2 Different names and concepts may signify the same things or properties, but they do not thereby generate different objective realities. There are at least two words that mean 'pot', but they do not signify different kinds of pots.

3 No two universals partially overlap with each other in their instances. There can be no 'cross-cutting'. This rules out 'beastness'.
4 No universal generates an infinite regress. Universals do not inhere in universals. In other words, there is no cowness-ness inhering in cowness.
5 No universal can destroy the nature of that in which it inheres. Although there is an infinite number of unique particularities (*viśeṣa*) individuating atoms, souls and minds, there cannot be a real universal '*viśeṣa-ness*' because the categories *jāti* and *viśeṣa* are mutually exclusive.
6 A universal must be capable of inhering in its instances. Every universal occurs in its instances by the relation of inherence. There cannot be a universal 'inherence-ness' common to all these relations. Inherence cannot be related to itself by the relation that it is.

Samavāya (the inherence relation)

Nyāya posits a universe consisting of innumerable objects and structuring factors. Enduring substances, qualities, movements and universal properties are all counted as entities. There has to be a sort of relation that can combine such realities into complexes while preserving the differences between types. *Samavāya* is the relation by which types are held together while retaining their own identities. It is the cement of the universe. It integrates the constituents comprising particular objects. It combines two items when one is inseparable from the other in the sense that the breaking of the connection means the destruction of one of the terms. It thus differs from conjunction (*saṃyoga* – which links individual substances), where both terms survive separation.

Inherence obtains between qualities and the substances possessing them, actions and substances to which they belong, real universals and their particular instances, and unique particularities and the permanent substances that they individuate. It also combines parts into wholes or integral unities. A complex substance is a whole (*avayavin*) inhering in each of its parts. Wholes differ from collections, aggregates, crowds, herds and flocks in that the latter are assemblages of members. But genuine wholes have no such members, though by definition they have proper parts.[12]

Qualities and action inhere in substances. The particular case of the quality blue that is a feature of some lotus needs the lotus for its occurrence. A quality is always a property *of* something. Although *we* never encounter a lotus without some quality or other, at the first moment of its existence, the substance has neither qualities nor actions. Quality presupposes substance, but substance does not presuppose quality. Qualities (and actions) only exist in some substance that supports them.

There is a problem about treating inherence as a relation in its own right that was exposed by the Advaita Vedāntin philosopher Śaṃkara in his *Brahma-Sūtra-Bhāṣya* 2.2.13. The inherence relation is just as much a real entity as the items that it connects. This generates an infinite regress since it seems that further connections are required to tie the relation to its terms. Further, the relation of contact (*saṃyoga*) is a *guṇa*, so it is tied to the substances that it connects by *samavāya*. To avoid this, the tradition holds that inherence relates itself to its terms – it behaves like glue in that it is 'self-linking' (*svarūpa-saṃbandha*).

In its account of causation (*asat-kārya-vāda*), Nyāya eschews the notion of potentiality and says that prior to origination, the effect did not exist in its underlying cause but is a totally new product, different from the factors out of which it is made. The rejection of the category of potentiality implies the view that only what is actual and concrete is real and can cause something else. Causation is not the actualization of what was potential but the generation, through rearrangement, of new entities out of already existent factors. A cause is defined as a necessary prior condition of an effect. There are three factors in a causal complex: the underlying cause which is always a type of substance (e.g. the threads comprising the cloth); the non-inherent cause which is always a quality or activity (e.g. weaving and colour of the threads); and the efficient or instrumental cause (*nimitta*) (e.g. the shuttle and other instruments). The weaver is the agent cause.

The category *Viśeṣa* (ultimate particularity)

These are unique features of the simple eternal substances (atoms, atmosphere, time, space, souls and minds) distinguishing them from each other. Whereas complex entities are differentiated by the different arrangements of their parts, eternal substances are partless. So each must have its own individuating feature. The presence of a *viśeṣa* accounts for the unique identities of these kinds of entity. The *viśeṣa* belonging to a 'soul' (*ātman*) is what differentiates it from every other soul. So released souls that have neither *karma* nor bodies remain different.

A problem here led to the ultimate abandonment of the category by Navya-Nyāya. If the *viśeṣas* are themselves distinguished by other individuators, there is an infinite regress. If they do not need to be distinguished by other individuators, they are unnecessary for individuation.

The category *Karman* (motions)

Motions characterize substances and are always transient. Included here are all varieties of changes in spatial position, as well as contraction and expansion. Motions are the causes of conjunctions and separations.

Motion is given a basic ontological status. Enduring substances really move through space. This counters the Buddhist view that there are no motions of entities, only reconfigurations of process.

The category *Abhāva* (absences)

Silence is the absence of sounds. Silences are real. Some absences are real. The absence of coffee in my cup is a fact. When absence is the absence *of something*, it is classified as a reality. That which is absent is technically termed the counterpart (*pratiyogin*) to the absence.

There are four varieties of absence. 'Prior absence' is the non-existence of an entity before its production by the rearrangement of other factors. Destruction is the dissolution of something that has existed for a period of time. Absolute negation covers logical and physical impossibilities. Mutual absence is another way of expressing difference. It is the denial of identity between two things such as a pot and a cloth.[13]

Epistemology: The *Pramāṇas* – Perception, reasoning and testimony

Classical Indian epistemological theory centres on the notion of *pramāṇa* or instrument of knowing. The number of such instruments differs according to the different schools of thought. Here we shall just look at perception, inference or reasoning, and testimony as methods of knowing. The seeker after truth wants to be sure that as many of his beliefs as possible are true. But he cannot know this by checking them one by one. Obviously, false beliefs do not admit the error of their ways. The truth-seeker wants to be in a position where his beliefs are justified, that is to say, that they are not merely true by chance. The best way to do this is to ensure that any beliefs that he acquires are produced by a reliable method that generally leads to true beliefs. *Pramāṇas* are such methods.

The Nyāya outlook is basically one of common sense or direct realism according to which perception is direct acquaintance with an external world. Although cognitive errors and hallucinations sometimes occur, for the most part our perceptions are reliable, and vigilance against specious reasons (*hetu-ābhāsa*) can ensure that inferences based upon them are sound. The Nyāya thinkers hold that cognitions are primarily and directly about objects and states of affairs belonging to an objective, mind-independent environment. Cognition, as we saw above, is the illumination or discovery of objects. Cognition is direct in the sense that no veil of representations, and no sense-data, fall between the subject and what is given. The extroverted mind is a centre of interactions with the physical environment. Mind is not a private inner arena isolated from the world. For the most part, what we see is the world about us and not ideas in our minds. We are not, as it were, watching an internal motion picture that has been constructed out of amorphous data supplied from outside. Rather, perceptual cognition puts us directly in touch with external reality.

A *pramāṇa* is an epistemic capacity (*śakti*) or process that produces *knowledge* rather than merely true beliefs, which may have been arrived at accidentally or by chance. To do so, it has to be functioning efficiently in the absence of defects (*doṣa*) that may prevent its proper operation. Etymology may be illuminating here. The word '*pramāṇa*' derives from the root '*mā*', which means measuring and ascertaining. A *pramāṇa* is that by which something is measured. It is an instrument for 'getting the measure' of something – understanding it as it really is in the face of some doubt or query that throws the veracity of a belief into question.

The sorts of defects that can impede the proper operation of the perceptual instrument include environmental factors such as poor lighting, haze or remoteness, physical factors such as short sight or jaundice which makes things appear yellow, and psychological factors such as inattentiveness, a tendency to jump to conclusions, greed in the case of shell mistaken for silver or timidity in that of the rope seen as a snake. That we can identify such defects and understand why we are sometimes mistaken underpins the basic reliability of perception as a means of epistemic access to reality.

Nyāya is a philosophy of direct realism according to which perceiving the world is to be directly related to matters that are outside you – seeing things that already exist prior to their being perceived as they really are. But the fact that cognitive errors and hallucinations occur suggests that this cannot be right. Surely in such cases what we are 'seeing' are sense-data or mental representations ('mere appearances') of reality that happen to be deceptive. Sometimes I look out of the window and think that it is raining. Sometimes I am right and sometimes wrong. *But the experiences are the same*. From the subjective or phenomenological point of view ('how it feels'), really seeing a real snake is the same as misperceiving a rope as a snake. Since both true and deceptive experiences feel the same way to the subject (they are phenomenologically or experientially indistinguishable), it appears that veridical experiences too are mediated by mental representations and we are not directly acquainted with the world. This may encourage the sort of idealist position according to which all experience is just a matter of ideas occurring to minds, there being no mind-independent physical world.

Nyāya has a response to these lines of thought. It says that we only make mistakes when things are similar in some respects. We never confuse a mountain with a mustard seed. When I see a rope as a snake, this is because the rope is similar to the snake in some respects. (Likewise in the case of seeing a piece of mother of pearl as silver.) Under the influence of weaknesses such as timidity and excessive caution, the appearance of the rope elicits memory traces of a snake. The memory trace of the snake triggers the operation of extraordinary perception (*alaukika-pratyakṣa*) that relates the subject directly to some snake that is outside one's field of vision. The appearance in the deceptive case is not an inner mental item, such as a sense-datum or a memory-image, but a real feature of the world. So the deceptive experience relates to something real, even though it is not actually present to the mind and senses. In other words, I am neither experiencing a purely mental representation or 'mere appearance' nor am I merely imagining a snake out of thin air. (Dreams, fictions and hallucinations are analysed as consisting of remnants of previous experiences of realities to which they refer.) It follows that although the true and deceptive experiences seem the same to the subject, in fact they are different in themselves. This denial of a common psychological process or mechanism shared by true and false perceptions (a version of 'disjunctivism'), despite how things seem to the subject, blocks the fundamental representationalist and idealist objections to the direct realist view because there is no need to invoke appearances or representations intervening between the subject and the world.[14]

A true belief is a piece of knowledge as long as it is produced by a properly functioning instrument. 'Without a means of knowledge, there is no understanding of objects. Without understanding of objects, there is no successful activity.'[15] It is not a necessary condition for being in a state of knowledge that the subject knows that he knows. Knowledge does not require subjective certainty. Validity is not *dependent* upon confirmation. What is required is that the cognitive state has been arrived at by an appropriate and reliable method. Nyāya philosophers hold that a cognition is true when it corresponds to some reality external to the mind. They recognize that we cannot check the truth of a cognition by stepping outside ourselves and comparing our thoughts with objective reality. Just as false beliefs do not declare their own falsity, so true beliefs do not display their own truth. Something more is required. Introspection (*anuvyavasāya*) may apprehend a primary belief about the world. We can know that a belief is veridical if successful activity proceeds from it. So we infer on the basis of confirmatory evidence that a belief is knowledge. When justification is required, we can appeal to successful activity consequent upon a cognition.

Nāgārjuna had raised the problem of how we know that the *pramāṇas* themselves are veridical. Is there not an infinite regress here? Nyāya thinks that the problem is specious. The Naiyāyikas admit that in principle there is a danger of infinite regress but that in practice the problem never arises. They make the points that we can see things before we know that we have a visual faculty and that we all recognize that a lamp illuminates both other things and itself. They also admit, in the light of the widely recognized principle that something cannot exercise its proper function on itself, that *while* we are subjects of the visual process of seeing an object, that process cannot itself be an object of observation. But that visual process can be scrutinized subsequently and assessed for validity ('Was the light bad? Did I have my glasses on? Did I have my mind on something else?').

Circumstances may arise when we want to check that what has been assumed to be a piece of knowledge is indeed that, or when we want to justify a piece of knowledge. Then, it is usually sufficient to appeal to successful activity consequent upon the use of the *pramāṇas*. This is what is meant by the notion that the validity of knowledge is extrinsic (*parataḥ-prāmāṇya*). The crucial point is that justification does not confer the status of knowledge. If we had to justify everything before we could treat it as knowledge, the process would have no end, and there would be no knowledge. It is worth noting that Gaṅgeśa simplifies matters, quite consistently with the tradition, by accepting that the validity of knowledge is intrinsic.

Knowledge by perception (*pratyakṣa*)

To begin with, it is worth observing that according to the Nyāya realist theory, perception is basically a physical process. Cognitions are understood as qualities residing in the soul-substance in the same way as the quality of blue occurs in a jar. Cognitions are products of a perceptual mechanism based on contact between sense-faculties and the external environment.

Nyāya-Sūtra 1.1.4 defines perceptual knowledge as a cognition produced by contact between a sense-faculty and an object that is faithful (*avyabhicāri*), focused (*vyavasāya*) and does not need to be expressed in words (*avyadapeśya*). This definition is elaborated by Vātsyāyana and all subsequent commentators in the Nyāya tradition. According to Annambhaṭṭa's *Tarka-Saṃgraha*, 'perception is the instrumental cause of perceptual knowledge. It is knowledge produced by contact between an object and a sense-faculty. It is twofold: non-conceptual (*nirvikalpaka*) and conceptual (*savikalpaka*). The former is a cognition whose content lacks specific components (*niṣprakāraka*), as when we say, "This is something." The latter includes specific components, as when we say "this man Ḍittha is a dark-skinned Brahmin"'.

Perception as a means of knowing is direct acquaintance, unmediated by sense-data, with the objective environment. The Nyāya direct realist stance is apparent in the view that memory is not a means of knowing. This is because it does not reveal an object in the past, but a *representation* of it. If the memory cognition is valid, that is because the original cognition was valid. After the middle of the fifth century, all writers respond to the view of the Buddhist Dignāga who says that perception is free from the *imposition* of concepts (*kalpanā*) on the given. Writing from a completely different metaphysical perspective, he thought that it is only perception that relates us to the real world of inexpressible unique momentary particulars. According to this view, perception never involves concepts. Any experience involving concepts and words he classifies as 'thinking' (*anumāna*) rather than perception. Thinking is at one remove from what is immediately given. (The opposite view is articulated by the grammarian and linguistic idealist Bhartṛhari, again from a different metaphysical perspective, for whom our world is the proliferation of meanings deriving from a single absolute meaning. Bhartṛhari says, 'There is no awareness that is not accompanied by language. All cognition appears as permeated by words. If the eternal identity of word and consciousness were to disappear, consciousness would not illuminate anything: because that identity makes reflective awareness possible.')

The Nyāya response to Dignāga is to distinguish two varieties of perception. They maintain that perceptual experience may or may not involve concepts. Non-conceptual perception is termed '*nirvikalpa*' and conceptual perception is termed '*savikalpa*'. The latter is knowledge that comprehends the relation between what is qualified (*viśeṣya*) and its properties (*viśeṣaṇa*) such as name, universal and qualities. This may be understood as the distinction between looking around the room without noticing anything in particular and directing one's attention to some particular feature and thinking 'that is a round table'. Alternatively, we may distinguish between mere seeing and understanding what one sees. Although there are different formulations of the distinction, they all posit a process of two stages. In the first stage ('mere seeing'), aspects of the perceptual field are sub-consciously registered. They may subsequently feature in the explicit content of conceptual perception, which grasps the relation between a complex qualified subject and its properties. A non-conceptual perception is an informational state that grasps the whole object as 'a something', but the generic features are not understood as shared by others, and the specific features are not grasped as peculiar to it. Although the generic feature is not grasped as such, the Naiyāyikas argue that it must be perceived implicitly: it belongs to the informational content of the state. We can only think that an object belongs to the same kind as others if it has been perceived as belonging to a certain kind in the first place. They think that it is a mistake to suppose that we can see any number of 'bare particulars' and abstract a general form from these indeterminate experiences.

A conceptual perception is a cognition of something that has attributes *as characterized* by those attributes. It involves an explicit manifestation of information that has already been received at the non-conceptual stage. So conceptual thought is not fabrication, but the organization and conceptual interpretation of what has been *discovered* at the non-conceptual stage.

This distinction surely makes sense. It has been argued by those who want to repudiate the 'myth of the given' that genuine understanding involves the capacity to make inferences and that this can only happen if the initial experiential content has propositional and therefore conceptual form.[16] But something is going wrong here, because on this account of perception, young children and animals do not perceive anything. They would be confined to their inner worlds of sensation. But they surely have experiences of an environment that has significance for them and are in receipt of information about it, although they do not think about it in words and concepts.

Anumāna: Knowledge by reasoning or inference

While perception is an instrument for the acquisition of knowledge about what is present to the mind and senses, inference (*anumāna*) is a means of acquiring knowledge about matters that are beyond the range of direct acquaintance. The outlook is empiricist (although we must remember that sensory experience is not restricted to particulars but includes universal properties and relations): inference depends upon information supplied by perception.

According to Nyāya, inference begins with a doubt, such as whether there is a fire on a remote mountain. The relevant observation is that we can see smoke. In this case, fire is termed the *sādhya* – that which is to be established. The mountain is called the subject (*pakṣa*), and the smoke is called the reason (*hetu*) in the inferential process. We already know that there is no smoke without fire (this invariable association is called *vyāpti*) and are familiar with other instances where they co-occur, such as the kitchen. By way of corroboration, we also know the truth of the contraposed version of the generalization 'no fire, no smoke' from cases like the lake. This negative example is intended to show that we have investigated the matter thoroughly and have not confused smoke with mist seen rising from a lake early in the morning.[17] We apply knowledge of the general principle to the case in question and can safely conclude that there is indeed fire on the mountain, although we do not see the fire.

A demonstrative inference (*prayoga*) used to persuade someone else (*parārtha-anumāna*) would be formulated by the Nyāya-Vaiśeṣikas as:

Statement of the position or uncertainty (*pratijñā*): 'There is fire (*sādhya*) on the mountain (*pakṣa*).'

Logical reason (*hetu*): Because there is smoke on the mountain.

General principle (*vyāpti*): 'Wherever there is smoke, there is fire'. This is supported by examples (*dṛṣṭānta*) – like a kitchen (*sapakṣa*); unlike a lake (*vipakṣa*).

Application: 'There is smoke on the mountain', which states that the subject under consideration has the logical reason that is always associated with (pervaded by or included in – *vyāpta*) the property to be proved.

Conclusion: Therefore, there is fire on the mountain.

Clearly, the notion of invariable concomitance or pervasion (*vyāpti*) is pivotal. Knowledge of pervasion is said to be the instrumental cause of a piece of knowledge arrived at by the inferential process. **A** is said to pervade **B** when it occurs in all or more of the instances where **B** occurs. Fire pervades smoke. Having an agent pervades being a created product. Impermanence pervades being a product. The factor of greater extent is called the pervader (*vyāpaka*) and that of lesser extent the pervaded (*vyāpya*). This means that **A** invariably accompanies **B:** smoke is always accompanied by fire and thus serves as a sign, logical reason or proving property (*hetu*) of the presence of fire.

In the background, there is the problem of justifying this sort of inference in the face of the fact that we are not acquainted with all possible circumstances. We cannot know that smoke is *always* accompanied by fire. There was a range of views about the nature of the statement of pervasion (*vyāpti*): some thought that it was just a generalization about many observed instances to which no counter-example has been found. If the proposition that there is no smoke without fire were just a generalization based on observations of instances seen so far, we could not be certain that it will hold tomorrow. The developed tradition resists scepticism by saying that nature is regulated in such a way that there is an invariable association (*vyāpti*) between universal properties such as 'being smoke' and 'being fire' such that whenever 'being smoke' is manifested, so is 'being fire'. The instances might be infinite, but the universal is single. On this account, knowledge of the general proposition that there is no smoke without fire is a type of non-sensory intuition of the invariable association between the universal smoke and the universal fire, of the pervasion of smoke by fire.

Both the Nyāya and the Buddhist logicians devote much energy to discussions of the many varieties of specious reasons (*hetu-ābhāsa*) in arguments. Among the most common are:

Anaikāntika-hetu (inconclusive reason) of which there are three varieties:

(a) The reason occurs in cases where what is to be proved is absent (i.e. it occurs in *vipakṣas*).

Example: The village is holy, because it is close to the Ganges. But there are unholy things close to the Ganges (called *sādhāraṇa-hetu*).

(b) Where the logical reason only applies to the subject of the inference (*asādhāraṇa-hetu*).

Example: 'Sounds are impermanent, because they are audible.' It is a condition of an inference's validity that we should be able to cite an instance other than the subject of the inference where both the logical reason and the property to be proved always occur together. But this is impossible here because nothing other than sounds have the property of audibility.

(c) Where the subject of the inference is universal.

Example: 'Everything is nameable, because it is knowable.' The invariable association is, 'Whatever is knowable is nameable.' Distinct from the universal subject, there can be neither a *sapakṣa* nor a *vipakṣa*, showing the invariable association between the logical reason and what is to be proved. Since the inference begins from a question about whether nameability applies to the subject, the invariant association, 'whatever is knowable is nameable', is itself doubtful.

The variety called *asiddha-hetu* (unestablished reason) occurs when the reason does not occur in the subject under consideration (*svarūpa-asiddha*), for example, 'sound is a property, because it is visible', and in cases where the subject of the inference does not exist or when its existence is controversial. Buddhists apply this to what are held by Hindus to be proofs of the existence of the soul and its properties. They say that no soul is perceived apart from experiences, and since it is the sort of thing that ought to be perceptible, its existence cannot be proved.

In a *viruddha-hetu* (contradictory reason), the reason is defective because it never occurs where the property to be proved occurs (i.e. it contradicts what one wants to prove). For example: 'There is fire on the mountain, because it is icy.' 'Sound is eternal, because it is produced.'

An inferential argument for the existence of God might run, 'The world has an omniscient creator, because it is a complex product, like a pot.' Here the pot example invites the accusation that the reason is contradictory because it leads to the conclusion that the world has a creator of finite intelligence.

There is another classification, shared by Sāṃkhya and Mīmāṃsā, of inferences into three varieties. This is variously interpreted. Inference from cause to effect (*pūrvavat*) is when we infer from the presence of clouds that it will rain. Inference from effect to cause (*śeṣavat*) is when we infer from a swollen river that it has rained. Inference from general observation (*sāmānyatodṛṣṭa*) draws conclusions about the supra-sensible. Observation that a heavenly body has changed place implies movement, albeit unseen. If qualities belong to substrata, and cognition is a quality, we can infer that there is some substance to which it belongs.

Śabda: Testimony and the transmission of true information

Among the philosophical traditions, Vaiśeṣika and Buddhism admit that we may obtain knowledge from words, but they say that testimony is a form of inference and not a method of knowing in its own right. Nyāya, and virtually everyone else, treat testimony as an independent *pramāṇa*, largely because of the problems attached to assimilating it to either perception or inference. At the same time, they are aware that of the things that we know, many are known on the basis of testimony and not perception or inference. They say that testimony is information supplied by someone who knows the truth and wants to tell it. Speech often misleads, but it is a method of knowing in so far as the speaker is well informed and sincere. As well as reliable information about matters belonging to our world, testimony also includes the Scriptures composed by the 'Seers' who originally heard the sound units comprising the Vedas. Later writers hold that the Scriptures are reliable because a benevolent and omniscient deity is their author.

It is assumed that the normal situation is that what the speaker states when he utters an assertoric sentence and what the hearer understands directly is a piece of verbal knowledge (*śābda-bodha*) about a state of affairs in the world. Let us bear in mind that it is possible to understand a proposition without believing it to be true and that it is possible to assent to a false proposition. So neither understanding nor assent is sufficient for knowledge. The Nyāya account of testimony establishes the conditions under which the hearer understands a proposition, assents to it and obtains a piece of knowledge.

One knows a proposition expressed by a sentence (i.e. there is *śābda-bodha*) when:

The hearer acquires a true belief about the world from hearing the sentence.
The speaker knows the truth and is reliable, sincere and competent.
The sentence expressing the proposition has these features:

(i) The words are uttered together or written together (*āsatti*).
(ii) It is grammatically correct (*ākāṅkṣā*). Just saying the word 'a pot' does not really signify anything. We need another word such as 'bring'.
(iii) It is semantically adequate (*yogyatā*). 'He cuts with a knife' makes sense, but 'he cuts with butter', albeit grammatically correct, does not.
(iv) If the sentence is ambiguous, consideration of the speaker's intention (*tātparya*) in the circumstances should solve the problem.

Words and sentences

The *Nyāya* view about individual words is that while each word has its own significative power (*śakti*), it is only in the context of a sentence that words are used to really mean anything. In short, sentences, both fact-asserting and action-guiding ones, are the vehicles of communication and understanding. Nyāya followers think that the relation between a word and its literal or primary meaning is created rather than innate. In some cases (e.g. Scriptural words and words in common usage like 'cow'), the word–meaning relation has been decreed by God. The rationale is that we have no knowledge of any original human stipulation that 'pot' should stand for pots. In other cases, the relation has been fixed by human convention – this applies especially in the case of proper names and in languages other than Sanskrit.

Words like 'pot' and 'cow' apply to innumerable individuals that share some property. If the word pot just stood for an individual, the word–object relation would have to be miraculously renewed every time someone mentioned a pot. Communication would break down. But if the word just expressed a common property, when someone said 'bring the cow' he would absurdly be saying 'bring the universal cowness'. So they argue that words like 'pot' and 'cow' have a complex signification. They express a universal feature common to a kind (*jāti*), a perceptible shape (*ākṛti*) and an individual (*vyakti*). A perceptible shape, a configuration of parts, indicates the kind of which the individual is a manifestation. In the case of a model or toy cow, it suffices for the application of the word. While most perceptible shapes indicate some *jāti*, not every *jāti* is indicated by such a shape. For example, clay and gold have no specific configuration. They are indicated respectively by their characteristic smell and colour. The variability of forms led the Navya-Nyāya philosophers to deny that shape (*ākṛti*) is an ingredient in the meaning of words. Finally, since there is no real universal 'cookness', the general term 'cook' is applied to anyone who works in a kitchen. The signification here is just a matter of human agreement, as in the case of proper names.

Further reading

An enjoyable starting point is Jayanta's play, *Much Ado about Religion*, (Dezsö 2005) Act Three of which sees a confrontation between Nyāya and Buddhist ideas.

Another way into the original material is Annambhaṭṭa's *Tarka-Saṃgraha* (Athalye 2003).

The *Nyāya-Sūtras* and the commentaries by Vātsyāyana and Uddyotakara are translated in Jha (1984).

There are summaries of works and a helpful introduction in Karl Potter (1977), which deals with Nyāya-Vaiśeṣika up to Gaṅgeśa, and in Potter and Bhattacharya (1993) for the later period.

Bimal Matilal, *Perception*, treats extensively the Nyāya debates with the Buddhists. Despite the title, its scope is wider than epistemology.

Chapters VI–XII of Matilal (2002) discuss the Nyāya realism in the light of some contemporary philosophical interests.

Jonardon Ganeri, *Indian Logic*, is a useful collection. The same author's *Semantic Powers* concerns Navya-Nyāya philosophy of language but says illuminating things about the earlier tradition. Ingalls (1951) is a lucid guide to key Navya-Nyāya concepts.

Kishor Chakrabarti (1999), *Classical Indian Philosophy of Mind*, also deals with questions about the self and the existence of God.

Scharf, *Denotation* (1996), has a section on Nyāya theories about linguistic meaning and reference and translates *Nyāya-Sūtra*, 2.2.58–69.

Halbfass, *On Being and What There Is* (1992), and Tachikawa, *The Structure of the World* (1981) focus on Vaiśeṣika.

The best, if not the only, work on the materialist tradition is Franco (1994), *Perception, Knowledge and Disbelief*.

Questions for discussion and investigation

1. Is the Nyāya concept of self a naturalistic one?
2. Do the Nyāya arguments for souls as persisting subjects succeed against the Buddhists?

Notes

1. For an elaborate version, see Burge (2010). For critiques of this sort of approach, see Robinson (1994) and Foster (2008).
2. Halbfass (1992).
3. v. Ingalls (1951) and Potter (1957).
4. For a more elaborate account, see Halbfass (1992), pp. 89–105. For the definition of substance as that which lacks the constant absence of qualities, see Tachikawa (1981), p. 89.
5. Chakrabarti (1992) and Ganeri (2000).
6. Butler (1813), Dissertation 1 ('Of Personal Identity'). Incidentally, Bishop Butler, like almost everyone else, misunderstands Locke on this point. What Locke means by 'consciousness' is synthetic mental activity, relating present to past, as well as anticipating future experiences. For Locke, see *An Essay Concerning Human Understanding* II, p. xxvii.
7. Ganeri (2001).
8. Matilal (1986), pp. 41–179.
9. Matilal (1986), pp. 201–20.
10. See Chakrabarti (1975) and Halbfass (1992), pp. 113–29 for more detailed exposition.
11. Jetly (1971), p. 23.
12. For the whole–part controversy between Brahmins and Buddhists, see Tola and Dragonetti (1994).
13. For an exhaustive treatment, see Matilal (1968).
14. The term 'disjunctivism' was coined by Howard Robinson for a position formulated by J. M. Hinton and Paul Snowdon. See Robinson (1994), pp. 152–9. The relevant material is collected in Byrne and Logue (2009).
15. *Nyāyabhāṣya* 1.1.5.
16. For the notion of 'the myth of the given', see Sellars (1997), and Gaskin (2006), pp. 53–64 and 141–9.
17. As suggested by Mark Siderits.

8

Sāṃkhya and Yoga

Chapter Outline

The Sāṃkhya vision

Sāṃkhya is one of the six orthodox Brahminical Hindu systems of salvation or 'visions' (*darśana*), and it is closely associated with the *Yoga* system of spiritual development. Although this tradition is ancient, its basic text is the *Sāṃkhya-Kārikās* of *Īśvarakṛṣṇa* (c.400–500 A.D.) upon which there are commentaries including the *Yuktidīpikā* (c.650 A.D.) and the *Tattvakaumudi* by Vācaspati Miśra (c.950–1000 A.D.). *Sāṃkhya* is basically a non-theistic, world-renunciatory and gnostic outlook, rather than a religion for the person immersed in daily life and ritual religion. Its goal is the elimination of suffering by the eradication of its ultimate cause. Religious practices, such as rituals and austerities, can only afford a temporary relief from suffering. What is required is discriminative understanding of the difference between the conscious subject, and material nature and its manifestations. In other words, we need to understand that the active embodied person is alienated from its true identity, which is tranquil, reflexive consciousness. The goal is freedom from determination by natural causal processes and the recovery of one's true nature.

Sāṃkhya posits a dualism of souls and matter. There is an infinity of souls (*puruṣa*), which are self-contained and inactive self-aware conscious monads whose true mode of existence is beyond space, time and matter. Souls are merely disinterested observers, and most definitely not active participants in the sphere of becoming. Somehow, some of these souls have become entangled in the material environment, including individual personality and the body. Sāṃkhya and Yoga aim to free the soul from this imprisonment by matter and rebirth.

Souls have become confused with limited and basically material forms. When there is an association between what is merely a static conscious monad and the material mind (*buddhi*), the latter is illuminated, irradiated by the light of consciousness, and becomes as-if conscious [SK 20]. The confusion is compounded when the activity of the *buddhi* is mistakenly attributed to the inactive soul. Thus, we have the origins of the individual person and the series of births marked by suffering. But the souls are really always purely passive spectators of human experiences, abiding in splendid isolation, each illuminated only by its own consciousness. It is, however, a basic tenet of Sāṃkhya that the experiences deriving from involvement with matter which bind the soul also operate for the sake of the soul's release (SK 21).

The other pole of the dualism is Prime Matter (*pradhāna* or *mūla prakṛti*). It is beginningless and ever-changing. Prime Matter spontaneously transforms itself (*pariṇāma*) into the real cosmos of material and psychological phenomena. The best we can say is that this just happens. There is no divinity initiating or superintending the process.

Prime Matter is said to consist of three strands (*guṇa*): *sattva* (goodness and light), *rajas* (dynamic energy) and *tamas* (heavy and dark). (The *Yuktidīpikā* interprets the triad as standing for happiness, distress and delusion.) Before the manifestation of the cosmos, they are in a state of equilibrium, cancelling out one another's properties. Their 'mere presence' is said to prompt the transformation of material nature. Matter (*prakṛti*) transforms for the sake of the human souls so that they have experiences that lead them to realize the difference between soul and matter. It might be asked how an unconscious cause can act for the sake of anything, let alone produce specific and organized realities. The Sāṃkhya position, however, is that the existence of the cosmos calls for explanation. The world consists of active and complex realties made of parts. Each has its own purpose, and we should assume a purpose for the totality. The Sāṃkhyas espouse a principle that *composite* entities exist for the sake of something else (*parārtha*) that is different in nature from them. So it is concluded that physical entities exist for the sake of conscious souls.

> 'Just as the unconscious milk functions for the nourishment of the calf, so matter functions for the sake of the liberation of the soul (*puruṣa*).' [SK 57]

> 'No *puruṣa* is really bound or liberated or reborn. Only matter in her various transformations is bound etc.' [SK 62]

> 'Through repeated meditation on the nature of the manifest world, there arises the intuitive insight that the *puruṣa* is not the individual personality and whatever it identifies with.' [SK 64]

Prime Matter evolves to produce the basic material and psychological realities (*tattva*, i.e. *buddhi* (mind/intellect); *ahamkāra* (one's sense of personality); *manas* (the co-ordinator of the separate sense-faculties and their deliverances); the five sense-faculties (*indriya*); physical organs; the essences of sounds, touch, colours, tastes and smells; and the gross elements – space, air, fire, water and earth which make up physical objects). These products contain the *guṇas* in differing proportions and compose the world we inhabit.

Individual objects are confluences of qualities (*guṇa-saṃdrava*) such as colours, shapes, textures, tastes and smells. The Sāṃkhyas reject the Nyāya view that there is a separate property-possessor (*dharmin*) that is distinct from the conglomeration of properties. They think that once we have, as it were, listed all the properties of an entity, there is no *extra* factor called the substrate. Such would be what is sometimes called a 'bare particular' or an entity without properties, and that makes no sense.

All that is required for the substantial unity of entities over time is that they be integrated in a suitable way. As the *Yuktidīpikā* puts it, 'When an entity without departing from its nature loses an earlier property and receives a new one, that is called modification (*pariṇāma*).'[1] This is true to experience. People and things change all the time and still remain identifiably the same. There can only be change, rather than replacement, if something stays the same.

Causal processes

Sāṃkhya propounds a theory of causation termed *satkārya-vāda* which says that future products pre-exist in a potential state in their underlying, substrative causes (*upādāna-kāraṇa*) prior to their actualization or manifestation (*abhivyakti*) as entities identifiable by their specific names and forms. Milk transforms into yoghurt. Milk is the underlying cause or substrate, and yoghurt emerges as a product (*kārya*) from it. Pots are transformations of the clay that is their substrative cause and in which their individual forms have implicitly pre-existed. Here the causal process involves a modification (*pariṇāma*) of a stable underlying reality and not the generation of a totally novel product. Hence there is a strong ontological link between the emergent effect and its causal substrate. We shall see the importance of this emanative model of cosmic causality for those forms of Vedānta that see the cosmos of souls and matter as real transformations of the divine being.

The Sāṃkhya theory of causation develops in opposition to that of the Nyāya-Vaiśeṣikas. That position is called *asatkārya-vāda* or 'the production of something new'. When parts combine, a new entity is produced. It results from the combination, but it cannot be reduced to them. Production here is not emergence. So prior to origination, the effect did not exist in its underlying cause but is a new reality, different from whatever it is made out of. Causation is not the actualization of what was potential but the generation, through rearrangement, of new entities out of already existent factors. A cause is defined as a necessary prior condition of an effect. There are three factors in a causal complex such as the manufacture of a cloth by a weaver out of threads: the substrative or underlying cause (*samavāyi-kāraṇa*) which is always a type of substance (*dravya*) – for example, the threads comprising the cloth (the new whole – *avayavin*); the non-inherent cause (*asamavāyin*) which is always a quality (*guṇa*) or activity (*karma*) – for example, the weaving and colour of the threads; and the efficient or instrumental cause (*nimitta*) – for example, the shuttle and other instruments. The weaver is the agent cause. The products of causal processes are integrated wholes (*avayavin*). The whole is a new creation with its own identity, over and above the sum of the parts in which it inheres. The whole entity cannot exist without the parts, but the parts can exist without the whole. It is distinct from the parts since it manifests a single specific universal. An individual object must be the substrate of a universal, such as cowness or potness – a collection of different parts will not suffice. That the whole is not reducible to its parts is crucial to the Nyāya-Vaiśeṣika resistance to the Buddhist reduction of objects to constituents and phases because they explain endurance through space and time in terms of integrated natures that are held together by the relation of inherence (*samavāya*). The Nyāya-Vaiśeṣikas adduce a number of reasons for their view that prior to origination, the effect does not exist in its underlying cause. Some of them are:

(a) The effect was not perceived in the causal substrate.
(b) If the pre-existent effect lacks specifiable properties, it is not identifiable and thus its existence does not fall within the province of inference.
(c) The agent's efforts would be superfluous if the effect already existed.
(d) A pile of threads is not called 'cloth' and vice versa.
(e) Difference in function of causes and effects: a lump of clay will not carry water.
(f) Difference in form or shape of causes and effects.
(g) Number: threads are many, the cloth one.

The human condition: Bondage to material causality

We said above that some souls have become entangled in and misidentify themselves with aspects of the material environment, in particular psychological faculties and events, and the body. The process occurs when the mind (the *buddhi*), a material product, captures the reflection of the light of some consciousness. The conscious spirit is then confused with some organic material configuration. We only function as individual conscious agents and experiences when conjoined with a body and psychological apparatus. We engage with the world through the operations of the physical *buddhi*. Immersed in daily life, where our natural drives and the acquisitive mentality encourages us always to be moving on, satisfying our interests and achieving our own purposes, we generate *karma* that necessitates further births in the here and now.

The Sāṃkhya distinction between consciousness as the transcendental presupposition of experience and consciousness as a stream of psychological events – cognitions, thoughts, feelings and desires – will become influential. Consciousness is constitutive of sentient beings, but sensory activity, perceptual cognitions and consequent conceptual thoughts that come and go are psychological functions that properly belong to the material mind and sense-faculties. *Sāṃkhya-kārikā* 5 says that perception is a judgement (*adhyavasāya*) about each of the sensory faculties' specific objects. *Sāṃkhya-kārikā* 23 says that judgement is a function of the physical *buddhi*. The *Yuktidīpikā* commentary elaborates: definite awareness is a conceptual apprehension involving a propositional belief such as 'This is a cow' or 'this is a man'. Primary experience is a function of the sense-faculties that assume the form of external objects. A thought such as 'This white cow is running' is a judgement based on sensory deliverances. Primary experience, mere observation or just seeing something, is restricted to the present time, but perceptually based thoughts and judgements can range over past, present and future. Sense-based primary experience is not conceptual. Concepts belong to the *buddhi*, which is able to discover generalities and is unrestricted where its objects are concerned. But although the mind apprehends the forms of objects once they have been grasped by the senses, being physical, it requires illumination by the consciousness that it has borrowed if psychological events are to mean anything. Hence we need to posit the conscious principle as the ultimate source of experiencing. But that principle is merely an observer rather than an active participant in experience. Such is the vision of the world renouncer. This is of course problematic because if the process by which the souls become enmeshed in physical conditions is a purely mechanical and automatic one, and since *prakṛti* and its works are eternally active, it is hard to see why it should not afflict the released soul again.

Liberation (*kaivalya* – 'wholeness', 'isolation') from the cycle of becoming and rebirth (*saṃsāra*) results from the discriminating insight, presupposing the discipline of *yoga*, that the purely conscious and inactive soul is distinct from both the physical and psychological spheres that are the evolutions of material nature. *Prakṛti* then ceases to function in relation to the enlightened centre of consciousness. Liberation occurs when the three *guṇas* are reabsorbed into *prakṛti*, whose functions cease. The spectator-soul recovers its true form, detached from mental modifications and other features of embodiment. Knowledge is enough to effect the soul's disengagement from the environments of experience.

The Yoga vision

Yoga accepts the Sāṃkhya metaphysic, but the Yoga tradition has its own identity. The foundational text is the *Yoga-Sūtra* of Patañjali, variously dated from the second century B.C. to fourth century A.D. The commentary by Vyāsa is probably a work of the sixth century. Vācaspati Miśra (950–1000 A.D.)

wrote a commentary called the Tattvavaiśaradi. The Yogasūtrabhāṣyavivaraṇa is probably much later.

In Indian culture, any discipline of physical and mental self-cultivation and self-transformation whose aim is that of freeing us from rebirth is called 'yoga'. The *Yoga-Sūtra* defines its subject as the restraint and suppression of all mental modifications – that is to say, all forms of thought and feeling, whose forms the soul has assumed. The goal is a disengagement from the life of action in which the soul recovers its true nature. This is achieved by constant contemplative practice and detachment, presupposing mental and moral cultivation. Detachment is said to be self-mastery on the part of one who no longer thirsts for perceptible objects or any of the transitory goals promised by the Scriptures. Active yoga consists in austerities, the recitation of mantras and the study of scriptures bearing on freedom from rebirth, and the direction of the mind to Īśvara – an exemplary soul (*puruṣa*) who has transcended the mutually dependent factors of *karma* and what are collectively termed 'the afflictions'. The latter are ignorance, selfishness, desires, animosity and attachments. Ignorance here means failure to discriminate what matters from what does not, the morally valuable from the corrupt, and what is one's true identity from one's personality and everyday identifications. The discriminating person has realized that everything is unsatisfactory because pleasures turn into frustrations, because of the weight of dispositions inherited from previous lives over which we have no control, and because our minds are always restless and at war within themselves.

The soul in its pure form is mere non-intentional awareness. When implicated in the conditions of space and time, it has an observer's perspective of the thoughts and feelings that are functions of the embodied mind with which it is associated.

The eight stages of the physical, moral and mental discipline of classical *Yoga* are:

Self-restraint, non-violence, honesty in thought, word and deed, sexual restraint and lack of greed.

Discipline: interiorization, tranquillity, asceticism, mantra recitation, the study of texts on liberation and attention to God.

Physical postures, exercising control over the psychosomatic complex.

Breath-control: regulation and reduction of the processes of inhalation and exhalation that increase psychophysical control.

Withdrawal of the senses from their objects and direction of attention to the inner self.

Attention: focusing the mind on a single point (i.e. an object of meditation).
Meditation: the uninterrupted continuity of awareness of the object of meditation.
Profound contemplative introversion in which there is no individual self-awareness.

Mental purification coincides with purification of the soul. The state of liberation from rebirth is one of wholeness and isolation (*kaivalya*) where consciousness experiences only itself. It occurs when the constituents of material nature no longer operate in relation to the individual centre of consciousness. The soul recovers its true form, disjoined from mental and physical modifications.

Further reading

For the *Sāṃkhya-kārikās*, see the classic work by Gerald Larson (1979).

Larson and Bhattacharya (1987) have a useful introduction and summaries of works, including the important *Yuktidīpikā*, which is edited in Wezler & Motegi (1998).

For the *Yoga-Sūtras* and commentaries, see Woods (1927) and Whicher (1998). For a philosophical analysis, see Burley (2007).

Chapter 11 of Halbfass (1992) is valuable for Sāṃkhya.

Questions for discussion and investigation

1. Can we make sense of there basically being more than one centre of pure consciousness?
2. Does it make sense to hold that material nature operates for the sake of the *puruṣas*?
3. Can the *puruṣas* be finally released from rebirth?

Note

1. Wezler and Motegi (1998), pp. 111 and 163.

9

The Mīmāṃsā Vision

Chapter Outline

The Buddhist Dharmakīrti's pithily expressed polemic against the religion of the Brahmins has been mentioned in an earlier chapter (p. 69):

> Accepting the authority of the Vedas, believing in individual agency, hoping for merit from bathing, taking pride in caste, undertaking rites for the removal of evils: these are the five signs of stupidity, the destruction of intelligence.[1]

This chapter surveys some of the ideas propounded by objects of his disdain.

Mīmāṃsā is one of the six visions (*darśana*) of classical Indian philosophy.[2] Its practitioners are specialists in the exegesis of the Vedas which were regarded as the sole and fundamental authority for the social and ritual duties (*varṇa-āśrama-dharma*) of twice-born Hindus. Mīmāṃsā is primarily the hermeneutics and defence of those parts of the Vedas that prescribe the performance of rituals and describe their results. Mīmāṃsā also includes philosophical reflection upon matters connected with the performance of rituals that are part and parcel of everyday life for orthodox (*smārta*) Hindus. In opposition to Buddhism, Mīmāṃsā thinkers articulate a realist view of the world as a mind-independent domain of objects and values. The pivotal values of purity and impurity are properties of things (*vastu-dharma*) outside the mind. This world is sustained and organized by rituals. The latter are performed by persisting human agents who may enjoy their fruits in this and in subsequent lives, ultimately achieving release from the series of births. A world safe for ritual expectations is one in which there are stable subjects of experience and an objective realm structured in such a way that the promised outcomes of religious and moral actions are guaranteed. The cosmos is a self-perpetuating process without beginning or end: things have never been other than they are. Given that the cosmos is self-sustaining, there is no need for a god who originates and preserves it.

The most important names are Śabara (probably during the second half of the fifth century A.D.), who wrote the earliest extant commentary on the Jaimini or Mīmāṃsā-Sūtras, which is the foundational text of the system; Kumārila (600–660 A.D.) whose *Ślokavārttika* is an explanation Śabara's work; and Prabhākara (c.650 A.D.) whose works include the Bṛhatī.

The central concept here is that of *dharma*, which encompasses the notions of natural law, right order, and social and religious duty. *Dharma* is revealed by the authorless, eternal and infallible Vedas. We act in accordance with *dharma* when we obey the Vedic injunctions, thereby entering into relation with the Highest Good.[3] What is to be done is dictated by scripture, not determined by human intellect and will.

It is the *dharma* of grass to grow and of the sun to shine. It is the *dharma* of members of the Brahmin caste to study and teach the Veda and the *dharma* of Vaiśyas to engage in agriculture or commerce. *Dharma* would be unknown were it not taught by the Vedas. The teachings of the latter are codified in rulebooks called the *Dharma-Śāstras*. As an ethical outlook, the concept of *dharma* is thoroughly deontological; a right action is one that an agent is obliged to do.[4] The good is understood as the outcome of right actions. This is in contrast to a consequentialist account where the notion of the good is specified first, and right actions are deemed those that contribute to the achievement of the goal in question. But for orthodox Brahmins, consequentialist goals such as welfare, pleasure and pain are irrelevant to the determination of what is right and wrong. The same applies to the biddings of conscience, divine commands or the cultivation of virtuous character.

Values are exclusively defined by Vedic injunctions and prohibitions, and are manifested in the 'conduct of the virtuous' that derives from strict observance of the Vedic rules separating the pure from the pollutant. *Dharma* is not a 'universal' ethic in that its demands vary according to one's caste and stage of life. One and the same type of action might be right for one person (*sva-dharma* or 'own *dharma*') and wrong for another because they belong to different castes. There was a widespread recognition of the principle that it is better to perform one's own *dharma* badly than that of another well.[5]

For the later Mīmāṃsaka theorists of ritual and social duty, the correct performance of both the public sacrificial rituals by Brahmin priests and the domestic rituals by householders of the highest three castes, in addition to observance of the obligations appropriate to one's caste and stage of life (*varṇa-āśrama-dharma*), controls, maintains and perpetuates order and stability in the universe. A properly performed rite automatically produces its result. It does not depend upon any divine action. The gods exist only in name, that is to say, only in so far as their names are mentioned in the course of rituals. Since they have no belief in an absolute divinity or unsurpassably great being, the Mīmāṃsakas are atheists. Their primary concern is the correct performance of the rituals, including the question of who is entitled to perform them and reap their benefits. Mīmāṃsakas are also concerned with questions about language (whether it is primarily referential and fact-asserting or primarily action-guiding), with the nature and relationship of words and sentences, and with whether words primarily signify individuals or express universal concepts. Kumārila is a figure of outstanding significance in virtue of his debates with Buddhists about inter alia the nature of human agents, the authority of scriptures, the objectivity of general properties, and the relation between perceptual and intellectual faculties.[6]

The authority of the Vedas (*Veda-prāmāṇyam*)

The Vedas are authorities on matters that are outside the scope of other means of knowing such as perception and inference. Without the Veda, we would have no reliable guide to the things that have to be done if we are to reach paradise. *Dharma* is not something that we ourselves could know by means of our natural capacities. Since it is something to be brought about, it is outside the scope of perception and those means of knowing that are founded upon perception. A perception is a cognition that is produced when the human sense-faculties are connected with an already existing object. It cannot be the grounds of knowledge of *dharma* since it only apprehends presently existing things. Only prescriptive Vedic language has the capacity to inform us about *dharma* as something that needs to be brought about.

Any religion that offers knowledge about the supernatural is going to need a source of authority that is not of this world. For Christians it is the revealed Word of God: both Jesus and the scriptural testimonies to him. Naiyāyikas, Śaivas and Buddhists hold that scriptures are authoritative when they have a promulgator (in the case of the first two, it is the God Śiva) possessed of appropriate virtues. For the Buddhists, the Buddha is himself a *pramāṇa* – a teacher of truth. His authority is indicated by the original and unprecedented character of his salvific message when he tells us about what is to be sought after and what avoided and the means of so doing. He teaches things that we could not know otherwise, as the Veda is held to do. Because he is a reliable guide (*avisaṃvādaka*) in matters to do with human life, he can be presumed to be an authority for non-empirical matters too.

For both Mīmāṃsakas and their Vedāntin cousins, the Vedas are authorities about what lies beyond the bounds of sense because they have no author, either human or divine. They are called '*apauruṣeya*', which literally means 'non-personal'). The Vedas are simply given, not created. The notion of the uncreated, non-personal nature of the meaningful sound units of the Vedas is foundational for the authority of those scriptures.

The validity of the Vedas is intrinsic to them (*svataḥ-prāmānya*). The notion is an epistemological one, and it basically means that the truth of a thought does not depend upon a later thought that verifies or establishes it. Were it to do so, an infinite regress would result and we could never be said to know anything. On this view, reliability does not depend upon verification or confirmation and may safely be taken for granted. Validity just means not being falsified. A statement may be presumed true if nothing falsifies it or makes it suspect.

Error can arise from a lack of distinctness in the objects of cognition, or it may occur because the complexity or subtlety of objects surpasses our capacities for cognitive discrimination. But it may also arise because the sense-faculties are somehow defective and thus fail to transmit information to the mind. Kumārila specifies the nature of the possible sources of fallibility which include such factors as greed, desire, hostility, pride, intoxication, passion and shame. These are emotional and moral defects of finite beings. It follows that a false speech-report is entirely the fault of the speaker. But the Vedas have no author, so cannot be open to doubts about their reliability on that score. Moreover, because the Vedas speak of what is absolutely imperceptible and non-empirical, there is no possible cognition that could falsify them. Mandates such as 'The person who desires paradise should perform fire-sacrifices' speak of things that can never be shown to be false.

The defence of the unquestionable authority of the infallible Veda is one reason why the Mīmāṃsakas argue against the existence of an all-knowing and all-powerful divinity, or an omniscient Buddha. Kumārila argues that neither perception nor inference can be used to establish an omniscient being. Obviously, such is never observed. It would be difficult to frame a non-question begging inference on a number of grounds, the most blatant of which is that there are no relevant supporting examples that would validate a statement of universal concomitance (*vyāpti*) between a reason and that which is to be established. In addition, the *arthāpatti-pramāṇa* (argument from 'otherwise-inexplicability' – 'fat Devadatta does not eat by day, so he eats by night') would not be applicable because it is not clear that there is anything that requires explanation by the postulation of an omniscient being. An omniscient being cannot be established by scripture because if it were supposed to be the author, the reasoning would be circular, and if the author is not himself omniscient, he cannot claim to know that there is an omniscient being.

The scriptures are classified in three ways:

Vidhi or *Codanā*: Passages commanding the performance of specific rites with specific results. Such injunctive statements are imperative in form (from the technical point of view of Sanskrit grammar, their verbs are in the optative mood). They maintain that language is properly meaningful only when it is injunctive or prescriptive – when it tells us to do something and how to go about it. Descriptive or fact-asserting statements are meaningful only in so far as they are connected with actions and injunctions to act. The argument for this is that children learn language by observing its application in various contexts of activities. The primary function of language is to produce some action – something to be done (*kārya*) or brought into existence. The ritualists draw the conclusion that those scriptural passages that appear to speak of already established realities must be construed as merely supplementary to the all-important passages enjoining ritual activity.

Arthavāda: Indicative statements describing the manner of performance of rituals and providing explanations. As we have just seen, these are subordinate to injunctions and not independently significant.

Mantras: Incantations invoking the presence of deities during the rites.

Words and sentences

The Mīmāṃsā view is that a Sanskrit word (*pada*) is a permanently fixed sequence of timeless, unproduced and imperishable phonemes (*varṇa*), which are manifested in audible sounds. It is the eternal sequence of phonemes that is the conveyor of meaning or signifier (*vācaka*). Words are essentially, and not merely by convention, correlated with the extra-linguistic realties that they express and that are their significations (*vācya*). The signifier–signified relation is an innate power (*śakti/sāmarthya*) in words to express their meaning. A given word stands for a limitless number of objects: 'We say, "The single word 'cow' is uttered eight times and not that there are eight words 'cow'"' The word–object connection (*śabda-artha-saṃbandha*) cannot be a human creation. It cannot be established every time we use a particular word. But we have no traditional recollection of anyone originally fixing the references of words.

Each word expresses its own meaning, and an uttered combination of word meanings is understood as a sentence. Sentences are not units of meaning over and above the words comprising them. This is the mainstream view espoused by Śabara and Kumārila, and it is called '*abhihita-anvaya*' or 'the connection of meanings that have been expressed'. There is another view propounded by Kumārila's contemporary Prabhākara that is called '*anvita-abhidhāna*' ('expressing interrelated meanings'). Prabhākara thinks that word meanings are primarily understood when used to prescribe actions and to bring things about rather than as referring to already existent objects. So the fabric of linguistic understanding consists of sentences that include a verbal meaning. Words have meaning only in the context of sentences. All meanings are relative to particular situations. The Prabhākara argue that a child does not learn individual words on their own but learns language through the insertion and removal of words in sentences. She hears, 'bring a cow', and sees someone do that. Then she hears, 'bring a horse'. By the removal and insertion of words in sentences, she learns the meanings of individual words. The theory of 'the expression of inter-related meanings' may also be interpreted as the view that it is only in the context of a sentence that a word has meaning: when we want to know the meaning of a word, we should look at its use in context and not scrutinize it in isolation.

Let us return to Kumārila's view that the real relation between a Sanskrit word and its extra-linguistic signification is inseparable and eternal. If the word–meaning relation is to be permanent and unbreakable, words must be primarily expressive of general concepts and the objects falling under them.

They do designate particulars when used in sentences in specific circumstances, but this is not their primary signification. The word–meaning relation obtains between a word and a natural or artificial kind (*ākṛti* or *jāti*). What words mean are the underlying structures shared by members of a kind. The relation is fixed (*niyama*) and natural (*autpattika*). The permanence of the word–object relation is of course consonant with the notion of the intrinsic validity of the Vedas. If the Vedic words were like names and primarily signified individuals, the word–meaning relation would be continually broken and reconstituted. But the form common to all cows is a structure comprising the essential properties that make something a cow. That structure is a basic feature of the cosmos, and it is endlessly manifested as individual (*vyakti*) cows. The *ākṛti* is not just the visible appearance of cows. Cows come in all sorts of shapes, sizes and colours. But each and every one shares the same genetic structure that we may call 'cowness' or 'bovinity'. It is that to which we refer when we speak of 'The Cow', meaning the species. The generic form of gold (what we would call its atomic number or molecular structure) is likewise common to all artefacts made of gold.

As Kumārila puts it, 'the kind (*jāti*) is called the physical structure (*ākṛti*) because it is that by which the individual (*vyakti*) is formed. The generic property (*sāmānya*) is the basis of a single concept under which individuals fall.'[7] The form is a generic property of many things. It is not identical with a configuration of parts (*saṃsthāna*) because there is no configuration of parts in the case of actions, qualities and substances like the self. Because a configuration perishes and differs for each individual, if that were the form, it could not be the generic property expressed by a word. The generic property, kind or form is a property constitutive of individuals and it is the object of a simple cognition. It is the form that is the primary signification of the word 'cow'. That is why it can apply to many. In everyday life and in Vedic usage, it designates an individual in the context of a sentence.

Kumārilabhaṭṭa's realism

Kumārila holds that the uncreated and therefore eternal cosmos, structured by universals and populated by individual knowers and agents confronting a plurality of objects, is independent of human minds. This sort of realism is integral to the ritualists' world view. If cognitions did not have objects that are independent of minds, the religion of ritual would be pointless, and the well-established categories of means of knowing, objects of knowing and agents of knowing would be abolished. People have to be confident that the rituals are valid, that what they are doing matters and has real consequences, and that they can expect to reap their benefits in the future. The objectivity of the world is underwritten by the theory that cognitions are acts, bearing no internal content of their own, belonging to a self who is their agent. As acts, they have an effect on objects, which already exist and are not brought into being by our thoughts. The effect that a cognitive act brings about in objects is the temporary incidental property of being known (*jñātatā*) or made manifest. This gives expression to the distinction, crucial to realism, between objects as they are in themselves and objects as known. One knows that one knows something not by introspection or by the internal luminosity of consciousness, but as the result of a process of reasoning in which one observes the production of an effect and concludes that it would not have occurred in the absence of cognition.[8] Of course, the theory here attracts the objection that we are not knowing the world as such, but only the world as modified by cognition.

The perceptual process and our experience of the world

Kumārila maintains that both sensory perception and discursive, conceptual thinking bring us into direct contact with the real external world. A direct realist such as Kumārila does not accept that perceptions are a veil of representations falling between the subject and the given. Rather they disclose the actual structures of reality. Kumārila confronts a range of Buddhist idealist and anti-realist views, all of which maintain that perceptual experience somehow misrepresents reality. Buddhists such as Dignāga and Dharmakīrti hold that universals are not real entities and that they are imperceptible. Universals, they say, are products of the generalizing and externalizing capacities of minds. They are mental and linguistic conventions, stored as concepts and superimposed upon configurations of particular sense-data (*svalakṣaṇa*). Both the Mīmāṃsā and the Nyāya realists are committed to establishing the reality of universals and kinds. One of the ways in which they did this was by establishing the perceptibility of universals, which are features of the mind-independent domain.[9]

There is an extended treatment of questions about perception in the fourth chapter of the *Ślokavārttika*.

The background here is the influential view of the Buddhist nominalist philosopher Dignāga (480–540 A.D.) that sense-perception (*pratyakṣa*) and reasoning (*anumāna*) are concerned with exclusive spheres. This appears to involve a severance between experience of the given, on the one hand, and its representation in thought, on the other. Dignāga defines perception as always free from conceptualization (*kalpanā*). Perception is pre-linguistic experience of unique, ineffable momentary particulars (*svalakṣaṇa*). The particulars are the only genuine realities and they do not fall within the referential capacity of language. Reasoning uses general concepts, which are mental constructs. There are five types of conceptual construction (*kalpanā*): the association of a cluster of particulars that have furnished a perceptual experience with a proper name; the association of a cluster with a universal ('this is a man'); the association of a cluster with a quality or qualities ('this is white'); the association of a cluster with actions ('this is running'); and the association of a cluster with something else that has been identified as a substance or individual entity ('this man is wearing glasses'). The meanings of words are the generalities (*sāmānya-lakṣaṇa*) constructed by conceptual thought.[10] The idea is that as soon as we start expressing what we experience in words and thoughts, we are distanced from the real world of momentary particulars.

The following passage forms part of Kumārila's response to nominalist anti-realism. The Buddhist opponent has just said that since inferential thought always involves concepts, it cannot depend upon perception because the deliverances of the senses are non-conceptual.

Ślokavārttika IV, 111–120

> As for the view that the logical reason (and other elements in an inferential sequence of thought) is not grasped by sensory perception because sensory perception does not involve conceptualizing: that view is false because concepts (*vikalpa*) are implicit in that they enable us to cognize the object. [111]

The idea is that any perception that is about some object (in contradistinction to a sensory impression that is of an object in the sense that it is caused by it) must be to some extent informed by conceptual thought. That Kumārila recognizes the non-cognitive character of sensation is apparent from verses 121–2 where he says that the sense-faculties are an instrumental cause of cognition but they are not cognitive.

> In the first place here is cognition (*jñāna*) that is just seeing (*ālocanā*) and it is free from concepts (*nirvikalpaka*). It is produced from the pure entity and is like the cognitions of infants and the mute. [112]
>
> Neither general (*sāmānya*) nor specific features (*viśeṣa*) figure explicitly in the content of awareness, but the individual that is their substrate is grasped. [113]

The next three verses refer to an Advaita Vedānta view that will appear in the writings of Maṇḍana Miśra (c.700 A.D.), who says that, 'Initially there is non-conceptual perception relating to the bare reality of an entity (*vastu-mātra*). The ensuing conceptual cognitions comprehend its peculiarities.' (*Brahma-Siddhi* 71.1-2).

> Others say that there is an ultimate universal called 'Substance' or 'Reality' that is the sole object of perception. [114]
>
> On the other hand, particularities (*viśeṣa*) are known by conceptual cognitions (*savikalpa-buddhi*). Some particularities are specific to an individual and others are shared by many. [115]
>
> But perception that arises without taking account of particularities as either shared or specific does not differ whether it arises in relation to a cow or a horse. [116]
>
> That is false because we apprehend a distinct form in the case of each individual entity. It is not the case that no differences are grasped just because we cannot apply a word to the object. [117]
>
> Even in non-conceptual awareness (*nirvikalpaka-bodhe'pi*), there is an implicit apprehension of an entity as having both shared and specific features, although only a simple form is grasped by the cognizer. [118]
>
> The entity is not identified in its uniqueness because it is not distinguished from others. A generic feature is not grasped because we do not notice any similarity with other entities. [119]
>
> A subsequent cognition by which an entity is grasped in terms of its properties such as its universal and its qualities is also considered a form of perception. [120]

The denial by Buddhists such as Dignāga (and Advaita Vedāntins) that sensory perception is always non-conceptual is open to question. The same can be said about the other extreme that perception always involves explicit conceptual content: if that is true, it follows that infants and animals lack perceptual experiences. We see the latter view in the thought of the grammarian Bhartṛhari, who says [VP 1.131-2], 'In this world there is no thought that is not associated with language. All cognition appears as pervaded by language. If the eternal linguistic nature of awareness disappeared, consciousness would not illuminate anything because it is that nature which makes identifications possible.'

There is the question of explaining the relationship between sensation and beliefs. Also, concepts are general but sense-perception engages with particulars. There is an argument that concepts and beliefs are abstractions from the data supplied by sensory experience, but this is not really Dignāga's view. He insists on a radical disjunction between perceptual experience and conceptualization because he wants us to realize that the everyday concepts and categories of thought to which we are attached do not mirror reality as it is in itself. Our concepts are at best impositions upon a given reality that is unstructured in the sense that it is unarticulated and amorphous until we organize it conceptually into persisting objects, kinds, properties and relations.

But if perception and thinking are two completely different modes of experience, it is not clear how the raw data of sensation can be translated into conceptual experience and perceptual judgements. If perception justifies (rather than just causes) beliefs, a perceptual experience must yield a reason to hold a given belief. But only an informational state with a least implicit conceptual content can furnish such a reason.

Dignāga's radical divorce of sensory perception and thinking provoked opposition from thinkers belonging to the orthodox Brahminical schools. They maintained that there is a single kind of mental activity called perception and that it puts us in touch with the real world. Perception has two varieties: non-conceptual (*nirvikalpa*) and conceptual (*savikalpa*). As we have just seen, Kumārila is party to this reaction to Dignāga when he says (as we saw above) that a cognition that grasps an entity as a manifestation of a kind (a persisting individual substance that possesses certain qualities and may be capable of certain types of action) is also a form of perception. The point is that the conceptual grasping of such structure is not a conceptual fabrication, imposition or invention but rather represents a discovery. The informational states, which a subject acquires on the basis of primary perception, are non-conceptual. Judgements about the world based upon such states necessarily involve conceptualization. For this to happen, information about an object and its properties must have been received and implicitly registered in the primary informational state. According to this outlook, conceptualization or judgement or belief takes the subject from an informational state with non-conceptual content to a cognitive state with conceptual content. Although judgements are based upon experience, this does not entail that they are about informational states. They are about the world. When one wants to check that a judgement is accurate, one looks again at the world and not at one's states.

An illustration may help here: I may be looking in the direction of a green expanse, although I might not even be explicitly registering that it is green because my mind is on something else. This is a perceptual informational state, but one that does not involve any specific thoughts about what is in the field of vision. Its content is non-conceptual. But I may shift the focus of my attention and register that the expanse is green and undulating. On closer inspection, I come to understand that I am seeing a golf course. I am now in an informational state whose content is conceptual. An animal or infant could be seeing the same area but could not believe that it is a golf course.

The problem with Dignāga's position is that it cannot accommodate the following distinctions:

(a) Sensations, or sensory impressions, are of objects in that they are caused by objects but they are not about objects. In other words, they are not cognitive.

(b) Some perceptual experiences are about objects without being discriminative or involving judgements. They may just be informational states of the subject that do not involve any commitment to beliefs about the object. But such states are cognitive and informed by meaning.

(c) Perceptual experiences that are explicitly discriminating ('This is a black laptop PC') and epistemic ('I know that there is a book on the desk').

The nature of ritual agents

Kumārila maintains that there is a subject or possessor (called *ātman*) of cognitions (always indicated as the same by the pronoun 'I') which remains constant through all its changing cognitive and affective states.[11] It is an eternal reality, the intuition of which does not reveal any conditioning by space and time. Contact, mediated by the psychological apparatus, with those conditions is a product of *karma*. *Karma* propels souls (*ātman*) through series of embodied lives in a hierarchy of worlds of experience.

For a ritualist like Kumārila, the primary significance of human individuals consists in their being agents of sacrificial causality. The ideal person is simply obedient to social and religious duty and free from the personal motivations that generate *karma*. It is *karma*, purposive intentional action, that personalizes the *ātman*. But truly disinterested action will not generate *karma*. Accumulated *karma* will be exhausted over the course of lives dedicated to duty for the sake of duty alone. A very long series of lives spent in disinterested conformity to *dharma*, in a spirit of 'duty for duty's sake' and not for any advantages that it might yield, will terminate in the release from rebirth of a depersonalized, timeless and featureless entity without contacts or cognitions of an environment.

But what about the selves that we are in the here and now? Fundamental to the Mīmāṃsā world view is the conviction that the person who performs an action is the same as the one who will enjoy its fruits. We would feel no motivation to act if we did not believe that we will experience the consequences. But if the *ātman* is inactive owing to its permanence and omnipresence, and if it is not really subject to pleasure and pain, how can it be the enjoyer of the fruits of its actions? And if when it experiences suffering or pleasure it undergoes a real change, how can it be permanent and immutable (*nitya*) because that which is permanent is incapable of any sort of causal activity, either simultaneously or successively? To questions like these, Kumārila responds that although the *ātman* is eternal, it can be connected with different states, and it can be both an agent and patient. The distinction between substantial entities and their states may be considered straightforward: I am the same Christopher Bartley, although my thoughts, feelings and moods are changing. I have a life history that is extended through time, but I cannot be identical with the events comprising that history. If I were, it would make no sense to say that on some particular occasion 'I could have done otherwise than I did' because that would be to talk about another life history.

The Buddhists, echoed by Derek Parfit in *Reasons and Persons*, promote a reductionist view of the self as a 'series person'. They deny that we are persisting individuals, enduring substances that maintain a stable identity throughout the course of their existence. What we really are is a causally related series or stream of psychological and physical occurrences (*skandhas*: body, feelings, sensory perceptions, conceptual thoughts and inherited traits), which may be described impersonally or from a third-personal point of view. Interrelated physical and mental events constitute a person's life. This is coupled with the thesis of the essential temporality of beings (*kṣaṇikatva*): mental events and acts are momentary and self-contained occurrences that somehow constitute themselves as streams.

In the course of the eighteenth chapter of his *Ślokavārttika*, Kumārila engages with this outlook and argues for a conception of the persisting self (*ātman*) as the ultimate subject of mental acts and experiences. Only such an entity can be the guaranteed recipient of the benefits of ritual. People are only going to be interested in ultimate release from rebirth if there is an identity that will be released. His arguments are transcendental ones: continuity of experience presupposes a single, enduring subject that is a further fact over and above the stream of experiences and life history. In fact, the resulting picture of 'the self' is a pretty minimalist one. There has to be a constant subject if we are to make sense of the synthesis of experiences. This subject is like Kant's purely formal 'I' that accompanies all representations. It is not the same as a personality or individual life.

The Buddhist interprets 'person' as meaning 'a series of experiences' (*saṃtāna*). Kumārila says that the expression 'series' may mean either a temporal succession of momentary psycho-physical events or a real unity that is not reducible to its components but which emerges from them. In the first case, the series is really impersonal and expressible in third-personal terms ('there is the thought P'; 'the feeling F is happening'; 'the decision D is being made'). As such, the series cannot be considered as a genuinely personal agent or subject. In the second case, the series might well be a single subject compatible with the diversity of its experiences. But now we are very close to the notion of a stable self. He observes that identifying something as 'this series' presupposes that there is some sort of unity present and this involves abandonment of reductionism about persons. Even if it were possible convincingly to reformulate reports of mental states in third-personal terms and still be true to the character of our mental lives, we would need to be able to relativize those reports to a 'series-life' because something has to own the experiences. We would still need some explanation of why a series of physical and mental events constitute one life. It is looking like the notion of a series-life is parasitic upon that of a person as usually understood.

It is not enough to take the 'stream' metaphor literally and say that we attribute unity to a flow of water when we call it a river. Rivers are physical entities and they have banks. It is not clear what the equivalent to the banks is where streams of experiences are concerned. If the self is really just a bundle of perceptions, what ties the bundle together, if not a persisting subject? (A physicalist may say that there is no problem here. Bodies, including neurological events, individuate and underwrite personal continuity through time. But the Buddhists are not physicalists, and they want to make sense of the possibility of rebirth which of course presupposes the possibility of disembodiment at death and re-embodiment at rebirth. This is not a problem for the Indian materialists or Carvākas because they do not believe in rebirth. Most Indian thinkers accept that the body cannot be the subject because (a) it is not conscious and (b) it is a collection of parts, and a number of parts only form a system when they are subordinate to another principle that makes them an organized structure.)

In an expression such as, 'I know', the pronoun 'I' expresses a constant subject that is immediately given. Its support, the basis of its use in language, is the persisting self. The crux in the debate between Kumārila and the Buddhists is whether the subject is a thinking substance (an enduring thing that thinks) or whether it is only an aspect specific to each successive mental event and so different in each and every case. Kumārila argues that if momentary ideas were the subjects of experience, as the Buddhists suppose, there could be no experience of recognition in the form, 'I previously saw this thing and now I am seeing it again.' Kumārila recognizes that the flow of consciousness is always both backward- and forward looking, retentive and anticipatory. Consciousness is fundamental to mental states in the sense that it can range over them. The condition of connecting past and present mental states ('I am looking at something that I saw yesterday') is a persisting conscious principle that is not identical with those states. Successive distinct, momentary and self-contained mental states cannot achieve this reconciliation. Now while recognitional thoughts about external objects or other people may be false, 'I-thoughts' are immune to error by misidentification. They cannot relate to anything other than the knowing subject. The subject is not identified in the ways in which external objects are, because there is no need for comparison and the assignment of an object to a kind. We might mistake a piece of shell for silver when, under the sway of avarice, stored sub-conscious traces (*vāsanā*) of a prior perception of silver are revived by the shining surface appearance of a piece of shell. The Buddhist holds that what we call the recognition of the self is a variety of this type of illusion resulting from confusion of similar moments in a continuum. But Kumārila points out that strictly speaking there is no recognition or memory of the self. It is not something contained in stored traces of prior experiences. If I have an immediate sense of myself as the same being over time (this is different from remembering what I had for lunch yesterday), this does not involve a process of recollection like that of the recollection of objects, facts or states of affairs. 'I-experience' is always simply given: it does not have to be recovered. I never have to establish to myself that I am now the same being that I was yesterday. The Buddhist may think that the 'sense of self' is a conventional misconception deriving from ignorance, desire and attachment. This may be a reasonable account of the mechanisms of selfishness. But ignorance, desire and attachment have to belong to something, and the best candidate appears some sort of persisting subject that makes the mistake in the first place.

Kumārila's epistemological stance is a strong version of common-sense realism recognizing that for the most part, cognitions are valid. He thinks that cognitions of a pre-existing objective physical world are always intrinsically true. Errors and hallucinations sometimes occur, but they can be explained as arising from identifiable defects in the perceptual apparatus, or from the indistinctness of objects. Cognitions can be trusted as valid if they are not contradicted by a subsequent perception. In short, there is no need to check everything. Reliability may be safely assumed. Intrinsically valid cognitions are true just in virtue of their occurrence. The Vedic sounds are heard to command the rituals and tell of the supernatural benefits accruing to their performers. (If what is promised is something concrete and it does not happen, this can be blamed on a mistake in the performance of the ritual.) In the cognition of the Vedic mandates, there is no scope for falsehood, no possible standpoint from which they might be criticized and countermanded, and no room for scepticism about their authority.

For a realist like Kumārila, the variety of experience depends upon differences between the objects grasped. The metaphor of 'grasping' is instructive, conveying that objects already exist, independently of any thinker. They are not created or produced by knowledge. There is no veil of representations intervening between the knowing subject, the agent of the act of knowing, and the given. Consciousness is not a repository of forms or concepts, but is more like a capacity for activity. When a cognition brings about the property known-ness in an object, that property is accidental: its loss or gain makes no real difference to the object.

We began this chapter with a reference to Dharmakīrti (600–660 A.D.), and we will conclude it with a summary of the Mīmāṃsā outlook composed by another Buddhist who lived slightly earlier. The following verses from the ninth chapter of Bhāviveka's *Madhyamakahṛdaya* describe the religion of ritual as seen by its Buddhist deniers:

1 There are those who deny that meditation and gnosis are the true way to liberation, stipulating that it can only be achieved by rituals.
2 On the basis of tradition (*āgama*), they hold that the only appropriate way to liberation is that of the scripturally prescribed rituals.
3 Human testimony is suspect because it is polluted by desire and other passions. It is understood that the Veda is the final authority because it does not have a personal author.
4 The Veda is believed not to have a personal author because no author is remembered. It is an authority because its transmission from generation to generation is uninterrupted.
5 Without the Veda there could be no inferential knowledge of super-sensory matters such as heaven and socio-religious duty for which there is no empirical evidence.
6 But timeless language, expressed in sounds, has a permanent connect with its referents. It is because of this that there can be understanding about (super-sensory) matters.
7 Vedic language is known to be eternal because it is recognized that its sounds have been transmitted without interruption.
8 Vedic scripture is an epistemic authority distinct from inference, just as perception is. The instances of understanding that it yields may be about one topic or several topics.
9 Vedic scripture is different from inference because it produces understanding of matters for which there is no empirical evidence.
10 Duty is manifested in ritual action, and ritual actions bring about liberation.
11 The ancient and shining path of the Vedas is traversed by gods and sages. It is logical that the Vedas are rejected by women and śūdras, who are excluded from the Vedic teachings.
12 What exists here in the Veda also exists elsewhere. What does not exist here, exists nowhere.
13 Cavilling about the Vedas with specious arguments, logicians who put too much weight on inference rejoice in their own conclusions.
14 But like blind people running on an uneven path guided only by their feet, they are prone to falling because of the excessive weight they put on inference.
15 And there is no omniscient person, because such is never seen. The omniscience of the Buddha has been invented to impress people.

16 The word of the Buddha is not an authority because it is something produced like the words of other people. The Buddha is not omniscient because he is just a human being.

17 The word of the Buddha is not an authority because it reviles the Vedic teachings.

Further reading

For the view that meaningful language is essentially prescriptive rather than fact-asserting (and the Vedāntic response), see Lipner (1986), Chapter 1.

Chapters III, IV and IX of Halbfass (1991) are about Vedic orthodoxy, ritualism and sacrificial causality.

Olivelle (1999) and (2005) translate the texts that concern the practical applications of *dharma*.

Act Four of Jayanta's *Much Ado About Religion* (Dezső 2005) sees a debate about the authority of the Vedas.

Matilal (1990) Chapter X ('Words and Sentences') expounds *abhihitānvaya* versus *anvitābhidhāna*.

Scharf (1996) has a long section on words and meanings, accompanied by translations of typical Mīmāṃsaka argumentation.

Eltschinger (2007) is a mine of information about Kumārila. For the latter's epistemology, Taber (2005) is invaluable and contains a richly annotated translation of the chapter on perception in Kumārila's *Ślokavārttika*.

Questions for discussion and investigation

1. Why do the ritualists put so much weight on the infallible authority of the Vedas?
2. Why is realism so important to them?

Notes

1. Dharmakīrti's own commentary on his Pramāṇavārttika Bk1, Verse 340.
2. It is called Pūrva-Mīmāṃsā when it is subordinated to its cousin Vedānta or Uttara-Mīmāṃsā, which calls itself the Higher Inquiry.
3. 'We claim that dharma connects a person with well-being. It is the aim of Vedic injunctions' (MS 1.1.2).
4. It appears that originally the observance of *dharma* meant the performance and patronage of elaborate and expensive sacrificial rituals generating worldly prosperity (*bhoga*) and post-mortem pleasures in paradise (*svarga*). Its neglect has all sorts of negative consequences ranging from personal misfortunes to the collapse of the universe into chaos. Thinkers in the early Mīmāṃsā tradition such as Śabara thought of *dharma* as the same as the performance of prescribed actions. But this makes *dharma* as transitory as those actions, with the consequence that it is difficult to establish a connection between an action and its consequences. Hence, the earlier thinkers said that the rituals generated an unseen factor called *apūrva* ('something new') or *adṛṣṭa* (something unseen) that transmitted the ritual's effect to the future. But its status and location were vague. Later writers favour the view that *dharma* is an eternal reality that is manifested in the rituals and their consequences. The concept of manifestation is invoked in various contexts to explain occasions where something eternal becomes perceptible in certain conditions. For example, timeless phonemes are manifested in audible sounds. A universal property (*jāti* or *sāmānya*) such as cowness is manifested in individual cows (*vyakti*). *Apūrva* is treated by Kumārila as a power (*śakti*) belonging to *dharma* that belongs to the sacrifices and to the identity of the sacrificers. It activates the fruits of the rituals.
5. BG 3.35.
6. See Arnold (2005), Chs 3 and 4. Taber (2010).
7. SV *Ākṛtivāda* 3.
8. Technically, this is called *arthāpatti*, involving *anyathā-anupapatti* or 'otherwise-inexplicability/impossibility'.
9. For more on this specifically as it applies to caste, see Eltschinger (2012), *passim*.
10. 'Words are born of concepts (*vikalpa*) and concepts are born of words. These do not touch reality.'

11. For the controversy about whether the use of the first-personal pronoun and the associated concept (*ahaṃ-pratyaya*) establish the permanent subject of transitory experiences, see Watson (2006), Chapter 3. The worry is that a subject established in reliance on concepts would not be the self-revealing and self-establishing permanent background consciousness. Of course, this is not a problem for Nyāya, whose thinkers are quite happy to accept that I-thoughts refer to a real self that falls under their system of categories as a substance.

10

Vedānta

Chapter Outline

The interpretation of the Upaniṣads

The word 'Vedānta' literally means 'the end of the Vedas', where end means the Upaniṣads. Vedānta is the systematic interpretation of the Upaniṣads (collectively termed '*śruti*' or 'what has been *heard*') either by direct commentary upon them or by elaborate explanations of the aphoristic summaries of their contents in the *Brahma-Sūtras*. The *Bhagavad Gītā* is also a key authority. With the Epics (the *Rāmāyaṇa* and the *Mahābhārata*) and *Purāṇas*, the *Gītā* is included in the category of traditional authorities called *smṛti* or 'what has been remembered'. The latter has the function of elucidating and corroborating *śruti*.

There are three antagonistic traditions of thought: *Advaita Vedānta*, which is a metaphysical monism saying that fundamentally reality is featureless and tranquil consciousness; *Viśiṣṭādvaita Vedānta*, which proclaims the unity of a complex reality; and *Dvaita Vedānta*, which combines strict monotheism and a realistic metaphysical pluralism.

They all agree that eternal scriptures called *śruti* or 'what has been heard' are the sole means of knowing (*pramāṇa*) about what is beyond the scope of sensory perception and inference. Vedāntins hold that it is the Upaniṣads, the 'knowledge portion' (*jñāna-kāṇḍa*) of the *Vedas* that reveal the truths that we need to know about the absolute Being (the *brahman*), the soul (*ātman*) and the relation between the two, the origin of the universe from the *brahman*, the consequentiality of actions (*karma*), transmigration (*saṃsāra*) as well as the means to and nature of ultimate liberation from rebirth (*mokṣa*/*mukti*).

All Vedāntins will agree with the grammarian Bhartṛhari's observation that even if something is inferred by clever logicians with a big effort, there will always be cleverer ones who come up with another explanation [*Vākyapadīya* 1.42]. As Rāmānuja puts it: 'A theory that rests exclusively on human concepts may at some other time or place be refuted by arguments devised by cleverer people.... The conclusion is that with regard to supernatural matters, Scripture alone is the epistemic authority and that reasoning is to be used only in support of Scripture' [*Śrī Bhāṣya* 2.1.12].

Vedāntins aim to construct a systematic and coherent interpretation of the Upaniṣads, in accordance with a principle that they form a single body of literature with a unified overall purport (*tātparya*). The Vedāntins follow common exegetical norms and techniques in order to identify specific coherent contexts of meaning (*eka-vākyatā*) and then demonstrate that these contexts themselves fit together. As far as possible, the exegete must construe the texts in their literal senses. The principal Upaniṣads were probably composed over a very long period of time (roughly 800 B.C. to 300 B.C.) and long before the first extant Vedāntic systematizations (c. 700 A.D.). Their contents are diverse. They do not obviously teach a single coherent message. Moreover, they are often obscure. The abbreviated summaries of the topics of which they treat (the *Brahma-Sūtras*) are frequently ambiguous. So there was ample scope for very different interpretations, and that is exactly what we find.

Whereas the theorists of ritual performance (*Pūrva-Mīmāṃsakas*) were concerned with and insisted upon the primary meaningfulness of Vedic action-commands (*vidhi*) bearing on ritual performance, Vedāntins focus upon the fact-asserting or descriptive texts (*arthavāda*) referring to already existent entities or states of affairs, rather than 'things to be done' (*kārya*). Both earlier and later Mīmāṃsā developed sophisticated techniques of textual exegesis and argued about whether ritual performance can be a path to salvation with or without intuitive insight into the true nature of reality (*jñāna*), devotion to God (*bhakti*) and divine grace (*prasāda*).

Most Vedāntins accept versions of the Sāṃkhya theory of *satkāryavāda* and say that effects are emanations that do not differ essentially from their underlying or substrative causes. It follows that there is some form of ontological nexus or parallelism of being (an *analogia entis*) between the world and the *brahman* that is its cause. *Madhva* is an exception here in that he denies that there is a real continuity of being between God and the world. He maintains (like the Śaiva Siddhāntins by whose outlook the Dvaita tradition is influenced) that God produces the cosmos out of eternally real Prime Matter that is distinct from him.

The Bhedābheda tradition of Upaniṣadic interpretation

Before turning to a consideration of some of the major representatives of the different Vedāntic schools, we will mention a tradition of theological thinking that is labelled 'Bhedābheda', meaning 'difference and no-difference'. The idea here is that the Supreme Being has two modes of existence: an unconditioned mode that is the *brahman* as it is in itself wherein all differentia have been suppressed, and a conditioned mode that is the emanated cosmos. The cosmos is understood as the real self-differentiation of the One, the substrative cause of all finite existences. The cosmos emerges out of the absolute Being. Freedom from rebirth is achievable through a combination of works and knowledge. It is the soul's dissolution into the foundational reality.[1]

We have here an attempt to hold together the transcendent unity of divinity and the reality of the plural world. (A version of this cosmography is to be found in Ādiśeṣa's *Paramārthasāra*.)

Rāmānuja radically modifies this outlook, but as a pupil of Yādavaprakāśa, he is a reliable source of information:

> Bhāskara and his followers say on the basis of the scriptures expressing unity that the Brahman although having every excellent quality such as freedom from evil is conditioned by a limiting condition (*upādhi*) and is bound and released, and is the substrate of transformations (*pariṇāma*) that are various imperfections. [*Vedārthasaṃgraha* para. 8]

> Because Bhāskara and his followers do not accept any realities other than the Brahman and the limiting conditions, given the association between the Brahman and the limiting conditions all the defects proper to the latter will apply to the Brahman itself. [*Vedārthasaṃgraha* para. 54]
>
> Yādavaprakāśa and his followers, explaining the exact meaning of the scriptures about unity say that the Brahman, an ocean of unsurpassable and immeasurable noble qualities proper to its nature, is by nature both distinct and not distinct from sentient beings, and the abode of many kinds of impure transformations. [*Vedārthasaṃgraha* para. 9]
>
> Given their assumption that the individual soul and the Brahman are both different and non-different, it follows that if the Brahman is essentially the same as the individual souls, all the defects belonging to them will belong to it also. If God is essentially constitutive of all the different creatures, then he is the nature of each and every one. Such being the case, all their pleasures and pains will belong to him. [*Vedārthasaṃgraha* para. 58]

In the course of his explication of *Brahma-Sūtra* 2.1.15, he attributes to these thinkers the view that the *brahman* is the primary cause – an entity that is undifferentiated Being possessed of every potentiality. Prior to the emanation of the cosmos it is self-luminous consciousness that is distinct from the insentient and in which all experiences, pleasant and painful, are stilled. But during the cosmic emanation, it exists in tripartite mode as experiencers, objects of experience and the controller. Because of the continuity between cause and effects and the non-difference between the *brahman* and the cosmos, all the good and bad features of the produced cosmos affect the *brahman*.

Proto-Vedānta from a Buddhist perspective: The description of Vedānta in Bhāviveka's *Madhyamakahṛdaya*

> 1 How is freedom [from rebirth] possible for those who say that there are no permanent identities, and that all conditioned entities are empty of intrinsic nature?

2 After contemplating the transcendent principle (*puruṣa*) beyond the darkness and radiant like the sun – the Maheśvara (Śiva) – a wise man survives death.
3 When seeing the golden one, he will see that God is the creator. Putting aside merit and demerit, he will attain equality (with Śiva).
4 All things past, present and future are included in the *puruṣa*.

He is within, without, near and far. As such he is the agent, the maker of all.

5 All entities are produced from him, like threads from a spider. Wise men are dissolved in him and do not enter upon another existence.
6 What is mortal cannot become immortal. Hence immortality is impossible unless one has awakened to the immortal *puruṣa*.
7 The cosmos is rolled out by the one first principle which is the unsurpassedly great being.
9 In that *puruṣa* (causal substrate and principle), all elements come into being. For the one who sees that reality, there is equality between learned and ignorant, between Brahmin and outcaste.
10 When a pot is produced or destroyed, the space it contains does not acquire those characteristics. Bodies are subject to birth and death, but souls are exempt from those processes.
11 If you say that the one is diversified if it is like the space in pots, the reply is that the space is not differentiated: although the pots are different individuals, the one space is the same for all.
12 Although the pots be different, the clay is the same.
13 Just as a single space contained by a pot becomes polluted by dust and smoke without that applying to space as a whole, so people have different experiences.
14 It is because he is unawakened that the one who does not know the soul collects *karma* and enjoys the welcome and unwelcome consequences – like the misconception during dreaming that the experiences are genuine.
15 Although embodied he is not sullied when he enjoys experiences as long as he is not attached. Like a king taking his pleasure, he is innocent of wrong-doing.

16 When a self-controlled yogin knows the *brahman* as one, omnipresent, eternal, transcendent and imperishable, he is not reborn.
17 It is eternal and beyond concepts, but words are applied to it by those whose minds are beguiled by differences.

Further reading

Nakamura (1983).

Note

1. v. Oberhammer (1997).

11

Advaita Vedānta

Chapter Outline

Liberating gnosis and disengagement from the world

Śaṃkara, who with his contemporary Maṇḍana Miśra was one of the founding fathers of Advaita Vedānta, probably lived around 700 A.D. His major work is a commentary on the *Brahma-Sūtras*. He also wrote commentaries on the *Bhagavad Gītā* and on individual Upaniṣads. Among the many other works attributed to him by the Advaita tradition, the 'Thousand Teachings' or *Upadeśa-Sāhasrī* stands out. His vision is that of the radical renouncer, which ultimately calls into question the values of mainstream orthodoxy by denying that there are any real individual thinkers, agents and acts.[1]

There is no question that Śaṃkara was an original genius, but it should be mentioned that the Advaitic tradition traces itself back to Gauḍapāda who probably lived around 450–500 A.D. and wrote the *Āgama-śāstra* about the *Māṇḍūkya Upaniṣad*. He likened the phenomenology of normal experience to that of dreaming and claimed that in both cases it is only the fact of consciousness that remains constant. Individual entities (*bhāva*) are mental constructs (*kalpanā*). The one Supreme Soul, the waveless absolute, imagines itself as conscious individuals.[2]

Gauḍapāda's contemporary, the grammarian Bhartṛhari, taught the 'non-dualism of meaning' (*śabda-advaita*). The idea is that the diversified phenomenal cosmos ('the proliferation of names and forms') is the emanation from a unitary sonic Absolute not of things but of meanings. It is the appearance of the transcendent 'meaning-reality' (*śabda-tattva*), otherwise known as the *brahman*. The absolute Being appears to transform itself through its innate powers into meanings, words and sentences. Words and what they mean are identical. The differentiated world of our experience is a product of diversification by language. Reality is a matrix of differentiated meanings rather than things or objects. Ignorance (*avidyā*), our default position as it were, is a function of linguistic proliferation into individual words and propositions. It consists in understanding the world in terms of the individual entities that are the referents of words and resting content at that level. Bhartṛhari's linguistic idealism exercised a considerable influence on Maṇḍana Miśra as well as on the monistic Śaiva traditions.[3]

Advaita means non-dualism or monism. Monism is the doctrine that reality is of only one kind. According to Advaita, the unconditioned reality (the *brahman*) is the coincidence of being, consciousness and bliss (*saccidānanda*). Central to Śaṃkara's position are the distinctions between being and becoming, and between gnosis and ignorance. Authentic reality that is eternal, uniform and unchanging is contrasted with the change, agency and multiplicity that characterizes everyday experience.

Vedānta is the systematic exegesis of the Upaniṣads, those parts of the infallible and authorless Vedic Scriptures (*śruti*), which according to orthodox Vedic Brahmins are the sole means of knowing (*pramāṇa*) about anything beyond sense-perception and inference. In short, the Scriptures are the only way of knowing about the *brahman*, soul (*ātman*) and the way to release from rebirth. The founders of the different Vedāntic schools understood themselves as interpreters of the Upaniṣads and the *Bhagavad Gītā*, and as expositors of the epitomes of the Upaniṣadic teachings called the *Brahma-Sūtras*.[4]

Advaitins say that the essential teaching of the Upaniṣads is that our experience of a differentiated world of conscious and non-conscious individual entities is really a gigantic misconception superimposed upon the undifferentiated and inactive *brahman* or Pure Being. That foundational reality is nothing other than the coincidence of Being and tranquil consciousness. Liberation is just the cessation of the ignorance or misconception (*avidyā*) that is responsible for our experiencing reality as fragmented and our misunderstanding ourselves as individual experiencers and agents. While religious activities, ritual and meditative, purify the mind and distract us from selfish pursuits, they cannot produce enlightenment and liberation from rebirth *directly*.

For Advaitins, the focal teaching of the Upaniṣads is that one's true nature (*ātman*) is the same as undifferentiated pure being (the *brahman*), understood as tranquil consciousness undisturbed by differences. But reality and truth are obscured by ignorance: an ignorance that generates the illusions of individuality and differentiation. Individual entities are constructs, limiting conditions (*upādhi*) superimposed upon the foundational conscious reality. Liberation (*mokṣa*) from rebirth (*saṃsāra*) means an intuitive realization of the coincidence of featureless being and tranquil consciousness. Liberation is just the elimination of mistaken thinking in terms of differentiation and the immediate realization that one's true nature is nothing other than tranquil, transcendental consciousness. Advaita is a gnostic tradition: intuitive knowledge will set you free from bondage to a cosmos that is a function of beginningless ignorance. It is the repudiation of religion as a set of beliefs and practices, and as a path to a goal that can be attained by means of rituals or devotion to deities.

At the beginning of his commentary on the *Bhagavad Gītā*, Śaṃkara gives mythic voice to an opposition that has been thought by some to be the key to understanding Indian religion.[5] That opposition is manifested in the dialogue between 'the man in the world' who gains merit by following the public Vedic religion (*dharma*) of ritual acts and social duties, and the renouncer who has disengaged himself from religious practices and social involvement in order to pursue his own salvation through gnosis (*jñāna*).

> The Lord produced the cosmos, and desiring to establish its perpetuation, he first created the Lords of Creatures and gave them the active path of social

> and religious duties (*pravṛtti-dharma*) that is sanctioned by the Vedas. Then he made others, and gave them the path consisting in the renunciation of ritual acts and social duties (*nivṛtti-dharma*) that is characterised by *gnosis* and dispassion.... The aim of the teaching of the Gītā is the Supreme Good, understood as the final cessation of rebirth and its causes. The Supreme Good arises from commitment to intuiting one's true nature (*ātma jñāna*), preceded by the renunciation (*saṃnyāsa*) of all ritual acts and social duties. The religion of activity is prescribed for members of castes and stages of life who are intent on prosperity and it may be the cause of the attainment of the world of the gods. When practiced in an attitude of devotion to a personal godhead, without any interest in the benefits of ritual acts, it produces purity of mind. The pure minded person approaches the efficient cause of the attainment of the Supreme Good – that cause being the onset of *gnosis* expressed in the enlightened mode of living.[6]

Śaṃkara was one of those who followed the way of renunciation of ritual and social engagement. This is the tradition of those who deny that extroverted religious activity can of itself deliver liberation from rebirth. Enlightenment arises from intuitive insight unmediated by thoughts and words, into the identity of one's inner nature (*pratyag-ātman*) and the *brahman*. This is the mystical realization of the equation of Being and Consciousness. It is the manifestation of what one always and already is. While insight obliterates all experience of differentiation and individuality, vestiges of such experience persist in the life of the enlightened one, who is 'liberated while alive' (*jīvan-mukta*) until his release at death.[7] One response on the part of the man who has seen the light is the renunciation of all ritual acts as well as all everyday responsibilities and obligations. Śaṃkara's radical vision is that of the world renouncer (*saṃnyāsin*) who rejects the view that liberation is the fruit of a combination of actions and gnosis. His contemporary Maṇḍana Miśra is more concerned with integrating liberating gnosis into the everyday life of the householder. He recognizes that renouncing social ties and the shared religion is not an easy option. He says that the Vedic rituals purify the mind and prepare the way for realization of one's true identity as the *brahman*. Understanding of that identity, conveyed by scripture, is intensified by ritual and contemplation that counteract the still forceful traces of the pluralistic mentality. He recommended the repetitive type of meditation called *prasaṃkhyāna* as a means of removing moral defects and hindrances (*kleśa*) and as a way of internalizing the Upaniṣadic statements conveying non-duality.

One of Śaṃkara's primary concerns is the justification of the path of detachment and inactivity in the face of mainstream Brahminical orthodoxy, which holds that it is the ritual actions of select human agents that keep the cosmos going. But Śaṃkara was also a mystic. The meditator absorbed in profound contemplation and isolated from the world of experience has neither thoughts nor feelings. There is just motionless, undifferentiated awareness that does not seek to accomplish any purposes. This is the state that Advaitins call 'pure consciousness' or 'mere knowing'. It knows no fluctuations and is neither directed towards nor about objects. It is not consciousness *of* anything, and it has no specific content. It is blissful, for it lacks nothing. There is no sense of selfhood or personal individuality: there is merely *being conscious*. This is the authentic reality, the *brahman*, the coincidence of being and blissful consciousness. It is on this non-discursive experience that Advaita is founded. This is the experience that is meant by Upaniṣadic statements such as '*tat tvam asi*' and 'I am the *brahman*', which Advaitins interpret as asserting the identity of the *brahman* and the *ātman*.[8] When the practitioner emerges from the state of absorption, the world around him with all its frustrations, its changes and chances, means and ends, seems thin, frustrating and unsubstantial. The Advaitin rejection of the categories of differentiation, relation, change and individual substance can be seen as flowing from a serene and self-authenticating contemplative experience in which one's sense of personal individuality and agency are obliterated. The construction of personhood and our sense thereof (*ahaṃkāra* – lit. 'I-maker') as well as our engagement with a diversified material world are attributed to the work of beginningless ignorance (*avidyā*). Broadly speaking, ignorance can either mean simply not knowing something or other, or it can mean being mistaken. The latter sense includes not just everyday mistakes about this and that but also fundamental misconceptions about the nature of the world, and of oneself. It is that sense with which the tradition is concerned. Encouraged by the tradition's use of metaphors comparing everyday experience to a mirage, to things seen in dreams, to a rope mistaken for a snake or mother of pearl taken for silver, there is a tendency to Advaita as 'illusionism'. But this is to take the metaphors literally. The description, however, is apt if it is understood as meaning that nothing in the world that we inhabit and know *really matters* since all unenlightened experience is conditioned by innate misunderstanding. The extent to which the vision is subversive of mainstream Brahminical orthodoxy must be emphasized. It follows from Advaitin premises that the beliefs that life is *saṃsāra* subject to *karma*, that the Vedas can point us to the summum bonum, and that caste distinctions are important are all mistaken.

Why do we encounter a diverse cosmos? Why do we think that we are individual embodied conscious agents? In the first part of his *Upadeśa-Sāhasrī*, Śaṃkara says that the *brahman*, unchanging in itself, activates a non-conscious world-creative principle that depends upon it. This primary substrative cause is called 'undeveloped name and form' (*nāma-rūpa*), and it is inexpressible (*anirvacanīya*) as this or that, as one thing or another. This is because entities have not yet been actualized, and there is nothing that could be identified. In the subsequent tradition, this idea will be reformulated as 'inexpressible as being or not-being' and will be taken in a variety of ways to mean that the world and its cause is ontologically indeterminable. Later writers will say that *avidyā* means the causal principle of the cosmos. When Śaṃkara describes 'name and form' as 'having the nature of *avidyā*' he just means that it is other than consciousness. From the substrative cause emanate the basic elements constituting the differentiated cosmos – where things with determinate identities can be called 'this' or 'that'. Śaṃkara holds that the products (*vikāra*) of the primordial causal substrate are less than fully real (*anṛta*). In other words, they are not the authentic reality or the 'genuine article'.[9] Whatever the sense in which the cosmos proceeds from its source, the source is unchanged. The *brahman* cannot change. If it did, it could not be a fully accomplished or perfect reality because it would always be becoming something else, becoming what it was not.

Inexplicably, there is the universal delusion, present prior to any possible experience of the world, that the one true purely conscious nature (*ātman* identical with the *brahman*) is divided into individual centres of consciousness, attached to bodies and social status, and actively engaged with an objective and differentiated world. As such, we misunderstand ourselves as different from the *brahman* and in our innate ignorance (*avidyā*) are subject to transmigration and all our woe. Śaṃkara is not really interested in questions about the ontological status of *avidyā*. To the question, 'to whom does it belong?', he replies, 'you, the questioner who does not know'. All our everyday secular and religious transactions (*vyavahāra*) that involve thinking in terms of individual subjects, objects and relations, agents, actions and results are infected by error. It follows that ritual and salvific gnosis are incompatible. Belief in the efficacy of ritual presupposes that an event (*kriyā*), the multiple factors (*kāraka*) of agency and action of which it is comprised, and its result are independent entities connected by relations. But gnosis concerns only the featureless absolute consciousness, knowledge of which reveals that the plurality of factors implicit in ritual action is the work of *avidyā*.

In the introduction to his *Brahma-Sūtra-Bhāṣya*, Śaṃkara defines the existential ignorance (*avidyā*) that is natural to the human condition as 'mutual superimposition' (*itaretara-adhyāsa*). He basically means by this the misattribution of the properties of one thing to something else, typified by false memories. More elaborately, it is the superimposition of the purely conscious internal sphere onto what is objective, insentient and mutable, and the reverse superimposition of the objective sphere onto consciousness, the inner identity and the detached witness of all experiences. Mutual superimposition is the misconception that one's true nature (*ātman*) is other than it is. This happens when the reflection of the radiant light of consciousness is captured in the mind (*buddhi*), which is both material and active. The mind assumes the character of consciousness, as a crystal assumes the colour of a proximal object, and the per se unchanging consciousness appears to become active. The basic case of mutual superimposition is self-understanding as an individual centre of consciousness and agency (*ahaṃkāra*), and self-misidentification as an embodied person having a caste status. Furthermore, there is the misconception that the accumulation of merit and demerit through the performance of intentional actions really influences one's true nature. The superimposition of the subjective on the objective occurs when we attribute consciousness to the activities of the material mental apparatus. This beginningless and endless innate practice of superimposition, whose nature is misconception, causes agency and enjoyment of finite experiences. It is the precondition of all secular and religious activities, of all behaviour (*vyavahāra*) involving means of knowing (*pramāṇa*) and knowable objects, and of all the Scriptures whether concerned with ritual injunctions or even liberation from rebirth. In everyday life (*vyavahārika*) where what are ultimately false beliefs are current, the world is treated as differentiated, and the distinctions between knowers and what is knowable, experiences and what is experienced, agents, actions and outcomes are taken for granted. Given that Scripture is recognized as *pramāṇa* and if the *pramāṇas* belong to the arena of *avidyā*, how can it convey knowledge about the *brahman*? The answer is that the existence of the *brahman*, a state of pure knowing (*jñapti-mātra*), is self-revealing and self-established and thus needs no *pramāṇa*. In any case, the *pramāṇas* yield intellectual '*knowledge that*' rather than the liberating experience that transforms one's view of reality and one's way of living. The purpose of scriptural exegesis is primarily to demonstrate that Advaita does not conflict with the *śrutis*. It is not to be expected, however, that Śaṃkara seriously entertained the possibility that the liberating awareness, that is unmediated experience of the *brahman*, could happen for one who was not familiar with the Advaita-*śrutis*. His position seems to have been that the liberating awareness happens to one who has reflected upon and internalized certain *śrutis* and whose mentality has been purified thereby. In short, scripture prepares the ground for liberating experience, although it does not bring it about.

The intuition of one's true nature or identity (*ātman*) *happens to* one who had formerly mistakenly understood himself as a centre of experience and agency, one whose mental life is a stream of ever-changing perceptions of and affective responses to external objects and who had deemed himself subject to caste-duties and ritual obligations. The intuition reveals that one's everyday sense of individual personality (*ahaṃkāra*) as the centre of that arena conceals our true nature as tranquil, objectless consciousness. It reveals that one is not essentially an individual agent of actions. The existential transformation occurs simultaneously with the non-discursive awareness, 'I am the *brahman*'. This knowledge obliterates *karma* and prevents the accumulation of fresh *karma*. Such is the condition of one who is liberated while still alive (*jīvan-mukta*), one who is the witness of rather than a participant in the stream of mental events and mundane transactions. The *brahman*'s being the true nature of beings who wrongly believe themselves to be individual agents is an already established fact. Knowledge of the *brahman*, like all knowledge, depends upon something already given as a reality. Liberation is not an achievement. It is not something that is brought about by religious strivings. It is simply the removal of an unenlightened mentality and thus does not require, indeed is antithetical to, anything that might be regarded as religious praxis since the latter presupposes mistaken belief in the reality of differentiation, of means and ends. Gnostic insight destroys error and reveals the truth that one is nothing other than permanently unchanging and non-intentional or 'pure' consciousness. The permanent background consciousness, one's true nature, both establishes its own existence and is always revealed as the unchanging witness of changing mental states. Everything other than consciousness needs consciousness for its revelation or manifestation by the means of knowledge. But consciousness is unique in that it needs nothing outside itself. It is simply given and undeniable, for only consciousness can deny anything. It is not subject to temporal limitations, for it may have a perspective on past, present and future all at once and is thus eternal. It is not limited by external objects, for it can imagine that things are other than they are. Once the scriptural teaching that the *brahman* is one's true nature is internalized, the misconception that there are individual selves with their own identities no longer operates. On that constitutive misconception was founded the belief that the entire matrix of worldly life (*vyavahāra*) has its own self-sufficient reality. With the removal of the primary misconception, that of the second follows.

Difference means limitation, so it cannot characterize the primal, unconditioned reality. The *brahman* is the transcendental precondition of there being anything at all. It transcends the determinations characteristic of finite beings. It is prior to all oppositions such as subject and object, knower and known, cause and effect. It has no features (*nirguṇa*) and is exempt from actions and changes (*niṣkriyā*). Since it neither owes its existence to anything else nor is conditioned by anything outside itself, it is beyond the categories of being and non-being if these are thought of as pertaining only to property-bearing entities that belong to kinds. It follows that the *brahman* eludes conceptual or linguistic description because the foundational reality is not *a being* or *a something* distinguishable from other finite things. This understanding of *ātman* and the *brahman* repudiates an already established tradition of emanationist Vedāntic theological interpretation called *pariṇāma-vāda* that posits a single, self-transforming divine substance that really constitutes itself as all individual souls and material entities.

Śaṃkara's via negativa

While the *brahman* per se cannot be signified by words for kinds, actions, attributes or relations, it may be approached along the path of negation by denials of what it is not. A sophisticated variety of the *via negativa* can be found in Śaṃkara's commentary on the statement in *Taittirīya Upaniṣad* 2.1.1: 'The *brahman* is reality, consciousness, infinite' ('*satyaṃ jñānam anantaṃ brahma*'). Some Vedāntins construe this as meaning that the *brahman* has features – it is *saguṇa* rather than *nirguṇa* – and thus is not simple. Śaṃkara thinks that when properly understood, the *śruti* makes an identifying reference to the *brahman* without implying that it is complex. It does this because the three grammatical predicates are used definitionally, as three different names of the same thing, rather than descriptively. He says that descriptively used predicates distinguish something from other members of the same class, while definitionally used ones demarcate their subject from everything else. The predicates are used to exclude their normal meanings and function together to intimate the *brahman*, even though it is really beyond the range of linguistic meanings. Śaṃkara resolves the *śruti* into three distinct identity statements: 'The *brahman* is reality.' 'The *brahman* is consciousness.' 'The *brahman* is infinite.' The statement has a simple sense (*akhaṇḍārtha*). The three descriptions, albeit functioning in different ways, name the same thing – the foundational reality that is infinite consciousness.

Śaṃkara begins by stipulating that something is real when it does not deviate from the form that is known to be its own. So by definition, the real is constant and immutable. Something is called unreal when it does deviate from its proper form. Hence, modifications are unreal. The definition, 'the *brahman* is reality' excludes modifications from the nature of the *brahman*. It also means that the *brahman* is the ultimate cause of the cosmos. Now the theory of causation termed *satkāryavāda* – the idea that effects pre-exist as potentialities in their causal substrate prior to their actualization – suggests that effects are ontologically continuous with their causal substrate. This may be taken as implying that substrative causes share the nature of their effects. Given that the effected cosmos is in part material, the impression may follow that the *brahman* contains *in potentia* elements of materiality. Hence it is said that 'The *brahman* is consciousness.' Śaṃkara says that the word (*jñānam*) for consciousness here has a stative sense of pure awareness (*jñaptimātram*), when it applies to the *brahman*.

The definition 'The *brahman* is infinite' excludes the possibility that the sort of knowing predicated of the *brahman* is ordinary cognitive agency that involves diversification by particular cognitions and objects of cognition. So when the 'knowing' is being used as a definition of the unchanging *brahman*, this is in an extraordinary sense different from the everyday meanings that are derived from the root sense of the verb. Śaṃkara explains the everyday process of cognition of which the soul (*ātman*) is the unchanging witness as follows: The embodied mind (*buddhi*), a limiting condition (*upādhi*) wrongly superimposed upon the *ātman*, becomes informed by sense-mediated phenomena such as sounds and colours. When those phenomena are irradiated by the light of the *ātman*-consciousness, they become its objects. Such limited presentations to the *ātman*-consciousness are what are usually meant by words for awareness and knowing. They are the root meanings of the verb 'to know'. It is such changing events that are wrongly supposed by the unenlightened to be real properties of the *ātman*.

'Infinite' also means that the sort of reality attributed to the *brahman* is unconditioned by space and time. The *brahman* is also infinite or unlimited in respect of its ontological status. Its reality is not like that of entities that belong to kinds and which are the possessors of various properties such that they may be spoken of as different from one another. For example, a cow is not a horse and vice versa. Also, individuals within each kind differ in respect of their physical characteristics. Differences of that kind cannot apply to the *brahman*. On the other hand, the *brahman* is said to be 'not other' than everything else (*sarvānanyatvam brahmaṇaḥ*) since it is the substrative cause of all entities. Does this mean that the *brahman* is the same as the cosmos? It does not. Rather it means that the *brahman* does not differ from finite entities because it has nothing in common with them. A cow and a horse share the nature of animality and differ because they are varieties of it. A man can be taller than another in respect of height. Red things differ from green ones in respect of their shared nature of being coloured. But there is no shared nature in respect of which the *brahman* may differ from the world of entities. It is in this sense that it is 'not other' than everything else.

It might be wondered how statements such as 'I am the *brahman*' and '*Tat tvam asi*' mean the identity of the *brahman* and the *ātman* given that the personal pronouns usually designate embodied centres of agency, thinking and feeling. Śaṃkara says that when they are purified of such connotations and used in grammatical co-ordination with terms signifying the absolute Being, they can discriminate a simple immaculate state. For instance, reflection on the pronoun 'I' may lead to an intellectual conclusion that the embodied ego is not the soul because it is objectifiable, and nothing that one can objectify can be one's true identity. We shall see below that such modifications are seen as illegitimate by those who interpret the Scriptures theistically and claim to be following their literal senses.

Maṇḍana Miśra

The other founding father of Advaita Vedānta, Śaṃkara's contemporary Maṇḍana Miśra, author of the *Brahmasiddhi*, concurs that our true nature is identical with the *brahman* that is other than conditioned reality, pure consciousness, blissful, unique, imperishable and ungenerated. He says that if the source is undifferentiated, so must be its products. All plurality is a function of beginningless innate error (*avidyā*). While Śaṃkara tends to characterize the *brahman* as 'pure consciousness', Maṇḍana prefers to formulate it as a unity of undifferentiated being that is also the universal identity common to all things.[10] The absolute Being is given as such in every act of pre-conceptual, pre-discursive perception. Initial perceptual experience is non-conceptual and relates only to being as such. It is the ensuing conceptual cognitions that comprehend particularities. Everyday thinking, which prompts activity and presupposes that there are real differences between individual entities, is mental construction (*vikalpa*). Constructive cognitions or representations (*avabhāsa*) that involve differentia and oppositions are erroneous (*bhrānti*) in that they disguise rather than disclose the nature of pure being. The organizing structures of our minds ('this is different from that', 'this is the difference between the two') derive from an inherited beginningless supply of constructive ideas. Maṇḍana argues that no sense can be made of the notion of difference as an entity, either substantive or attributive, in its own right. Difference, and hence the finite individuality of demarcated entities, is not substantial (*niḥsvabhāva*) and does not enter into the fabric of reality. It is simply manifested by constructive thoughts and language, and as such cannot be truly real. The world of differentiated individual entities is a fabrication, manifested due to beginningless error (*anādi-avidyā*). Like Śaṃkara he thinks that it is the ultimately unreal individual selves, mistakenly constructing themselves as centres of awareness and agency different from the *brahman*, that are the bearers of *avidyā*. Its object (*viṣaya*) is the *brahman*, whose nature we misunderstand if we view it as the source of real plurality. By contrast, most later Advaitins following Padmapāda (700–750 A.D.) and his contemporary Sureśvara say that *avidyā* is a causal force, analogically called *māyā* (illusion – it is what the magician produces), responsible for the complex, shared virtual reality that is the cosmos, and that it is a power (*śakti*) of the *brahman*. But Maṇḍana says that it is the individual identities (*jīva*) that are polluted by error, not the *brahman* that is always pure and constant light. Maṇḍana thinks that there is a mystery here, since the very constitution of individuality is a case of *avidyā*. But he is explicit that if error belonged to the *brahman*'s nature, it would never cease and there would be no possibility of release from rebirth. Moreover, it would be the *brahman* that transmigrates and the *brahman* that is released from rebirth. Further, the release of one would entail the release of all, because by seeing plurality it is just the *brahman* that transmigrates and by seeing non-difference it is released. Hence it is the individuals transmigrating due to error that are released by knowledge.

After c.950 A.D., two schools of thought about this question appear. One is called the *Bhāmatī* school, named after Vācaspati Miśra's (950–1000 A.D.)

commentary on Śaṃkara's *Brahma-Sūtra-Bhāṣya*, and the other is called the *Vivaraṇa* school, named after Prakāśātman's commentary on Padmapāda's *Pañcapādikā*. The *Bhāmatī* school follows Maṇḍana and says that it is the individual selves that are the substrate of *avidyā* and that the *brahman* is its object. There is a problem here. How can the individual selves be the substrate or support of *avidyā* when the experience of individual selfhood is itself a product of *avidyā*? They do not exist in advance, unaffected by ignorance, in such a way that they could be its substrate. Rather, they are constituted by ignorance. The response is simply that the association between individuals and *avidyā* is beginningless. In other words, it is something for which there is no explanation. The *Vivaraṇa* school says that since the *brahman* is the sole reality, it has to be both the substrate and the object of *avidyā*. In this they can appeal to the authority of Sureśvara, who makes the point that since the *jīva* is a product of *avidyā*, it cannot be its support. But is it not a contradiction to hold that the *brahman*, which is pure knowing, is the very basis of ignorance? The reply is that the problem is only apparent. The *brahman* is the substratum of error only in the sense that it is the substratum of all cognition and the precondition of all subjective and objective experiences. One might suggest that the view of Sureśvara, Sarvajñātman, Padmapāda, Prakāśātman and their followers to the effect that the *brahman* is both the substrate and the object of *avidyā* is an aspect of a mentality that understands cosmic variety, whose nature and occurrence is mysterious, as ultimately having a transcendent source. The alternative view, articulated by Maṇḍana and Vācaspati Miśra is perhaps more inclined to blame the tendency of imperfect beings to conceive themselves as separate from the source of their being.

Śaṃkara had applied the expression 'inexpressible (*anirvacanīya*) as one thing or another' to the amorphous primary causal state that is prior to the differentiation of names and forms. Maṇḍana modifies the formula to mean 'inexpressible as real or unreal' and applies it to *avidyā* and its consequences. He says that error is neither the nature of the *brahman* nor is it anything else. It is not absolute non-being, like a pure fiction, because erroneous cognitions (*bhrānti*) occur and have practical consequences. But it is not an authentic reality because errors are corrected. Were it real in an absolute sense, it would never cease, and liberation would be impossible. It would be another reality in addition to the *brahman* – indeed, one that is antithetical to the nature of the *brahman*. But were we to say that it is non-existent, it would be difficult to explain the phenomenon of bondage to rebirth and our everyday experience of practical transactions (*vyavahāra*). To count as real, something must have a determinate identity. But that is what error lacks, and hence it is indeterminable as real or unreal. Maṇḍana thinks that to be inexpressible is to be unintelligible and that what is unintelligible cannot be authentically real. We see here the origin of what will become the established principle that the working of *avidyā* and the very occurrence of the differentiated cosmos are essentially mysterious. Evidently, any philosophy saying that the complex world (including persons), as we know it, is the consequence of error and that the authentic reality is simple consciousness is bound to acknowledge that the occurrence of error is a mystery. Cognitive errors are also mysterious in the sense that until they are corrected by knowledge, they seem perfectly real and are accepted as true for the time being. The magician's illusions are convincing while they last. Dreams are only recognized for what they are from the standpoint of the waking state. There is the phenomenon of 'brainwashing' or the spontaneous social construction of myths that condition the minds, language, behaviour and purposeful activities of almost everyone. Cultures entertain long-standing beliefs that turn out to be false, but they enabled people to inhabit the world. Such cases of operative false beliefs or uncontradicted assumptions about the nature of things, the tradition will call '*saṃvṛti-satya*' or '*vyavahārika-satya*'. Those expressions mean provisional, conventional and everyday reality in contradistinction to some conception of fundamental reality. The argument that the success of everyday beliefs requires only an ultimately false *assumption* that reality is as it ordinarily appears to us – an argument primarily directed at the Nyāya-Vaiśeṣika realists, who maintain that knowledge is only knowledge if it refers to a structured domain of objects existing prior to and independently of cognition – will be developed by Śrī Harṣa (1125–1180 A.D.) in his *Khaṇḍanakhaṇḍakhādya*. It should be noted that after Prakāśātman, most Advaitins are careful to distinguish the fictions and illusions (*prātibhāsika*) from long-standing uncontradicted false beliefs.

Śaṃkara insists that gnosis is both necessary and sufficient for release from rebirth, an existential transformation that may be the condition of one still living (*jīvan-mukti*). Indeed, for him continued engagement with religious practices of any sort is antithetical to enlightenment. (The matter is elaborately dealt with in the commentary on *Brahma-Sūtra* 1.1.4.) By contrast, Maṇḍana believes that the repeated practice (*abhyāsa*) of ritual actions and meditation on one's discursive understanding of the *mahāvākyas* are useful in that they intensify the insights received from those scriptural statements of non-duality and counteract the still forceful residual traces of ignorance. This difference between the two seminal figures will remain controversial in the subsequent tradition, for it concerns the questions of the role of scripture and whether basically linguistic understanding that occurs within the arena of *avidyā* can produce enlightenment. There is also the more general question about the importance of religious practices: the 'radicals' follow Śaṃkara and hold that the observance of obligatory ritual duties is unnecessary for the enlightened person, while those of a more conservative disposition say that the performance of social and religious duties is still required.

Padmapāda, Prakāśātman, Vimuktātman and Sarvajñātman

Padmapāda belonged to the generation after Śaṃkara and composed the *Pañcapādikā* on the first five parts of his mentor's *Brahma-Sūtra-Bhāṣya.* Whereas Śaṃkara had understood not knowing (*avidyā*) as error and the confusion of one's true identity with what it is not, Padmapāda is innovative in treating *avidyā* as a basic metaphysical category when he says that it is the power of misconception in the transcendental consciousness that appears as the objective world. He also introduces the terminology of *vivarta* (phenomenal manifestation), expressing the idea that effects are less real (*viṣama-sattā*) than their causal substrate (*upādāna*). This will be interpreted as meaning that the cosmos is an apparent transformation of its cause rather than a real one (*pariṇāma-vāda*) where the effects have the same degree of reality as their substrative cause.[11] Basically, we see here the idea that what truly is – the coincidence of being and consciousness – appears as something other than what it is. This notion of *vivarta* is congruent with the idea that the world and its source are inexpressible as one thing or another. From the point of view of the *brahman*, the cosmos is false or unreal (*mithyā*), but from our point of view it *exists*. This leads naturally to the formulation that *avidyā* and its works are indeterminable as real or unreal. The notion of falsity (*mithyātva*) is perhaps evaluative rather than primarily ontological. To say that the physical and mental domain with all its changes, imperfections and limits is false is to say that it is not authentically real or that in the final analysis *it is not what really matters*. This is not to deny that it exists. It seems that this is what they are trying to capture in the formulations that the world and its source are neither real nor unreal.

Padmapāda says that the *brahman* is the root cause on the basis of which the proliferated cosmos 'unfurls' or appears (*vivartate*). The pure *brahman* is the substrate of the appearance of the infinite number of individual centres of experience (*jīva*) that are constituted due to beginninglessly established *avidyā*. It is *avidyā* that is responsible for phenomenal plurality, and *avidyā* is a power (*śakti*) of the *brahman*. It is sometimes called '*māyā*'. He characterized *avidyā* as a non-conscious (*jaḍa*) principle. The rationale is that if *avidyā* is other than *vidyā* and *vidyā* has the nature of consciousness, then *avidyā* cannot be conscious. We might consider here the familiar modern claim that there are non-conscious, or sub-conscious, psychological functions, over which we have no control. Perhaps the Advaitins would be prepared to put natural and inherited *avidyā* in this category. This causal *avidyā* is the substrative cause of both the world-appearance and of mundane cases of misconceptions. *Avidyā* thus construed veils the luminous nature of the *brahman*-nature present in the mistaken construction that is the individual soul. In association with the workings of *karma* and the mental apparatus, it produces the experience of limited selfhood that is the substrate of individual experience and agency. Śaṃkara had identified *avidyā* (error) as the mutual superimposition of the subjective and the objective. It is a universal human failure, a constitutive imperfection in human nature. But for Padmapāda, it is rather the cause of the notion of the individual ego, of the process of superimposition and of all misconceptions. Most significantly perhaps, we see here the first statement of the view, rejected by Maṇḍana and Śaṃkara, that it is the *brahman* that is the ultimate substratum of *avidyā* and the consequent mistaken belief that we are individual personal agents.

The doctrine that the cosmos is a phenomenal manifestation (*vivarta*) of the transcendent *brahman*, understood as objectless, undifferentiated consciousness, when it is concealed by a power called *avidyā* becomes explicit in the works of the tenth-century thinkers Prakāśātman, Vimuktātman and Sarvajñātman. Prakāśātman (c.950 A.D.) wrote the *Vivaraṇa* on Padmapāda's *Pañcapādikā*, and developed that thinker's views. His most influential innovation is the reification of *avidyā* as something positive and effective (*bhāva-rūpa*), rather than as a privation of knowledge. Ignorance as something positive, as opposed to the mere absence of knowledge, is exemplified by cases where we recognize that we do not know some matter of fact. The example is held to explain that ignorance does not obliterate the light of consciousness. The point is that ignorance construed as such is not opposite in nature to knowledge. Hence it is compatible with it and will not be eliminated by the state of pure knowing that is the *brahman*.

Sarvajñātman (c.950 A.D.), the author of the *Saṃkṣepaśārīrakam* and the *Pañcaprakriyā*, explicitly states that the distinctive mark of monistic Vedānta is its view that the plural cosmos is a phenomenal manifestation (*vivarta*) of its causal substrate (*vedāntapakṣas tu vivartavādaḥ*), rather than a real transformation or self-differentiation of the one divine substance. He calls this phenomenal manifestation the 'state of *avidyā*'. When that obtains, the pure *brahman* appears to be the ultimate cause of cosmic plurality through the instrumentality of the principle of positive ignorance and its effects. That power of misconception depends upon the *brahman*, which is also its object. *Avidyā* has two functions: it conceals the nature of the absolute Being as the pure light of consciousness, and it projects phenomenal diversity. In the fifth chapter of the *Pañcaprakriyā*, Sarvajñātman propounds the theory that the pure *brahman* appears to be the efficient cause of the material cosmos, the presiding deity and the internal witness known to each individual conscious being. In other words, it appears to be diversified as the plural world, it appears to be the divine creator and regulator, and it appears to be the innermost constitutive element in the individual souls (*jīva*). The real inner nature (*pratyagātman*), which is nothing other than the purely conscious *brahman*, becomes individuated as a knower, an experiencer, an agent and as one who is subject to Vedic mandates in virtue of connection with the physical elements constituting the cosmos. The individual soul is just the *brahman* that is implicated in finite conditions (*brahmaiva saṃsarati*) due to its own *avidyā*, and it is the *brahman* that is released thanks to its own knowledge. The *saṃsāra* of the *brahman* means its being the substrate of the plural cosmos, its being the sovereign divinity and its being the individual souls. Liberation is the destruction of those conditions. *Avidyā* is held to 'belong' to the *brahman* that is its ultimate substrate, because otherwise it would be an independent 'rival' principle. It is only in virtue of its modality as the inner identity of the finite souls (*jīva*), its being the precondition of finite experiences, that the *brahman* is said to be the substrate of knowing and not knowing. He argues that the view that it is the *jīva* that is the ultimate subject of knowing and non-knowing lacks explanatory value, because the *jīvas* are constituted as such due to the workings of *avidyā*. In addition, the view that it is the finite selves that are the ultimate substrata of *avidyā* implies that they are realities in their own right, identities distinct from the *brahman*.

Vimuktātman (c.950 A.D.) wrote the *Iṣṭasiddhi*, where much attention is paid to discussions of cognitive error. The work contains a succinct statement of the monistic metaphysic: what is unreal never comes into being. Whatever is, is indestructible. Hence, being is always just being. Hence being never changes. Hence it does not show itself in virtue of a connection with anything else. Hence when it appears, it is self-luminous consciousness and free from duality. Hence, material things that are complex and changing are manifested due to *avidyā*. They seem as if real like things in dreams before one wakes up.

The first part of the *Iṣṭasiddhi* identifies the unconditioned reality (the *brahman*) as consciousness (*anubhūti*) that establishes its own existence. As such, it is independent of anything else (*an-anyādhīna*). We saw above that the undeniable fact of consciousness is unique in that while everything else requires consciousness for the revelation of its existence, consciousness does not need anything outside itself. Intrinsically reflexive consciousness is self-establishing. Vimuktātman argues that were consciousness ever the object of experience in the way in which physical objects such as pots are, its insentience would be entailed. He argues that what establishes its own existence exists necessarily. Hence it is unoriginated and exempt from modifications and cessation. What are perceived as different objects are not properties of consciousness. Being free from limitations, it cannot be measured (*ameya*). Having no finite properties, it is infinite. Finally, what is not originated can have no intrinsic parts because there is no possibility of composition out of pre-existing factors. Hence consciousness is simple. He continues to say that non-dual (*abheda*) consciousness is a single (*ekam*) reality that does not differ from anything else because there is nothing else. It is never the object of knowledge because that would entail its dependence upon something else and the denial that it is 'without a second'. As has been said, consciousness is self-revealing and self-establishing. Its singularity is not a property.

Some dazzling dialectic follows – a style of reasoning that will be deployed at great length and to great effect by Śrī Harṣa (1125–1180 A.D.) in his *Khaṇḍanakhaṇḍakhādya*. Vimuktātman argues that it is not possible to specify a difference between subject and object, between the perceiver and the perceived, because the former, being simply given but never perceived, cannot be identified in relation to anything else. The suggestion that the perceiver differentiates itself in virtue of its being self-revealing introduces a discussion about the nature of difference. If difference were the same as the essential nature as an entity, then it would not require correlatives. It would also follow that nothing would really be separate from everything else, entities effectively merging into one another. Difference understood as essential nature serves to only prove identity. If it cannot be the essence, it would be a property, and understood by a distinct mode of cognition: there would be 'difference-perception' parallel to taste-perception and colour-perception. But if 'being different' is a further real *property* (*dharma*) of an entity parallel to its colour etc., it would have to be different (another property) from its substrate. This would be to treat difference as an entity that is different from the entities that differ. Each case of difference would require the postulation of further differences. An infinite regress results, and the notion of difference becomes inexplicable. In the light of this, it is difficult to see how we could say that there is any difference between the perceiver and the perceived, between subjectivity and objectivity. The foundational reality of intrinsically reflexive consciousness is indubitably self-established. If there is no difference between consciousness and what is experienced, experienced diversity must have the nature of consciousness. But this seems to introduce variety and change into consciousness, which is supposed to be uniform. In response, Vimuktātman says that experiential variety is insubstantial or not truly real (*avastu*). Experiential variety is fabricated like a magical illusion (*māyā*): it is insubstantial, but we are still taken in. He uses an analogy in which permanent background consciousness is likened to a wall, and the manifold contents of experience are likened to a picture painted upon it. The wall does not contribute to the matter of the picture painted on it. The picture is not a modification of the wall in the way that pots are modifications of clay. Nor is it a change in the qualities of the wall. The wall was there before the picture and will remain after it has been washed away. But the painting needs the wall.

Experiential variety is attributed to an error-generating metaphysical power (*avidyā-śakti*). Its operation explains why there are experiences of matter and plurality when the truth is that reality is just pure consciousness. Neither the *avidyā-śakti* nor the world of experience that it produces is authentically real, nor are they non-existent. It is knowledge of the *brahman*, understood as the self-manifestation of transcendental pure consciousness that counteracts the *avidyā-śakti*, destroys misconceptions and leaves consciousness shining in its own radiance. For everyday purposes, the means of knowledge (*pramāṇa*) operate successfully in the sphere where oblivion of the truth of non-duality prevails. But since Scripture (*śruti*) is such a means of pseudo-knowledge, how can it reveal the truth? We see the answer here. The truth is self-revealing and needs no *pramāṇa*. Scripture as a means of knowing does not produce anything: it simply destroys misconceptions by conveying the falsity of the experience of duality. It does not need to tell us anything new.

Śrī Harṣa and his *Khaṇḍanakhaṇḍakhādya*

Śrī Harṣa denies that conceptual thought can reveal the truth, and he seeks to demolish the arguments of those who think that reason can establish the nature of a genuinely real mind-independent world. He does this by demonstrating that all the definitions of the means of knowing, varieties of correspondence theories of truth and basically real categories offered by realists are incoherent. Common sense revolts against the amazing Advaitin claim that authentic reality is tranquil undifferentiated consciousness. So he sets about demonstrating that the common-sense world view is infected by contradictions and cannot be true. Śrī Harṣa does not offer any 'theories' of his own, being content with the one unassailable truth that consciousness is the sole self-revealing and self-authenticating reality.

A typical line of argumentation runs like this: Difference may be understood as a sort of relation. But under analysis it can be seen as something that unites rather than separates. If two or more items are 'internally related', their being so connected is an aspect of their natures. Since the relation is a two-way affair, they are really united and not different. So the notion of internal relations leads to monism. If we say that relations are external, meaning that they connect two different items without affecting the natures of their terms, then it is not clear that they are really related at all. If we want to avoid this conclusion, we might say that relations are realities in their own right: a + R + b. But now we need other real relations to connect R to a and R to b. An infinite regress results, and it follows that nothing can ever be connected. So all relations are internal and monism must be true.

Scriptural exegesis and the significance of coreferential constructions

The Advaita tradition is inspired by certain Upaniṣadic passages suggestive of the identity of the soul and the absolute Being such as:

'You are That' (*Chāndogya Upaniṣad* 6.8.7: '*tat tvam asi*').

'In the beginning, all this was just Being, one only without a second' (*Chāndogya Upaniṣad* 6.2.1).

But many of the scriptures have a dualistic sense, some clearly suggesting a difference between the *brahman* and the individual souls and the cosmos, others talking in terms of distinct agents, instruments and goals that are aspects of external religious practices, and others obviously supposing that the Supreme Principle is a being with glorious characteristics. Advaita Vedānta draws a distinction between the ultimate authority of texts teaching non-difference and those that cannot possibly be construed in a non-dualistic fashion. While this may appear controversial, it is not unprecedented for the Mīmāṃsakas had already distinguished between those texts that prescribe actions (*vidhi*) and those that merely describe how and why to do things (*arthavāda*).

We have seen that Advaitins believe that some scriptures, such as 'That thou art' ('*Tat tvam asi*') and 'I am the *brahman*' ('*Ahaṃ brahma asmi*'), mean the featureless character of reality, and the identity of the soul and the *brahman*. Many of those statements have a grammatical form known as co-referentiality or grammatical co-ordination (*sāmānādhikaraṇya*). The grammarians define this as the reference to one thing of a number of words having different grounds for their application (*pravṛtti-nimitta*). The interpretation of such statements is central to Vedāntic theological dialectic. It is central because it is the language of the Scriptures (*śruti*) that provides the only means of knowledge of anything that transcends the bounds of sense-perception, and *a fortiori* inference. But language is often susceptible of different interpretations, so a philosopher's theory of meaning, of how language works and what verbal formulations convey to the understanding, will exercise a considerable influence on this metaphysics. The Advaitin position here is that certain scriptures, albeit on the surface exhibiting complex linguistic form, have a unitary simple meaning (*akhaṇḍārtha*) and thus convey a non-relational and featureless essence. Where the *sāmānādhikaraṇya* constructions are concerned, the Advaitins put the emphasis on the unity of reference and construe the coreferential constructions as statements of identity. They have a simple, impartite sense (*akhaṇḍārtha*). They maintain that this is compatible with the words' having different grounds for their operation. A distinction can be made between what a word or sentence refers to and the mode or modes under which it presents the referent. Their view is that an expression may include different such modes of presentation while signifying a single simple reality. They also appeal to a familiar distinction between what is usually, literally and primarily meant by words (*mukhyārtha*) and what is non-literally or secondarily indicated (*lakṣaṇā*) in order to explain how certain scriptural statements convey an undifferentiated essence, despite surface appearances. In certain circumstances, a non-literal interpretation of a statement is the only possible one. The stock examples illustrating non-literal usages are the expressions, 'Devadatta is a lion', whose purport (*tātparya*) of course indicates that he is brave, and 'The village on the Ganges', which indicates that it is on the bank of the river. In both cases, the literal sense is impossible and is thus suppressed. The impossibility or absurdity of the literal sense triggers a transference from the literal semantic content to a non-literal one.

The Advaitin theory is that in the case of coreferential constructions whose purport is an undifferentiated essence, incompatible primary senses are superseded in the process of semantic transference, while those aspects of the primary meanings that are compatible are retained. Advaitins such as Sarvajñātman and Prakāśātman say that coreferentiality is the non-literal reference (*lakṣaṇayā vṛtti*) to a single entity by means of the discrimination of the referent. The semantically modified terms in grammatical co-ordination are held to indicate obliquely a unitary sense (*akhaṇḍārtha*) and convey an undifferentiated essence. This form of partial oblique predication is technically termed '*jahadajahallakṣaṇā*'. They use the statement of identity about a person, 'This is that Devadatta' (*So'yaṃ Devadatta*), as an example of this non-literal semantic function. The demonstratives 'this' and 'that' primarily signify different times and places. So taken literally, the statement would mean something like, 'This man standing in front of me now is the same one whom I saw yesterday in the market.' They hold that the grammatical co-ordination of the two pronouns means simple essential identity (*svarūpaikyam*). For each to denote just the man Devadatta, purely referentially, the pronouns have to be understood non-literally. When the meaning components expressing the different times and places are eliminated, the terms corefer to the individual essence of Devadatta. In this way, the statement is understood as having a unitary sense.

This may be illustrated by examples from the second chapter of Sarvajñātman's *Pañcaprakriyā*. He says that release from rebirth follows only from understanding the meaning of the principal scriptural statements (*mahāvākya*) such as 'I am the *brahman*'. Understanding such a statement arises from discriminative knowledge of the meanings of the two terms 'I' and '*brahman*'. There are two sorts of meaning: the literal and usual (*vācya*), and what is non-literally indicated (*lakṣya*). The former is complex and the latter pure and simple. The word 'I' is complex in that it literally signifies both the inner conscious reality and the body, mind and senses with which it is wrongly associated. The word '*brahman*' is complex in that it literally signifies non-dual blissful consciousness when it is associated with the *avidyā* that is the causal substrate of embodiment. Because the non-dual blissful consciousness signified by the word '*brahman*' is imperceptibly associated with the inner conscious reality signified by the word 'I', the meanings of 'I' and '*brahman*' can be co-ordinated and refer to the same state (*sāmānādhikaraṇya*) without any conflict. This is because when the incompatible elements of meaning peculiar to each are eliminated, they both indicate (*lakṣyete*) a pure and simple meaning. When the connotations of embodiment are eliminated, the part of the meaning that is inner awareness is indicated by 'I'. By eliminating the meaning of causal *avidyā* that is responsible for embodiment, the word '*brahman*' indicates non-dual blissful consciousness. The coalescence of the suitably 'purified' indicated meanings produces a unitive experience that is described as the freedom enjoyed by one who is still alive in the world (*jīvan-mukta*).

In the case of '*Tat tvam asi*' ('That thou art'), which may be construed either as a relational statement or as one of identity, the two pronouns appear to differ in their literal senses. Accordingly, the Advaitin has to eliminate aspects of those meanings in order to secure an impartite sense. Sarvajñātman says that the word '*Tat*' literally expresses the *brahman* as associated with *avidyā* and hence understood as the cause of the cosmos. The personal pronoun '*tvam*' ('thou') usually means the individual self (*jīva*) that is misidentified with the body. But in another aspect of its meaning, it signifies the purely conscious inner identity (*pratyagātman*). The individual self, as the passive witness that is distinct from its experiences, really shares the same nature as the supreme identity or the pure *brahman* (*tat*) in that both are without features (*nirguṇa*), impartite, without attachments, eternally pure consciousness, always released, authentically real and supremely blissful. When the term '*Tat*' is purified of connotations of cosmic causality through *avidyā* and the term '*tvam*' is purified of connotations of personal individuality and finite experience, they are understood together in the identity statement 'That thou art' as obliquely indicating the nature of the purely conscious reality.

Illustrative extracts from Śaṃkara's works

For Śaṃkara, constancy is a mark of the real. So the fact that the phenomenological character or 'subjective feel' of awareness is the same in all cognitions, regardless of what they are about, is held to show that consciousness is basically real. In his commentary on the *Bhagavad Gītā* 2.16 ('Of the non-existent, there is no coming into being: there is no ceasing to be of the existent. The difference between the two is seen by those who understand the truth.') Śaṃkara formulates a substantial conception of 'Being' as the changeless basis of all finite and transitory existences. 'Being' thus understood is not involved in causal relations and is outside space and time. In the background here is a reaction to Dharmakīrti's espousal of dynamic causal efficacy as criterial of reality, with its entailment that anything permanent, in so far as it is static, would be unreal.[12]

Unconditioned being is the foundational cause of the cosmos. Its general features (*jātīyaka-dharma*), as opposed to those conditions (*upādhi*) that we, or some scriptures, might superimpose upon it, are universal presence, eternity, omniscience, omnipotence and its being the true nature of everyone. Nothing finite and nothing whose existence depends upon its relation to other things can be truly real. The same applies to anything that is a product. Products are transformations (*vikāra*), and a transformation (being a derivation) lacks a nature of its own. Thought expresses something truly real when it is constant and unvarying, and when a thought expresses something that comes and goes, then it concerns what is other than Being.

Bhagavad Gītā 2.17 asks the question, 'What is "Being" that exists timelessly?' Śaṃkara replies that it is the condition of the possibility of anything: Everything is pervaded by the *brahman*, called Being. This Reality never deviates from the nature that is its own because it has no parts. It cannot suffer loss because it has no properties. It is the true identity (*ātman*) of everyone. Commenting on *Gītā* 2.18, he says that this timeless, changeless and indestructible nature cannot be determined by any of the means of knowing (*pramāṇa*). Dismissing the suggestion that it is determined by scripture and by perception, he responds that consciousness establishes its own existence (*svataḥ siddha*). It is only if such consciousness, *qua* knowing subject, is already a given that the truth-seeker's use of *pramāṇas* is possible. We could not act with a view to understanding knowable objects unless we had already understood ourselves as subjects. The transcendental subject is a given, a presupposition of the sort of experience that we have. Scripture is the ultimate *pramāṇa* in the sense that it has its epistemic authority about the transcendental subject only by stripping away properties that have been mistakenly superimposed upon that identity, and not by providing us new information about something previously unknown.

From Śaṃkara's Upadeśa-Sāhasrī (p. 68):

> Permanently unchanging consciousness, whose nature is self-luminosity, establishes its own existence since it does not need a means of knowing for itself. [Everything in the world requires consciousness to reveal or establish its existence. But consciousness is unique in not needing anything external to establish it: it is self-revealing.] Anything other [than consciousness] that is insentient exists for the sake of something else, since it functions in complexes. And in so far as that which exists for the sake of the something else produces experiences of pleasure, pain and delusion, it follows that it is what is not the self. Hence its existence (*astitva*) is not authentically real (*paramārtha*). Just as the contents of illusions have no real existence apart from consciousness, so everyday experience of differentiation has no real existence apart from consciousness. And the permanently unchanging nature of the light of consciousness, the authentic reality, follows from its uninterrupted presence. Consciousness is uniform because it is unvarying in the midst of all the different ideas, which come and go. Just as the different ideas that come and go in dreams are said not to exist in reality, so the different ideas inconstantly presented to waking consciousness must be unreal too. Because there is no perspective on consciousness other than that of consciousness itself, it is not the sort of thing that can be accepted or rejected, and there is nothing else.

Brahma-Sūtra-Bhāṣya 1.1.31

Scriptures such as '*tat tvam asi*' ('You are that') and '*ahaṃ brahma asmi*' ('I am the Brahman') show that what is called the 'individual self' is not ultimately distinct from the Brahman. It is the *brahman* that is called 'individual person', the agent and the experiencer, when it is regarded as diversified as a result of properties (*upādhi*) superimposed upon it, such as body, mind and sense-faculties. Some passages reveal the true nature of Pure Being by negating differentia resulting from the superimposition of features. They focus attention on one's inner identity (*pratyag-ātman*).

Brahma-Sūtra-Bhāṣya 2.3.7

> But surely soul (*ātman*) is different from the atmosphere etc., so must it not also be an effect?
>
> The Soul is not a modification because that would mean that it is an effect.
>
> We cannot deny the reality of soul without self-contradiction. It is not a contingent property of anything else since it establishes its own existence and that existence is not established by any of the means of knowing (*pramāṇa*). One uses the means of knowing to establish previously unknown objects of knowledge. But the soul, because it is the basis of the exercise of the means of knowing, is established prior to their functioning. The rejection of a reality of that sort is impossible. A person may deny the existence of some entity or another, but he cannot deny the subject doing the rejecting.
>
> In expressions such as 'I know something present', 'I have known something past' and 'I shall know something future', the objects known differ as present, past and future, but the knower does not change because by nature it is wholly present through the entire course of experience.

Most followers of the Nyāya-Vaiśeṣika tradition hold that while the synthetic and unified nature of human experience presupposes an enduring subject (*ātman*), these subjects are not intrinsically conscious. They say that cognitions (and feelings, desires and intentions) are contingent properties that occur when the embodied *ātman* is connected with a mind (*manas*), the material faculty that co-ordinates sensory data. Śaṃkara addresses this view under *Brahma-Sūtra-Bhāṣya* 2.3.18:

> [The opposing view]: If consciousness were a permanent feature it would persist in the states of deep sleep, swoon and demonic possession. But people report that they did not experience anything in such states. But in normal life, people are actively intelligent. Hence, given that consciousness is not constant, the *ātman* is only contingently conscious.

We reply that knowing consciousness is permanent, and it is one's real identity because it is not produced. Unchanging pure being exists as the individual person when it is associated with superimposed properties. Scripture reveals that consciousness is the true nature of pure being in definitional passages like, 'The Brahman is knowledge and bliss' and 'The Brahman is reality, consciousness, infinite'. If the individual really shares the nature of the unconditioned reality, then permanent consciousness is its essential nature.

Brahma-Sūtra-Bhāṣya 2.3.30

As long as one's identity is that of a transmigrator, as long as the *saṃsāric* state has not been terminated by the realization of one's true identity, association of the soul with some mind and personality continues. And while there is a relation to the superimposed property (*upādhi*) that is the mind, then there is individual personality and the series of births. But in reality there is no individual person apart from the nature that is fabricated by relation to the superimposed property that is the mind. This relation of the superimposed property that is the mind to one's real identity presupposes misconception (*mithyājñāna*), and misconception continues until knowledge arises. So as long as there is no comprehension of Pure Being, connection with the superimposed property that is the mind obtains.

Brahma-Sūtra-Bhāṣya 2.3.40 answers the question whether agency is innate and natural (*svābhāvikam*) to one's identity, or is it a superimposed property?

Agency does not belong to one's true identity because it would follow that there could be no liberation from rebirth. Were agency an essential feature of identity, it could never be separated from it, just as heat is inseparable from fire. The ultimate human good cannot happen unless one is free from agency because agency always involves suffering.... Agency is not essential because it is one of the properties superimposed upon the fundamental identity.

The enlightened realize that there is no individual person, no agent and no enjoyer of experiences, all of which are concepts superimposed upon the true nature.

But surely if there are no real personal agents distinct from body, mind and sense-faculties and distinct from the transcendent nature, then it must be the transcendent nature that is the transmigrator, the agent and the enjoyer.

No – because agency and experience are presentations due to *avidyā*. Scriptures reveal that being an agent and experiencer belongs to the sphere of *avidyā*. Agency is not an essential feature of the Soul.

It could be argued that agency must be an essential feature of one's identity because otherwise the scriptures enjoining actions would have no purpose.

We respond that scriptural injunctions teach that certain things are to be done and thus presuppose an appropriate sort of agency. But it is not the case that this agency is essential to the soul, because the scriptures teach that one is identical with unconditioned being. The scriptural injunctions presuppose the type of agency that is fabricated by ignorance. Passages such as, 'the agent, the person whose nature is understanding' (Praśna Up. 4.9) refer to the agency fabricated by ignorance.

Brahma-Sūtra-Bhāṣya 2.3.46

The painful experience of the individual person is not something truly real but is occasioned by a mistaken failure to discriminate between one's true identity and the superimposed properties (mind, body and sense-faculties) that are fabricated by ignorance.

Brahma-Sūtra-Bhāṣya 3.2.11

Some scriptural passages refer to the *brahman* as possessing differentia (*sa-viśeṣam*), while others say that it lacks differentia (*nirviśeṣam*). Does this mean that the *brahman* has both a conditioned and an unconditioned nature?

Śaṃkara responds that the unconditioned reality cannot intrinsically possess two natures because it is illogical that one and the same reality should both intrinsically have and lack characteristics such as colour and shape. Relation to superimposed properties (*upādhi*) does not involve a change in the real nature of an entity. A brilliant crystal does not become dim by being related to a projected red feature. And the superimposed properties in relation to the *brahman* are projected by *avidyā*. We must understand that of the two descriptions, the one of the *brahman* as void of every differentia and beyond discursive thought is the true one.

Brahma-Sūtra-Bhāṣya 3.2.14-15

The *brahman* has no forms (*ākāra*) such as colour and shape. As scripture says, 'The Brahman is without before and after. There is nothing inside or outside of it. The Brahman is the nature that experiences everything' (*Bṛhadāraṇyaka Upaniṣad* 2.5.19). These passages refer to the transcendent (*niṣprapañca*) nature of pure being, so it must be understood that it is formless.

Other scriptural passages that refer to the *brahman* as having form are not primarily about the *brahman*, but are instructions to contemplate the supreme reality in certain ways.

There is no problem about the fact that some texts teach meditation on the *brahman* as having some specific forms. This sort of attribution of characteristics does not compromise our view that the *brahman* does not have a twofold nature although properties are superimposed upon it. When something is due to a superimposed property (*upādhi*), it cannot be a genuine property of an entity. And the superimposed properties are fabricated due to ignorance. We have already explained that primal ignorance is the precondition of all religious and secular dealings.

Brahma-Sūtra-Bhāṣya 3.2.18

Because the nature of unconditioned pure being is consciousness, void of differentia, beyond mind and language and conveyed by the negation of all finite characteristics, the scriptures teaching freedom from rebirth use the simile of the sun reflected in water, meaning that the *brahman's* having different features is not the real truth because those features are properties that have been superimposed.

Brahma-Sūtra-Bhāṣya 3.2.21

Being and consciousness coincide in the *brahman*. They are not distinct properties. The supposition that the *brahman* has a mode of being that excludes consciousness and another mode that has the form of consciousness that is other than being implies that it is internally complex. Being is just consciousness and consciousness is just being. They are not mutually exclusive, so conceptual analysis (*vikalpa*) about whether the *brahman* is either Being or consciousness or both is groundless. Scriptural texts that speak of the *brahman* under certain forms have their own positive purpose: they do not merely have the significance of denying that finite features of the cosmos pertain to the *brahman*. When features of the cosmos are mentioned in passages enjoining meditation – such as, 'It is made of mind: the vital breaths are its body; its appearance is light' – the text does not have the purpose of suppressing plurality but that of enjoining meditation.

The ineffability of the *brahman*

We have seen that one's true identity as the *brahman*, and the unreality of all differences and individuality, are revealed by some of the scriptures. But the nature of the unconditioned being cannot be expressed by concepts and words. Śaṃkara understands *Bṛhadāraṇyaka Upaniṣad* 2.3.6 as referring to the *brahman* and reads the passage as, 'Now there is the teaching, "It is not this. It is not that." There is no better expression than "not this." This is the designation of the truth about reality.'

> It expresses something that has no distinguishing features (name, form, actions, differences, class-property or qualities) that are the reasons for the application of words. The *brahman* has no distinguishing features. Therefore it is not possible to describe it as such and such. The *brahman* may be described by means of names, forms and actions that are superimposed upon it. But when we want to express its proper form that is devoid of every specific limiting condition, then it is not possible to describe it in any way. There is only one way left – namely, the designation, 'Not this, not this' i.e. by the negation of all possible descriptions.[13]

Brahma-Sūtra-Bhāṣya 13.12b

> 'The highest reality is beginningless. It is not said to be Being or non-Being.'

This text is tremendously influential in the Advaitin tradition. Among other things, it was taken as stating that there can be no continuity of being (*analogia entis*) between the *brahman* and anything belonging to the cosmos. (The formula 'Inexpressible as being or non-being' was also applied to *avidyā* and its works.) What Śaṃkara actually says here is that it means that the absolute Being is not the sort of empirical thing that either could or could not exist. It is not an entity on the same level as other entities. It is not knowable by conventional means adapted to our world, but only by Scripture. He also says:

> It stands to reason that the unconditioned reality cannot be directly expressed by words such as 'being' and 'non-being' for words are ordinarily used to reveal some object, and when they are heard they convey a conventional meaning, by expressing the kind to which an object belongs, or some action, quality or relation. Thus 'cow' and 'horse' express kinds, 'he cooks' and 'he reads' express actions, 'white' and 'black' express qualities, and 'having wealth' and 'possessing cows' express relations. But the *brahman* is not *an entity* that belongs to a kind or class, so it cannot be expressed by words such as 'being' or 'non-being'. Because it is without characteristics, it has no qualities such that it might be expressed by words for them. Because it is unchanging, it cannot be expressed by action-words. Because it is non-relational, unique, non-objectifiable and the Inner nature of all, it cannot be expressed by any word.

What about those Scriptures that speak of the absolute Being in anthropomorphic terms? The answer is:

> 'That which is *totally other* than the cosmos is explained by the provisional attribution of features to it, followed by a demonstration that they are inappropriate.'

Śaṃkara and the Buddhists

Śaṃkara and his followers were sometimes described as 'closet Buddhists'. Buddhists and Advaitins agree that the sense of personal individuality is an illusion, which is created by the interactions between our modes of experiencing and the world. Moreover, like the Buddhists, Śaṃkara envisages the evaporation of personal individuality once enlightenment dawns, and blames suffering on ignorance. But the accusation is far from the truth. Śaṃkara's metaphysic is totally different from the Buddhist temporalism that rejects the very notion of enduring identities or substances in favour of successions of phases. Śaṃkara believes that 'behind' the array of changing phenomena, there is a single unconditioned reality: the static coincidence of pure being and consciousness. Relative to unconditioned Being (the *brahman*), the world that we experience is less than fully real – not the genuine article – but in the state of liberation (*mokṣa*), what is truly real is enjoyed by consciousness and as consciousness. In other words, the cosmos has a real cause (*sat-kāraṇa-vāda*), even if we must be agnostic about the ontological status of entities that 'cannot be determined as either real or unreal'. This is because every phenomenon is unreal when mistakenly considered as having its own subsistent, but real in so far as it participates in the general reality or the *brahman*.

Let us see what he says about various Buddhist schools:

Brahma-Sūtra-Bhāṣya 2.2.18

There are three traditions of Buddhist thought:

> Those who say that both material and mental phenomena are real. [Sarvāstivāda]
>
> Those who say that only mental phenomena are real. [Yogācāra]
>
> Those who say that there are no timeless essences. [Mādhyamaka]
>
> To begin with, we refute those who admit the reality of physical factors as well as minds and ideas. By physical they mean the four elements and the sense faculties as well as their respective objects. They say that earth, water, air and fire are combinations of four different kinds of atoms. The five constituents (*skandhas*) – body, perceptions, feelings, conceptual thoughts and inherited dispositions – make up human lives and underlie all interpersonal dealings.
>
> At this point, it must be said in reply that Buddhist theory about the two different sorts of combinations – that of atoms into material elements and the five constituents into persons – is unintelligible. The argument is:
>
> The atomic components of the material combinations are non-conscious.
>
> The emergence of sentience depends upon the prior existence of some combination.

They do not accept any other persisting conscious subject or director who could combine the basic factors.

It cannot be the case that the atoms and *skandhas* operate spontaneously because that would entail that they would never cease from activity.

Brahma-Sūtra-Bhāṣya 2.2.19

The Buddhist: Although there is no persisting subject of experience or director who combines the basic factors, the world process is sustained by the interactive causality of factors such as ignorance etc. (*pratītya-samutpāda*). [The factors are] ignorance, habits, perceptions, name and form, the six types of sensation, touch, feeling, grasping, birth, old age and death, sadness, pain, frustration and discontent form a self-perpetuating circle of causes and effects. The reality of those facts of life is accepted by everyone. The cycle of factors, each conditioning the other as effect and cause, presupposes that there are real combinations [such as bodies and mind].

Śaṃkara responds:

You are only talking about the originating causes (*utpatti-mātra nimittatvam*) that connect the elements in the series and overlooking the sort of organizational causality that would account for the formation of combinations. The latter is impossible if there are only momentary atoms and no subjects of experience. Perhaps the factors beginning with ignorance are the causes of the formation of aggregates. But how can they cause that which is the necessary condition of their existence?

Moreover, you do not think that the combinations are formed in the interests of enduring conscious subjects so that they might experience the fruits of their *karma* (*bhogārtham*). Hence, experience is just for the sake of experience and is not sought by anything or anyone else. So freedom from rebirth (*mokṣa*) is just for the sake of itself, and there is no one by whom it is sought. A being with an interest in both experiencing the fruits of action and gaining freedom from rebirth would have to exist contemporaneously with those processes, and such persistence would conflict with your belief in the temporality of beings (*kṣaṇikatva*).

So while there may be a relation of originative causality between the members of the series, this does not suffice to explain their organized combinations. Śaṃkara goes on to establish the stronger claim that the Buddhist position cannot even make sense of originative causality between members of the series. He begins by arguing that a strictly instantaneous reality does not last for long enough to bring about the existence of anything else.

Brahma-Sūtra-Bhāṣya 2.2.20

The theory that realities are instantaneous implies that when the later moment originates, the earlier one no longer exists. So it is not possible to establish the relation of cause and effect between the two moments. Something that has ceased to be cannot function as a cause. The claim that as soon as a prior moment is fully actualized it becomes the cause of the later one is not intelligible because the hypothesis that a fully actualized entity exercises a causal function (*vyāpāra*) means that it is connected to another moment [which contradicts universal instantaneity].

Nor does it make sense to say that the causal function simply is the existence of the prior entity [and not the exercise of a causal property]. This is because origin of an effect that is not tinged by the nature (*svabhāva*) of its cause is impossible. If one accepts that the effect is tinged by the nature of its cause, the nature of the cause continues in the effect and that entails the abandonment of the hypothesis of instantaneity. Nor can it be argued that there could be a cause–effect relation without the nature of the cause's influencing the effect, because if that happened there would be chaos.

Moreover, what the Buddhist understands as simultaneous 'origin and cessation' would be either the same as the proper form (*svarūpa*) of an entity, or two phases of its existence, or another entity. If they are the same as the proper form, the words 'origin and cessation' and 'entity' would be synonymous. If the terms 'origin' and 'cessation' mean two phases that are the beginning and end of an entity whose existence is what occurs between them, the entity would not be instantaneous because it would be connected with three phases – beginning, middle and end.

If origin and cessation are completely different from the entity, then the entity would not be associated with them. It would follow that the entity is everlasting.

The doctrine of momentariness (*kṣaṇikatva*) extends to human personality, which the Buddhists understand as just a series of experiential phases. The doctrine implies the momentariness of the perceiver as the perceived. So there is no enduring principle of identity or soul that unifies the phases and converts them into a continuum. Śaṃkara argues that the phenomenon of memory shows that the Buddhist view is impossible.

Brahma-Sūtra-Bhāṣya 2.2.25

Moreover, the nihilist (Vaināśika – literally the believer in the spontaneous destructibility of all entities) accepting the instantaneity of everything must apply instantaneity to the subject of experiences. But that is not possible because of the phenomenon first-personal memory [of the form, 'I remember myself doing that']. Such memory is produced by the re-occurrence of an experiential awareness, and it is only possible if the one who remembers is the same as the original subject. One man does not remember the awareness of another. How could there be the experience of the awareness 'I saw that and am seeing it now' if there were no single subject that sees the earlier and the later? We all know that the experience of recognition occurs only when there is a single subject of both seeing and remembering.... The nihilist knows himself to be the one subject of seeing and remembering whenever he thinks, 'I saw that'. He does not deny that the past perception belongs to him any more than he denies that fire is hot and light.

Since one and the same agent is connected with the two moments of seeing and remembering, the nihilist must give up his acceptance of the universal temporality of beings. If he recognizes that all his past and future experiences belong to one and the same subject, and accepts that there is sometimes synthetic awareness of both successive and simultaneous cognitions, how can the nihilist who asserts universal instantaneity maintain his position?

The Buddhist may say that recognition and synthetic awareness derive from the similarity of the momentary cognitions [and this generates the misapprehension that there are persisting objects and the illusion that there is an enduring self]. But similarity is a relation between two different things. Someone who says that although there is no single perceiver of two similar things, synthetic awareness is based on similarity is talking nonsense. If he admits that there is a single perceiver of the similarity between the earlier and later moments, he thereby grants that there is one thing enduring through two moments and this contradicts the hypothesis of instantaneity.

When a universally accepted reality is denied by philosophers, whatever they may say in support of their own view or in finding fault in that of others, they convince neither themselves nor others. When it is known that something is such and such, it must be expressed accordingly. Their thesis about similarity fails to accord with the facts of experience. The act of recognition is an understanding about one and the same thing and not of something that is similar to something else. It may be that sometimes there is a doubt about whether an external object is the same one or something similar to it. But there is no room for doubt about whether the perceiving subject is identical to itself or just something similar.

Śaṃkara now turns his critical attention to the Buddhist 'consciousness-only' theory that says that what are usually taken to be physical things outside the mind are really just ideas internal to awareness. Of the basic factors (*dharmas*) posited by the Buddhist schools, they say that only the mental ones are real (*vijñapti-mātra*).

Brahma-Sūtra-Bhāṣya 2.2.28:

The Buddhist opponent says:

The Enlightened One taught that there really is an external world in consideration of those followers who were convinced about the reality of things external to minds. But this was not his own belief, which was that among the five constituents of personality (*skandhas*), only the perceptions (*vijñāna*) were real. According to the 'perceptions-only' theory (*vijñāna-vāda*), we can make sense of everything to do with our cognitive experiences if both the sources and the objects of knowing are purely internal to minds. Even if there were external objects, the process of knowing would not get under way without minds.

But how is it known that this entire process is internal and that there are no objects independent of perceptions?

Because there cannot be external objects. If external objects are accepted, they would be atoms or combinations of atoms, such as pillars. But atoms are not discerned in our awareness of pillars etc. because they cannot be represented in consciousness. External objects cannot be combinations of atoms because we cannot determine whether they are the same as or different from the atoms. Moreover, although all cognitions have the same nature in that they are consciousness, they may express different objects. This would not happen unless the differentia were internal to awareness, so it must be accepted that a cognition has the same form as its object (*viṣaya-sārūpya*). Once this is granted, given that the representation of the object is determined by cognition (and not the other way round), the postulation of external objects is superfluous. Moreover, given that the object and the awareness of it always occur simultaneously (*sahopalambha-niyamād*), it follows that there is no difference between a cognition and its object. Cognition and its object are always apprehended together. They never occur separately. This would not make sense if the two were different in nature.

Perception of objects is comparable to dreams. Just as ideas in dreams manifest the form of the apprehender and the apprehended although there are no external objects, so in the waking state one must understand that representations of solid objects occur without external objects. This is because from the point of view of felt experience, there is no difference between the forms of awareness.

Now if there are no objects external to minds, how is the variety of representations (*pratyaya-vaicitrya*) explained? It is explained by the variety of residual impressions (*vāsanā-vaicitrya*) left by previous ideas. In the beginningless series of births, an impression causes a perception which in turn leaves an impression, and so on. This explains the variety of representations. Moreover, we understand by reasoning from positive and negative concomitance that the variety of cognitions is just caused by residual impressions. We both admit that in dreams and hallucinations, in the absence of external objects the variety of cognitions is caused by residual impressions. But we do not accept that there can ever be any variety of cognitions without residual impressions. Hence there are no objects external to awareness.

Śaṃkara replies:

It is impossible to make sense of the non-existence of external objects because things are perceived as such. It is the external object – represented in thought – that is perceived. What is being perceived in this way can't be held not to exist. [Two points implicit here: we are aware of both thoughts and objects as distinct; that perceptual experience is about an external world is a basic phenomenological fact about consciousness.]

The Buddhist may claim, 'I do not say that I am not aware of objects. What I do say is that I am not aware of any object apart from perception.' But objects independent of perception must be accepted simply because of the nature of perception itself. No one perceiving a pillar or a wall is just conscious of a perception. But everyone perceives pillars and walls precisely in so far as they are given in perceptions. Even those who deny the reality of external things implicitly grant their existence when they say that representations internal to consciousness (*antar-jñeya-rūpam*) appear as if external. If we accept that immediate experience is a guide to truth, it is logical to accept that it is precisely something external that is manifested in consciousness, not something that is merely a semblance of the external.

The Buddhist argues that the 'external-like' is what is manifest because of the impossibility of external objects. This can't be right because what is possible and what is impossible is ascertained by the means of knowing (*pramāṇa*), and the means of knowing do not depend on what we might imagine to be possible and impossible. What is possible and what not is understood by the use of some means of knowing. External objects are apprehended as they are in themselves by all the means of knowing. How can it be said that they are not possible on the basis of specious argumentation, given that they are perceived. And it is not the case that there are no external objects because of the conformity between cognitions and objects. If there were no objects, conformity between the representation of the object in awareness and the external object would be impossible. Moreover, the object is represented as external. That is why the co-occurrence of thought and object (*sahopalambha-niyama*) is due to the fact that a relation of mode of presentation and object-presented obtains between thought and object. It does not derive from the identity of thoughts and objects. Moreover, two successive but discrete thoughts, self-illuminating and confined to their own instantaneous occurrences, cannot be related as the subject (*grāhaka*) and the object perceived (*grāhya*). There needs to be a perceiver who witnesses the successive perceptions.

But does this not lead to an infinite regress? If a perception needs illuminating by a perceiver, would not the perceiver need illumination by something else, and so on? That is why the Buddhist says that each perception is self-illuminating.

[Reply] The problem of an infinite regress does not arise if there is a witness of the perceptions. Since the witness and the ideas are different in nature, they may be related as cognizer and cognized. Moreover, the witness is self-established and undeniable. Self-illuminating perceptions do not reveal anything because they are not manifest to anyone.

How does this differ from the Buddhist theory?

The Buddhist says that perceptions are transient and diverse in nature, while the witness is single and permanent. Hence it is proved that perceptions need a separate witness if they are to mean anything.

Brahma-Sūtra-Bhāṣya 2.2.29

According to the Vijñānavādin, dreaming shows that we may have experiences (with a subject–object structure) that are phenomenologically indistinguishable from waking ones, in the absence of external objects. Vijñānavādins go further and say that since dreaming and waking are both varieties of conscious experience, what happens in dream experience is the same as what happens in waking experience. The reply appeals to the evidence of the difference between dream experience and waking experience. In short, we have a perspective upon dream experience from the vantage point of waking experience, but the converse does not hold. Dream experiences differ from waking experiences so it is impossible to conclude that waking experiences are false because they share the same nature as dream ones.

Brahma-Sūtra-Bhāṣya 2.2.30

Turning now to the doctrine that the variety of perceptions is explained by the variety of impressions (*vāsanā*) of prior experiences without reference to external things, it is replied that the Buddhist cannot make sense of the occurrence of the impressions because he does not admit cognitions of external things. If the impressions arise from cognitions of objects, on what basis would the variety of impressions arise if external things are not perceived. A beginningless series without a starting point would exclude the possibility of everyday life and communication.

Brahma-Sūtra-Bhāṣya 2.2.31

There is the supposition that the storehouse-consciousness (*ālaya-vijñāna*) is the substratum of the traces. But since that is admitted to be momentary in nature and essentially transient, it cannot be the substrate of impressions. Without a single, stable continuous factor, a witness of all one's experiences, which is connected with past, present and future, ordinary experience involving synthetic acts of memory and recognition that presuppose traces dependent upon times, places and occasions would not be possible.

Further reading

Śaṃkara's *Brahma-Sūtra-Bhāṣya* is translated in Thibaut (1904). Mayeda (1979) translates the *Upadeśa-Sāhasrī* and has a useful introduction.

Potter (1981) has an introduction and summaries of works by Śaṃkara, as well as Maṇḍana's *Brahma-Siddhi* by Allen Thrasher. The latter's *Advaita Vedānta of Brahma-Siddhi* is stimulating, as are Ram-Prasad (2001 and 2002). Comans (2000) is an illuminating exposition of early Advaita.

Suryanarayana Sastri (1971) translates a classic of Advaita epistemology and metaphysics.

Some aspects of the debates between the Advaitins and theists about scriptural exegesis are described in Bartley, *Theology of Rāmānuja* (2002).

See Granoff (1978) for Śrī Harṣa.

For Bhartṛhari, see John Brough's classic essays on 'Theories of General Linguistics in the Sanskrit Grammarians' and 'Some Indian Theories of Meaning' in Hara and Wright (1996). Also Matilal (1991).

For Gauḍapāda, see V. Bhattacharya, *The Agamaśāstra of Gauḍapāda*. See King (1995), for connections with Buddhism.

For an account of a modern articulation of the Advaitic outlook, see Bartley (2013) on Radhakrishnan.

Questions for discussion and investigation

1. In what senses is Advaita subversive of mainstream orthodoxy? Does it represent the implicit rejection of Hindu *dharma*?
2. Why would anyone suppose that Śaṃkara was a closet Buddhist?

Notes

1. Parts of this chapter draw on material in my article 'Advaita and the Schools of Vedānta' (Bartley 2011).
2. See Bhattacharya, V. (1989).
3. Nemec (2011), pp. 146–210.
4. Advaita is informed by Scriptures such as 'At first the world was just being, one only without a second' (Ch.Up. 6.2.1), 'I am the *brahman*' (BAU. 1.4.10), 'This whole world is the *brahman*' (Ch.Up. 3.14.1), and 'Whatever is the finest essence, that is the true nature of everything, that is authentic reality, and that is what you are (*tat tvam asi*)' (Ch.Up. 6.8.7).
5. Dumont (1980), Appendix B: 'World Renunciation in Indian Religions', and Biardeau (1997).
6. *The Bhagavad Gītā with Eleven Commentaries*, pp. 2 and 4.
7. Fort (1998).
8. Bartley (2002), Ch. 4.
9. These questions are illuminatingly treated in a series of publications by the late Paul Hacker. See Halbfass (1995), Ch. 4.
10. His doctrine is what Paul Hacker called a 'radical ontologism'. See Halbfass (1995), pp. 198–9.
11. *Vedāntaparibhāṣā*, p. 37: *Pariṇāma* means producing an effect of the same degree of reality as its causal substrate. *Vivarta* means producing an effect whose reality is inferior to that of the causal substrate. The source is Appaya Dīkṣita's *Siddhāntaleśasaṃgraha*, p. 67.
12. v. supra Ch. 4.
13. *Bṛhadāraṇyaka Upaniṣad with Śaṃkara's Commentary*, Agase (1891) pp. 315–16.

12

Viśiṣṭādvaita Vedānta

Chapter Outline

The religious context

In the centuries after 700 A.D., we see the gradual rise to predominance within Hinduism of the sort of personalist theism found in the *Bhagavad Gītā* and the *Purāṇas*, accompanied by a decline in the religion in which the Vedic rituals are central. This is not to say that ritual practices disappear. Rather, they are assimilated to modes of practice that are more concerned with worship of a deity conceived personally whose grace or favour is accessible to those human souls who love him (*bhakti*). From this perspective, God is thought to be concerned with the destinies of finite beings. Moreover, the cosmos is understood as creation for the sake of sentient beings rather than as a hierarchy of spheres of existence (*tattva*), through which souls may or may not progress naturally in accordance with their *karma*, understood as an automatic mechanism. There develops a theological concept of the soul and a notion that human beings are essentially lovers, enjoyers and knowers of God. According to this sort of devotional monotheism, the person is constituted by God and the meaning and fulfilment of its life is to be found in relationship to God.

Viśiṣṭādvaita Vedānta is the doctrinal articulation of the theistic *Śrī Vaiṣṇava* religious tradition that still flourishes in Tamil Nādu. It is a pluralist ontology and epistemological direct realism about a complex universe whose basic constituents are kinds of property-bearing enduring substances. The term '*Viśiṣṭādvaita*', frequently mistranslated as 'qualified non-dualism', is held by the tradition to mean 'the integral unity of complex reality'.[1] *Vedānta* is the systematic hermeneutic of the Upaniṣads, the brief summaries of the teachings of the latter in the *Brahma-Sūtras*, and the *Bhagavad Gītā*.

The *Śrī Vaiṣṇava* tradition developed in interaction with the enthusiastic devotion (*bhakti*) towards a personally conceived deity found in the hymns of the Tamil *Ālvārs*, the temple and domestic rituals and theology of the Tantric (i.e. non-Vedic) *Pāñcarātra Āgamas*, and a reflective Vaiṣṇava *smārta* orthodoxy. The last found expression in the philosophical theologies of Nāthamuni (980–1050 A.D.), Yāmuna (c.1050–1125 A.D.) and Rāmānuja (c.1100–1170 A.D.).[2] Rāmānuja was a creative genius who adopted ideas from Yāmuna and an earlier commentator on the *Brahma-Sūtras* called Bodhāyana, and synthesized them with beliefs current in the tradition to articulate a realistic and pluralistic philosophical and theological system. As a practitioner of Vedānta, he related the beliefs of his tradition to the normative scriptures (*śruti* and *smṛti*) such as the Upaniṣads and *Bhagavad Gītā*, seeking to establish that those beliefs are precisely what those authorities teach.

Influential Viśiṣṭādvaitins and their works include:

Nāthamuni (980–1050 A.D.): *Nyāyatattva* (known only from quotations).

Yāmuna (1050–1125 A.D.): *Ātmasiddhi, Īśvarasiddhi, Saṃvitsiddhi; Āgamaprāmāṇyam* (on the validity of the Pañcarātra cult and its scriptures).

Rāmānuja (1100–1170 A.D.): *Śrī Bhāṣya* (commentary on the *Brahma-Sūtras*), *Vedārthasaṃgraha* (précis of the former); *Bhagavadgītā-bhāṣya*.

Paraśara Bhaṭṭa (1170–1240 A.D.): *Tattvaratnākara* (quotations from Vedānta Deśika).

Vedavyāsa (Sudarśanasuri) (1120–1300 A.D.): *Śrutaprakāśikā* (commentary on *Śrī Bhāṣya*), *Tātparydīpikā* (commentary on *Vedārthasaṃgraha*).

Vedānta Deśika (Veṅkaṭanātha) (1270–1350 A.D.): *Tattvamuktākalāpa*, *Sarvārthasiddhi*, *Nyāyapariśuddhi*, *Nyāyasiddhāñjana*, *Tātparyacandrikā* (commentary on Rāmānuja's *Gītābhāṣya*), *Tattvaṭīkā* (commentary on *Śrī Bhāṣya*), *Pāñcarātrarakṣā*.

Śrīnivāsadāsa (1600–1650 A.D.): *Yatīndramatadīpikā*.[3]

The formation of the Śrī Vaiṣṇava tradition

We have to reckon with a confluence of various trends and factors. There is the intense ecstatic devotional religion of the Tamil *Ālvār* poets, who thought of all devotees equally as servants of God. They model the soul's relationship with God upon that between human lovers, and sing of the agony of separation and the bliss of reunion.[4] The theologians, at least in their prose works, in which they were concerned to demonstrate the concordance of their beliefs and practices with the normative religion of social and religious duty (*varṇāśramadharma*) that respects distinctions of caste, tended to suppress the ecstatic emotionalism and incipient social inclusivism of the *Ālvār* tradition. Nevertheless, they belonged to a monotheistic devotional milieu in which one is encouraged to delight in the awareness that one exists to be a servant of the divinity Viṣṇu Nārāyaṇa. God is a person, a being with will, agency and purposes, upon whom one is radically dependent and in whom one may take refuge. God is a compassionate being who attracts praise and love. This entirely self-sufficient deity creates and sustains the cosmos for no purpose other than his own delight (*līlā*). He is immanent both as the inner guide, the innermost constitutive element guide (*antar-yāmin*) of persons, and also as present in the consecrated temple icon. The reconciliation of mainstream orthodoxy and devotional theism appears in the soteriologies of Yāmuna and Rāmānuja when they say that performance of the duties appropriate to one's caste and stage of life, informed by understanding of the natures of the individual and divine natures, combined with ritual worship and devotion, invites the grace of the Supreme Person.[5] In the first verse of his *Summary of the Meaning of the Gītā*, Yāmuna says that *Nārāyaṇa*, who is the *brahman*, is only accessible by devotion (*bhakti*) that is the outcome of observance of one's social and religious duty, knowledge and dispassion.[6]

Bhakti is not just a matter of feeling. It accords with the belief that if God is the foundational cause of one's very being and everything one does is also an action of God. This does not mean that one's free actions do not flow from the will. It means that it is in virtue of its divine ensoulment or animation that the dependent soul is an *entity* in the first place.

A further factor constitutive of the *Śrī Vaiṣṇava* tradition is the non-Vedic or Tantric *Pañcarātra* system of theology and ritual, which informs the liturgies enacted in South Indian *Śrī Vaiṣṇava* temples. This tradition is probably as old as the Christian era, but it is unlikely that any of the surviving texts were composed before c.850 A.D.[7] Pañcarātra is an ancient form of Viṣṇu worship.[8] Viṣṇu is believed to pervade and sustain the cosmos, as well as underpinning stable social structures. Pañcarātra is believed by its adherents to derive from a no longer extant branch of the Vedic scriptures called the *Ekāyana Śākhā*. Tantric cults are monotheistic, and the *theos* here is called Viṣṇu Nārāyaṇa. He is accompanied by his female partner named Śrī or Lakṣmī, who personifies the creative divine energy (*śakti*). The divinity, conceived as a person having will, agency and purposes, may be gratified by adoration and displeased by neglect and evil practices. He is a being upon whom human souls are radically dependent and in whom they may take refuge in their distress. This entirely self-sufficient deity, lacking nothing and not subject to any kind of internal or external necessity, creates the cosmos purely and simply for the sake of sport or play (*līlā*).[9] The cosmos is the arena in which souls can be rid of the burdens of accumulated *karma* by experiencing the consequences of their previous morally significant acts. As well as constituting souls (*jīva*) as entities adapted to life in the world, the deity is also their inner guide (*antar-yāmin*) who helps them on the path of righteousness (*dharma*), understood as devotion (*bhakti*) and diligent religious practice and morality, towards salvation from the cycle of rebirth. In general, Tantric traditions promise to released souls experiences that are rather more alluring than the liberated states (*mukti*) envisaged by the orthodox. For the Pāñcarātrins, supreme felicity consists in the adoration of God in heaven, which is of course a form of experience anticipated in the temples of this world.

Tantric traditions advertise themselves as more accessible alternatives to the mainstream traditionalist (*smārta*) path that deems itself normative. They are not normally in conflict with that path, since they often define themselves as extensions of it, both in virtue of their provision of access to supernatural powers and in the promise of exalted forms of liberation from rebirth in space and time. Nor are such cult movements on the fringes, adhered to only by eccentrics. Indeed, it appears that Tantric sects were sometimes vehicles of upward social mobility, the vertical axis reaching even up to the royal court. Involvement with the mainstream Vedic religion is the preserve of members of the three higher castes. By contrast, the Tantric cults are far less restrictive where initiation into membership is concerned. They thus offered paths to salvation through religious discipline and devotion to god for those who were excluded by accident of birth from participating in the mainstream traditionalist religion.

Rāmānuja defends the soteriological value of the Pañcarātra in his *Śrī Bhāṣya* commentary on *Brahma-Sūtras* 2.2.42-5, insisting that it is divinely promulgated and in perfect harmony with the normative Vedic tradition. He stresses the Pañcarātra belief in the accessibility of a divinity who is well disposed towards human beings. Pañcarātra, says Rāmānuja, teaches the nature of the godhead and the proper methods of worshipping him. The doctrine is intended to ease appreciation of the sense of the Vedas which on their own are difficult to understand. And he quotes with approval the Paramasaṃhitā, one of the Pañcarātra scriptures:

> I have read, Lord, the Vedas and the extensive authoritative writings based upon them. But in all these I do not discern anything that is indubitably pertinent to the attainment of the highest good by which its achievement might be reached.
>
> The wise Lord Hari, moved by compassion for his devotees, collected the essentials in the Upaniṣads and condensed them into an easy form.

The scriptures (called Āgamas or Saṃhitās) of the cult are no ordinary compositions but are believed to be records of divine utterances.[10] The literary corpus includes the liturgical forms of the daily offices owed to god by the devout, directions for the performance of rituals in the temple that is the site of the icon embodying the divinity, and guidance about the consecration of one's life to Viṣṇu. Of particular note here is the use of *mantras*, which are sonic forms of the deity. These are recited in rites of entheosis (*mantra-nyāsa*) wherein they are imaginatively infused with one's body. They are also deployed in the interests of the acquisition of extraordinary powers (*siddhis*) that are useful both to initiates who might have an interest in exercising control over others as well as to the often powerful and sometimes royal associates of the cult. But above all, according to Pañcarātra the goal of life is the glorification of the godhead. That divinity is understood to be accessible to human beings, an availability mediated not only through the consecrated icon that occupies the most sacred space in the temple, but also in the hearts of devotees as their inner guide (*antar-*

yāmin) and the soul of their souls. Such a theology is of course concordant with the enthusiastic devotional religion of the Tamil *Ālvār* poets.

Finally, there is a lineage of learned *Vaiṣṇava* teachers (*ācārya*) specializing in *Upaniṣadic* exegesis and adept in sophisticated *śāstric* traditions, *Smārta* Brahmins who take refuge in Viṣṇu as their patron deity (*iṣṭa-devatā*). Nāthamuni, Yāmuna, Rāmānuja and their successors belong to this tradition of realistic and pluralistic interpretations of the Scriptures in the face of the monism found there by the gnostic renouncers of the Advaita tradition. The Śrī Vaiṣṇavas seek to demonstrate that the *brahman* of which the Upaniṣads speak is not some unconditioned impersonal ground of being but rather the personal god Viṣṇu Nārāyaṇa. Rāmānuja's sophisticated theological formulation of the *bhakti* religion in opposition to the world-renunciatory Advaitic gnostic tradition was not new.[11] But Advaitic monism flourished after the seminal works of Maṇḍana Miśra and Śaṃkara (fl.c.700 A.D.). They held that ordinary experience of a plurality of individual conscious and non-conscious entities is a beginningless global misconception (*anādi-avidyā*) superimposed upon an inactive and undifferentiated *brahman* characterized as non-intentional pure consciousness. On this view, the liberation of the soul from rebirth is simply the cessation of ignorance about the true nature of reality. It is the intuitive realization that one's true identity (*ātman*) is non-intentional awareness (*jñapti-mātra*) and that one is not an individual agent subject to ritual duties and transmigration. This outlook is obviously at odds with the realist tradition of *Upaniṣadic* exegesis, which sees the real cosmos as an emanation (*pariṇāma*) of the absolute Being, as the real self-differentiation of the Supreme Soul – the substrative cause of all existents. The basic *Viśiṣṭādvaitin* doctrine that the world of conscious and unconscious entities is an organic complex that is both essentially dependent upon God and intrinsically distinct from him is a development of that realistic tradition of thought.

Knowing God only from Scripture

Like all Vedāntins, Rāmānuja assumes that the truth about God can only be known from the timeless Vedic scriptures, primarily the Upaniṣads, the knowledge portion (*jñāna-kāṇḍa*) of the Vedas. Although only scriptural language, and not perception and inferences based upon it, can reveal the truth about what transcends the bounds of the senses, Rāmānuja does say [*Śrī Bhāṣya* 1.1.2] that we have natural knowledge of God as that which possesses unsurpassable greatness, since this is the meaning of the verbal root *bṛh* from which the term 'Brahman' is derived. Unsurpassable greatness includes powers such as omniscience and omnipotence that are properties of that which is both the material and efficient causes of the cosmos. Further content may be added to this concept by texts such as *Taittirīya Upaniṣad* 2.1.1. 'The Brahman is reality, consciousness, infinite', which he interprets as implying three distinct properties belonging to the divinity, in contradistinction to the Advaitins who think that what appear to be predicates are names serving to differentiate the *brahman* from all else.

Only the Scriptures, and not human reason, can reveal anything about the nature and existence of God. Rāmānuja [*Śrī Bhāṣya* 1.1.3] uses philosophical argument to show that argument cannot prove the existence of God. He adduces a number of considerations against the standard inferences for the existence of God, all of which rely on the general principle (*vyāpti*) that products require an intelligent maker with the appropriate capabilities. For example, although we can infer a producer from human artefacts, we have no knowledge of the ultimate origination of natural features such as mountains and oceans and their existence supplies no reason to suppose that they have one all-powerful and all-knowing maker. The philosophical inferences cite as examples the production by potters of objects such as pots that are unequivocally single whole entities. But can we really treat the cosmos as a whole as a single great big object? The complex world consists of many different types of effects and as such cannot license the inference of a single maker. Assuming that the universe can be treated as a single product, was it made at one time or at different times? We have neither observational nor purely conceptual grounds for supposing that it was made at one time. But if it is made at different times, it is also possible that it has more than one maker. In our experience, agents, however capable, are finite and embodied. All our everyday valid inferences about who produced what concern finite and embodied makers. The *brahman* is different in kind from everything else. Thus we cannot infer that it is an agent in the sense in which we understand agency.

Response to Advaita[12]

The Advaitic concepts of the Absolute as impersonal, static, consciousness, and of the non-individual soul (identical with that Absolute principle) as utterly transcendental and detached from personal individuality, are the fruits of the mystic renouncer's contemplative experience in whose light the everyday world appears as less than fully real. But these visionary insights are problematic when it comes to explaining the genesis of the finite universe and its relation to the unconditioned reality that has nothing in common with the world. The developed Advaita tradition attributes the plural universe and our experience thereof to the operation of a positive force (*bhāva-rūpa*) called *avidyā* (as the substrative cause of the cosmos, it is obviously different from everyday notions of ignorance and misconception) which projects diversity and conceals pure being. The undifferentiated pure conscious reality falsely appears as the plural world when it is obscured by *avidyā*. *Avidyā* explains why we unenlightened beings mistakenly but inevitably think in terms of different individual entities. Causative *avidyā*, and its product, the cosmos, are indeterminable or inexpressible (*anirvacanīya*) as either real or unreal. The Viśiṣṭādvaita tradition rejects the latter claim as incoherent: if something is not real, it is unreal. If it is not unreal, it is real. If it is neither real nor unreal, it is both real and unreal. If *avidyā* is different from the *brahman*, monism is compromised. If it is the same as the *brahman* then it exists either absolutely or never. They insist that ignorance cannot be a subsistent entity with causal efficacy. It is just the absence of knowledge. Moreover, the putative causal ignorance must have a substrate. It cannot be the *brahman*, which is pure knowledge. Nor can it be the individual self which, according to Advaita, is itself the product of ignorance. Also, since the scriptures, in common with all the *pramāṇas*, belong to the sphere of *avidyā*, their capacity to reveal the truth is undermined.

The Advaitic proposition that reality is unitary and undifferentiated quickly attracted the objection that there is no means of establishing its truth (*pramāṇa*). There is already an instance of difference if the operation of the means of knowledge presupposes a duality of act and object. Rāmānuja argues that we cannot make sense of the notion that there is any sort of reality, ultimate or otherwise, that is undifferentiated and non-intentional consciousness (*nirviśeṣa-cinmātra*). He is an epistemological direct realist, holding that all cognitions are intrinsically valid (*svataḥ-prāmāṇyam*) just in virtue of their occurrence. He holds that intrinsically reflexive consciousness is always *about* something external. In addition, apprehension is always of the real (*sat-khyāti*): all perceptual cognition, even when misleading (*bhrama*), is in accordance with what is the case (*yathārtha*) independently of our thinking. There are no intrinsically false cognitions. Ultra-realism involves minimizing or explaining away what are ordinarily viewed as perceptual errors and hallucinations. There is an ancient theory that all material things are compounded out of the same elements. When mother of pearl is mistaken for silver, we are actually detecting traces of silver in the mother of pearl. Cognitions are intrinsically formless (*nirākāra*) and assume the forms of their objects. The lack of subjective contribution eliminates perceptual distortion. It is the extra-mental environment, consisting of stable objects that endure through space and time, that is responsible for mental variety. Truth is correspondence, understood as structural isomorphism, between knowing and the known. The subject–object structure of cognition is held to be self-evident and encoded in normal language. There simply are no cognitions lacking an agent and external object.

Implicit in Rāmānuja's critique of the Advaitic tenet that authentic reality is featureless and non-intentional consciousness is an appeal to a principle upheld by the Indian dualist traditions: whatever is, is knowable and nameable. All the means of knowledge refer to entities having properties. The notion of an object without properties is unintelligible because thought and language are possible only with respect to entities identifiable by their specific characteristics (*viśeṣa*). The language of the Scriptures, like all language, is composite and relational, and its complexity mirrors that of its objects. This is a crucial point. Scripture is our only means of knowing about the transcendent. If scriptural language is complex and language is isomorphic with what it expresses, complexity must obtain at the ultimate level.

He continues with the argument that sensory perception (*pratyakṣa*), whether non-conceptual (*nirvikalpa*) or conceptual (*savikalpa*), cannot establish the existence of a non-differentiated reality. We have seen that thinkers of the Nyāya-Vaiśeṣika and Mīmāṃsaka traditions tried to distinguish the two types of perception in various ways. The problem is difficult: to what extent can non-conceptual perception lack specificity while still referring to something? Is it possible to apprehend a 'bare particular' devoid of specific and generic features? Following Maṇḍana Miśra, Advaitin thinkers appeal to the example of non-conceptual perception in arguing that there can be pure uninterpreted experience that is the same as 'pure being' or featureless reality. The Viśiṣṭādvaitins reject the mainstream view upheld by Naiyāyikas and Mīmāṃsakas that *nirvikalpaka* perception grasps a bare reality (*vastu-mātra*) without reference to features such as names, quality, substance and generic property. Rāmānuja says that the content of *savikalpa-pratyakṣa* (conceptual perception) is complex since it explicitly refers to that which is qualified by several categorial features (*padārtha*: i.e. *jāti*, *guṇa*, *dravya* and *kriyā*). But the object of non-conceptual perception (*nirvikalpa*) is also complex since such a prior sensational state is a condition for the comparison of already experienced differentiated entities at the subsequent conceptual stage. Non-classificatory perception is the apprehension of an entity as lacking some differentia, but not of every differentiating feature, since apprehension of the latter kind is never encountered and is in any case impossible. Every cognition arises in virtue of some differentia and is specifically verbalized in the form, 'this is such and such a kind of thing'. The difference lies in the fact that in non-conceptual perception a complex entity, analysable in terms of the categories of substance, specific and generic properties, is cognized, but what is missing is knowledge of the recurrence (*anuvṛtti*) of those features in other entities of the same kind. In *nirvikalpa-pratyakṣa* we cognize an individual and its concrete generic structure (*jāti*, construed as *ākṛti* or *saṃsthāna*) as distinct. But since the structure has been seen in but one individual, we cannot generalize and form a concept. The key point is that since non-classificatory perception is complex and since there is a structural isomorphism between knowing and the known, it cannot yield knowledge of an undifferentiated reality. Finally, inference (*anumāna*) relies upon perceptual data and is thus incapable of revealing anything without features.

The individual self: Agency

The Advaitin opponents say that one's soul or true nature (*ātman*) is inactive, impersonal consciousness without any content because it is identical with the *brahman*. Everyday first-personal experience is a mirage, concealing one's true nature as unconditioned being and consciousness. But devotional theism requires that the self is an individual thinking, acting and feeling entity, capable of responding to God. Advaitin gnostics and Viśiṣṭādvaitin theists attach quite different meanings to the term '*ātman*'. Viśiṣṭādvaita maintains that we really are individual souls, enduring substantial entities that are really distinct from the bodies that they animate and which they can objectify. Souls have experiences while not being reducible to streams of experiences. Each soul has its own ineffable identity that is known only to itself. Every subject of experience enjoys a unique sense of itself as an enduring being somehow distinguished from oneself as a physically, psychologically and socially constituted person. It is this feeling that individuates the souls, whatever their circumstances. The soul is a permanent principle of identity that underpins the synthetic unity of experience in the present and through time.[13]

Viśiṣṭādvaitins think that agency, which requires some form of embodiment, is always an accidental and not an essential feature whether the soul is bound or released. Nevertheless, embodied agency is a reality, not a misconception.[14] The Viśiṣṭādvaitin philosophers propound defences of common-sense realism about the self as a persisting centre of reflexive awareness that is in contact with mind-independent realities. Embodiment is crucial in that it enables agency and sorts of experience that exhaust the accumulated *karma* of souls in bondage to rebirth.

Where contexts of theistic belief are concerned, it may sometime appear that God's universal primary causality excludes the possibility of freely chosen human actions. There may be a suggestion that God is ultimately responsible for human decisions. Rāmānuja responds that God allows us to be free and that this freedom includes the ability to make the wrong choices. The matter receives attention in both his *Vedārthasaṃgraha* (§ 89–90) and in the *Śrī Bhāṣya* commentary on the *Brahma-Sūtras* (2.3.40-1), where he tries to accommodate both universal divine primary causality of everything that happens and individual moral responsibility.

Rāmānuja envisages the following objection:

> It has been stated that the Supreme Being is the Inner Guide (*antar-yāmin*) of all creatures and that everything is under his governance. If this is the case, then there is no one who can be a proper subject (*adhikārin*) of the injunctions and prohibitions found in the *śāstras*. For only someone who is able to act or not act just as a result of his own decisions can be a fit subject of injunctions and prohibitions of the kind 'one should do this' and 'one should not do that'. But there is none such. From what has been said about universal divine governance, it follows that it is God who causes our actions and that he is the driver of all the activities of everyone. As the Kauśītaki Upaniṣad (3.8) puts it: 'He incites to right actions the person whom he wishes to guide upward beyond the world, and he incites to wrong actions the one whom he wishes to bring down.' Does this not mean that God is cruel because he causes us to perform good and evil actions?[15]

To this Rāmānuja responds:

> The Supreme Being has provided conscious beings equally with all the equipment in terms of thought and action that they need for performing or

> refraining from activity. To accomplish this, the deity who is the very basis of their existence and that for the sake of whose glorification they exist has entered them and exercises control *in the sense of permitting them to act*. It is the individual who thus empowered by the godhead engages in actions entirely of its own accord. Observing what is being done, the deity does not interfere. Such creation of the possibility of the performance of good and bad actions is relative to individuals [and not arbitrary]. When a person of his own accord acts in a way that is approved, God is pleased with him and enhances his virtuous disposition, thereby helping him to remain steady in virtue. But when a person is habituated to actions that are displeasing to god, God responds by giving him a bad disposition and thus drives him to perform misdeeds of his own accord.

The question is also discussed in the *Śrī Bhāṣya* (2.3.40-41). The question is whether the agency of the individual soul is autonomous and independent, or does it depend upon God? The prima facie reply is that personal agency is entirely self-determining for if it were dependent upon God, it would follow that scriptural mandates and prohibitions would be meaningless. This is because injunctions can only apply to someone who is capable of making their own decisions to act or not act. But surely some scriptures teach that the agency of the individual soul arises from God because they say that God causes that agency? Rāmānuja takes such scriptures to mean that the godhead, as the soul's inner guide (*antar-yāmin*), observes the soul's intentions and enables it to act by granting permission. The decisions are made by the soul, but their enactment is not possible without the permission of the godhead. So it follows that the scriptural injunctions and prohibitions do make sense since they are directed at responsible agents.

Rāmānuja illuminates the relevant sense of consent and permission here with an analogy: Take the case of two owners of a piece of land. One wishes to sell it. To do so he must obtain the agreement of the co-owner. This consent or permission is a necessary condition of the deal's going through. But the process is the result of intention and actions on the part of the partner who wants to sell the land. The other merely makes it possible. Rāmānuja's point is that God makes possible the actions of the soul, and in this sense, causes them. It does not follow that it is God who is performing the soul's actions and that consequently personal agency is a mirage. In Rāmānuja's view, from the facts that God provides us with the capacity to make decisions and that God gives us the capacity to execute decisions, it does not follow that God is causing the action in the sense of making the decision. In short, God provides the conditions that enable free decisions on our part.

Indeed, another implication of God's permitting action is that the embodied soul is thereby granted the autonomy that is denied to purely material beings whose wholly causally determined behaviour is just an expression of physical processes.[16] As we said above, Rāmānuja, in common with all the Vedāntic traditions, holds that the self is not an agent by nature. It becomes an agent when subject to spatio-temporal conditions. Where activities in the sphere of *saṃsāra* are concerned, the self's activity is not due to its own nature but to its contact with material nature. When embodied and subject to space and time, the soul is in bondage to a series of natural causes and effect. God confers the sort of supernatural freedom that is required for moral responsibility. The principle of divine consent or permission means that embodied souls are free personal agents relative to their circumstances and the causes of their own acts in spite of their entanglement in matter, an entanglement that includes the decision-making process that is 'located' in the physical *buddhi* or mind, which faculty is an evolute of material nature (*prakṛti*).

If *karma*, the system of right and wrong actions, punishments and rewards is understood as an automatic mechanism, then it poses a problem for theistic schools. How is such a mechanism related to the godhead? The question was often raised with reference to the manner of God's arranging the universe at the beginning of a cosmic epoch. This is a fresh start for the cosmos, but not for individual souls who retain their karmic inheritance. When deciding the status on individuals in the new creation, does God take account of their accumulated *karma* or not? The dilemma is this: if he does assign each soul's initial status in accordance with the moral quality of its karmic inheritance, it might seem that he is bound to accept the dictates of the *karma*-mechanism. In that case, God is not omnipotent. If on the other hand, God disregards the karmic inheritance of individuals when assigning status in the new world order, he is open to charges of arbitrary partiality towards some and cruelty towards others.

These matters receive attention in *Śrī Bhāṣya* 2.2.3, where the objection is countenanced that a perfect being whose purposes are ever realized could not be the creator because such a being would have neither reason nor motive to create anything. Moreover, the inequalities in creation imply that the creator is cruel. Rāmānuja responds to the first challenge that it is quite intelligible for a being that has everything that it needs to engage in play or sport. Such activity does not imply any sort of lack or deficiency. In response to the second, he says that it is only the previous deeds of the embodied souls that are responsible for the unequal arrangement of the world. This is because God has regard to karmic inheritances when inaugurating a new cosmic epoch.

There follows an objection to the effect that if the organization of the new creation is an automatic response to the good and bad actions of souls, then there is no need of divine superintendence. Material nature will be conditioned by the good and bad actions of the souls, and will be appropriately transformed in different ways in accordance with human deserts [i.e. the conditions will be such that sentient beings may experience the fruits of their *karma*]. The response is that this objection belies ignorance of the natures of good and bad actions, something that can only be learnt from the Vedic scriptures [and is hence not a matter to be decided by humans]. Those scriptures teach that the essence of right actions is that they please the Supreme Person and that the essence of wrong actions is that they displease the godhead. The ethical value of an action consists in whether or not it is agreeable to the godhead. What is right is determined by what is good, where goodness means the same as being pleasing to God.

We see here the solution to dilemma raised by the question of God's relation to the *karma*-mechanism. Rāmānuja's tradition cuts the Gordian knot by a reinterpretation of the meaning of *karma*.[17] For here, *karma* is not a self-regulating mechanism independent of the divine will and intellect. It makes no sense to treat it as something that the divinity might take notice of or not when arranging the initial distributions at creation. Rāmānuja thinks that morality is a matter of obeying divine commands. He holds that the notions of the morally good and morally bad have meaning only in relation to what God wills. Virtuous actions are by definition actions that please God. Indeed they are forms of worship. Possessing good *karma* means the same as being favoured by god. The rewards for good actions and punishments for bad ones are not automatically occurring products: rather, they are divinely willed.

Individual selves: Consciousness

The Viśiṣṭādvaitins agree with the Advaitins that consciousness is unique in that it does not require anything else to establish its existence (*svataḥ siddha*).[18] But they differ from them in denying that the true self may be understood simply as consciousness. Were that the case, selves could not be individuals. Rather, reflexive and intentional consciousness is an essential *property* of individual selves that are its agent and substrate. It is one's true nature that is incorrigibly revealed as the 'I' in every conscious state. Our everyday sense of selfhood is not a mistake concealing another authentic 'inner self'. Thoughts are properties that require an enduring thinking subject. That consideration is used by the Naiyāyikas as an inference for the existence of a persisting subject. But Rāmānuja and his tradition think that such an inference is superfluous because we are immediately aware of ourselves as enduring individual conscious agents. The self is not known in the same ways as objects and states of affairs in the world are known, because it is phenomenally given in direct intuition. Each of us is known to ourselves in an immediate and special way. Everyone always knows who they are.

The Self is the agent of conscious acts that illuminate objects. Conscious acts are both intentional and reflexive. The tradition defines consciousness in terms of two factors: its intentionality – its being directed towards objects other than itself – and its reflexivity or 'self-awareness'. They hold that all conscious states are intentional: they are acts on the part of a subject directed towards some object or state of affairs. But Rāmānuja resists the externalist view that experience is necessarily and not just causally dependent upon interactions with an objective environment by insisting that all conscious acts and states are always self-illuminating or intrinsically reflexive (*svayaṃ prakāśa*). That is to say, when a subject cognizes something, *simultaneously and in virtue of the same act*, he is aware of himself as cognizing that reality. Even in intentional cognitive acts that are, as it were, absorbed in the object by being fully attentive to it, there is also an element of subjective awareness.

We have seen that the Viśiṣṭādvaitins rule out the possibility of non-intentional blank awareness (*nirviśeṣa-cinmātra*). Awareness is always complex and always about something. Moreover, consciousness is in a state of flux. Were it identical with the self, it would be impossible to recognize something seen today as the same thing seen the previous day. The self is not a bundle of fleeting experiences. It is the persisting subject that has the experiences – a principle of continuity with a witness' perspective upon the states that it co-ordinates. The normal self keeps track of itself through time. It is the agent of mental acts, and its permanence as such and the momentary nature of those acts are both directly perceived. Distinctively, Viśiṣṭādvaitins think that the self both has the form of consciousness (*cid-rūpa*) and has consciousness as its quality. They say that consciousness is both substance (*dravya*) and an attribute (*guṇa*), and its nature is to render entities susceptible of thought, speech and action. As the essential property (*svarūpa-nirūpaṇa-dharma*) of the soul, it can be considered as substance, but as discrete mental acts possessed by the self, it exists as an attribute.

The Advaitic tradition says that one's everyday feeling of personal identity (*ahaṃkāra*), the sense of oneself as an individual agent subject to religious and social duties and confronting a world of objects, is a mask concealing the identity of consciousness with the impersonal, inactive Absolute beyond differentiation. The illusion occurs when the light of consciousness is confused with the activity of the material intellect (*buddhi*). As we saw above, Rāmānuja's tradition denies that our everyday feeling of continuous personal identity is an illusion or a case of mistaken identity. It is integral to *bhakti* theism that the self that understands itself as a servant and lover of God should be the authentic self. The 'I' that thinks, intends and acts is the real self. The pronoun 'I' ultimately stands for the inner self that is itself animated by God, its inner guide and sustainer. As Nāthamuni puts it in the Nyāya-tattva, 'If "I" did not refer to the true self, there would be no interiority belonging to the soul. The interior is distinguished from the exterior by the concept "I". The aspiration "May I, having abandoned all suffering, participate freely in infinite bliss" actuates a person whose goal is liberation from rebirth (*mokṣa*). Were it thought that liberation involved the destruction of the individual, he would run away as soon as the subject of liberation was suggested.... The "I", the knowing subject, is the inner self.' In other words, if salvation through gnosis means the destruction of the person, we would have no interest in it.

The soul–body model

Rāmānuja's basic ontology is a hierarchy of three really distinct categories. At the summit there is the perfect being, the personal god Nārāyaṇa, the first cause and sovereign of the cosmos who is also immanent in individual souls as their existential support and guide. Next there are the souls themselves that are individual subjects of experience. They exist to glorify God but they are burdened by *karma* or the accumulated consequences of actions performed in past lives. Inherited *karma* is responsible for a contraction of the souls' cognitive and imaginative powers. It restricts the capacity for moral discernment and sensibility. It brings about the misconception that one's embodied present circumstances define one's identity. Thirdly, there are the physical things populating the material environment that is the arena in which experiences are undergone. Rāmānuja's most significant contribution to Śrī Vaiṣṇava theology is his systematic elaboration of the Vaiṣṇava idea that the cosmos of souls and matter is the body of God. The notion derives from such scriptural passages as Brihadāraṇyaka Upaniṣad 3.7.3-23, verse 14 of which reads:

> This soul of yours who is present within but is different from all beings, which all beings know not, whose body is all beings, and who guides all beings from within – he is the inner guide (*antar-yāmin*), the immortal one.

In a nutshell, the idea is that the relation between God and the world is loosely analogous to the relation between an individual soul (*jīva*) and its material body. God animates the world as the *jīva* animates its body. This is not intended as a provisional model – a fruitful way of thinking about divinity. Rather, it is the literal truth as stated by the scriptures (*śruti*) that are our only means of knowing (*pramāṇa*) about the transcendent.

The key features of the analogy are difference and dependence. Soul and body are distinct, but the body is essentially dependent upon the soul in the sense that the soul is its only raison d'être. But there is an even stronger kind of dependence: a given lump of matter is only constituted as a determinate corporeal entity when it is animated by a soul. So, extending the analogy into the sphere of human interests: our being bodies of God – alternatively, our being divinely animated – means that the purpose of our existence is that we might serve and glorify God, and that we only exist as entities because God has ordained it to be the case.

The soul–body model is succinctly stated in *Vedārthasaṃgraha* Section 76:

> The relation between soul and body is that between existential ground (*ādhāra*) and dependent entity (*ādheya*) that is incapable of separate existence, between director and thing directed, and between principal (*śeṣī*) and subordinate (*śeṣa*). One term is called *ātman* because it is the substratum, the director and the principal. The other term is called body because it is an inseparably dependent mode (*apṛthak-siddhi-prakāra-bhūta*), a thing directed and a subordinate. Such is the relation between the individual soul and its body. Because all conscious and non-conscious entities are modes of the Supreme Soul because they are his body, all words for such beings apply in their primary senses to the Supreme Soul.

And as Rāmānuja puts it in *Śrī Bhāṣya* 1.1.1 (pp. 114–15):

> The self is the sole unique substratum of the body since when it is separated from the body, the latter perishes. The self is the body's sole raison d'être since it exists only so that the soul may experience the fruits of its *karma*.

And again from *Śrī Bhāṣya* 2.3.18:

> The *brahman* always has as its essentially dependent modes the conscious and non-conscious entities that compose its body. When that body of beings is in a super-subtle, potential condition, they cannot be designated as separate from the *brahman*. That is the *brahman*'s causal condition. When the body is in its gross condition, there is a distribution of names and forms applied to entities. That is the *brahman*'s effected condition.

The specialized definition of a body as 'any substance that a sentient being is able to control and support for its own purposes and which is entirely subordinate to that entity' (Śrī Bhāṣya 2.1.9) is a response to those who say that the world (let alone souls!) neither looks not behaves like the range of items usually designated by the term 'body'. Indeed, Rāmānuja remarks that in ordinary language, the word 'body' differs from words such as 'pot', whose denotation is restricted to things of a single form, because it is applied to items of radically different character.

Rāmānuja's formulation of the relation between God and the world of finite beings in terms of the soul–body model was in part a response to two alternative ways of thinking, both of which he saw as objectionable. One was that of the Advaita Vedāntins who held that the absolute reality (the *brahman*) was undifferentiated and inactive consciousness, and that the merely apparent individual selves are identical with that. In truth, there are no individual entities of any sort, and thinking in terms of difference is a mistake. It follows that the phenomenal world about us and our experiences of ourselves as personal individuals are ultimately speaking a mirage concealing a changeless absolute totally detached from the realm of becoming. All plurality of selves and actions, thoughts and objects, results from the operation of a beginningless force that generates misconceptions (*bhāva-rūpa-avidyā*) about the true nature of reality. As Rāmānuja puts it, 'The one simple conscious reality when concealed by *avidyā* manifests (*vivartate*) the cosmos' (Veds § 35).[19] To Rāmānuja's mind, Advaita denies not only the reality and value of personal individuality and experience, but also the reality of suffering and evil.

Most schools of Vedānta (that of Madhva is an exception) say that the *brahman*, or the unsurpassingly great being, is both the material (or substrative) and the efficient cause of the cosmos. They accept the *Sāṃkhya* system's *satkārya-vāda* theory of causation, which states that effects pre-exist in subtle or potential form in their material causes prior to their emergence as determinate entities with name and form. This can be interpreted as meaning that cause and effect are substantially the same, while effects are treated as different because they acquire their own additional properties and functions. Material causes were deemed to transform themselves into their effects: milk turns into yoghurt, pots and plates are made from clay, and jewellery is made from gold. The one material 'stuff' is scattered throughout the world. When this idea is applied in cosmogonic contexts to the *brahman*, the cosmos is thought of as emerging from the being or substance of that unconditioned reality. It is that being that is distributed as the cosmos. Obviously, this notion that the world and everyone in it is the self-transformation of the divinity has parallels with the idea that there is an *analogia entis* between God and the world. There is a strong ontological continuity, a shared nature, between the *brahman* and the emergent cosmos.

Advaita Vedānta accepts a version of the *satkārya-vāda* view of causation. They say if the substrative cause is undifferentiated and inactive awareness, its effects must be also. Hence, phenomenal plurality, individuality and activity are not ultimately real. Another form of Vedānta (sometimes called 'Bhedābheda-vāda') sought to defend realism against Advaitin *vivarta-vāda*. But it posed an equally serious challenge to devotional theism. This was because its pantheistic claim that the world is a real transformation (*pariṇāma*) of the substance of the *brahman* could be read as meaning that the essence of the Supreme Being and the total cosmos are one and the same. According to this view, the *brahman* becomes the cosmos and the cosmos is what the absolute has changed into. Some of these people say that the *brahman* is the all-encompassing universal Being of which all entities are instances. They believed that souls and matter emanated from the godhead, a single divine substance that transforms itself into all subjects and objects of experience. Such views were objectionable to Rāmānuja who thought that by recognizing the conversion of unconditioned reality into finite realities, they implicated divinity in imperfections including suffering and rebirth. This has the undesirable consequence that release from the series of births is impossible (*Śrī Bhāṣya* 2.3.18).

Rāmānuja describes the view of Bhāskara and his school as follows:

> They say that the effected cosmos is real. The difference between the individual soul and the *brahman* is contingent [brought about by limiting conditions]. By nature, they are non-different. The duality of the *brahman* and matter is natural. Given that there are no realities other than the *brahman* and the limiting conditions (*upādhi*), and given the connection of a limiting condition with the undivided and partless *brahman*, it is the *brahman* as it is in itself that is transformed into inferior modes of being. (*Śrī Bhāṣya* 2.1.15)

> Bhāskara and his followers say that the *brahman* although having every exalted quality such as freedom from evil is connected with a limiting condition so that it is bound and released, and becomes the basis of a transformation into imperfect modes of being. (*Vedārthasaṃgraha* § 8)

And in the cognate view of Rāmānuja's teacher Yādavaprakāśa:[20]

> The *brahman* is the substrative cause of the cosmos. It is hyper-essential substance that is just undifferentiated being. But it possesses all potentialities. In that condition the properties of being an experiencer, being an object of experience and being the regulator are elided.
>
> Prior to the emergence of the cosmos, the substrative cause albeit self-luminous rests like one asleep, all experiential variety having ceased. At creation, just as the substance clay acquires the forms of pots and plates and the water of the ocean becomes foam, waves and bubbles, so the substrative cause constitutes itself in tripartite form whose parts are: subjects of experience, objects of experience and the director. The properties of being subjects of experience, objects of experience and the director as well as the virtues and defects attendant upon them are distributed as the cosmos. They are one in being, just as pots and plates etc. are constituted by clay. It is just the substance, simple undifferentiated being, that underlies all the different states and conditions. In this sense, the world is not different from the *brahman*. (*Śrī Bhāṣya* 2.1.15)

Rāmānuja says that it follows from the Advaitin view that 'The *brahman* itself is deluded by beginningless *avidyā*. It follows from one version of the emanationist view (that of Bhāskara) that the reality of the limiting condition (*upādhi*) applied to the *brahman* is that the *brahman* itself is in a state of bondage to space, time and rebirth. It follows from the other version (that of Yādavaprakāśa) that because the *brahman* is transformed under manifold aspects, it experiences the unpleasant fruits of action (i.e. is subject to *karma*). Furthermore, God cannot be identified simply as undifferentiated being for two reasons. In the first place, pure being is admitted to be but one aspect of the godhead, and in the second place, all being is differentiated. In terms of the opponent's formulation, the divinity is but one of three aspects of the substrative cause. It follows that the divinity is part of the whole that is undifferentiated being and hence subordinate to that whole' (*Śrī Bhāṣya* 2.1.15).

One of the reasons why Rāmānuja developed the three-level ontology (God, souls and material things) was to counter the claims of such *pariṇāma-vādins* and *vivarta-vādins*. He insists that entities at each of the three levels of the hierarchy are essentially distinct and that there is no substantial intermingling of the properties of being the sovereign, being subjects of experience and being objects of experience. He replaced the *brahma-pariṇāma* theory, which sees the world as a transformation of the divine substance, with the *brahma-śarīra-pariṇāma* theory. According to the latter, the cosmos is what happens when the body of the *brahman*, 'containing' all souls and material things in potential forms, moves from its causal to its effected condition. The occurrence of the cosmos is a reality, a real transformation initiated by and continuous with the divinity, but change and imperfection occurs in the sphere proper to the conscious and non-conscious entities that are essentially dependent modes in that they constitute the body of the *brahman*. The transcendent divine essence is unsullied by involvement in finite conditions, albeit ones of its own making. The divine perfection is preserved. The soul–body model may be viewed as panentheistic. It is a theology which seeks to accommodate divine transcendence, the qualitative otherness and infinite perfection of the deity, and divine immanence in the world. The *brahman* is 'in' the world as that which sustains and pervades it. This total pervasiveness underlines its otherness from the finite. The soul–body model also articulates the belief that God is the innermost constitutive element (*antar-yāmin*) in man. Since soul and body are intimately related as well as categorically distinct, the idea holds together immanence and transcendence. Just as the body is existentially dependent upon its animating self, so the individual selves are utterly dependent upon the Supreme Being. The categorical difference between self and body means that when the *brahman* is regarded as the self of his body or the cosmos of souls and matter, he is untouched by imperfection.

> The individual self being related to the Supreme Being as Its body, its properties do not affect the godhead any more than infancy, youth and other features of the material body touch the individual soul. (*Śrī Bhāṣya* 1.1.13)

Being free from evil is of course an aspect of the divine perfection. The precise sense is that the godhead is free from *karma*: a mode of being that is the preserve of the Supreme Being and released souls. This expresses divine transcendence, the total otherness of the creator's essence from the world process. Individual selves are, however, bound by the consequences of their *karma*, which is responsible for a contraction of their innate cognitive and imaginative powers. It is not a constraint upon agency, because the souls are agents only when embodied and subject to space and time in modes appropriate to their *karmas*. Since they are not agents by nature, such limits are not limitations. Furthermore, the godhead has arranged the diversity of creation in accordance with the different *karmas* of individual souls (*Śrī Bhāṣya* 2.1.35).

The soul–body model and the interpretation of scripture[21]

'Since everything forms the body of the Supreme Person, he is directly signified by every word.' The soul–body model enables Rāmānuja to interpret many scriptural statements that had been treated as favourable to Advaitic monism in a theistic way. Rāmānuja has a semantic principle that the signification of words for essentially dependent modal entities (e.g. bodies) extends to the mode-possessor.[22] Whenever something is essentially in an attributive relation to something else (this includes the relations between qualities, generic properties (*sāmānya, ākṛti*) and the individual substances (*dravya*) to which they belong as well as that between souls and bodies), the terms for the attributes may also signify the possessor. God has created the expressive power (*vācaka-śakti*) of words together with the entities which they signify. Any self is a mode of the *brahman* since it is included in the *brahman's* body. Human bodies are modes of their souls. Words for bodies signify in their primary senses both the sentient entities that animate their respective bodies and God *qua* the inner controller and guide (*antar-yāmin*) of the self. God's immanence as the soul of each embodied soul is the basis of the literal reference of some scriptural passages to him.

It is in the field of scriptural exegesis that the soul–body model comes into its own.[23] The interpretation of coreferential (*samānādhikaraṇa*) statements such as '*Tat tvam asi*' ('That thou art' expressing a relation between the self and the *brahman*) and '*Satyaṃ jñānam anantaṃ Brahma*' ('The Brahman is reality, consciousness, infinite': *Taittirīya Upaniṣad* 2.1.1) is central to Vedāntic theology. *Samānādhikaraṇa* means the co-occurrence of two or more items, for example an individual substance and its property, in the same locus or substrate. In grammatical usage, it is 'the reference to a single object by several terms having different grounds for their application'. Such constructions appear in scriptures expressing the relationship between God and the world, and God and the self, or in the case of '*Satyaṃ jñānam anantaṃ Brahma*' as saying something about the divine nature.

Vedāntins believe that the language of revealed *śruti* is our only means of knowledge (*pramāṇa*) about transcendent reality. We have no cognitive access to God independently of the infallible and authorless scriptural authorities. Rāmānuja is a realist holding that there is an isomorphism between knowledge and the known. There is also a structural isomorphism between scriptural statements and the reality of which they speak. It is not just the meanings of words that are informative. Grammatical constructions reflect the nature of reality. There is a sense in which a thinker's theory of meaning determines their metaphysics. Advaitins emphasize the singularity of reference and construe coreferential constructions as identity statements conveying an impartite essence (*akhaṇḍārtha*). This usually involves attributing non-literal senses (*lakṣaṇā-artha*) to the co-ordinated words, and this is recognized as an exegetical weakness. Rāmānuja's tradition maintains that the grounds for the application are differences belonging to what is signified. Co-referentiality is thus the reference to a complex reality by words expressing its different features. Rāmānuja says that it expresses a single entity qualified by its essentially dependent modes. He interprets co-referential statements about God and features of creation as expressive of the soul–body relation. In the case of '*Tat tvam asi*' ('That thou art'), the Advaitins attribute an extraordinary sense to each term: 'that' stands for the impersonal Absolute, and 'thou' has to be purged of its everyday connotations of individual personality so that it may signify the inner self that is identical with the *brahman*. The statement expresses the identity of the two. But according to the Viśiṣṭādvaita exegesis, the 'that' stands for the creator God, the inner guide of the soul, of whom all entities are modes since they form his body. 'Thou' stands for an individual self, an essentially dependent mode of God. '*Tat*' denotes the Highest Self, which is the cause of the universe, whose purposes are ever-actualized (*satya-saṃkalpa*), who possesses every exalted quality and who is devoid of every trace of imperfection. '*Tvam*' denotes the same *brahman* embodied by the individual self, along with the body of the latter. The grammatical co-ordination conveys the unity (not identity) of the two. The coreferential terms apply in their primary senses.

Let us conclude with some of Rāmānuja's own words:

People unlearned in Vedānta do not see that all objects and all individual souls participate in the nature of the Brahman. They think that the referential scope of all words is restricted to the entities that they usually signify that are in fact only part of their meanings. Once they have learnt about the Vedānta passages, they understand that all words signify the Brahman who constitutes his various modes since everything participates in the Brahman in so far as he is the Inner Controller and that everything is created by him. (Vedārthasaṃgraha, p. 21)

The body may be thought of in co-ordination with the Self in that it is the essential nature of bodies to exist in an attributive relation with selves since they would not exist independently of them. This is comparable to the relation between generic properties such as cowness and their individual instances. (*Gītā Bhāṣya* 13.1)

We have interpreted the manifold scriptural statements consistently with each other and without sacrificing their literal senses. The Scriptures saying that the Brahman does not change retain their primary senses by rejecting transformations of its essential nature. The Scriptures saying that it is without qualities are established as denying undesirable ones. Denials of diversity are preserved because they assert that the Brahman has everything as its modes in that he is the soul of all because all conscious and non-conscious things are entities only because they are embodied modes of the one Brahman. Passages saying that the Lord is different from his modes and has all perfections may be taken at their face value. Statements that he is pure consciousness and bliss are taken literally because they convey a self-luminous reality having blissful awareness as an essential property. Statements of unity are well established because the coreferential constructions in their primary senses express a soul–body relation.

Is the overall purport of the Upaniṣads difference or non-difference or difference-cum-non-difference? It is all three. Non-difference is established because the one Brahman has everything as its modes because he is embodied by everything. Difference-cum-non-difference (*bhedābheda*) is established because the *one* Brahman exists as multiplicity having conscious and non-conscious entities as his modes. Difference is established because non-conscious entities, conscious entities and the Lord differ in respect of their essential natures and activities and are not intermingled. (*Vedārthasaṃgraha*, pp. 84–5)

Further reading

The *Śrī Bhāṣya* is translated in Thibaut (1904) and the *Vedārthasaṃgraha* in van Buitenen (1956). The commentary on the *Gītā* has an English précis in van Buitenen (1953).

Svāmī Ādidevānanda's edition and translation of the *Yatīndra matadīpikā* is a useful primary source.

There is a classic monograph by Carman (1974), which can be supplemented by Lipner (1986) and Bartley (2002).

For God as the 'inner-controller', see Oberhammer (1998).

For the devotional religious context, see Hardy (1983).

For Pañcarātra, Schrader (1973) is still the standard work. There is interesting material in Sanderson (2001). See also Sanjukta Gupta (2000), *Lakṣmī Tantra*.

Questions for discussion and investigation

1. Does Rāmānuja have a pantheistic *vision* of the world as the body of God, or is the notion better understood as an exegetical device?
2. Why is Rāmānuja so resolute in his opposition to Advaita?

Notes

1. The compound word resolves as *viśiṣṭasya-advaita*, meaning 'unity of something complex'.
2. For Yāmuna, see Neevel (1977). For Rāmānuja, see Lipner (1986) and Bartley (2002).
3. The chronology proposed here works back from Vedānta Deśika.
4. See Hardy (1983).
5. Vedārthasaṃgraha, p. 3.
6. van Buitenen (1953), pp. 179–82.
7. Sanderson (2009) pp. 58–70 and Sanderson (2001)(historyx).
8. The earliest references are in the *Mahābhārata*, dating to the two or three centuries prior to the Common Era. See Schrader (1916).
9. See Śrī Bhāṣya 2.1.33.

10. The most revered are the *Sātvata-āgama*, the *Jayākhya-saṃhitā* and the *Pauṣkara-saṃhitā*.
11. In *Vedārthasaṃgraha*, pp. 92–3, he gives a long list of earlier teachers belonging to the Vedāntic tradition of Upaniṣadic exegesis who taught that *bhakti* alone, expressed in action and involving profound understanding, is the path to god.
12. See also Bartley (2011) for more about theistic reactions to Advaitin metaphysics.
13. Bartley (2002), pp. 48–64.
14. Lipner (1986), Ch. 4.
15. *Vedārthasaṃgraha*, p. 89.
16. Śrī Bhāṣya 2.3.33.
17. See also the Pāñcarātra scripture *Lakṣmī Tantra* 3.32-7 (Gupta 2000): 'O Goddess, born of the milky ocean, if you distribute pleasure and pain having regard to *karma*, what has become of your complete freedom? Reply: Karma is my instrument when I am creating. The dependence of an agent upon an instrument does not impede his autonomy. Do not look for a reason: [creation] is just for playfulness (*līlā*)'. The notion that creation is divine play enjoys currency in all the Tantric traditions.
18. For more, see Bartley (2002), pp. 49–64 and Lipner (1986), Ch. 3.
19. *Pariṇāma* says the world is a modification of a basic reality and that the substrative cause and its effects are equally real. *Vivarta* names a process wherein less than fully real effects emerge from a real substrative cause. See Vedānta Paribhāṣā Section 85.
20. Oberhammer (1997).
21. For a more detailed treatment, see Bartley (2002), Ch. 4.
22. Because the body is a mode of the embodied entity and because the meanings of words for modes extend to the mode-possessor, there is the principle that the meanings of words signifying bodies extend to what is embodied. Whenever we think, 'This is such and such', the mode is understood as the aspect that is 'such and such'. It is logical that the mode culminates in the mode-possessor since it depends upon that entity and its being apprehended depends upon that entity. Thus, a word signifying a mode extends to the possessor (*Śrī Bhāṣya* 1.1.13).
23. Because all conscious and non-conscious entities are modes of the Supreme Soul in that they are his body, all words for such beings apply in their primary senses to the Supreme Soul (*Vedārthasaṃgraha*, p. 75).

13

Dvaita Vedānta and Madhva

Chapter Outline

Dvaita is a realist form of metaphysical pluralism. It is the philosophical articulation of radical *Vaiṣṇava* monotheism. Madhva and his followers insist that the Scriptures are first and foremost revelations from and about the one god called Viṣṇu. Madhva's thinking is theocentric, rather than anthropocentric or cosmocentric, to a remarkable degree. Anything that we may know about God, we learn from the Scriptures. There can be no natural knowledge of God. The tradition extends the canon of Scripture beyond the revealed *śrutis* and traditional *smṛtis* that are accepted by all Vedāntins to include many specifically Vaiṣṇava sectarian compositions, many of which appear to be very late compositions.

Madhva lived in Udīpi in Karnataka from 1238 to 1317 A.D. and wrote commentaries on several Upaniṣads, the *Bhagavad Gītā*, the *Brahma-Sūtras* and the *Bhāgavata Purāṇa*, in addition to many compositions of his own such as the *Viṣṇutattvavinirṇaya*. Other exponents of Dvaita Vedānta are the acute logicians Jayatīrtha (1365–88 A.D.) and Vyāsatīrtha (1460–1539 A.D.), both of whom commented on Madhva's works.

Basic to their ontology is the distinction between the only independent and self-determining (*svatantra*) reality that is the unsurpassably great godhead, and the dependent sentient and insentient existences whose very being is sustained by God. The universe is real creation, but it has no intrinsic tendency to continue in existence. The world only continues in existence beginninglessly and perpetually because it is *always* known and sustained by God. Viṣṇu is omnipotent, omniscient and blissful. Indeed he is possessed of the host of glorious characteristics elaborated in the *Pāñcarātra* scriptures. All his attributes are eternal and in no wise different from him. He is different from all other beings, but this difference does not affect him. There is no plurality in the divine nature parallel to that of the world. There are no differences intrinsic to the divine nature, which is simple. God's uniqueness consists in there being no difference between his essence and his existence. In other words, it is his essence to exist, whereas the existences of finite beings are dependent.

The cosmos is structured by five types of real difference: the difference between God and the individual soul, that between material objects and God, differences between individual souls, difference between individual souls and material objects, and differences between material objects. Souls and matter are eternal realities. So the notion of divine creation should be understood as an articulation of a relation of absolute dependence rather than a process of emanation from the divine substance.

The cosmos is real and has no beginning. If it has a beginning it would perish. But it does not perish, and it is not constructed by mistaken thinking (*na bhrānti-kalpita*). Were it is thus constructed, it would cease. But it does not cease. Only the mistaken could say that duality does not exist! The wise know that the plural world is real because it is known and protected by Viṣṇu. There are many individual selves, and the complex physical world exists independently of consciousness. An attitude of common-sense direct realism pervades his work. The basic principle is that in direct acquaintance (*anubhava*) with environment that we inhabit, our minds are not creative and constructive. We are confronted by a world outside us, before our minds get to work. He calls this primary, pre-reflective and pre-discursive experience 'pure knowing' (*kevala-pramāṇa*). Truth is correspondence between the mind and an objective state of affairs. Correspondence here should be taken in the strong sense of congruence or conformity, rather than just the sort of correlation that we find between a map and a territory. He says that knowing (*pramāṇa*) is ascertainment (*niścaya*) that conforms to its object (*yathārthyam*). The word '*pramāṇa*' can be analysed as having two senses: a state or piece of knowledge (*pramiti* or *pramā*), and an instrument of knowing – an intentional act by which the real nature of an entity is ascertained or measured.

Madhva's Vedānta is not only opposed to non-dualism that denies the reality of difference and maintains that the absolute Being and the soul are identical, but also to other theistic forms of Vedānta such as *Viśiṣṭādvaita*. The latter posits links between God and the world of conscious and non-conscious entities. This is held to compromise God's transcendent perfection. He disagrees with the Viśiṣṭādvaitin view that there is a continuity of being (*analogia entis*) between God and finite existences. Conceiving of the relation between God and the world in terms of a model such as that between soul and body is to conform God to our ways by using our ways of thought. It posits too close a parallelism between the divine and human orders of being.

Each entity is a unique individual (*viśeṣa*). This individuality is directly and non-discursively intuited (*anubhavād jñāyate*). The unique individuality of an entity has to be known before we can apply words and concepts to it. This is crucial: on this account entities are not constituted, constructed or individuated by our thoughts. We immediately know entities, and ourselves, in their uniqueness without having to compare them with anything else. The notion of *viśeṣa* eliminates the problem of explaining how released souls lacking personal individuality are distinguished from one another. There are three categories of souls: those who are liberated, possible candidates for liberation and those who are beyond salvation (those who explicitly reject the sovereignty of Viṣṇu).

Liberation, in which the soul retains its essential individuality, consists in the realization of a state of innate consciousness and bliss focused on the divinity and is unattainable without a combination of intense devotion (*bhakti*) and divine favour (*prasāda*). Only Viṣṇu saves: liberation is not a human achievement. Love follows acceptance of the unique sovereignty of the Creator and Sustainer, and the understanding of the fivefold difference that characterizes the cosmos in contrast to the absence of internal differentiation in God.

Madhva departed from mainstream *Vedānta* in denying that God is the material or substrative cause of the world. God is only the efficient cause or creator in that he actuates an independent material principle that is subject to his governance. The gulf between the absolute Being and finite beings is spanned by the divine will's sustaining and supporting the limited world.

The examination of Viṣṇu's nature

Madhva's doctrines are attractively and succinctly presented in a work called the *Viṣṇu Tattva Vinirṇaya*.[1]

> If we say that there is no text without an author (*apauruṣeya*) the notions of right (*dharma*) and wrong and the other matters of which the scriptures speak that are accepted by all philosophical traditions lack any foundation. Someone who denies right and wrong does not help the world and only encourages violence. There is no point in his trying to serve mankind since he admits no supernatural reality.
>
> Right and wrong cannot be established by human opinions because people are liable to ignorance and dishonesty.
>
> That the Vedas are not human compositions is self-evident because there is no tradition testifying to their authorship. Positing an author when one is not known is an uneconomical hypothesis.
>
> The epistemic authority (*prāmāṇyam*) of the Veda is intrinsic. Otherwise there is the problem of an infinite regress.
>
> Modes of knowing (*pramāṇa*) like perception and inference have no epistemic authority independently of scripture in matters such as what is right and wrong because the latter are out of their range.
>
> The Vedas are eternal and subsist in the mind of Viṣṇu. They are manifested but not originated when uttered by God.
>
> The Vedas assert facts. They speak of already existing things as well as things to be done. In ordinary language, meanings are primarily grasped in respect of things that already exist. Language is primarily informative and descriptive. It is only once one has understood that something is a means to an end that one acts accordingly.
>
> The overall purport of scripture is not the identity of the individual soul and God.
>
> Passages stating that they are different are not uninformative repetitions of what is already known by some other means because the existence of God is not established without scripture.
>
> God's existence cannot be proved by inference because inference can also prove the opposite.

The argument, 'The world must have a creator because it is an effect, like a jar' is countered by 'The world has no creator because it is not a single whole object.'

If the reality of difference is established by perception and inference within whose province it falls, scriptures asserting non-difference must be false because they are contradicted by those modes of knowing.

Even if scripture is stronger than perception in some contexts, it cannot be valid when it conflicts with it.

Self-evident experience establishes the difference between the individual soul and God. Everyone knows that they cannot do everything. Scripture is not an authority if it contradicts this sort of self-evidence.

If difference is established by a means of knowing other than scripture, it is self-evident that it cannot be denied.

If it is not so established, scriptures teaching difference will still be authorities because they inform us about something that would otherwise be unknown.

As non-difference is contradicted by all the means of knowing it is not the purport of scripture. Rather, the purport of scripture is the unsurpassable greatness of Viṣṇu.

The goals of human life such as *dharma* have results that are ultimately transitory and mixed with unhappiness (since one knows that they won't last for ever). Only freedom from rebirth (*mokṣa*) is the supreme felicity to be sought by those wandering in *saṃsāra*.

Freedom is not attained without the grace of God. God fells affection for those who recognise his superior virtues but not for those who insist on their identity with him.

Difference

The logical arguments against the reality of difference advanced by Advaitin thinkers are unsound because difference is the proper form or essential nature (*svarūpa*) of an entity.

Examples of such arguments are:

There is proof of difference by the existence of the relation between attribute and substrate or quality and qualified. But relation between attribute and substrate depends upon difference.

> Knowledge of difference depends upon cognition of the counterparts to the subject. But the cognition of those counterparts depends upon cognition of the subject from which they differ.
>
> These arguments are circular and lead us to conclude that since we cannot properly formulate an understanding of difference it does not exist.
>
> Madhva replies: But just because difference implies that there are counterparts to the subject, it does not follow that it is not the proper form of the subject. That the number one is not the number two does not compromise its identity.
>
> Difference is established whenever a proper form is identified. We see the proper form of an entity as unique and other than everything else. The expression, 'the difference of this', is parallel to the expression, 'the proper form of the entity'.
>
> If the proper form is not also the difference, the difference of the entity from all others would not be known when the entity is seen. If such individuality is not already known, it would be possible to doubt whether one's self is not a jar.
>
> Having cognised individuality and the general difference of the entity from everything else, one might sometimes question whether the entity is in fact the same as something else that it resembles. But one never doubts whether one is the same person.
>
> Cognition of a universal like potness occurs only once the identity of an object has been cognised. Entities are unique to begin with. They are not made individual by their properties or modes because they must be distinct identities in the first place if they are to acquire different features.
>
> Individual identity is directly intuited.
>
> When we say that something is different from a pot and that something is different from a cloth, the 'being different' is not the same in both cases.
>
> The hypothesis that individual entities cognised by the means of knowing are unreal (*mithyā*) is an obfuscation since it contradicts the means of knowing.
>
> Reasoning (*tarka*) on its own cannot refute what has been established by the means of knowing. What is directly perceived cannot be dismissed as error just by reasoning.

We move on to the rejection of the Advaitin theory that just as illusions and mistakes cannot be categorized as real (because they are subsequently corrected) or unreal (because they have real effects), neither can the plural cosmos be real or unreal because it is a product of *avidyā*.

> There is no means of knowing something that is neither real nor unreal. [143]
>
> When someone says, 'We cannot be aware of what does not exist', is he thinking about non-existence or not? If he is not thinking about non-existence, he cannot deny that non-existence was a real content of thought. If he is thinking about non-existence, the same applies.
>
> Without a concept of non-existence, the difference of something from the non-existent cannot be known. When we mistake a piece of shell for a piece of silver, it is not the case that the silver is neither existent nor non-existent because the corrective experience is, 'Non-existent silver appeared there'. We cannot say that it was objectively real just because it was experienced. Illusion means thinking that something unreal is real or thinking that something real is unreal.
>
> In illusions there is a thought of something that was not present in a certain set of circumstances.
>
> We do not need to claim that the content of illusions is neither real nor unreal. Introducing that category introduces more problems than it solves. For instance, is it real or not? The idea flies in the face of experience. Everyone thinks in terms of things either existing or not existing.

Sections 160–308 provide dualistic and theistic interpretations of scriptural passages to which Advaitins appeal as the foundations of their position. Madhva says that we cannot rationally reject the difference between the individual soul and the *brahman* when it is taught by many scriptures. The Advaitin distinguishes between scriptures teaching the truth of non-duality and the rest whose authority is secondary. Madhva points out that this amounts to saying that some scriptures are false. So why should we accept that the ones teaching identity are true? We have no way of evaluating scripture apart from scripture. The purport of the scriptures is the unsurpassable greatness of Viṣṇu. It cannot be the identity of the individual and the *brahman* when this is contradicted by every means of knowing. Such identity is contrary to experience. No one thinks, 'I am omniscient' or 'I am the Lord of all' or 'I am free from sorrow' or 'I am perfect.'

Chāndogya Upaniṣad 6.8.7 says: 'That which is the subtle essence, that is the nature of the cosmos, that (*tat*) is the reality, that is the *ātman*, and that (*tat*) is what you are.' (*Sa ya eṣo'ṇimaitadātmyaṃ idaṃ sarvam. Tat satyam. Sa ātmā. Tat tvam asi*).

Advaita Vedāntins read 'That thou art' as an identity statement. Rāmānuja understood it as expressing the relation of inseparable dependence between body and soul, and between the soul and God. Madhva reads it as 'You are not that.' He contrives this by ignoring the natural break between '*ātmā*' and '*Tat tvam asi*' so that it becomes '*ātmātat tvam asi*', which is analysable as '*ātmā atat tvam asi*'. The long **ā** may indicate the coalition of an initial letter **a** with the letter **a** or **ā** at the end of the preceding word. The form 'atat' means 'not that'.

Sections 309–62 are devoted to a critique of a form of subjective idealism which reduces to solipsism. As he puts it, 'There is no way of proving that the whole cosmos is a figment of the imagination of a single soul.'

The word '*prapañca*' is a common expression for the plural cosmos. Madhva analyses it by the *nirukta* method and finds that it means the five kinds of differences. '*Pañca*' means five, and '*pra*' abbreviates '*prakṛṣṭa*' meaning expansion. Because this *prapañca* is called '*māyā-mātram*', it cannot be unreal. What does he mean? *Māyā*, he says, means God's consciousness. That which is known (*māna*) and preserved (*trāṇa*) by God's consciousness is *māyā-mātram* (*mā* + *tra*). 'Since it is known and protected by God, the plural world is not fabricated by misconception.' 'There can be no perceptual error when one sees directly. Viṣṇu knows everything directly. He sees the universe, so it cannot be unreal.'

Direct epistemological realism

> If the world is fabricated by misconception, there would be two worlds (one fabricated and another in which someone or something is doing the fabricating). There is no mistaking a piece of shell for silver unless there is real shell, real silver and similarity between the two. Even in dreams when traces of prior experiences are active, a world appears to the mind as existing externally. In cases like the conch seen as yellow and the sky as blue, the subject is related to the properties yellow and blue. They exist elsewhere although not concretely instantiated in those circumstances. There are no perceptual errors without two similar real entities. This is why it makes no sense to speak of the superimposition of what is not the self (i.e. features of the world) on the self. [343ff.]

There are further considerations in defence of realism in verses 389–95:

The theory that something that is directly seen as real, is in fact unreal, needs the support of stronger evidence than observation. But if there is no such evidence, there is no need to suspect observation. What is known by perception cannot be refuted by reasoning alone without other more authoritative perceptions. We know on the basis of perception and reasoning that large objects appear small in the distance. This is not a perceptual error. We can understand that this is the way things appear to us. We can use perception to establish the scope of perception, but there could no way of establishing that all our perceptions are false.

* * *

The trouble with *avidyā*

The Dvaita philosophers present a battery of arguments against the various ways in which the Advaitin thinkers attempt to account for the appearance of the many when the truth is that Absolute Reality is single and unchanging. Advaita blames the appearance of plurality on ignorance (*avidyā*). The theory that ignorance is a cosmic force inexplicably connected with the *brahman* had become established as the canonical doctrine long before Madhva's time. The argument that if the plural universe were just a mistaken mental construction, it would cease to exist whenever anyone understood that it was such, recurs throughout his works. If the universe is but an ultimately unreal construct and *avidyā* is always associated with the *brahman*, there is no genuine possibility of liberation.

Madhva applies the principle that illusions and cognitive errors only occur when there is some similarity between two things. But this cannot apply globally because there is no similarity between the *brahman* and the cosmos.

The view of Maṇḍana Miśra and Vācaspati Miśra that *avidyā* belongs not to the *brahman* but to the individual self can quickly be dismissed because the very concept of individuality is fabricated by misconception in the first place. Moreover, if the soul that has *avidyā* is really identical with the *brahman*, then *avidyā* belongs to the *brahman* too. Some Advaitins argue that the apparent difference between the soul and the *brahman* derives from some sort of imagined feature or unreal qualification (*upādhi*) that becomes superimposed upon the *brahman*. But this is unconvincing. If the *upādhi* is constructed (*kalpita*), this act presupposes ignorance in the first place, and the argument becomes circular: *avidyā* produces the *upādhi*, and the *upādhi* is responsible for ignorance. If the *upādhi* is not constructed and is a beginninglessly real feature of the individual soul, it follows that there is something that originally differentiates the individual soul from the *brahman*. If the qualification really belonged to the *brahman*, it would compromise its perfect simplicity.

The idea that the *brahman* is the substrate of ignorance was intended to avoid these problems. But if this is true, the released soul will be subject to ignorance too since the Advaitins suppose it to be the same as the *brahman*. If ignorance is somehow implicated in the very being of the *brahman*, it must be real. If such ignorance is responsible for plurality, then plurality is real and it would be impossible to escape from ignorance-based *saṃsāra*.

Further reading

Sarma (2003) is a good start. It needs to be supplemented by Mesquita (2000). Gerow (1990) translates a text from the subsequent tradition and is excellent on the details of the controversies with Advaita. The *Viṣṇu-Tattva-Vinirṇaya* is in Raghavachar (1959) with a translation.

Questions for discussion and investigation

1. Is Madhva right to think that Rāmānuja's soul–body model compromises God's perfection?
2. In what sense does he have a concept of God as a personal being?
3. Some people have suggested Christian influences. Do you detect any?
4. The Mādhvas were originally Śaiva Siddhāntins. Can you see any connections?

Note

1. Raghavachar (1959).

14

Tantra and some *Śaiva Thinkers*

Chapter Outline

Between 700 and 1100 A.D., Kashmir was home to an extraordinarily rich and sophisticated religious and intellectual culture.[1] Most prominent were monistic and dualistic schools of Śaivism or the worship of forms of the God Śiva, sometimes accompanied by his female partner or Śakti.[2] There were also a significant number of Vaiṣṇavas or votaries of the deity Viṣṇu. All these traditions of ritual and belief had their own scriptures, called Tantras or Āgamas. The latter present doctrines, describe rituals for public and private use, and teach types of yoga and proper conduct. They also contain instructions about the construction and consecration of temples. For the most part, followers of these traditions recognized the validity of the religion and scriptures of orthodox Brahmanism and accepted its basic tenets. But they claimed that their religious disciplines were the superior ones, surpassing mainstream orthodoxy in respect of accessibility and availability, as well as providing superior benefits both mundane and transcendent.

We shall look at a version of ritual-based monotheism called Śaiva Siddhānta, which understands the world as a real creation for the sake of individual conscious souls, as well as at some of the monistic Śākta cults worshipping forms of the Goddess and the fearsome god Bhairava.[3] The latter follow scriptures that are sometimes abhorrent to followers of the Vedic tradition, prescribing as they do practices involving the violation of taboos as means of acquiring extraordinary powers, the expansion of consciousness beyond inhibitions deemed to originate in social conventions, and the propitiation of antinomian deities. They think that freedom from rebirth is the recognition of one's true nature as nothing other than the single dynamic consciousness that is the source of everything. Both Śaivas and Śāktas accept the authority of a corpus of twenty-eight divinely revealed Āgamas or Tantras, but the Śāktas expanded the canon significantly and of course claim finality for their own scriptures.

Śaiva Siddhānta dualism

This is a Tantric (i.e. non-Vedic) ritual cult teaching that there are three permanently distinct eternal categories of reality: the godhead named Śiva, individual conscious souls, and material and psychological realities. Its scriptural authorities are twenty-eight texts called *Tantras* or *Āgamas* that are believed to be the revealed word of God. This religion flourished in Kashmir between the eighth and the eleventh centuries A.D., and its most important theorists are Sadyojyotis (c.700 A.D.), Nārāyaṇakaṇṭha (925–975 A.D.), his son Rāmakaṇṭha (950–1000 A.D.) and Aghoraśiva (c.1150 A.D.). Sadyojyotis wrote a work called 'The Examination of God and the Soul' (expounded by Rāmakaṇṭha as the *Nareśvara-parīkṣā-prakāśa* [NIPP]), a commentary on the *Svayaṃbhūva-āgama*, as well as a number of shorter works. Nārāyanakaṇṭha wrote a commentary on the *Mṛgendra Āgama*.

Rāmakaṇṭha's most significant works, in addition to that just mentioned, include commentaries on the *Mataṅgapārameśvara Āgama* [MPAV] and the *Kiraṇa Tantra*.

Śaiva Siddhāntins believe that ritual worship of Śiva, consequent upon initiation into the religion (*dīkṣā*) through the imposition of mantras by one who has undergone a higher consecration (*ācārya*) and is held to be a human expression of the deity, is the only means to the human soul's liberation from rebirth at death. Initiation and liberation are entirely thanks to the descent of Śiva's grace (*anugraha-śakti-pāta*). Only Śiva saves. Initiation removes some of the restrictions on the soul's potentially infinite innate powers of knowledge and agency. These, however, cannot be fully manifested in the context of human life. So initiation does not wholly destroy all the limiting factors proper to the human condition. The portion that remains is gradually eliminated over the course of one's life by the prescribed daily ritual and meditative observances. Following the prescribed religious path for its own sake prevents the production of personalizing *karma* that binds one to rebirth. The latent accumulated *karma* that would otherwise have generated further finite existences is wiped out in the initiation ritual.

The innate capacities for universal knowledge and agency of some souls have been suppressed by an innate defect called '*mala*'. *Mala* is also responsible for those souls' subjection to bondage by *karma* and rebirth. The concept of *mala* as a substantial and irreducible entity in its own right (*vastu*) is of cardinal importance for the Śaiva Siddhāntins because it explains why the souls undergo subjection to bondage, that is, karmically bound experiences, in the sphere of materiality in the first place. There has to be such a primal and irreducible defect obscuring the soul's dual faculty (*śakti*) of knowledge and action, because there is no other satisfactory explanation for the process of transmigration. Originally pure souls would not become involved in rebirth. (Rāmakaṇṭha discusses this in the sixth chapter of his commentary on the *Mataṅgapārameśvara Āgama* [MPAV, p. 208 ff] and in the second chapter of *Kiraṇatantra-vṛtti*.) This original stain, the root cause of bondage to rebirth, is categorized as a material substance (*dravya*) that attaches itself to souls. Knowledge would be sufficient for liberation if bondage to rebirth were just a misconception. Indeed, the monistic Śaivas identify it with ignorance and thus say that it can be removed by knowledge. But knowledge of the presence and nature of a material substance is insufficient for its removal. Such a substance can only be removed by action – specifically, the Śaiva Siddhānta initiation ritual (*dīkṣā*). *Mala* is like an ocular cataract, awareness of which does not prevent its efficacy. Its removal requires the action of the surgeon's instrument. When Śiva decides that a human soul, who longs for liberation from rebirth and accepts the Śaiva teachings, is morally fit for liberation, he induces that soul to approach an *ācārya* and solicit initiation. That ritual weakens *mala* and enables participation in Śaiva ritual life. The real nature of Śiva is revealed to the initiate for the sake of the manifestation of his power of cognition. Thus illuminated, he appears like Śiva and he becomes a Śiva at the death of the body.

Initiation leaves caste, understood as a physical property, intact. The Śaiva Siddhāntin is thus able to fulfil his Brahminical social and ritual duties. His exigent life of Śaiva ritual duty is thus compatible with the observance of mainstream orthodox Brahminical duty and caste purity (*varṇa-āśrama-dharma*). The tradition holds that the daily and occasional obligatory rites must still be performed because there is a danger of reversion to *saṃsāra* if they are omitted. Indeed, one should not transgress the practices of one's caste and station in life. (Some of the monistic Śaiva traditions say that their votaries are in everyday life Vedically orthodox (i.e. observant of *varṇa-āśrama-dharma*), in religion a Śaiva (i.e. a Śaiva Siddhāntin), but in secret a Kaula (i.e. an initiate into a visionary cult whose power-seeking practices violate the norms of conventional religion).)

So the Śaiva Siddhānta is primarily a religion of ritual from initiation until death. *Mala* obfuscates the awareness that Śiva and the soul are equals (not, for example, master and servant). Initiation enables the realization of this truth. But it does not destroy every imperfection. Some *karma* (were it totally obliterated, the initiand would die) remains, and one is still embodied and enmeshed in the impure cosmos. Post-initiation performance of ritual eliminates the residual imperfections. Such observances are not mindless and mechanical but an enlightened path of active gnosis or understanding-in-action. Knowledge is only effective when acted upon, and action presupposes understanding. Daily worship is preceded by a rite in which the practitioner imagines himself as Śiva, sanctifying himself by the imposition of *mantras* on his body and faculties, in accordance with the principle that only Śiva can worship Śiva. Initiation marks the start of a new way of life and the transformation of one's being. Liberation, occurring at death, is understood as equality with Śiva – meaning a state of qualitative identity in which the soul's innate capacities for knowledge and action are fully realized. (In order to avoid a clash of purposes, the released selves choose not to exercise their omnipotence.) It should be noted that the tenet that the capacity for *agency* is an essential property of the selves in all their conditions is one of the factors that demarcates the Tantric from those mainstream orthodox traditions that treat agency as ultimately either illusory or derivative.

Three categories: *Pati*, *Paśu* and *Pāśa*

Pati includes Śiva and released souls. The deity is the efficient (*nimitta-kāraṇam*) but not the substrative cause (*upādāna-kāraṇam*) of the cyclical emanation, stasis and dissolution of the universe. As well as the cosmogonic functions, the deity also has the powers (*śakti*) of concealment (*tirodhāna-śakti*) and grace (*anugraha-śakti*). The former is understood as the compassionate provision of environments in which finite beings may experience the fruits of their *karma*, thereby exhausting its potency, and in which they may work towards their salvation. Saving grace is primarily manifest in the initiation ritual. Śiva is the efficient cause in that he activates the real and beginningless substrative cause, called the *māyā-tattva*, out of which evolves the cosmos of inferior worlds. This differs from the view, characteristic of the Vedānta taught by Śaṃkara and Rāmānuja (but not Madhva), that the Supreme Being is the material as well as the efficient cause of the cosmos that emerges from the divine being. The Siddhāntins reject this on the grounds that the implicit ontological continuity between God as the substrative cause and the world as the arena of effects would implicate the totally transcendent divinity in the finite, imperfect and physical aspects of the cosmos.

The cosmos comes about so that finite beings may perform actions and experience their results. The worlds, or spheres of experience, are organized in accordance with the accumulated *karma* of finite beings. World production is a compassionate act for the sake of bound souls who need spheres of experience if they are to be freed from *karma* and *mala*. It follows that the cosmos is ultimately friendly to human beings. The world is shaped by and for human interests, and there is the possibility for freedom and fulfilment of our highest aspirations.

While the existence of the supreme divinity is revealed by the Śaiva scriptures, Nārāyaṇakaṇṭha and Rāmakaṇṭha hold that it can also be proved by argument from effect to cause. And the occurrence of an effect permits the inference of its own causal factor (*sva-kārakam*). Just as fire is inferred from the observed presence of smoke, so the existence of God can be inferred from the exercise of his creative powers. We conclude that an object such as a pot has a maker because it is an effect or product. There is an invariable association (*vyāpti*) between something's being and effect and its having a maker, just as there is between smoke and fire. Effects require makers with the appropriate knowledge and power. The success of the causal inference for the existence of God depends upon accepting that the cosmos as an integral whole can be considered as an effect. The Mīmāṃsakas deny that the world is an effect because it does not have a beginning ('things have never been otherwise'). But Rāmakaṇṭha claims that the world must be an effect because it is complex (*saṃniveśa/sāvayava*) and composed of gross matter (*sthūla*). As such it cannot be self-created and must have a maker with the knowledge and power appropriate to its complexity. Thus we establish the existence of God.

There is a specific challenge at this point from the Buddhist Dharmakīrti (600–660 A.D.) who argues that while we can infer in respect of specific cases of *composition* that each has a controlling agent, we cannot infer that all effects have a single maker. In other words, from the proposition 'every effect has a cause', we cannot infer 'there is one cause of every effect'. Pots and mountains are both effects, but they are effects of different kinds. Rāmakaṇṭha thinks that this is a quibble that undermines inference: it is established that every sort of effect is invariably concomitant with some kind of maker.[4]

But perhaps the world just emerges from the material elements. So why try to prove another cause called God that is absolutely unseen? Rāmakaṇṭha's reply is that a non-intelligent cause could not generate the regular and structured diversity that the world displays. Without supernatural governance, the emergence of entities from matter would be chaotic. It is true that the world is organized in accordance with the good and bad *karma* of sentient beings. But *karma* is non-conscious, so such organization requires superintendence by a single deity who has the requisite understanding of the diverse *karma* of beings.

Paśu

This is the category of bound souls that are individual centres of reflexive awareness and agency potentially capable of existing beyond space, time and matter. Each has the essential properties of being a knower and being an agent. While potentially omniscient and omnipotent, some of them have become enmeshed in inferior physical and mental existences in the realm of *māyā* where their deliberate and intentional actions generate residues which personalize and remain with the agent until circumstances appropriate for their fruition occur (*karma*). Human souls are subject to *mala*, *māyā* and *karma*. Such souls are equipped with five derivatives from māyā that are called *kañcukas*:

1 A limited capacity for agency (*kalā-tattva*) bestowed upon souls who would otherwise be paralysed by *mala*.
2 A limited capacity for sensory perception and other intellectual acts (*vidyā-tattva*). In verse thirteen of his *Tattvasaṃgrahaṭika*, Aghoraśiva says that '*vidyā* is the means by which one knows the intellect (*buddhi*) in its various aspects such as judgement, memory, imagination and concepts'.
3 A principle of causal regularity (*niyati-tattva*) ensuring that the results of actions (*karma-phala*) accrue to the agent.
4 An interest in the objects of experience on the part of the otherwise apathetic *mala*-afflicted selves (*rāga-tattva*).
5 Our experience of time and its successiveness (*kāla-tattva*). Time is a created reality and plays no part in the lives of Śiva and released souls.

Pāśa

These are the bonds including *māyā*, *karma*, *mala* and Śiva's power of concealment. In addition to the five *kañcukas*, the products of *māyā* are Prime Matter (*prakṛti-tattva*) consisting of the three *guṇas* (*sattva*, *rajas* and *tamas*), intellect (*buddhi*), mind (*manas*), the sense of ego (*ahaṃkāra*), the five sense-faculties and the subtle forms of their objects, the organs of speech and movement, and earth, water, air, fire and space. The mental apparatus, being inert and material, is not intrinsically conscious, but it may assume the form of awareness. Mental faculties are purely instrumental, helping bound souls to find their way around the world. Rāmakaṇṭha says that the instrument of knowing may be said to be conscious only metaphorically.

Rāmakaṇṭha on the enduring individual soul and its experiences

Embodied human souls are self-conscious individual agents of knowing (*grāhaka*) endowed with a psychological apparatus. They are neither merely consciousness nor just a stream of experiences. Their perceptual cognitions grasp mind-independent realities. We can distinguish between objects as known and objects existing mind-independently. Immediate perceptual acquaintance, prior to any conceptualization that may lead to sceptical doubts, tells us that the objects of awareness are external things that have effect upon us. Indeed, our being confronted by a world of objects upon which our thinking has no effect may be reckoned to be the most basic phenomenological fact that there is.

A Buddhist philosopher of idealist bent may argue that everything and everyone is really undifferentiated consciousness variously expressing itself. He may say that we do not apprehend any difference between the *forms of awareness* (*ākāra*) of objects and cognitions because they are always co-experienced. A Mādhyamika may argue for emptiness (*śūnyatā*): because there are no essences or intrinsic natures (*svabhāva*), everything is relative. There are no absolute truths apart from what humans may agree on and no possibility of an absolute conception of reality independent of particular human interpretations. Rāmakaṇṭha points out that either is going to need some means of substantiating his thesis. Hence whatever we understand the world to be, that will have to become the object of some means of knowing (*pramāṇa*). There will thus be some sort of relation between the means of knowing and the objects known. That relation presupposes that there exists at least one kind of duality. Without a means of knowing, he cannot establish emptiness. The world is *objectified* (*viṣayīkṛta*) whenever someone seeks to establish (*vyavasthāpāyitum* – identifying the nature of something and discriminating it from others) anything by a means of knowing. It is impossible to establish anything about that which has not been made an object. Because of the reality of the process of objectification, the world cannot be empty in the Madhyamaka Buddhist's sense. That is to say, there really are objective standards by which truths can be known.[5]

Rāmakaṇṭha rejects the Buddhist idealist claim that there is non-apprehension (*anupalambha*) of the difference between the forms of objects and our cognitions of them. He says that this is contradicted by the fact that we recognize the difference between establisher and established. Were it otherwise, we could not establish anything. The Buddhist agrees that there are methods of establishing the nature of reality. But such methods cannot just be operating on themselves because there is a contradiction in something's performing its proper function on itself. Hence if there are such methods, they must have objects external to themselves.[6]

Let us remind ourselves at this point of the difference between the Buddhist idealists (*vijñaptimātra-vādins*) and the Buddhist representationalists

(*Sautrāntikas*). The latter hold that there is a significant difference between the way things are and the ways our minds work. They accept that there are real mind-independent realities (*bāhyārtha*), but we have to *infer* (*anumeya*) their existence as the ultimate *cause* of experiences. But those experiences are always human interpretations. There is an external domain consisting of instantaneous unique particulars (*svalakṣaṇa*), but it does not figure in the contents of our thoughts. By contrast, the idealist theory denies that there is a real domain independent of perceptions. Mental variety derives from the accumulation of traces laid down by prior perceptions. When Dharmakīrti said that there is no difference between the colour blue and the cognition of blue because they always co-occur, he did not mean that there was no mind-independent reality.[7] Rather, the point is that we always understand the world from a human perspective, and the argument recommends agnosticism about the true nature of reality: an agnosticism that should wean us away from our conventional mentality structured by the subject–object dichotomy. The point was, however, taken by Buddhists and non-Buddhists alike to be an idealist thesis.

Dharmakīrti had said that 'Although awareness is undifferentiated, it is considered by the misguided to be differentiated into objects, perceivers and thoughts.' This can be interpreted in two ways. If it means that in reality everything is internal to awareness, it is consistent with the idealist outlook. But it is also consistent with the Sautrāntika representationalist's anti-realism if it is taken as meaning that we naturally understand the world in terms of subjects, objects and experiences, although those categories do not mirror reality as it is in itself. Rāmakaṇṭha follows the idealist reading. The idealist will say that an experience of a pot is precisely that: just an experience. Believing in a world of mind-independent material objects is just such a matter of experience. But there is a problem here. Rāmakaṇṭha observes that two sorts of consciousness are pre-reflectively *given* in everyone's experience (*anubhava-siddham*): there is the awareness of oneself as the perceiving subject (*grāhaka*), and there is awareness of objects apprehended (*grāhya*). Also, from the phenomenological point of view, there is a difference between the sorts of awareness that we have of our cognitions on the one hand and of objects on the other. Moreover, the subject is given in its internality as the constant and uniform perceiver, but the contents of its awareness of objects known are always changing. So Dharmakīrti's claim that consciousness is uniform fails. Dharmakīrti thought that the notion of a constant subject was an illusion, a product of mental construction. But Rāmakaṇṭha points out that while all sorts of imagination and mental fabrications are possible, the basic identity of the subject cannot be a construct because it cannot exercise the process of conceptualization (*vikalpa*) on itself. The constructor cannot produce itself as a result of its own constructive activity. It has to be there in the first place. Rāmakaṇṭha argues that the Buddhists cannot make sense of the notion of concept formation (*vikalpa*) if everything is instantaneous. A momentary awareness is no sooner come than gone. If there is no temporal duration, there can be no mental synthesis of earlier and later. It follows that recognition, memory and conceptual construction, all of which require both duration and a single subject capable of uniting separate cognitions, are impossible.[8]

Rāmakaṇṭha argues for a conception of the self as an enduring principle of identity, whose essential properties are reflexively known consciousness and agency. The self is that which always reveals objects. It is established by its own self-awareness as the stable and continuous illuminator of objects. Embodied human souls inhabit a ready-made structured environment consisting of kinds of persisting objects that are not of our mental making. The world really is as it appears to us. It is irrefutably given in pre-reflective experience that external things are the objects of awareness in that they are causally effective as they impinge themselves upon us.[9]

To say that the self is an enduring substance is to treat it as a stable entity that is not a property, state or feature of something else. It is numerically one and the same at different times. Although some of its accidental properties may change, it retains its essential character. Its fundamental stability does not preclude its being involved in time and matter through the process of embodiment. We may contrast this notion of substance with that of an event, which is a reality that has temporal parts or phases. Examples are plays and cricket matches, which are spread out in time. Substances and events can be conceived as persisting through time in different ways. Events consist of phases, and no one part may be present at more than on time. Substances persist thanks to an intrinsic self-maintaining power and principle of unity, which may be embodied in matter. This applies to the classical understanding of *ātman*, and it is stated explicitly by Śaṃkara.[10] The *ātman* is involved in processes through the life of the body, mind, senses and public circumstances with which it is associated. Occurrences comprise the life history of such a continuant, and it makes sense to speak of phases of this history. But it is a mistake to suppose that such stages of the *ātman*'s history when embodied are also parts or stages of that which has the history. On this understanding, events in one's life are not parts of one's essential identity but parts of the life with which it is associated.

We have seen that Buddhist philosophers adhere to an ontology of processes and events (*nairātmya* – non-substantiality), rather than one in which enduring substances are the ultimate constituents of the worlds. They typically reduce whatever is conventionally considered as a stable substance to sequential occurrences: the human subject is an essentially temporal succession of phases.

Rāmakaṇṭha refers to four traditions of Buddhist thought as he introduces his polemic against Buddhism:[11]

> The Vaibhāṣikas and the Sautrāntikas who accept the existence of entities external to the mind (*bāhyārthavāda*); the Mādhyamaka relativists who say that the constituents of reality postulated by the *bāhyārthavādins* lack intrinsic identities (*svabhāva-śūnyatā*); and the Yogācārins who hold that everything is dependent upon minds.
>
> They all agree that there is no entity called 'soul' which is distinct from transient cognitions, because we have no knowledge of it.

The argument from non-cognition (*anupalabdhi*), characteristic of Dharmakīrti, is that when an object or state of affairs satisfies the conditions for knowability or perceptibility, it is not being cognized allows us to conclude that it does not exist. Dharmakīrti maintains that the soul is the sort of thing that would be knowable by us (*upalabdhi-lakṣaṇa-prāpta*) as separate from ephemeral episodes of awareness. But it is not thus known, and so we may conclude that it does not exist.

Rāmakaṇṭha attributes to his Vaibhāṣika Buddhist opponents the view that there is no personal identity but only a succession of experiences, continuously subject to change:

> If differences are real, cognition, which is the basis of the distinction between individual personality and the impersonal external world and which is different at each moment and in relation to each object, is shown by immediate experience to be the perceiver. There is no further fact called soul: it is difficult to maintain the existence of something that is never perceived although it is a possible object of cognition.[12]

The Buddhist says that we see consciousness appearing in many forms such as joy and despondency and concludes that we are a stream of impermanent cognitions. He further argues that were the knowing subject permanent, it would be invariant and so could not shift the focus of its attention from object to object. As Dharmakīrti (to whom Rāmakaṇṭha refers frequently) puts it:

> There is no permanent way of knowing because knowledge is authoritative when it applies to real things. Given the impermanence of knowable objects, knowing cannot be static.[13]

According to Dharmakīrti, what is permanent cannot be causally effective either in the present moment or successively. It follows that there are no permanent identities but only streams of experiences in which cognitions differ from object to object.

To cite Dharmakīrti again:

> Although awareness is undifferentiated, it is considered by the misguided to be differentiated into objects, perceivers and thoughts.[14]

All of this is anathema to Rāmakaṇṭha, who is adamant that we are directly aware of the soul as an enduring substance:

> The soul is defined as that which is established by its own reflexive awareness (*svasaṃvedana-siddha*) as a stable continuant (*sthiratayā*) in as much as it is always the illuminator of objects.
>
> The self, which is the ever-uniform stable conscious perceiver, is not a conceptual construct in that it is reflexively given to each person as the observer of all objects.[15]

> Given that perception proves the nature of the subject as the conscious agent of the direct perception of all objects, it is not possible to establish the non-existence of the self since it is self-evident. Being a subject of karmic experience means being a cognizer. That is the true form of the soul and it is self-evident to everyone.[16]
>
> That whose nature is to have knowing as its essential property is the soul that is the subject of experiences. The soul is proved to exist for everyone because it is manifest in one's own immediate intuition.[17]

This timeless soul is constantly manifest as the same in all mental acts. The individual consciousness that is an essential property of everyone is self-manifesting or reflexive. The reflexivity of consciousness means that when a subject is aware of some object or fact, *simultaneously and in virtue of the same act*, he is aware of himself as the subject or possessor of the experience. It is important to remember that in this sort of 'self-consciousness', the self does not appear as an object. As Rāmakaṇṭha puts it: 'It is not the case that there are two cognitions: one of the object and another of the self. Rather, when an awareness of an object is also aware of itself, the nature of the self is established in that reflexive cognition.'[18]

Rāmakaṇṭha has to reconcile the diverse and flowing character of our mental life with the continuous integrity of the soul that is its subject. The self is not reducible to the states that are its stream of consciousness. The self cannot be the same as the states because it is the very condition of those states occurring as a unified stream. The Buddhist takes the opposite position when he argues that consciousness is always changing: we only find awareness appearing in various modes such as joy and despondency but never encounter a separate entity called self.[19] He concedes that even if the cognitive capacity of the perceiver is not momentary, it definitely is not permanent because it comes and goes – as expressed in experiences like 'I have a headache', 'this feels nice', 'my sorrow has gone away or it will pass'.[20] Given that we experience our cognitions as transitory, it follows that personality is a state of constant flux, and a bundle of perceptions is all we are.

Rāmakaṇṭha responds by distinguishing two modes of awareness: the cognitive discrimination (*adhyavasāya*) and the permanent background consciousness. The former is variable because it is a property of the essentially material and mutable mind (*buddhi-dharma*). The latter is the awareness that is a constitutive feature of the human condition (*pauruṣam*). Its absence is never experienced as it is always known as the uniform perceiver.[21] The distinction enables him to say that thoughts and feelings may come and go, the succession of experiential states may indeed be variable, but the enduring subject of experiences remains constant, always appearing as the same.

It is undeniable that we experience a stream of consciousness, but this is different from saying that we are such a stream. Consciousness is a unity with a perspective upon its different states. The unity of consciousness means that at any given moment I may be looking at something, feeling something, thinking about something else, wanting something and deciding to do something without falling into a schizophrenic morass. The different conscious acts do not mean that my consciousness is fragmented. My awareness of the different objects and contents of those states is unified. Consciousness encompasses the range of mental operations.

Rāmakaṇṭha's response to the Buddhist account of experience appeals to two types of argument – one from the phenomenology of consciousness, and a hypothetical inference (*arthāpatti*) from the intelligibility of activity that has future goals:

> Everyone knows that he is a knowing subject on the basis of immediate pre-conceptual experience. The question is whether the perceiver is an appearance

of mere moments, differing in earlier and later experiences, new every moment and in relation to each object, or is it something that never changes? The answer is that the constant light of consciousness is given for everyone in reflexive awareness. It knows no schism in itself despite being conditioned by the objects of awareness. In past, present and future, it is exempt from prior non-existence and destruction. Although experiencing the coming and going of many mental events such as the various means of knowing, the sense that one is the constant perceiver is unshaken. In the gaps between mental events, the light of consciousness is uninterrupted. Self-consciousness is unbroken in states such as deep sleep. It is called '*ātman*' because it is always known as self-illuminating.

It is in reliance on this unchanging and unfailing background consciousness that people undertake actions with future consequences. Were it momentary, all activity would collapse. Who would act, where and for what reason if no experience could extend to another moment, instantaneous thoughts just ceasing to be? Activity would be impossible for someone supposing that they lived only for a moment, thinking that in another moment, 'that is not me, it is not mine'. Everyone would become inert, absorbed only in the light of their own natures, lacking conscience of right and wrong and empty of the many types of mental activities. This contradicts the immediate experience of everyone because all these things depend upon the consciousness of a stable perceiver.[22]

Some Buddhists say:

It is undeniable that there is the appearance of a stable and uniform perceiver. But that perceiver is not reflexively given. Rather, experience reveals a flow of perceiver-moments and unity is superimposed upon the stream by misleading synthetic cognitions arising from perceptions of the similarity of the perceiver-moments, just as we attribute unity to flow of water and call it a river. But that is a mistake. This grasping at a stable identity (*ātmagraha*) is the root of all evil and it is what the Buddhist teaching aims to suppress.[23]

Indeed, belief in the soul derives from beginningless ignorance (*anādi-avidyā*) and since it causes rebirth should be rejected by seekers after liberation who should practice repeated contemplation of the non-existence of soul.[24]

Rāmakaṇṭha replies that this cannot be right because we are aware of the inner self as something different in kind from objects. If it were the product of superimposition, it would appear like an object and as different from whatever was performing the superimposition. But our experience is not like that. Rather, given that it is the illuminator of objects, its nature is that of the internal perceiver. The superimposer would have to be a stable subject of awareness. Were it manifest as purely momentary, superimposition would be impossible because it requires an enduring consciousness capable of a synthetic cognitive grasp of earlier and later.[25]

According to Buddhists of Dharmakīrti's school, an instant has no before or after. A thought is no sooner come than gone if it is momentary. Its origin coincides with its destruction. Hence, given the absence of endurance, how are memory and conceptual thought possible since the agent of the synthesis of thoughts is the consciousness that is proper to the self? Memory and the synthesis of experiences involve conceptualization (*vikalpa*) which requires the mental synthesis of earlier and later by a constant background awareness. But momentary cognitions cannot perform those functions [MPAV, p. 159]. Moreover, how can an instantaneous perceiver objectify itself in such a way that it can mistakenly impute permanence to itself?

Finally, Rāmakaṇṭha of course rejects the Nyāya-Vaiśeṣika view that the existence of what for them is a non-experiential principle of identity has to be inferred since it obviously cannot reveal itself. Nyāya-Vaiśeṣika posits what they call 'soul' as the single principle that is necessary for the unification of diverse sensory experiences, for example, touching, tasting and seeing the same thing. Such a metaphysical subject also explains the possibility of the synthesis of earlier and later experiences over time. Because cognitions, volitions, pleasures, pains, efforts, merit, demerit and inherited tendencies are qualities (*guṇa*), they need a substrate (*āśraya*) that is a substance (*dravya*) and that substance is the self. Rāmakaṇṭha simply does not accept the Nyāya-Vaiśeṣika ontology about the relationship between qualities and their possessors. His view is that a substance or basic particular (*dravya*) is a concurrence of properties (*guṇasaṃdrava* or *guṇasamudāya*). This is not the same as the Buddhist reductionist position because substance here means endurance, the stability of an entity that is an integration of properties. Such a whole is not conceived as distinct from its properties or parts. Rāmakaṇṭha concludes that because cognition, feelings and intentions are not separable qualities in their own right, it is on the basis of self-evidence, and not inference, that we establish that the capacity for knowing belongs to the soul's nature as its essential property.[26]

Personal agency

The self is not just a stable cognizer or detached observer (as the Sāṃkhyas think); it is also a centre of free agency with causal powers (*kriyā-śakti*).

But the Buddhist cannot make sense of the phenomenon of action since if the subject of experience were ephemeral, it could not perform actions. When something is done by a single instantaneous cognition, its fruition would be another instant of cognition that would not occur in a later life of the instigator. Since the instants differ, the experiencer of the fruits of action will differ from the instigator. The enjoyer of the fruit would be other than the conscious subject who is the agent of action. In fact, there would not be an enjoyer of the fruit.[27]

The Buddhist denies that when one person has done something, its fruits are experienced elsewhere on the grounds that actions and their consequences constitute different streams of experiences. Rāmakaṇṭha replies that the question, 'which stream is which?', has no determinate answer if the streams just consist of momentary entities where an earlier moment is followed by a later one. That would not be sufficient to yield real distinctions such that we could identify separate streams. In short, there would not be any individual streams. The Buddhist claims that a relation of similarity between moments individuates them into streams consisting of the five *skandhas* (the body, feelings, sensory perceptions, habits and conceptual thoughts). Rāmakaṇṭha says that there would have to be some sort of intimate connection between the moments. It cannot be produced by space or time since the Buddhist does not accept that they are realities in their own right. Nor can it derive from the essential natures of entities. There are two points here. Buddhists reject essences or unchanging natures. But in so far as anything may be conventionally treated as having a nature, such a nature derives from its place in a system of relations. So the notion cannot be appealed to as an explanation of the generation of those systems. Rāmakaṇṭha concludes that here is no proof of the existence of integrated streams of experiences because discrete instants cannot produce stable identities.[28]

The Buddhist doctrine of the essentially temporal nature of all entities involves a rejection of the theory upheld by mainstream Brahminical orthodoxy that actions are to be analysed in terms of specific factors (*kāraka-vāda*) such as a fixed starting point, the autonomous agent, the recipient, the object desired and means. They espouse a theory of causation according to which there are just processes or sequences of events (*kāraṇa-vāda*) in which individuals, whether agents or patients, are just aspects of a causal event, enjoying no special significance. The Brahminical view, according priority to substances and agents as causal factors, is succinctly expressed in the verse, 'The master of the factors in relation to action and inaction, whether it is currently active or not, is the factor called the agent.'

It is soteriologically crucial for Rāmakaṇṭha that the persisting self-conscious individual substances, embodied and enduring intact through time, are autonomous ritual and moral agents spontaneously capable of initiating novel sequences of events that follow from their decisions and that are not wholly produced by antecedent causal conditions. That is to say, souls are individual substances possessing innate causal powers that are dispositions to act in certain ways in appropriate circumstances. Where events involving human actions are concerned, souls are, as it were, the glue that holds the members of a sequence of ephemeral events together as a causal process and thus account for its continuity. As we have seen, the stable and enduring *—ātman*, the transcendental enabling condition of experience, which is given in experience but not produced by it, is exempt from determination by time. Its agency is not *determined* by sequences of events.

Personal agency, as opposed to behaviour which may be merely reactive, instinctive and non-conscious, is necessarily connected with consciousness and is introspectively manifest to oneself as the reason for one's physical exertions and movements. In the case of other people, it is analogously inferred from their bodily actions. Personal agency, which has the nature of autonomy (*svātantrya*) in that it is the rational basis for the functioning or non-functioning of all the factors involved in events (*kāraka*), is directly experienced as being responsible for effort and physical movements, and the performing of religious and everyday actions having seen or unseen results. It cannot be denied because, like the state of being a cognizer, it is directly known to everyone that each is the inner driver of the factors implicit in events.[29]

Rāmakaṇṭha claims that the Buddhist theory implies that it does not matter whether Devadatta provides services for monks or kills them. Since service and killing are equally treated as contributory causal aspects of an event, the merit and demerit proper to each would accrue indiscriminately to Devadatta and to the mendicants. Where could the difference lie if everything is just an aspect of a causal process that is a sequence of events? The Buddhist reply that the causal process is differentiated into streams that are the individual Devadatta as the instigator, service as the intended purpose and the mendicants as the beneficiaries amounts to acceptance of the *kāraka-vāda* which involves the categories of agent, object and instrument and not the process theory of causation (*kāraṇa-vāda*). And if the *kāraka* theory is established, so is the self's agency.[30]

Śākta Śaiva traditions

As well as the *Śaiva Siddhānta* dualists, there were many worshippers of forms of Śiva and the Goddess who subscribed to a non-dualistic or monistic (*advaita*) metaphysic.[31] While believing that it is knowledge and not ritual that is essential for liberation, adherents of these cults enjoyed a rich liturgical life. Some rituals confer specific benefits and powers. But ritual practice may also help to consolidate belief, deepen commitment and keep alive an original inspiring insight by preserving a sense of immunity from the frustrations, changes and chances of daily life. Enlightenment is understood as recovery by recognition of one's true identity as the deity. Salvific realization may be achieved by ritual informed by gnosis, or by gnosis alone, or it may simply happen unexpectedly thanks to a purely fortuitous descent of divine grace. While enlightenment and liberation, understood as the salvific expansion of consciousness bestowed in initiation, are possible in the course of one's life (*jīvan-mukti*), most initiates have to wait for death, which is coterminous with the exhaustion of the residual *karma* appropriate to this life, to experience it fully. The life of ritual practice confirms and intensifies the original liberating experience, purifying it of conceptual elements. Thus enlightened, one sees the world in a new light.

Utpaladeva and Abhinavagupta

Utpaladeva (925–975 A.D.) follows Somānanda (900–950 A.D.), who was the original theorist of the *Pratyabhijñā* school.[32] Somānanda's Śivadṛṣṭi expounds a form of absolute idealism: the denial that material things could exist independently of consciousness understood as the sole original principle. Central to this philosophy is a critique of the notion that our thoughts represent physical objects that exist independently of consciousness. The argument is that what appear as external, physical objects really depend upon consciousness. In other words, their intrinsic natures are conscious. Realists suppose that material objects impinge upon minds. The idealist argues that activity and hence causal efficacy are exclusively properties of conscious beings capable of volition. So matter cannot be the primary cause.[33] Moreover, since only an idea can be like and thus represent an idea, consciousness would not represent matter if matter were something totally different from it. We cannot experience anything that does not share the nature of consciousness. It makes no sense to say that consciousness represents things that are mind-independent and different in nature from it because as soon as something is represented by consciousness, it is no longer mind-independent. It has been brought into a relation with some mind. If there were a real difference in nature between consciousness and material objects, knowledge of the world would be impossible. Dualists says that material things, whether atoms or concrete wholes, and consciousness belong to completely different categories. It follows that they are not connected. But a relation between two categories is by definition possible only when they have something in common. A relation between thinking minds and objects is possible if consciousness is the common factor present in everything.

Universal consciousness (*saṃvit*) or *Cit* is identified as the supreme godhead usually understood as Śiva and his energy (*śakti*), which makes everything to exist. Consciousness is understood as active power (*kriyā-śakti*), as well as contemplation or knowing (*jñāna-śakti*) and the will to expand (*icchā-śakti*). It is the deity that projects all worlds and all beings, and the deity that causes them to appear (*prakāśayati*). Hence, everything expresses the divine nature and has no independent subsistence. Human problems start when we just think of ourselves as isolated individuals with caste-based social identities confronting a separate material environment. The point of religious practice is the recovery of one's true identity as Śiva, achieved by the expansion of awareness.

Somānanda criticizes those *Advaita Vedāntins* to whom he attributes the view (*vivarta-vāda*) that the differentiated cosmos is an illusory manifestation of the static and featureless unconditioned substrate (*brahman*). He rejects the version of idealism taught by the Buddhist *Vijñānavāda*, which views our experience of the material world as merely mental construction out of vestiges of prior experiences. Moreover, Buddhist temporalists cannot allow that there is a stable subject who performs the feat of imaginative construction. Common-sense realists are criticized for admitting individual centres of consciousness and agency but distinguishing them from their physical environments in such a way that no sense can be made of their relation to it. *Śaiva Siddhānta* dualists are castigated for positing themselves as individuals independent of godhead.

It is Utpaladeva (925–975 A.D.) who provides a philosophical defence and articulation of the sort of visionary spirituality that is central to the Krama cult.[34] His works include the *Īśvarapratyabhijñā-kārikās* [IPK] (with his own commentaries), a treatise in the Nyāya style proving the existence of

God called the *Īśvara-Siddhi*, a work called the *Ajaḍapramātṛ-Siddhi* (about the knowing subject) and a treatment of the topic of relations called the *Saṃbandha-Siddhi*.

Abhinavagupta (975–1025 A.D.) was an influential theologian, philosopher and aesthetician of remarkable profundity and intellectual sophistication and erudition who belonged to the Tantric *Trika* cult. The *Trika* (meaning 'triad') was a system of ritual originating and developing in Kashmir whose goal is the acquisition by the votary, who has undergone a caste-obliterating initiation ritual, of the supernatural powers of a triad of female deities. The latter personify both the benign and the terrifying and destructive aspects of existence. Associated with this cult was that of the eight mother goddesses and their expressions in families of female spirits called *Yoginīs*.[35] They may be invoked and pacified, in the impure cremation ground on the margins of society, with offerings of impure and hence potent substances such as blood, flesh, wine and sexual fluids. The cult adopted the horrific, all-devouring *Kālasaṃkarṣiṇī* form of the Goddess *Kālī* as the unifying form of the original three goddesses. From 900 A.D. the *Trika* was in competition with the Śaiva Siddhānta dualistic system of ritual and theology, according to which individual souls inhabit a physical world essentially. Assimilating the sophisticated Pratyabhijñā philosophy, the *Trika* was able to defeat the challenges posed by dualism, Vedāntic illusionism and Buddhism. Its explicitly sexual rituals underwent a process of domestication and internalization. This trend appears in the thought of Abhinavagupta where orgasm is understood as obliterating one's self-centredness and manifesting the expansion of that blissful self-awareness that is the same as the universal consciousness projecting all phenomena. The ritual use of impure substances, which had been understood as sources of magical powers, is held to induce ecstasy, a sense of freedom arising from violation of the taboo. Bondage to rebirth is understood as a state of ignorant self-limitation that understands the orthodox values of purity and impurity as objective realities. Enlightenment presupposes the realization that anxious concern about caste and related values such as one's Vedic learning, family's status, prescribed conduct, conventional virtues and prosperity is an aspect of an inauthentic identity. Freedom consists in the realization, typically through yoga and meditation, that one is a condensation of the universal consciousness, followed by an explosion of personality transcending rapture.[36]

Abhinavagupta's philosophical works include commentaries on Utpaladeva's *Īśvarapratyabhijñā-kārikās* and on the *Mālinīvijayottara Tantra*, the *Tantrāloka*, abbreviated as the *Tantrasāra*, which voluminously expounds the doctrines, yoga and rituals of the *Trika* cult, the *Parātrīśikā-Vivaraṇa*, the *Bodhapañcadaśikā* (translated below), and the *Paramārthasāra*, a translation into Śaiva categories of a Vaiṣṇava work attributed to Ādiśeṣa.[37]

As well as demonstrating the coherence, soteriological value and finality of the forms of Śaivism to which he was personally committed, these works include sustained critiques of the dualism of the *Śaiva Siddhānta* ritualism, the *Vedāntic* illusionism maintaining that all normal human experience is infected by ignorance of the truth about reality, and the Buddhist rejection of enduring substances (*nairātmya*), including the soul. Indeed, there is a sense in which we find here a polar opposite to Buddhism. While for the Buddhists, the world is at base an impersonal process of events where we who mistakenly think of ourselves as persisting centres of thinking and willing are in fact but expressions of external forces over which we have no control, for these Śaivas the world, pervaded by the divine consciousness, is not ultimately inimical to our best interests.[38]

Abhinavagupta develops the absolute idealism taught by Somānanda and Utpaladeva. According to this doctrine, the world derives from a single, universal, autonomous and dynamic consciousness (*saṃvit*), which expresses itself in an infinite variety of subjects, objects and acts of awareness. The seeker after release from rebirth should meditate upon the nature of consciousness, which is depicted as dynamic. The dynamism is a result of the internal oscillation (*spanda*) between two inseparable aspects: the manifestation of objects (*prakāśa*) on the one hand and reflexive awareness (*vimarśa*) on the other.[39] Consciousness pulsates between expansion and contraction. There are degrees of awareness extending from the most universal and expanded to the most restricted and specific, singular and concrete. It is the latter mode that presents itself as the sphere of objective matter – the lowest rung of the ladder.

In everyday individual awareness, the representation of what appear to be external objects, and hence duality, predominates. The adept should reflect that what is experienced as the objective world is nothing other than the self-expression of transcendent consciousness, the synergistic union of Śiva and Śakti, manifestation and reflexive awareness. The subject–object polarity is described as internal to consciousness. Ritual, yoga and meditation enable us to deconstruct that polarity, with a consequent collapse of all discursive thought. Contracted self-awareness is thus dissolved, and with it the misconception that the world is an arena of external objects confronted by individual agents.

Following Somānanda and Utpaladeva, Abhinavagupta believes that the mind-independence of matter is impossible. But trans-individual consciousness (*saṃvit*) causes the manifestations that we experience to appear *as if* distinct from the subjects of experience. While *Advaita Vedānta* understands the foundational consciousness as unchanging and quiescent (*śānta-brahma-vāda*), for this school, *saṃvit* is a triad (*trika*) of self-conscious awareness (*jñāna*), activity (*kriyā*) and will (*icchā*) positing itself as apparently other than itself.[40] *Saṃvit* projects phenomenal manifestations (*ābhāsa*), which are both the finite subjects of experience and agency and the objects that are experienced by them as external. Like Utpaladeva, he argues against Buddhism that there has to be a self-conscious subject as the permanent background to experience. There must be a stable unity that unifies the manifold of experience. The principle of the unity of reflexive awareness (*svasaṃvedana*) is crucial here. There is one and the same sovereign and independent self-aware consciousness that is common to present experiences and memories. It is the link between the two varieties of cognition. This is something that the Buddhist theory to the effect that each momentary and self-contained cognition is just aware of itself cannot explain, because Buddhists have no concept of a single consciousness over and above discrete mental episodes that could connect them.[41] It is difficult to explain how such a mélange of cognitions could conceive of itself as a series, let alone as a persisting identity. Abhinavagupta appeals to the phenomena of memory, recognition, as well as the interconnectedness of thoughts to prove that there is a constant conscious subject, which is the grounds of the possibility of cognitive synthesis.

Absolute idealism

The philosophical articulation of the Śākta cults is a form of absolute idealism: the view that everything is a manifestation of a single trans-individual consciousness, which is the only reality that has independent existence.[42] This sort of idealism is not philosophical scepticism about the existence of the external world. It is the affirmation of the real world as a partial expression of the divine nature. The world really is independent of human minds. It is not fabricated by individual perceivers. Still, the world exists only as its representation in consciousness: it is not the case that there are two types of substance, the mental and the physical. There is a single dynamic conscious reality, the coalescence of first-personal awareness, conscious activity and contemplation, which projects both finite centres of awareness and the experiences of the objects that they enjoy.

In his *Śivasūtra-vimarśinī*, Abhinavagupta's successor Kṣemarāja puts the idealist view as follows:

> Consciousness manifests itself both internally [as thoughts and feelings] and externally [as things and events] in a variety of forms. Because objects only exist in relation to consciousness, the world has the nature of consciousness. For entities cannot be known without consciousness. So it is concluded that consciousness has assumed the forms of entities. By contemplating entities, we can rationally understand that knowable phenomena share the nature of consciousness. Consciousness and its objects have a single nature because they are experienced simultaneously. [ad Sūtra 30]

In addition to the difficulties about finding a coherent conception of matter (that which keeps physics in business) and the philosophical problems of explaining our perception of the physical world, there are a number of considerations that encourage people to think that consciousness, not matter, is the basic reality, and to adopt the idealist outlook. Try to imagine a cosmos in which there never has been and is no conscious life. Remember that there are no observers, no experiencers, no intelligences. What would it be like? Your initial thoughts may be that it is all black, hard, soft, fluid, hot, cold. But it is not even that. Any of those characterizations presuppose that there is an observer or experiencer. As Abhinavagupta says,

> Regarding the modes of thinking, 'I know', 'I knew', 'I shall know', which are founded upon reflexive subjectivity, what else is there to know? If these did not shine, the cosmos would be dense darkness, or rather *it would not even be that*. 'How does the knower know itself?' If one denies the conscious subject, what question and what answer would there be?[43]

We find that by strictly eliminating observers or intelligences, nothing has any meaning. In the lifeless world there is not really any-thing: there literally are no things. This is because the identification and classification of entities requires conscious observers. In the dead world of chaotic matter, there cannot be any *intrinsic* structures, organization, repeatable forms or natural laws. Such organizing principles have to come from the outside. They cannot emerge from within. That which imposes order cannot arise from the indeterminate morass upon which it then imposes order. If natural laws impose regularities, they must be different from that which they regulate. They have to be external factors. Now our 'bleak and blank' chaotic world is by definition purely physical. So if there are to be external factors, structuring principles that necessarily are external, they must be other than the physical. And what is non-physical is conscious. Leaving imagination to one side, can we even conceive of a world without consciousness? A conception of reality as it is in itself not involving mention of human perceptual capacities would be a conception of a complex mathematical structure. But that is not our world because experiences of matter have now been excluded.[44]

Perhaps the best we can say is that there would be something there, but it would not mean anything. Indeed, merely saying, 'there would be something' does not really mean anything. So some people think that it is senseless to say that there could be anything at all if there were no consciousness, and this is what idealists mean when they say that there can be no unexperienced reality. Everything depends upon consciousness. Consciousness, not matter, is basic. There is another sense in which everything may be considered to depend upon consciousness. Let us not be afraid of the obvious and accept that there are physical objects in space. If what such objects are is to be understood or determined, if their nature is to be *established* (*vyavasthāpya*), if they are to mean anything, some sort of intelligence different from those objects is required. But consciousness differs in a crucial respect from physical objects. It reveals or establishes its own nature and its own existence. It knows its own nature simply by being what it is. It does not need anything outside itself to do this. This is another sense in which it is consciousness, not matter, which is basic.

The intrinsic dynamism of consciousness: *Prakāśa* and *vimarśa*

People initiated into these Śaiva Śākta traditions accept the categories recognized by their dualistic co-religionists but claim that they are ultimately aspects of the one purely conscious divine reality. One of the ways in which they differ from the Advaita Vedāntins is in their insistence that the unconditioned creative consciousness is dynamic, not inactive. The trans-individual consciousness (*saṃvit*) is the pure actuality of self-awareness. It knows itself. It is fully realized, perfect and self-sufficient, ever and always wholly present to itself. It is a state of peaceful repose (*viśrānti*) where actuality and potentiality are in equilibrium. Unconditioned by space, time or form, this state of perfect balance lacks nothing and so has nothing to accomplish.

The divine sovereignty consists in perfect freedom (*svātantryam*). This inherently creative consciousness generates the finite realm of multiplicity and relations. Divinity, understood as the co-inherence of Śiva and Śakti, spontaneously contracts itself to produce the matrix of individual knowers and agents, all experiences and acts of knowing, and all phenomena that appear as if they were separate from it. We shall see how this activity is conceived not as impersonal and unspecific surges of energy, but on the model of the processes of finite intelligence. Unconditioned consciousness is the freedom of self-determination. Creation is neither necessary to the Divinity, nor does it require an independent material principle.

Śiva and Śakti correspond to *prakāśa* and *vimarśa*, two modes of the one consciousness. These terms are rich and complex in meaning. *Prakāśa* literally means light – in this context, the light of consciousness. *Vimarśa* means self-awareness or reflexivity, and representation. The divine consciousness is an eternal dynamic and vibrant interplay between these facets. To grasp the difference, we need to explore some aspects of the internal variety of the notion of mind. We can distinguish *psychological* states and *phenomenal* consciousness. We can think of perceptions and cognitions as sometimes purely functional psychological states. Information is received by perceptions and stored as memories. In terms of this outlook, a subject is in a perceptual state whenever his or her psychological apparatus is receiving and processing data from the environment. A subject can have a perception in this sense of being in an informational state even in the absence of a corresponding subjective experiential awareness. This is what is sometimes called 'being on automatic pilot'. My field of vision at the present moment is greater than what I am seeing. Sometimes I walk down the road, oblivious of my surroundings, on automatic pilot, as it were. But what we call *experiences* are *phenomenal* conscious states. There is something that *it is like* to have them or to be in the state. This is sometimes called the subjective character of experience – what *it feels like*. A state is phenomenally conscious if there is something it is like to be in that state. This is one of the meanings of *vimarśa*. Abhinavagupta says that it is the life, the vitality of awareness (*prakāśa*). Items of belief and knowledge, when they are being stored, are potentially conscious states that can be brought to mind and made explicit in awareness. A thought or representation is 'alive' if it is being used in reasoning and in the direct rational control of action and speech.

The illumination (*prakāśa*) of objects means their objective manifestation, their potential to become objects of explicit awareness. *Prakāśa* is likened to a light shining in a dark room. But this in itself is insufficient for understanding. This is where the complex concept of *vimarśa* comes in. At its most basic, *vimarśa* means explicit awareness on the part of the subject that he is undergoing a certain experience. If the appearing of something blue is a case of *prakāśa*, the corresponding *vimarśa* is one's recognizing that one is seeing blue. Moreover, a subject's explicit awareness of itself as a centre of cognition and agency is called 'I-representation' (*aham-vimarśa*). Consciousness without reflexivity (*vimarśa*) would be blind.[45] In addition, it is *vimarśa* that determines the nature (*vyavavasthāpayati*) of the manifestations uncovered by the light of consciousness. Reflexivity is both Śiva's power (Śakti) of self-awareness and his representation of objects (and perceivers) within and to himself.[46] We said that *prakāśa* is like a light introduced into a dark room. Although there is illumination, this is insufficient for understanding. When the Nyāya-Vaiśeṣikas say that cognition is just the illumination of objects (*artha-prakāśa-buddhi*), they are treating consciousness as a searchlight illuminating objects in the world. Take the case of immediate sensory perception and think of it as pure observation. A video camera does something functionally analogous, but it does not *understand*. The view of Utpaladeva and Abhinavagupta is that *vimarśa* must be implicit even in immediate sensory perception if the perception is to *mean* anything. For a perception to mean anything, it has to be raised to the level of explicit consciousness. There has to be a phenomenal experiential aspect (*vimarśa*). Also, for the perception to really mean anything, it must be connected with other thoughts, and this sort of synthetic experience (*anusaṃdhāna*) is also *vimarśa*.

We may abstract from the flow of our conscious experience and analyse it into discrete moments, both simultaneous and successive. It may be misleadingly compared with the frames composing a film. But of course we do not see bare objects or simple things. Experience is not a collection of fragments. Even the notion of *present* experience may be a misleading abstraction. In conscious experience we bring to bear a mentality informed by retained memories and expectations for the future. I am looking at a cup on the table in front of me. (I don't think, 'there's an object above another object at such and such a distance' and then identify the objects and relations in the state of affairs.) I know that it holds the coffee that I made earlier. I reach out, pick it up and take a sip. I enjoy it. I know that it will be there later to be enjoyed again. This ordinary experience is replete with acts of cognitive identification, synthesis and separation. It is also pervaded by language. This is *vimarśa*.

The intimacy of Śiva and Śakti, *prakāśa* and *vimarśa*, is expressed in a text belonging to the Krama tradition as follows:

> Śiva's tranquil state is the highest form of self-awareness. But there is an even higher state that is ever so slightly distinct, and that is the abode of the Goddess. The whole of reality comes from the creative light of consciousness (*prakāśa*), itself deriving from the sheer delight that lacks nothing and which itself finds its rest in the uncreated light wherein there are no traces of awareness of differences. The Goddess is the unsurpassable tranquil state that has consumed the traces of awareness of existences that had remained in the uncreated light. Śiva's nature is the tranquil state that devours time. The Goddess is the perfection of that tranquillity.[47]

Reinterpretation of Śaiva Siddhānta concepts

Not only does the divinity always know itself, but it also knows itself in and through the creative process. Individual transmigrating selves are modes of the Divinity that permits its own contraction by *māyā*, *karma* and *mala*. Divinity enjoys a plenum of experiences by enacting itself in finite lives. Whereas the Śaiva Siddhāntins understand *mala* as a material substance attaching to the souls and restricting their powers of knowledge and action, the non-dualists think that it is ignorance in the form of the unenlightened acceptance that one is just a limited individual bound to rebirth and subject to caste and social and religious obligations. This ignorance also expresses itself in the belief that the Brahminical values of purity and impurity are objective properties of things. There is also the misconception that one is in danger of pollution by objectively real impurities that hinder spiritual progress, and that freedom (*mokṣa*) is but a remote possibility, difficult of attainment. This manifold ignorance causes bondage. Ignorance at base means the mistaken belief that there are individual entities, including souls, which are capable of existing independently of the Divinity. This ignorance is *constitutive* in that it establishes individuality.

Māyā, for the Siddhāntins the substrative cause of all objects, physical and mental faculties and experiences in the impure levels of the cosmos that we inhabit, is understood as the projection of the whole differentiated realm of objectivity so that it appears as if it were other than the Divinity, and from the many distinct and finite subjects of experience. It may also be understood in terms of thinking of oneself as a limited individual who confronts a mind-independent objective order. Similarly, *karma* is not a factor external to selves. Rather, it is the self-limiting subject's mistaken belief that good and bad deeds really have a bearing upon one's destiny.

Bondage to rebirth just is the *belief* that one is limited resulting from a failure on the part of people caught up in the conventional dualistic outlook, with its bifurcation of individual conscious subjects and material objects, to understand that their true identity is pure, autonomous consciousness. Liberation is the non-discursive (*nirvikalpa*), direct and fully expanded experience (i.e. not merely a propositional thought *that* one is identical with the Divinity) of being nothing other than the transcendent consciousness (*parā saṃvit*), perpetually delighting in itself. In short, one becomes the divinity: 'I am Śiva and this whole world is my self-representation.' Śaiva Siddhāntins may imaginatively identify themselves with the deity in liturgical contexts, but they do not believe that they are essentially the same as God. Therein lies the crucial difference between the dualistic and non-dualistic religious paths.

We have seen that the ultimate goal is to lose all sense of personal individuality by recovering the awareness that one is not different from the Divinity. This is sometimes expressed as immersion (*samāveśa*) in the realization of the all-encompassing supremacy of Śiva, who is autonomous and undivided consciousness uniting *prakāśa* and *vimarśa*, where the universe is experienced as non-different from one's identity. In its extroverted mode, trans-individual consciousness projects all experiencing subjects and all phenomena in a kaleidoscopic manifestation that is always aware of itself. In its introverted mode, consciousness simply delights in itself. What we experience are the multifarious self-representations of the trans-individual consciousness that contains within itself all the projections. Experiencers, as well as phenomena, are modes of consciousness contracted by time, place and form.

The Krama cult and the Pratyabhijñā philosophy

The *Pratyabhijñā* philosophy is a sophisticated reflective articulation of the *Krama* cult, central to which is the attainment of liberating gnosis through a liturgy known as the 'Worship of the Twelve *Kālīs*'. Freedom from rebirth is just re-cognition (*pratyabhijñā*): the recovery of knowledge by someone who had previously considered himself as an individual thinking agent confined by space, time and embodiment that his true nature is nothing other than the trans-individual consciousness that projects all phenomena, experiences and limited subjects. *Saṃvit* diversifies itself into limited subjects and objects. The boundaries are termed '*upādhis*' ('superimposed conditions' rather than genuine properties). The point is that while they seem real to us, any changes in and of them do not affect the ultimate consciousness, which is pure act without any passivity. This is an absolute idealism according to which everything that is experienced by us as material and everything apparently individual is projected by a single consciousness. It is argued that whatever causes the physical world must be non-physical because the world needs a source that is external to it and different in kind from it. Since individual centres of consciousness are localized by matter, the ultimate source must be unconditioned, creative universal consciousness. They argue that we can only make sense of the coherence and continuity of our experiences, memories and interpersonal communications if we are persisting conscious subjects that inhabit a stable world regulated by objective structures. This is extended macrocosmically: the universe of subjects and objects holds together because it has a single conscious source that preserves it in being. The co-ordination of diverse subjects and objects is possible only if they are aspects of a single, universal field of experience. Universal consciousness causes objects of awareness to appear as if distinct from the limited subjects of experience. The specific forms figuring in our awareness express the general manifestations (*ābhāsa*) projected by the universal consciousness.

The goal of religious practice is the transcendence of limited individual subjectivity, indeed of any subjectivity whatsoever in so far as it implies passivity. The state of bondage to rebirth means thinking that one is a self, a person or personality. Real freedom means the obliteration of petty selfhood. Enlightenment is the realization that the subject that has mistakenly and selfishly considered itself as an individual is identical with the universal transcendental conscious energy called the Śiva–Śakti state. Freedom from rebirth is just the recognition that 'I am Śiva, and this whole world is my self-expression'. One's authentic identity is already present as the constant and undeniable self-awareness that is in the background of all experiences, but it must be re-cognized and reflected upon as the ultimate conscious principle manifesting itself as all limited subjects, acts and objects of experience.

Krama practice

The Worship of the *Kālīs* is a meditative sequence of twelve phases (each symbolized by one of the twelve Kālīs) that effects an expansion of consciousness from the confines of limited personality to an enlightened form of awareness in whose light the everyday world becomes transfigured. In other words, what had been experienced as the merely mundane is recognized as reflecting the nature of the Divinity. In the course of this worship, consciousness is transformed as it 'devours' both its own contents and its appearance as limited. One contemplates the emanation (*sṛṣṭi*) of the cosmos from its transcendent source, its conservation in being or stasis (*sthiti*) and its withdrawal (*saṃhāra*) into that source, followed by a further emanation. That process of cosmic emanation is mirrored on the microcosmic level in the sequential structure of normal cognition that reaches out to objects, focuses attention upon them and absorbs them into itself. A clue to the nature of the divine activity is found in such modalities of human consciousness which mirror creation, conservation and withdrawal. Our states may be more or less self-aware. Sometimes we are in an extroverted state, totally absorbed in something and not really self-aware. But self-awareness brings consciousness to life. The interplay of extroversion and introversion in our own minds is held to be a microcosmic imitation of the divine nature. In the *Krama* ritual, one symbolically contemplates the cyclical process of cosmic emanation, stasis and reabsorption as represented by the path of cognition from its starting point as the initial state of the knowing subject (*pramātā*), via the internal mental faculties and the extroverted faculties of will, cognition and action (*pramāṇa*), to its intentional object (*prameya*), and then back again as the object is internalized in the subject. The phenomenal representations of the objects are withdrawn into the knowing subject, which is the terminus or resting point (*viśrānti*) of the process ending with something understood. Worship culminates in 'the phase of the nameless' (*Anākhya-cakra*), the unifying basis of the process of projection, conservation in being and withdrawal. This is the dissolution of all differentiated modes of cognition into the radiance of consciousness that is common to all mental acts and states. The final phase is symbolically expressed as the Goddess *Kālī*. She is beyond being and non-being, an abyss of pure light in which the powers of knowledge and action have merged, and where the distinctions between subjects, acts and objects of knowing have collapsed. From her unconditioned nature the diversified cosmos is manifest. She is attainable only in mystic gnosis. As Abhinavagupta's successor Kṣemarāja (1000–1050 A.D.) puts it in his *Pratyabhijñāhṛdayam* 19:

> By means of the internal trance of the *Krama* he remains immersed in expanded consciousness while still living in the world, and in this way achieves the final goal. In this process, he enters in from outside. By the very force of this penetration, he enters from within into his outer identity.

The language of penetration, emission, immersion and withdrawal may be suggestive of sexual activity. Indeed, Abhinavagupta says that such is an appropriate context. In fact, any ecstatic experience engenders an elevated sensibility or aesthetic rapture (*camatkāra*).[48]

Let us now look at what Utpaladeva and Abhinavagupta have to say in some of the Verses on the Recognition of the Divinity (*Īśvarapratyabhijñā-kārikā* in Torella, 2002) and their explanations of them. They think that by considering the operations of finite minds, which are microcosmic expressions of the 'Divine Mind', we can achieve some insight into the nature of the transcendent consciousness.

Illustrative extracts from *Īśvarapratyabhijñā-kārika* and commentaries

Īśvarapratyabhijñā-kārika 1.4.1

> The free consciousness that is the perceiver of the object previously perceived, and that is still in existence at the later time, realizes that the present object is the one previously perceived. This is called remembering.

At the end of the third section of the first chapter of his *Īśvarapratyabhijñā-Kārikās* (IPK), Utpaladeva mentions the three divine powers of knowing, memory and differentiation (referred to in the *Bhagavad Gītā* XV.5):

> 'If there were not one conscious Divinity who contains the infinite universe within himself and who has the powers of knowledge, memory and differentiation, the harmonious functioning (*sthiti*) of the human world, which stems from the synthesis by consciousness (*anusaṃdhāna*) of different and separate thoughts, would cease.'

Most Brahminical philosophers accept the definition of memory in *Yoga-Sūtra* 1.11: 'memory is the retention of an object previously experienced'. The alternative Buddhist account says that some perceptions leave a vestige or trace (*saṃskāra*) in a stream of experiences. But while their theory may be an adequate account of the mechanical transmission of information, it leaves out the subjective, phenomenal component that is integral to memory. The Buddhists say that the trace is revived at a later time when an experience calls to mind us of something similar about the past. But there are problems here. Experiential memory (as opposed to my recall of the stored information that the Sanskrit word for horse is '*aśvaḥ*') is both memory of the past object and of the previous perceiving. If everything is momentary and in a flux, the stream of experiences is in a different state, and past objects and events have ceased to exist. Memory cannot be the recovery of a past *experience* if that has not been retained. The trace is neither the original experience nor the object as it was cognized. Hence we are not in a position to know that the present perception resembles the past one. The account also fails to do justice to the phenomenology of memory experience. We do not just recall past objects and events: we often remember *what it was like for us* to experience them and the account leaves this out.

Experiential memory presupposes a unitary and active consciousness that surveys different moments of time. This subject is the agent that can relate cognitions occurring at different times. Given this, we can say that the past and present perceptions are the same in their phenomenological aspects, in their self-awareness (*svasaṃvedana*), and that this provides the link between them.

The idea is that if all minds and phenomena are aspects of a single conscious field, we can explain how we can understand what is going on in other minds, and communicate with one another. We can now overcome what is sometimes thought to be a problem for types of mind–matter dualism: how can there be any sort of relation between such completely different realities as consciousness and insentient matter?

Īśvarapratyabhijñā-kārika (IPK) 1.4.3-5

> There would be no manifestation of the object being remembered if it appeared as separate from the memory [i.e. were it not manifested in the present as an idea internal to consciousness but as something external and distinct from consciousness]. Therefore the unification of cognitions occurring at different times presupposes that there is a persisting subject of experiences. In memory the former experience does not appear like a separate external object, since it appears as resting within the self and is expressed as, 'I experienced this in the past.'

In his introduction to the fifth section of the first chapter of his *Īśvarapratyabhijñā-Vimarśinī*, Abhinavagupta says that Utpaladeva begins with the power of knowing (*jñāna-śakti*), and proceeds to say that the light of consciousness is the essence of objects. The text then establishes the existence of realities independent of finite minds by refuting the Vijñānavāda view that mental variety derives from stored traces or vestiges (*vāsanā*) of prior perceptions. He then rejects the direct realist view that sense-perception establishes the true nature of external objects. Next he rejects the view that the existence of external objects is known by inference. Then he shows that we know by reflective awareness that the true nature of external objects is that they are included in the absolute consciousness. He goes on to argue on the basis of pre-reflective immediate perception (*anubhava*), scripture and logic that self-awareness is the *very life* of the knowing subject's consciousness. Then he states that reflexive consciousness is foundational because it constitutes the ideal types of knowable objects (*jñeyam śuddham*) and the form of the knowing subject that contains them. Although consciousness is uniform, it is diversified into acts and subjects of knowing. He then says that just as reflexive awareness pertains to knower, it is also the very life of thoughts which may be non-conceptual or conceptual in form.

IPK 1.5.1

> 'The manifestation as external to consciousness of entities that are manifested in present experience is possible only if they are internal to consciousness.'

Abhinavagupta supplies the question to which the verse is an answer: Direct perception (*anubhava*) is held to be the basis of memory and conceptualization. If objects appear in direct experience as separate from the knowing subject, should they not appear like that in memory and conceptualization also? But they do not. So how can memory and conceptualization depend on direct perception?

Abhinavagupta explains that the verse deals with the nature of direct experience, which is a form of the power of knowing (*jñāna-śakti*) and of the sense in which objects are experienced as external to consciousness. He says that the clear and distinct perception of objects as distinct from the finite knowing subject is rationally intelligible only if they are one with the unconditioned subject that is pure consciousness and which makes them appear as separate. The divine *jñāna-śakti* effects the manifestation as different from the finite subject of what is internal to unconditioned consciousness.

IPK 1.5.2

> If the object were not of the nature of the light of consciousness (*prakāśa*), it would remain unilluminated as it was before it was known. The light of consciousness is not different from the object. The light of consciousness is the nature of the object.

Abhinavagupta says: Objects have to be illuminated by an external source. If they revealed themselves, every object would always be apparent to everyone. The same applies if we understand cognition as illuminating objects external to consciousness that were previously 'in darkness'. This is Kumārila's view that consciousness introduces a new feature, luminosity, into objects. It would be difficult to explain in these circumstances why the object does not appear to everyone.

Without consciousness, nothing can be established and universal blindness would follow. If objects are not constituted by *prakāśa*, they would be as unmanifested at the rise of cognition as they were prior to that.

He rejects the dualist view that there are two categorically distinct realms: material objects and consciousness. How could they be connected? The problem does not arise if we accept that consciousness is the essence of objects that are non-different from it.

If cognitions are unique in the case of each object, they could not be synthesized because each discrete cognition would be confined to itself. This is avoided if consciousness is unified awareness of which individual cognitions and the different conscious operations are modes.

If consciousness that is totally separate from objects is the illuminator of objects, we encounter another problem:

IPK 1.5.3

> If the light (*prakāśa*) were intrinsically undifferentiated and different from objects, objective reality would be confused. The object that is illuminated must itself be of the nature of the light of consciousness because that which does not have that nature cannot be established.

Utpaladeva explains: Undifferentiated light that is different from objects would illuminate every object equally. So there would be no basis for the specific discrimination of individual objects.

The absolute idealist's argumentative strategy for there being a single all-encompassing light of consciousness that projects the variety of manifestations has three stages:

The rejection of direct realism about objects perceived as occupying a mind-independent domain.

The rejection of the representationalist version of anti-realism, according to which the mind-independent domain is inferred but not perceived.

The rejection of forms of subjective idealism that drift into solipsism.

Utpaladeva and Abhinavagupta hold that we can explain mental variety and complexity only if it derives from a single conscious source. It is the Sautrāntikas who think that the mind-independent realm of unique particulars must be inferred as the cause of such variety, and to a statement of their outlook we now turn:

IPK 1.5.4

> If the light of consciousness is undifferentiated, it cannot be the cause of a diverse and complex manifestation. Because such a manifestation is inexplicable in these terms, we must infer external objects as its cause.

IPK 1.5.5: An argument against a Vijñānavāda Buddhist idealist

> A differentiated revival of karmic residues cannot be the cause [of mental variety]. Because in that case there would be the question of what causes the variety in such revival.

Abhinavagupta summarizes the Representationalist position: the cause of successive variety in intrinsically undifferentiated consciousness is the reflection of external forms that correspond to the reflections. The external is to be inferred, but we still call it perceptible. The reasoning is: awareness is intrinsically undifferentiated – its true form is just light. Undifferentiated light cannot be the cause of different representations. This leads us to infer an external domain separate from cognition that consists of many different forms which successively cast reflections of their nature in consciousness. The reflections are similar in form (*sārūpya*) to what is reflected, and there is a sort of correspondence between them.

The Sautrāntika contends that the idealist's explanation of mental variety as deriving from the re-awakening of sub-conscious latent traces (*vāsanā*) of prior perceptions does not make sense. We know that such re-awakening is responsible for memory, but here we are looking for the cause of variety in present experiences. Let us provisionally accept the theory that the latent traces are powers enabling cognitions to produce ideas of objects. Their re-awakening means their fitness to produce their own effects. In this way arises the variety of ideas. The problem here is that if although the representations in our minds do not strictly mirror reality, still their causes must be real if they are genuinely productive. If the traces are the causes of ideas, they must be both different from consciousness and objectively real. So this theory is a version of realism about the external disguised under a different name. Let there be a variety of sub-conscious traces. In that case, given the idealist view that there are no entities, space or time distinct from consciousness that could be the cause of variety by activating the traces, variety would appear simultaneously if consciousness is uniform. It is false that other cognitions occurring in a stream are the causes of the awakening of diverse ideas because if all mental states (pleasures and pains, cognitions of objects, and awareness of places and times) are just awareness and awareness is essentially just light, given the indivisibility of essence, there is no differentiation in awareness.

With respect to other mental states constituting other knowing subjects (which the Buddhist calls 'streams'), there is the same lack of individuation. If we restrict ourselves to the point of view of subjective awareness, we cannot form an objective conception of there being more than one such stream. We can only conceive of thoughts happening for that one stream. The Sautrāntika's conclusion is that we cannot account for mental variety by appealing to a sub-conscious store of latent traces. So it is established that if consciousness is undifferentiated pure light, and so cannot cause different ideas, it is necessary to infer an external realm.

Utpaladeva now states his own view:

IPK 1.5.6

> That may be the case. But why posit the external on the grounds that we cannot explain things otherwise, when all everyday activities *can* be explained if all things are manifestations of the single divine consciousness?

Abhinavagupta comments that there is no need to posit an external domain since all worldly life can be explained in terms of manifestations (*ābhāsa*). It is impossible to establish the existence of things independent of consciousness. We cannot make sense of the notion of material substance. The Nyāya theory that wholes inhere in their parts is invalid because there is no proof of inherence. No sense can be made of the Buddhist theories about the composition of macroscopic entities out of atoms.

The theory of the *ābhāsas* is crucial to Abhinavagupta's metaphysic. They are the primary realities that the trans-individual consciousness manifests. They are objective principles that can be grasped by everyone. *Ābhāsas* are universal properties. They are instantiated as objects, and the states of affairs arising from those objects' interactions, by their mutual delimitation and by their connection with space and time. The *ābhāsas* space and time are particularly important in that they impart particularity, and suppress the notions of eternity and omnipresence which produce the form of universality. The synthetic mental faculty (*anusaṃdhāna*) identifies the individual entities that are constituted by these manifestations. According to this account of general manifestations as objective types, when anyone has an experience of blue, the idea (*ābhāsa*) 'blue' is the same whatever the relevant mental connection (which may be seeing, imagining, remembering or delighting in). Likewise the idea 'seeing' is the same whether it is connected with a pot or a cloth. A round blue pot is the coalescence of the ideas round, blue and pot.

IPK 1.5.7

> Like a Yogin, just by the power of will, the Divinity whose nature is consciousness, manifests all phenomena lying within him as external without needing any independent substrative cause.

IPK 1.5.8-9

> We can only use inference if what is to be established has been perceived somewhere before. The sensory faculties are only inferred in very general terms as causes.

Objects that are totally external to consciousness are never manifested to consciousness at all. Thus their existence cannot be established through inference.

We can infer the presence of fire from the presence of smoke because we are familiar with smoke, fire and their relationship. But inference cannot operate when one of its terms is totally unknown (especially in this case where that which is to be established is by definition noumenal and outside the range of our cognitive capacities). This is not inference but pure speculation. It looks like Utpaladeva may be going too far here. We can infer the existence of the sensory faculties from the occurrence of perceptions, although, *ex hypothesis,* we never perceive those faculties. What he is in fact saying is that we do not infer the actual natures of the sense-faculties but only their generic characteristic of being something that has a causal function. So we are not inferring and understanding concrete realties but only the abstract concept of causal efficacy. Thus we have not left the sphere of thinking and entered the territory of external reality as understood by the Representationalist.

IPK 1.5.10

It is true that there is manifestation of beings that already exist within the Lord. Otherwise the act of reflexive awareness (*āmarśa*) that is deliberate willing (*icchā*) would not occur [they would not appear unless the Divinity knew them and desired that they be manifest].

IPK 1.5.11

Reflexive awareness (*vimarśa*) is the essence of manifestation by consciousness. Otherwise the light of consciousness (*prakāśa*) although tinged by the objects would be lifeless like a crystal.

[This is a response to the dualist view that understands consciousness on the model of a searchlight operating on an independent sphere of objects.]

IPK 1.5.12

That is why one's real nature is consciousness, meaning the acts of awareness and the state of being the agent of conscious acts. By that, one is distinguished from the insentient.

IPK 1.5.13

The act of awareness is reflexive, the repository of all meanings and spontaneously arising. This is real freedom, the sovereignty of one's real nature.

IPK 1.5.14

It is this that is the vibrancy of consciousness, unconditioned Being unlimited by place or time. This reality is expressed as the essence and the heart of the Divinity.

IPK 1.5.15

By virtue of this he makes himself the objects of awareness. But the field of cognition does not subsist independently of him. If he depended on knowable objects independent of himself, his freedom would cease.

IPK 1.6.1

The reflexive awareness 'I', whose nature is the light of consciousness, although expressed by a word, is not a concept (*vikalpa*) because a concept is an act of mental discrimination that presupposes the possibility of affirmation and exclusion, and this awareness has no opposites.

IPK 1.8.1-2

Sometime the manifestations (*ābhāsa*) are grasped in present sensory experience, but at other times they do not depend upon present experience, as in the cases of a blind person or in darkness. But there is no difference in the reality of the manifestations of objects featuring in thoughts, whether they concern past, present or future.

Abhinavagupta comments: When we say 'I see this *blue* thing' or 'I imagine it' or 'I remember it' or 'I make it', the manifestation 'blue' is essentially uniform. The manifestation 'seeing' remains uniform when 'I see' relates to something yellow. The manifestations are joined or separated by the creative divine power. In this way we can make sense of the variety of everyday life in past, present and future.

IPK 1.8.3-4

Even when feelings like pleasure and their occasions are real, and their manifestations are real conscious states, if they belong to the past their external conditions are not given. Still, if feelings are intensely reproduced by imagination, then they are felt by the subject as if the past object were present since he experiences the feeling so vividly.

IPK 1.8.5

Externality is a property imposed (*upādhi*) upon the manifestations of beings and non-being.[49] Being external is not the nature of manifestations. The manifestations are internal and always exist [whether some finite subject thinks them or not].

IPK 1.8.7

The manifestations, in so far as they are of the nature of consciousness, always exist within [the trans-individual consciousness]. When they are manifested as external thanks to the power of *māyā*, they are experienced as external.

IPK 1.8.9

Owing to the will of the Lord, mental representations and feelings of pleasure are manifested as if relating to what is external to consciousness.

IPK 1.8.10

Without the unification of cognitions, there would be no worldly life. The unification of cognitions is based on the unity of trans-individual consciousness. There is one knowing subject common to all [called the Supreme Self].

IPK 1.8.11

It is Śiva only that is the Divinity by virtue of his constant self-awareness and representation of things to himself. Reflexivity (*vimarśa*) is the pure knowledge and action of the deity.

IPK 2.2.1

The concepts ('*buddhayaḥ*', which is glossed as '*satya-ābhāsās*') of action, relation, universal property, individual substance, space and time, which apply in the sphere of unity and multiplicity, are considered true because of their permanence and utility.

The theory of manifestations recognizes the categories and the *pramāṇa* framework that are recognized by the realist Nyāya-Vaiśeṣika school. Utpaladeva and Abhinavagupta accept the validity of some features of their scheme, as long as it is construed within the overall framework of absolute idealism. This contrasts with the argument of an absolute idealist such as

F. H. Bradley who says that ordinary concepts such as space, time, causation and personal identity are ultimately incoherent and do not apply to reality as it really is. This is because we cannot identify them individually due to their relational nature. The contradictions inherent in whatever is posited by ordinary thought show that they are mere appearances and not realities. But the Theory of Ideas recognizes our everyday concepts as valid in that they are contained in and projected by the Divine Mind. They are not merely human conceptual constructs, useful in helping us to find our way around the world. Unity and multiplicity are compatible because phenomena are joined and separated within the all-encompassing divine consciousness.

Fifteen Verses on Consciousness

We conclude with Abhinavagupta's succinct overview of this theology called the *Bodhapañcadaśikā* or Fifteen Verses on Consciousness

> That single principle which is both within and external, whose form is radiance unlimited in light and darkness, that is the Divinity that is the essence of all beings. Its sovereign *śakti* produces entities. [1-2]
>
> The *śakti* does not desire to be different from its possessor. The shared nature of the two is permanent, like that of fire and burning. [3]
>
> This is the deity Bhairava who sustains the cosmos because by his *śakti* he has made everything appear as reflected in the mirror of his own nature. [4]
>
> The *śakti* is the transcendent Goddess who delights in contemplating his essence. Her perfect state neither increases nor diminishes in relation to finite beings. [5]
>
> The Divine Omnipotence eternally delighting in play with the Goddess simultaneously dispenses the emanations and reabsorptions of the worlds. [6]
>
> His impossibly difficult unsurpassable activity is total freedom and sovereignty whose nature is consciousness. [7]
>
> The distinctive feature of what is insentient is its being a limited manifestation. Consciousness is other than the insentient by which it is not limited. [8]
>
> The emanations and reabsorptions of the worlds are established as fissions of the autonomous innate *śakti*. [9]

In them there is infinite variety of spheres of experience and their regions, as well as pleasant and unpleasant experiences. [10]

When the unconditioned divine freedom is not understood, there is a cycle of birth and death that terrifies the unenlightened. This too is his power. [11]

Divine grace is accessible for one who has gone to a teacher or from scripture. [12]

God-given understanding of the truth is freedom from birth and death, and it is perfection for the enlightened ones. This is known as being liberated while still alive. [13]

Both bondage and freedom proceed from God. They are neither really different from each other, nor different from God. [14]

In this way Bhairava exercising his threefold *śakti* of will, action and knowing is the true nature of all beings. [15]

Further reading

For the Siddhānta, see Sanderson (1992).

Filliozat (1994) translates Sadyojyoti's commentary on the *Svayambhuvāgama*.

For Rāmakaṇṭha's thought about the self, Watson (2006) is invaluable.

Goodall (1998) provides a text and lucid translation of the first six chapters of Rāmakaṇṭha's *Kiraṇa Tantra* commentary. The *Mataṇga* commentary is in Bhatt (1977). It has not been translated. Nor has Rāmakaṇṭha's *Nareśvaraparīkṣā-prakāśa*. A (rather doubtful) text is Shastri 1926. Watson (2006) presents a critical version of much of Book 1.

Elaborate arguments for the existence of God were also formulated by Naiyāyikas beginning with Jayanta (850–900 A.D.) They are mentioned in *Much Ado About Religion* (Dezsö (2005)). By Jayanta's time, personalist theism had long surpassed automatic ritualism as the dominant type of religiosity in many parts of the subcontinent. A useful source here is Krasser (2002), which describes both Buddhist and Nyāya thought stemming from Dharmakīrti's arguments against an omnipotent and omniscient creator. The atheistic position is examined in Patil (2009). Also very interesting is Frank Clooney's *Hindu God, Christian God*.

For the traditions that we have labelled Śākta, see Sanderson (1985 and 1992) to begin with and move on to Sanderson (1990 and 1995 'Meaning in Tantric Ritual'). 'The Śaiva Exegesis of Kashmir' (2007).

Kṣemarāja's *Pratyabhijñāhṛdayam* is in Singh (1982) and his *Śiva Sūtra-vimarṣinī in* Singh (1991).

For Utpaladeva's *Īśvarapratyabhijñākārikā* with the author's own commentary, see the text and translation in Torella (2002). Abhinavagupta's *Vimarśinī* commentary is in Subramania Iyer and Pandey (1986).

The *Bodhapañcadaśika* is in Shastri (1947).

Chapter III of Kahrs (1998) deals with Kashmiri scriptural exegesis. Padoux (1990) is a classic study of the powers attributed to words in the Hindu traditions.

Questions for discussion and investigation

1 How does the idealism of Utpaladeva and Abhinavagupta differ from the Advaita Vedānta outlook?
2 Can the views of Somānanda, Utpaladeva and Abhinavagupta fairly be characterized as a version of theistic idealism?

Notes

1. Sanderson (2009K) for an overview.
2. Such cults are called śākta.
3. For a ground-breaking piece of philological theology, see Kahrs (1998), pp. 57–97.
4. See Goodall (1998), p. 275.
5. MPAV, pp. 154–5.
6. MPAV, p. 155.
7. See above p. 75.
8. MPAV, pp. 159–60.
9. MPAV, pp. 155–6.
10. BSBh 2.3.7: *na jñātur anyathā-bhāvo 'sti sarvadā vartamānasvabhāvatvāt.* 'There is no change in the knower, since it is always by nature present.'
11. MPAV, p. 150.
12. NIPP, p. 8.
13. *Pramāṇa-vārttika, Pramāṇa-siddhi,* verse 10 (Pandeya 1989).
14. NIPP, p. 20 quoting *Pramāṇavārttika, Pratyakṣaparicheda,* verse 354 (Pandeya 1989).
15. NIPP, p. 166 and MPAV, p. 158.
16. NIPP, p. 13.
17. Goodall (1998), p. 53.
18. MPAV, p. 157.
19. MPAV, p. 150.
20. MPAV, p. 172.
21. *Kiraṇatantra,* Goodall (1998), p. 54.
22. NIPP, pp. 13–14; cf. MPAV, pp. 172–3.
23. NIPP, p. 14.
24. MPAV, p. 151.
25. NIPP, p. 15.
26. NIPP, pp. 10–11; cf. MPAV, p. 153.
27. MPAV, pp. 165–6.

28. MPAV, p. 166.
29. NIPP, pp. 95–6.
30. MPAV, p. 171.
31. Sanderson (1992).
32. Nemec (2011).
33. For the argument, see IPKV II.4.1-9.
34. Sanderson (2007) treats this tradition exhaustively.
35. The word for family is *kula*, hence the term *Kaula* for forms of worship allied to the *Trika*. See White (2003) and Padoux (2013).
36. The ideas here are from Sanderson (1985).
37. Bansat-Boudon (2011) for the *Paramārthasāra*.
38. Basic to his eirenic outlook is a belief that other doctrinal systems are not to be treated as opponents but as aspects of the self-expression of the supreme conscious reality. He formulates an inclusive hierarchy of belief systems in accordance with how closely they approximate to the view that ultimate reality is dynamic universal consciousness.
39. The term *Spanda* designates a corpus of literature. See Dyczkowski (1992) for translations of texts.
40. For the critique of Advaita, see IPKV II.4.20.
41. The same argument can be directed against the Nyāya concept of an per se non-conscious subject of experiences (see supra, pp. 122–3). Such a subject cannot move between cognitions, uniting and separating them, let alone synthesizing past and present experiences. Only a single sovereign and independent consciousness capable of ranging over different cognitions can accomplish such unifications.
42. Since there has been some controversy about whether some of the Indian thinkers who have usually been called idealists really are idealists, I should say that I take idealism to mean the rejection of the possibility of material substance that exists independently of some consciousness. On this interpretation, Vasubandhu and his followers in the Vijñānavāda tradition, as well as Utpaladeva, Abhinavagupta and Kṣemarāja, are idealists.
43. IPKV I.1.4.
44. Dummett (2006), Ch. 8.
45. IPK 1.5.11.
46. Śakti is personified by the Goddess.
47. *Mahānayaprakāśa* 3.104-11. Cited in Sanderson (2007), p. 309.
48. Torella (2002), pp. 118–19.
49. *Bhāvābhāva* means 'everything in heaven and earth'.

Glossary

A note on pronunciation

A macron [**ā, ī, ū**] signals that a vowel is long. **ā** as in father
The letter **a** is very short. English pundit is Sanskrit *paṇḍita*
The letter **ī** is ee. [English 'suttee' is Sanskrit *satī*. 'Juggernaut' is Sanskrit *jagan-nātha*]
The letter **e** is sounded é or ay (as in 'made' and decayed).
ai as in 'bite'
au as in sound
o as in hope
ṛ is sounded ri [**kṛt** is krit] or er.
c is pronounced ch
ñ is pronounced nya or gya [*prajñapti* is most easily pronounced pragyapti]
ś is pronounced sh
ṣ is pronounced sh
kha, gha, cha, jha, ṭha, ḍha, tha, dha, pha, bha are just aspirated forms of **ka, ga, ja, pa, ta** etc.
This means that **ph** is *not* as in Philip and **th** is *not* as in that.
Consonants with a subscript dot 'can be pronounced like' those without.

ābhāsa	manifestation; appearance in consciousness
abhāva	absence; non-being
abhidheyatva	nameability
abhūta-parikalpa	mental construction
adhiṣṭhāna	substrate
adhyāsa	superimposition
adhyavasāya	judgement
aham	I
āgama	scripture; tradition

ahaṃkāra	personality; 'I-maker'
akhaṇḍārtha	simple meaning/sense
akhaṇḍopādhi	simple imputed property
ākṛti	physical form
ālambana-pratyaya	objective ground
ālaya-vijñāna	storehouse-consciousness
anirvacanīya	inexpressible; indeterminate
anitya	impermanent
anumāna	inference
anupalabdhi	non-cognition [as leading to a true judgement]
anuvyavasāya	introspective cognition
apoha	exclusion
artha	thing; meaning
arthakriyā	causal effectiveness; activity
asat	non-being
asatkāryavāda	idea that an effect is a new product
astitva	existence
ātman	nature; soul; identity
avayavin	whole [greater than sum of parts]
avidyā	ignorance; misconception
bhāva	entity; presence
bhāva-rūpa-avidyā	misconception as a real force
bheda	difference; individuality
brahman	foundational being, unconditioned reality
buddha	enlightened
buddhi	cognition; cognitive faculty
cetanā	intention
cit	consciousness
cittam	mind
citta-viprayukta-dharma	factors dissociated from mind
darśana	vision; doctrinal system
dharma	natural order/right; duty; attribute
dharma (*Abhidharma*)	basic factor/element
dhyāna	meditation
dravya	substance
dṛṣṭānta	example (in inference)
dṛṣṭi	point of view; theory
dukkha (*Pāli*)	suffering; unsatisfactoriness

duḥkha	suffering; unsatisfactoriness
dvaita	duality
eka	one
ekatva	unity
grāhaka	perceiver
grāhya	object perceived
guṇa	quality; property
hetu	reason (in argument); cause
hetu-ābhāsa	fallacy in argument
icchā	will, impulse
indriya	sensory faculty
jāti	natural kind; birth; caste
jīva	individual life
jīvan-mukti	liberation while alive
jñāna	cognition
jñeyatva	knowability
kalpanā	conceptual construction; imagination
kāraka	factor involved in action
kāraṇa	cause
kāritra	causal efficacy
kārya	effect; product
kleśa	moral/mental afflictions
kriyā	action, event
kṣaṇa	*moment*
kṣaṇika-vāda	momentariness theory
līlā	divine delight in creation
manas	mind
mokṣa; mukti	freedom from rebirth
nairātmya-vāda	no-substance theory
nibbāna (Pāli)	extinction of greed, hatred and delusion
nikāya	Buddhist scriptures; traditions
nirvāṇa	extinction of greed, hatred and delusion
nirvikalpa	non-conceptual
nirviśeṣa	featureless; undifferentiated
nitya	permanent
padārtha	ontological category; entity
pariṇāma	real transformation of substrative cause
prajñā	wisdom
prajñapti	conventional designation

prakāra	mode
prakāśa	light (of consciousness)
prakṛti	material nature
pramā	truth
pramāṇa	means of knowing
prāmāṇya	epistemic validity; veridicality
prameya	knowable object
prāṇa	vital breaths
pratibhāsa	mental representation
pratītya-samutpāda	interdependent origination
pratyakṣa	sense-perception
puruṣa	person
rūpa	physical form; visible form
śabda	sound; word
sādhya	something to be inferred
śakti	power
samādhi	profound meditation
sāmānya	generality
samavāya	inherence
sambandha	relation; connection
saṃjñā	name; conceptual identification
saṃnyāsa	renunciation
saṃsāra	realm of rebirth
saṃskāra	traces of prior experiences; inherited character
saṃsthāna	configuration of parts
saṃvit	consciousness
saṃvṛti	concealment; conventional truth
śarīra	body
sārūpyam	conformity
sat	being
satkāryavāda	theory that the effect pre-exists in its substrate
savikalpa	conceptual
skandha	constituent of personality
śruti	'heard'; scriptural authority
śūnya	empty
śūnyatā	emptiness
sāmānādhikaraṇya	coreferentiality
svabhāva	'own-being'; essence
svalakṣaṇa	unique particular

svarūpa	proper form
svasaṃvedana	reflexive awareness
svasaṃvitti	reflexive awareness
tantra	religious system
tattva	reality; entity; level of reality
upādāna-kāraṇa	substrative/material cause
upādhi	imputed property
upalabdhi	cognition; perception
upalabdhi-lakṣaṇa-prāpti	in principle perceivable
Upaniṣads	Hindu scriptures
vāda	doctrine; theory
varṇa-āśrama-dharma	duties pertaining to caste and stage of life
vastu	actual entity
vedanā	feeling; sensation
Vedas	Hindu scriptures
vidyā	knowledge; wisdom
vijñāna	perception; cognition
vikalpa	concept; dichotomy
vikāra	modification; product
vimarśa	reflexive awareness
viṣaya	object of awareness; cognitive field
viśeṣa	specific feature
viśeṣaṇa	determiner; property
viśeṣya	determinable; subject
vyakti	individual instance
vyāpti	invariable association between *hetu* and *sādhya*
vyavahāra	everyday life

People

Buddhist

Nāgārjuna (150–250 A.D.): *Mūlamadhyamakakārikā, Ratnāvalī, Vigrahavyāvartanī.*
Āryadeva (200 A.D.): *Catuḥśataka.*
Vasubandhu (c.350 A.D.): *Abhidharmakośa, Abhidharmakośabhāṣya, Viṃśatikā-vijñaptimātratāsiddhi, Trisvabhāvanirdeśa, Triṃśikā, Karmasiddhiprakaraṇa.*
Dignāga (480–540 A.D.): *Nyāyamukha, Pramāṇasamuccaya, Ālambanaparīkṣā.*
Sthiramati (550 A.D.): *Madhyāntavibhāgaṭīkā.*
Bhāviveka (550–600 A.D.): *Madhyamakahṛdaya.*
Candrakīrti (600 A.D.): *Prasannapadā* (on MMK).
Dharmakīrti (600–660 A.D.): *Pramāṇavārttika, Pramāṇaviniścaya, Nyāyabindu, Saṃtānāntaraduṣana, Saṃbandhaparīkṣā.*
Śāntarakṣita (700–750 A.D.): *Tattvasaṃgraha.*
Kamalaśīla (725–775 A.D.): *Tattvasamgrahapañjikā.*
Śāntideva (750 A.D.): *Bodhicāryāvatara, Śikṣā-samuccaya.*
Jñānaśrīmitra (980–1040 A.D.): *Apoha-prakaraṇa, Kṣaṇabhaṅga-adhyāya, Sākārasiddhi-śāstra.*
Ratnakīrti (990–1050 A.D.): *Apohasiddhi, Sarvajñasiddhi, Īśvarasādhanadūṣaṇam, Kṣaṇabhaṅgasiddhi-anvayātmika, Kṣaṇabhaṅgasiddh-vyatirekātmika, Citrādvaitaprakāśavāda, Santānāntaradūṣaṇam, Pramāṇāntarbhāva-prakaraṇa, Vyāptinirṇaya, Sthirasiddhidūṣaṇam.*
Mokṣākāragupta (1150 A.D.): *Tarkabhāṣa.*

Hindus

Nyāya and Vaiśeṣika Schools

Kaṇāda, *Vaiśeṣika-Sūtras* (first century A.D.?)
Gautama Akṣapāda (c.150 A.D.), the author of the fundamental *Nyāya-Sūtra.*
Vātsyāyana (350–400 A.D.), author of the *Nyāya-Bhāṣya* on the *Nyāya-Sūtra.*

Praśastapāda (c.500 A.D.), author of the *Padārthadharmasaṃgraha.*
Uddyotakara (550–600 A.D.), author of the *Nyāyavārttika.*
Jayanta Bhaṭṭa (850–900 A.D.), author of the *Nyāyamañjarī.*
Bhāsarvajña (900–950 A.D.), author of the *Nyāyasāra* and *Nyāyabhūṣaṇa.*
Vācaspati Miśra (950–1000 A.D.), author of the *Nyāyavārttika-tātparyaṭīkā.*
Śrīdhara (fl.991 A.D.), author of the *Nyāyakandali* on the *Padārthadharmasaṃgraha.*
Udayana (c.1050–1100 A.D.), author of the *Lakṣaṇāvalī, Ātmatattvaviveka, Nyāyakusumañjali and Kiraṇāvalī.*
Gaṅgeśa (c.1300 A.D.), author of the *Tattvacintāmaṇi.*
Raghunātha (1475–1550 A.D.), author of the *Padārthatattvanirūpaṇa* and *Dīdhiti* on the *Tattvacintāmaṇl.*
Viśvanātha (1600–1650 A.D.), author of the *Bhāṣā-pariccheda.*
Annambhaṭṭa (1700 A.D.), author of the *Tarkasaṃgraha.*

Mīmāṃsā School

Śabara: Commentary on *Mīmāṃsā-Sūtras* of Jaimini.
Kumārila Bhaṭṭa (600–650 A.D.): *Ślokavārttika.*
Prabhākara Miśra (625–675 A.D.): *Bṛhatī.*

Vedānta

1 Advaita

Śaṃkara (c.700 A.D.): Major works include commentaries on *Brahma-Sūtras, Bhagavad Gītā* and major *Upaniṣads.* A host of works have been ascribed to him, of which the *Upadeśa-Sāhasrī* is authentic.
Maṇḍana Miśra (c.700 A.D.): *Brahmasiddhi.*
Sureśvara (*Naiṣkarmyasiddhi*) and Padmapāda (Pañcapādikā) belong to the generation after Śaṃkara and expound his works.
Vācaspati Miśra (950–1000 A.D.): *Bhamatī* commentary on Śaṃkara's *Brahma-Sūtra-Bhāṣya and Tattvasamīkṣā* on Maṇḍana's *Brahmasiddhi.*
Prakāśātman (900–975 A.D.): *Pañcapādikāvivaraṇa.*
Sarvajñātman (950 A.D.): *Saṃkṣepaśārīraka.*
Vimuktātman (950 A.D.): *Iṣṭasiddhi.*
Śrī Harṣa (1125–1180 A.D.): *Khaṇḍanakhaṇḍakhādya.*

Citsukha (1250–1300 A.D.): *Tattvapradīpika.*
Madhusūdhana Sarasvati (C16): *Advaitasiddhi.*

Vidyāraṇya (d.1386): *Vivaraṇaprameyasaṃgraha* (on *Pañcapādikāvivaraṇa*), *Pañcadaśī*.

Sadānanda (1450 A.D.): *Vedāntasara*.
Appaya Dīkṣita (1549–1613 A.D.): *Siddhāntaleśasaṃgraha*.
Dharmarājādhvarīndra (C17): *Vedāntaparibhāṣā*.

2 Viśiṣṭādvaita

Nāthamuni (980–1050 A.D.): *Nyāyatattva* (known only from quotations).
Yāmuna (1050–1125 A.D.): *Ātmasiddhi*, *Īśvarasiddhi*, *Saṃvitsiddhi*, *Āgamaprāmāṇyam* (on the validity of the Pañcarātra cult and its scriptures).
Rāmānuja (1100–1170 A.D.): *Śrī Bhāṣya* (commentary on the *Brahma-Sūtras*), *Vedārthasaṃgraha* (précis of the former), *Bhagavadgītā-bhāṣya*, *Vedāntasāra*, *Vedāntadīpa*.
Paraśara Bhaṭṭa (1170–1240 A.D.): *Tattvaratnākara* (quotations from Vedānta Deśika).
Vedavyāsa (Sudarśanasuri) (1120–1300 A.D.): *Śrutaprakāśikā* (commentary on *Śrī Bhāṣya*), *Tātparydīpikā* (commentary on *Vedārthasaṃgraha*).
Vedānta Deśika (Veṅkaṭanātha) (1270–1350 A.D.): *Tattvamuktākalāpa*, *Sarvārthasiddhi*, *Nyāyapariśuddhi*, *Nyāyasiddhāñjana*, *Tātparyacandrikā* (commentary on Rāmānuja's *Gītābhāṣya*), Tattvaṭīkā (commentary on *Śrī Bhāṣya*), *Pāñcarātrarakṣā*.
Śrīnivāsadāsa (1600–1650 A.D.): *Yatīndramatadīpikā*.

3 Dvaita

Madhva (1238–1317 A.D.): Commentaries on *Brahma-Sūtras* and *Bhagavad Gītā*, as well as the *Viṣṇutattvanirṇaya*.
Jayatīrtha (1365–1388 A.D.): *Tattvaprakāśika*.
Vyāsatirtha (1460–1539 A.D.): *Nyāyāmṛta*, *Tatparyacandrikā*.
Viṣṇudāsācarya (1390–1440 A.D.): *Vādaratnāvalī*.

Śaiva Thinkers

Siddhānta Dualists

Sadyojyotis (c.700 A.D.), *Nareśvaraparīkṣā*, *Svayaṃbhūvasūtrasaṃgrahaṭīkā*, *Tattvasaṃgraha*, *Tattvatrayanirṇaya*, *Bhogakārikā*, *Ratnatrayaparīkṣā*, *Mokṣakārikā*, *Paramokṣanirāsakārikā*.
Nārāyanakaṇṭha (925–975 A.D.): *Mṛgendrāgamavṛtti*.

Rāmakaṇṭha (950–1000 A.D.): *Nareśvaraparīkṣāprakāśa, Mataṅgapārameśvarāgamavṛtti, Kiraṇavṛtti, Nādakārikā, Mokṣakārikāvṛtti, Paramokṣanirāsakārikāvṛtti.*
Aghoraśiva (c.1150 A.D.): *Tattvasaṃgrahaṭīkā, Mṛgendrāgamavṛttidīpikā, Tattvatrayanirṇayavyākhya, Bhogakārikāvṛtti, Ratnatrayaparīkṣollekhinī, Nādakārikāvṛtti, Mahotsavavidhi* (liturgical): *Kriyākramadyotikā* (liturgical).

Śākta Śaivas

Somānanda (900–950 A.D.): *Śivadṛṣṭi.*
Utpaladeva (925–975 A.D.): *Īśvarapratyabhijñākārikās and -vṛtti and -vivṛti, Ajaḍapramātṛsiddhi, Īśvarasiddhi, Saṃbandhasiddhi, Śivadṛṣṭivṛtti.*
Abhinavagupta (975–1030 A.D.): *Mālinīvijayavārttika, Tantrāloka, Tantrasāra, Paramārthasāra, Parātrīśikāvivaraṇa, Īśvarapratyabhijñāvimarśinī, Īśvarapra tyabhijñāvivṛtivimarśinī, Bodhapañcadaśikā.*
Kṣemarāja (1000–1050 A.D.): *Pratyabhijñāhṛdayam, Netratantroddyota, Svacchandatantroddyota, Śivasūtravimarśinī , Spandasaṃdoha.*

Bibliography

Acharya, D. (ed.) (2006), *Vācaspatimiśra's Tattvasamīkṣā: The Earliest Commentary on Maṇḍanamiśra's Brahmasiddhi*. Stuttgart: Franz Steiner Verlag.

Agase, K. S. (1891), *Bṛhadāraṇyakopaniṣat with Śaṃkara's Commentary*. Pune: Ānandāśrama Sanskrit Series.

Athalye, Y. V. (ed. and trans.) (2003), *Tarkasaṃgraha of Annaṃbhaṭṭa*. Pune: Bhandarkar Research Institute.

Bareau, A. (1955), *Les Sectes bouddhique du petit vehicule*. Paris: EFEO.

Bartley, C. J. (2001), 'Jainism', in Oliver Leaman (ed.), *Encyclopedia of Asian Philosophy*. London: Routledge.

Bartley, C. J. (2002), *The Theology of Rāmānuja*. London: RoutledgeCurzon.

Bartley, C. J. (2011), 'Advaita and the Schools of Vedānta', in Knut Jacobsen (ed.), *Brill's Encyclopedia of Hinduism*, Vol. III. Leiden and Boston: Brill.

Bartley, C. J. (2013), 'Radhakrishnan', in Knut Jacobsen (ed.), *Brill's Encyclopedia of Hinduism*, Vol. V. Leiden and Boston: Brill.

Basham, A. L. (1967), *The Wonder that was India: A Survey of the Culture of the Indian Sub-Continent before the Coming of the Muslims*, 3rd edn. London: Sidgwick and Jackson.

Bechert, H. and Gombrich, R. (1984), *The World of Buddhism*. London: Thames and Hudson.

Bhatt, N. R. (ed.) (1977), *Mataṅgapārameśvarāgama (Vidyāpāda) avec le commentaire be Bhaṭṭa Rāmakaṇṭha*. Pondichéry: Institut Français d'Indologie.

Bhattacharya, K. (1998), *The Dialectical Method of Nāgārjuna: Vigrahavyāvartanī*. Delhi: Motilal Banarsidass.

Biardeau, M. (1997), *Hinduism: The Anthropology of a Civilisation*. Delhi: Oxford University Press.

Bronkhorst, J. (2000), *The Two Traditions of Meditation in Ancient India*. Delhi: Motilal Banarsidass.

Buitenen, J. A. B. van (1953), *Rāmānuja on the Bhagavad Gītā*. The Hague: Smits.

Buitenen, J. A. B. van (1956), *Rāmānuja's Vedārthasaṃgraha*. Poona: Deccan College.

Burge, T. (2010), *Origins of Objectivity*. Oxford: Oxford University Press.

Burley, M. (2007), *Classical Sāṃkhya and Yoga: An Indian Metaphysics of Experience*. London: Routledge.
Burton, D. (1999), *Emptiness Appraised*. Richmond: Curzon Press.
Butler, J. (1813), *The Analogy of Religion*. London: T.Hamilton.
Byrne, A. and Logue, H. (2010), *Disjunctivism: Contemporary Readings*. Cambridge: MIT Press.
Carman, J. B. (1974), *The Theology of Rāmānuja*. New Haven: Yale University Press.
Carpenter, A. D. (2014), *Indian Buddhist Philosophy*. Durham: Acumen.
Chakrabarti, A. (1992), 'I Touch What I Saw', *Philosophy and Phenomenological Research*, 52 (1): 103–16.
Chakrabarti, K. (1975), '*The Nyāya-Vaiśeṣika* Theory of Universals', *Journal of Indian Philosophy*, 3: 363–82.
Chakrabarti, K. (1999), *Indian Philosophy of Mind: The Nyāya Dualist Tradition*. Albany: SUNY Press.
Clooney, Francis X. (2001), *Hindu God, Christian God*. New York: Oxford University Press.
Collins, S. (1982), *Selfless Persons*. Cambridge: Cambridge University Press.
Comans, M. (2000), *The Method of Early Advaita Vedānta*. Delhi: Motilal Banarsidass.
Conze, E. (1959), *Buddhist Scriptures*. Harmondsworth: Penguin.
Crosby, K. and Skilton, A. (trans.) (1996), *Śāntideva: The Bodhicāryāvatāra*. Oxford: Oxford University Press.
Danielson, H. (ed. and trans.) (1980), *Ādiśeṣa: The Essence of Supreme Truth* (*Paramārthasāra*). Leiden: Brill.
Dezső, C. (ed. and trans.) (2005), *Much Ado About Religion by Bhaṭṭa Jayanta*. New York: New York University Press.
Doniger, W. (trans.) (2005), *The Rig Veda*. London: Penguin Classics.
Duerlinger, J. (2003), *Indian Buddhist Theories of Persons: Vasubandhu's Refutation of the Theory of a Self*. London: Routledge Curzon.
Dummett, M. (2006), *Thought and Reality*. Oxford: Oxford University Press.
Dumont, L. (1980), 'World Renunciation in Indian Religions', in L. Dumont (ed.), *Homo Hierarchicus*. Chicago: Chicago University Press.
Dundas, P. (1992), *The Jains*. London: Routledge.
Eltschinger, V. (2007), *Penser l'autorité des Écritures*. Wien: Österreichischen Akademie der Wissenschaften.
Etschinger, V. (2012), *Caste and Buddhist Philosophy*. Delhi: Motilal Banarsidass.
Filliozat, Pierre-Sylvain (ed. and trans.) (1994), *The Tantra of Svayaṃbhū: Vidyāpāda with the Commentary of Sadyojyoti*. Delhi: Motilal Banarsidass.
Flood, G. (1996), *Introduction to Hinduism*. Cambridge: Cambridge University Press.
Fort, A. (1998), *Jīvanmukti in Transformation*. Albany: SUNY Press.

Foster, J. (2008), *A World for Us*. Oxford: Oxford University Press.
Franco, E. (1994), *Perception, Knowledge and Disbelief*. Delhi: Motilal Banarsidass.
Frauwallner, E. (1995), *Studies in the Abhidharma Literature and the Origins of the Buddhist Philosophical Systems*. Albany: SUNY Press.
Ganeri, J. (1999), *Semantic Powers*. Oxford: Clarendon Press.
Ganeri, J. (2000), 'Cross-Modality and the Self', *Philosophy and Phenomenological Research*, 61: 639–58.
Ganeri, J. (ed.) (2001), *Indian Logic: A Reader*. London: Curzon.
Ganeri, J. (2001), 'Objectivity and Proof in Classical Indian Number Theory', *Synthese*, 129 (3): 413–37.
Garfield, J. (trans.) (1995), *The Fundamental Wisdom of the Middle Way*. New York: Oxford University Press.
Gaskin, R. (2006), *Experience and the World's Own Language*. Oxford: Oxford University Press.
Gerow, E. (trans.) (1990), *The Jewel-Necklace of Argument*. New Haven: American Oriental Society.
Gethin, R. (1998), *Foundations of Buddhism*. Oxford: Oxford University Press.
Gethin, R. (trans.) (2008), *Sayings of the Buddha*. Oxford: Oxford University Press.
Gold, J. (2015), *Paving the Great Way: Vasubandhu's Unifying Buddhist Philosophy*. New York: Columbia University Press.
Gombrich, R. (1992), 'The Buddha's Book of Genesis?', *Indo-Iranian Journal*, 35: 159–78.
Gombrich, R. (1996), *How Buddhism Began*. London: Athlone.
Goodall, D. (ed.) (1998), *Bhaṭṭa Rāmakaṇṭha's Commentary on the Kiraṇatantra*. Pondichéry: Institut Français de Pondichéry and École Française d'Extrême-Orient.
Goudriaan, T. (ed.) (1992), *Ritual and Speculation in Early Tantrism: Studies in Honour of André Padoux*. Albany: SUNY Press.
Granoff, P. (1978), *Philosophy and Argument in Late Vedānta: Śrī Harṣa's Khaṇḍanakhaṇḍakhādya*. Dordrecht: Reidel.
Gupta, S. (trans.) (2000), *Lakṣmī Tantra*. Delhi: Motilal Banarsidass.
Hahn, M. (ed.) (1982), *Nāgārjuna's Ratnāvalī*. Bonn: Indica et Tibetica Verlag.
Halbfass, W. (1991), *Tradition and Reflection*. Albany: SUNY Press.
Halbfass, W. (1992), *On Being and What There Is: Classical Vaiśeṣika and the History of Indian Ontology*. Albany: SUNY Press.
Halbfass, W. (ed.) (1995), *Philology and Confrontation: Paul Hacker on Traditional and Modern Vedanta*. Albany: SUNY Press.
Hara, M. and Wright, J. C. (eds) (1996), *John Brough: Collected Papers*. London: SOAS.
Hardy, F. (1983), *Viraha-Bhakti*. Delhi: Oxford University Press.
Hattori, M. (1968), *Dignaga, On Perception*. Cambridge, MA: Harvard University Press.

Hayes, R. (1988), *Dignaga on the Interpretation of Signs*. Dordrecht: Kluwer.

Ingalls, D. H. H. (1951), *Materials for the Study of Navya-Nyaya Logic*. Cambridge, MA: Harvard University Press.

Jaini, P. S. (1979), *The Jaina Path of Purification*. Berkeley: University of California Press.

Jaini, P. S. (2000), *Collected Papers on Buddhist Studies*. Delhi: Motilal Banarsidass.

Jamison, S. and Witzel, M. (2003), 'Vedic Hinduism', in Arvind Sharma (ed.), *The Study of Hinduism*. Columbia: University of South Carolina Press.

Jayatilleke, K. N. (1980), *Early Buddhist Theory of Knowledge*. Delhi: Motilal Banarsidass.

Jetly, J. S. (ed.) (1971), *Kiraṇāvalī*. Baroda: Gaekwad's Oriental Series.

Jha, G. (trans.) (1984), *The Nyāya-Sūtras of Gautama with the Bhāṣya of Vātsyāyana and the Vārttika of Uddyotakara*, IV Vols. Delhi: Motilal Banarsidass.

Johnson, W. J. (1994), *The Bhagavad Gītā*. Oxford: Oxford University Press.

Kahrs, Eivind (1998), *Indian Semantic Analysis*. Cambridge: Cambridge University Press.

Kajiyama, Y. (1998), *An Introduction to Buddhist Philosophy: An Annotated Translation of the Tarkabhāṣa of Mokṣākāragupta*. Wien: Universität Wien.

Karmarkar, R. D. (ed. and trans.) (1953), *Gauḍapāda-Kārika*. Poona: Bhandarkar Oriental Research Institute.

King, R. (1995), *Early Advaita Vedānta and Buddhism*. Albany: SUNY Press.

Krasser, H. (2002), *Śaṅkaranandanas Īśvarāpākaraṇasaṅkṣepa*, 2 Vols. Wien: Österreichischen Akademie der Wissenschaften.

Lamotte, E. (1988), *History of Indian Buddhism*, S. Boin Webb (trans.). Paris: Louvain La Neuve.

Larson, G. J. (1979), *Classical Sāṃkhya*. Delhi: Motilal Banarsidass.

Larson, G. J. and Bhattacharya, R. S. (eds) (1987), *Encyclopedia of Indian Philosophies: Volume IV Samkhya*. Delhi: Motilal Banarsidass.

Lindtner, C. (1982), *Nagarjuniana*. Copenhagen: Akademisk Forlag.

Lipner, J. (1986), *The Face of Truth*. Basingstoke: Macmillan.

Lipner, J. (2010), *Hindus: Their Religious Beliefs and Practices*. London: Routledge.

Matilal, B. K. (1968), *The Navya-Nyāya Doctrine of Negation*. Cambridge: Harvard Oriental Series.

Matilal, B. K. (1986), *Perception: An Essay on Classical Indian Theories of Knowledge*. Oxford: Clarendon Press.

Matilal, B. K. (1990), *The Word and the World*. Delhi: Oxford University Press.

Matilal, B. K. (2002), *Mind, Language and World*. Delhi: Oxford University Press.

Mayeda, S. (1979), *A Thousand Teachings*. Tokyo: Tokyo University Press.

Mesquita, R. (2000), *Madhva's Unknown Literary Sources: Some Observations*. Delhi: Aditya Prakashan.

Mookerjee, S. (1975), *The Buddhist Philosophy of Universal Flux*. Delhi: Motilal Banarsidass.
Norman, K. R. (1991), 'Theravada Buddhism and Brahmanical Hinduism: Brahmanical Terms in a Buddhist Guise', in T. Skorupski (ed.), *The Buddhist Forum*. London: Routledge.
Oberhammer, G. (1997), *Materielen zur Geschichte der Rāmānuja-Schule, III, Yādavaprakāśa, der vergessene Lehrer Rāmānujas*. Wien: Österreichischen Akademie der Wissenschaften.
Oberhammer, G. (1998), *Materielen zur Geschichte der Rāmānuja-Schule, IV, Der 'Innere Lenker' (Antar-yāmī)*. Wien: Österreichischen Akademie der Wissenschaften.
Oetke, C. (1994), *Studies in the Doctrine of Trairupya*. Wien: Universität Wien.
Olivelle, P. (1986), *Renunciation in Hinduism: A Medieval Debate*. Vienna: Universität Wien.
Olivelle, P. (1993), *The Āśrama System: The History and Hermeneutics of a Religious Institution*. New York: Oxford University Press.
Olivelle, P. (ed. and trans.) (1998), *The Early Upaniṣads: Annotated Text and Translation*. New York: Oxford University Press.
Olivelle, P. (1999), *Dharmasūtras; The Law Codes of Apastamba, Gautama, Baudhayana and Vasistha, translated from the original Sanskrit*. Oxford: Oxford University Press.
Olivelle, P. (ed. and trans.) (2005), *Manu's Code of Law*. Oxford: Oxford University Press.
Padoux, A. (1990), *Vāc: The Concept of the Word in Selected Hindu Tantras*, Jacques Gontier (trans.). Albany: SUNY Press.
Padoux, A. (2013), *The Heart of the Yoginī*. New York: Oxford University Press.
Pandey, K. C. (ed. and trans.) (1986), *Īśvara-pratyabhijñā-vimarśiṇī of Abhinavagupta: Doctrine of Divine Recognition*. Delhi: Motilal Banarsidass.
Pandeya, R. (ed.) (1989), *The Pramāṇavārttikam of Ācārya Dharmakīrti*. Delhi: Motilal Banarsidass.
Patil, P. (2009), *Against a Hindu God: Buddhist Philosophy of Religion in India*. New York: Columbia University Press.
Potter, K. H. (ed.) (1977), *Encyclopedia of Indian Philosophies: Vol. II, Indian Metaphysics and Epistemology: The Tradition of Nyaya-Vaisheshika up to Gangesha*. Delhi: Motilal Banarsidass.
Potter, K. H. (ed.) (1981), *Encyclopedia of Indian Philosophies: Vol. III, Advaita Vedanta up to Śaṅkara and His Pupils*. Delhi: Motilal Banarsidass.
Potter, K. H. (1996), *Encyclopedia of Indian Philosophies: Vol. VII, Abhidharma Buddhism to 150 A.D.* Delhi: Motilal Banarsidass.
Potter, K. H. and Bhattacharya, S. (eds) (1993), *Encyclopedia Of Indian Philosophies: Vol. VI, Indian Philosophical Analysis; Nyāya Vaiśeṣika from Gaṅgeśa to Raghunātha Śiromaṇi*. Delhi: Motilal Banarsidass.

Pradhan, P. (1967), *Abhidharmakośabhaṣyam of Vasubandhu*. Patna: K. P. Jayaswal Research Institute.

Pruden, L. (trans.) (1988), *Abhidharmakośabhaṣyam*. Berkeley: Asian Humanities Press.

Raghavachar, S. S. (ed. and trans.) (1959), *Śrīmad-Viṣṇu-Tattva-Vinirṇaya of Śrī Madhvācārya*. Mangalore: Sri Ramakrishna Ashram.

Rahula, W. (1969), *What the Buddha Taught*. London: Gordon Fraser.

Ram-Prasad, C. (2002), *Advaita Epistemology and Metaphysics*. London: RoutledgeCurzon.

Rhys Davids, T. W. (1995), *Dialogues of the Buddha*, Part 1. Oxford: Pali Text Society.

Robinson, H. (1994), *Perception*. London: Routledge.

Rocher, L. (ed.) (1988), *Studies in Indian Literature and Philosophy: Collected Articles of J. A. B. van Buitenen*. Delhi: Motilal Banarsidass.

Ronkin, N. (2005), *Early Buddhist Metaphysics*. London: RoutledgeCurzon.

Sacks, M. (2000), *Objectivity and Insight*. Oxford: Oxford University Press.

Sadhale, G. S. (ed.) (2000), *The Bhagavad Gītā with Eleven Commentaries*. Delhi: Primal Publications.

Sanderson, Alexis (1985), 'Purity and Power among the Brahmins of Kashmir', in M. Carrithers, Steven Collins, Stephen Lukes (eds), *The Category of the Person*. Cambridge: Cambridge University Press, pp. 190–216.

Sanderson, Alexis (1990), 'Śaivism and the Tantric Traditions', in F. Hardy (ed.), *The World's Religions: The Religions of Asia*. London: Routledge, pp. 128–72.

Sanderson, Alexis (1992), 'The Doctrine of the Mālinīvijayottaratantra', in T. Goudriaan (ed.), *Ritual and Speculation in Early Tantra: Studies in Honor of André Padoux*. Albany: SUNY Press, pp. 281–312.

Sanderson, Alexis (1995a), 'Meaning in Tantric Ritual', in A-M. Bondeau (ed.), *Essais sur le rituel III*. Louvain, Paris: Peeters, pp. 15–95.

Sanderson, Alexis (1995b), 'The Sarvāstivāda and its Critics', in *Buddhism in the Year 2000: International Conference Proceedings*. Bangkok and Los Angeles: Dhammakāya Foundation, pp. 37–49.

Sanderson, Alexis (2001), 'History Through Textual Criticism', in François Grimal (ed.), *Les sources et le Temps. Sources and time. A colloquium*. Pondichéry: Institut Français de Pondichéry and École Française d'Extrême-Orient, pp. 1–47.

Sanderson, Alexis (2007), 'The Śaiva Exegesis of Kashmir', in D. Goodall and André Padoux (ed.), *Mélanges Tantriques à la mémoire d'Hélène Brunner*. Pondichéry: Institut Français de Pondichéry and École Française d'Extrême-Orient, pp. 231–442.

Sanderson, Alexis (2009), 'Kashmir', in Knut Jacobsen (ed.), *Brill's Encyclopedia of Hinduism*, Vol. I. Leiden and Boston: Brill.

Sanderson, Alexis (2009), 'The Śaiva Age', in Shingo Einoo (ed.), *Genesis and Development of Tantrism*. Tokyo: University of Tokyo.

Sarma, D. (2003), *An Introduction to Mādhva Vedānta*. Aldershot: Ashgate.

Scharf, P. (1996), *The Denotation of Generic Terms in Ancient Indian Philosophy: Grammar, Nyāya, and Mīmāṃsā*. Philadelphia: American Philosophical Society.

Schrader, F. Otto (1916), *Introduction to the Pāñcarātra and the Ahirbudhnya Saṃhitā*. Madras: Adyar Library.

Sellars, W. (1997), Empiricism *and the Philosophy of Mind*. Cambridge, MA: Harvard University Press.

Shastri, J. L. (ed.) (1980), *Brahmasūtra- Śaṅkarabhāṣyam*. Delhi: Motilal Banarsidass.

Shastri, J. Z. (1947), *Bodhapañcadaśika* of Abhinavagupta. Srinagar: Kashmir Series of Texts and Studies.

Shastri, M. K. (ed.) (1926), *The Nareshvarapariksha of Sajyojyoti with the commentary by Ramakantha*. Srinagar: Kashmir Series of Texts and Studies.

Siderits, M. (1991), *Indian Philosophy of Language: Selected Issues*. Dordrecht: Kluwer.

Siderits, M. (2003), *Personal Identity and Buddhist Philosophy: Empty Persons*. Aldershot: Ashgate.

Siderits, M. (2007), *Buddhism as Philosophy*. Aldershot: Ashgate.

Siderits, M. and Katsura, S. (2013), *Nāgārjuna's Middle Way: Mūlamadhyamakakārikā*. Boston: Wisdom.

Singh, J. (1982), *Pratyabhijñāhṛdayam*. Delhi: Motilal Banarsidass.

Singh, J. (1991), *Śiva Sūtras*. Delhi: Motilal Banarsidass.

Streng, F. J. (1967), *Emptiness: A Study in Religious Meaning*. New York: Abingdon Press.

Subramania Iyer, K. A. (ed.) (1964), *Vākyapadīya of Bhartṛhari (Kāṇda I)*. Poona: Deccan College.

Subramania Iyer, K. A. and Pandey, K. C. (eds) (1986), *Īśvarapratyabhijñā-vimarśinī of Abhinavagupta*, 3 Vols. Delhi: Motilal Banarsidass.

Suryanarayana Sastri, S. S. (ed. and trans.) (1971), *Vedāntaparibhāṣa of Dharmarāja Adhvarin*. Madras: The Adyar Library and Research Centre.

Suryanarayana Sastri, S. S. and Barnett, L. D. (ed. and trans.) (2003), *The Paramārthasāra of Ādi Śeṣa and The Paramārthasāra of Abhinavagupta*. Fremont: Asian Humanities Press.

Suthren Hirst, J. G. (2005), *Śaṃkara's Advaita Vedānta*. Abingdon: Routledge Curzon.

Svāmī Ādidevānanda (ed. and trans.) (1949), *Yatīndramatadīpikā*. Mylapore: Sri Ramakrishna Math.

Svami Dvarikadasa Shastri (ed.) (1994), *Nyāyabinduprakaraṇam*. Varanasi: Bauddha Bharati.

Swāmi Jagadānanda (1941), *Upadeśa Sāhasrl of Śrī Śaṃkarācārya*. Mylapore: Sri Ramakrishna Math.

Taber, J. (2005), *A Hindu Critique of Buddhist Epistemology: Kumārila on Perception: The 'Determination of Perception' Chapter of Kumārila Bhaṭṭa's Ślokavārttika Commentary*. London: RoutledgeCurzon.

Tachikawa, M. (1981), *The Structure of the World in Udayana's Realism*. Dordrecht: Reidel.

Thibaut, G. (trans.) (1904a), *The Vedanta-Sutras with the Commentary of Ramanuja*. Oxford: Clarendon Press.

Thibaut, G. (trans.) (1904b), *The Vedanta-Sutras with the Commentary of Shankaracarya*, 2 Vols. Oxford: Clarendon Press.

Thrasher, A. W. (1993), *The Advaita Vedanta of Brahma-siddhi*. Delhi: Motilal Banarsidass.

Tillemans, T. J. F. (1999), *Scripture, Logic and Language*. Boston: Wisdom Publications.

Tola, F. and Dragonetti, C. (1994), *The Avayavinirākaraṇa of Paṇḍita Aśoka*. Tokyo: International Institute for Buddhist Studies.

Tola, F. and Dragonetti, C. (2004), *Being as Consciousness*. Delhi: Motilal Banarsidass.

Torella, R. (ed. and trans.) (2002), *The Īśvarapratyabhijñākārikā of Utpaladeva*. Delhi: Motilal Banarsidass.

Watson, Alex (2006), *The Self's Awareness of Itself: Bhaṭṭa Rāmakaṇṭha's Arguments against the Buddhist Doctrine of No-Self*. Wien: Publications of the De Nobili Research Library.

Westerhoff, J. (2009), *Nāgārjuna's Madhyamaka*. Oxford: Oxford University Press.

Westerhoff, J. (2010), *The Dispeller of Disputes*. Oxford: Oxford University Press.

Wezler, A. and Motegi, S. (1998), *Yuktidīpikā*. Stuttgart: Franz Steiner Verlag.

Whicher, I. (1998), *The Integrity of the Yoga Darśana*. Albany: SUNY Press.

Williams, B. (1978), *Descartes: The Project of Pure Enquiry*. Harmondsworth: Penguin.

Williams, P. (1989), *Mahayana Buddhism*. London: Routledge.

Williams, P. (1998), *Altruism and Reality*. London: Curzon Press.

Wood, T. E. (1991), *Mind Only: A Philosophical and Doctrinal Analysis of the Vijñānavāda*. Honolulu: University of Hawaii Press.

Woods, J. H. (1927), *The Yoga Sūtras*. Cambridge, MA: Harvard University Press.

Wynne, A. (trans.) (2009), *Mahābhārata Book XII. Peace. Volume Three. The Book of Liberation*. New York: New York University Press.

Index